LONDON CEMETERIES

Nunhead Cemetery: a fallen angel

LONDON CEMETERIES

An Illustrated Guide and Gazetteer

HUGH MELLER & BRIAN PARSONS

Cover Illustrations: *Front*: Brompton Cemetery, 2006 © Stephen Edgar; *Back*: *Upper*: Tomb of pugilist Thomas Sayers at Highgate Cemetery; *Lower*: Abney Park Cemetery, Stoke Newington, Hackney, London, 4 September 2005 © Fin Fahey.

First published in 1981 by Avebury Publishing Company, Amersham, England.
Second, third and fourth editions published in 1985, 1994 and 2008.

This fifth edition published in 2011 by
The History Press
The Mill, Brimscombe Port
Stroud, Gloucestershire, GL5 2QG
www.thehistorypress.co.uk

© Hugh Meller and Brian Parsons, 1981, 1985, 1994, 2008, 2011

The right of Hugh Meller and Brian Parsons to be identified as the Authors of this work has been asserted in accordance with the Copyrights, Designs and Patents Act 1988.

All rights reserved. No part of this book may be reprinted or reproduced or utilised in any form or by any electronic, mechanical or other means, now known or hereafter invented, including photocopying and recording, or in any information storage or retrieval system, without the permission in writing from the Publishers.

British Library Cataloguing in Publication Data.
A catalogue record for this book is available from the British Library.

ISBN 978 0 7524 6183 0

Typesetting and origination by The History Press Ltd
Printed and bound in Great Britain

Contents

	The Cemeteries	vii
	Map of the Cemeteries	x
	Illustrations	xiii
	Authors' Note	xxi
	Introduction	xxiii
1	History	1
2	Planning	13
3	Monuments and Buildings	21
4	Epitaphs	57
5	Flora and Fauna	63
	Gazetteer	71
	Notes	367
	Bibliography	381
	Index of the Deceased	387
	Index of Architects, Landscapers and Sculptors	421

The Cemeteries

1. Abney Park Cemetery, Stoke Newington High Street, N16 — 71
2. Acton Cemetery, Park Royal Road, NW10 — 78
3. Alperton (Wembley) Cemetery, Clifford Road, Wembley, Middx. — 79
4. Bandon Hill Cemetery, Plough Lane, Wallington, Surrey — 80
5. Barkingside Cemeteries, Longwood Gardens, Ilford, Essex — 81
6. Barnes Common Cemetery, off Rocks Lane, SW13 — 81
7. Battersea New Cemetery (Morden) & North East Surrey Crematorium, Morden, Surrey — 83
8. Battersea St Mary's Cemetery, Bolingbroke Grove, SW11 — 84
9. Beckenham Cemetery, London Road, Bromley, Kent — 87
10. Bexleyheath Cemetery, Banks Lane, Broadway, Bexleyheath, Kent — 88
11. Brockley and Ladywell Cemetery, Brockley Road, SE4 — 89
12. Bromley Hill Cemetery, Bromley Hill, Bromley, Kent — 91
13. Brompton Cemetery, Old Brompton Road, SW10 — 92
14. Brookwood Cemetery, Cemetery Pales, Brookwood, Woking, Surrey — 105
15. Bunhill Fields, City Road, EC1 — 108
16. Camberwell Cemetery, Forest Hill Road, SE22 — 115
17. Camberwell New Cemetery & Honor Oak Crematorium, Brenchley Gardens, SE23 — 118
18. Carpenders Park Cemetery, Oxhey Lane, Watford, Herts — 120
19. Chadwell Heath Cemetery, Whalebone Lane North, Mark's Gate, Essex — 120
20. Charlton Cemetery, Cemetery Lane, SE7 — 121
21. Cherry Lane Cemetery, Shepison Lane, West Drayton, Middx. — 125
22. Chingford Mount Cemetery, Old Church Road, E4 — 126
23. Chiswick New Cemetery, Staveley Road, W4 — 129
24. Chiswick Old Cemetery, Corney Road, W4 — 130
25. City of London Cemetery and Crematorium, Aldersbrook Road, E12 — 132
26. Croydon Cemetery and Crematorium, Mitcham Road, Croydon, Surrey — 141
27. Crystal Palace District Cemetery & Beckenham Crematorium, Elmers End Road, SE20 — 142
28. Ealing and Old Brentford (South Ealing) Cemetery, South Ealing Road, W5 — 145
29. Eastbrookend Cemetery, The Chase, Off Dagenham Road, Dagenham, Essex — 146
30. Eastcote Lane Cemetery, Eastcote Lane, South Harrow, Middx. — 147
31. East London Cemetery and Crematorium, Grange Road E13 — 147
32. East Sheen Cemetery, Sheen Road, Richmond, Surrey — 148

33.	Edmonton Cemetery, Church Street, N9	151
34.	Edmonton and Southgate Cemetery, Waterfall Road, N11	153
35.	Eltham Cemetery and Crematorium, Rochester Way, SE9	153
36.	Enfield Cemetery and Crematorium, Great Cambridge Road, Enfield, Middx.	154
37.	Forest Park Cemetery and Crematorium, Forest Road, Hainault, Essex	155
38.	Fulham Cemetery, Fulham Palace Road, SW6	155
39.	Golders Green Crematorium, Hoop Lane, NW11	157
40.	The Great Northern Cemetery (New Southgate Crematorium), Brunswick Park Rd, N11	166
41.	Greenford Park Cemetery, Windmill Lane, Greenford, Middx.	169
42.	Greenlawn Memorial Park Cemetery, Chelsham Road, Warlingham, Surrey	169
43.	Greenwich Cemetery, Well Hall Road, SE9	170
44.	Grove Park Cemetery, Marvels Lane, SE12	171
45.	Gunnersbury Cemetery, Gunnersbury Avenue, W4	172
46.	Hammersmith Cemetery, Margravine Road, W6	176
47.	Hammersmith New Cemetery and Mortlake Crematorium, Clifford Avenue, SW14	177
48.	Hampstead Cemetery, Fortune Green Road, NW6	177
49.	Harrow Cemetery, Pinner Road, Harrow, Middx.	184
50.	Hatton Cemetery, Faggs Road, Feltham, Middx.	184
51.	Hendon Cemetery and Crematorium, Holder's Hill Road, NW4	185
52.	Hertford Road Cemetery, Hertford Road, Enfield, Middx.	187
53.	Highgate Cemetery, Swains Lane, N6	187
54.	Hillingdon and Uxbridge Cemetery, Hillingdon Hill, Hillingdon	207
55.	Hillview Cemetery, Wickham Street, Welling, Kent	208
56.	Hither Green Cemetery and Lewisham Crematorium, Verdant Lane, SE6	208
57.	Huguenot Burial Ground, East Hill, SW18	210
58.	Isleworth Cemetery, Park Road, Isleworth, Middx.	210
59.	Jewish Cemetery, Alderney Road, E1	211
60.	Jewish Cemetery, Brady Street, E1	212
61.	Jewish Cemetery, East Ham, Sandford Road, E6	213
62.	Jewish Cemetery, Fulham Road, SW3	213
63.	Jewish Cemetery, Hoop Lane, NW11	214
64.	Jewish Cemetery, Kingsbury Road, N1	216
65.	Jewish Cemetery, Lauriston Road, E9	217
66.	Jewish New Sephardi, Mile End Road, E1	217
67.	Jewish Old Sephardi, Mile End Road, E1	218
68.	Jewish Cemetery, Montagu Road, N18	219
69.	Jewish Cemetery, Plashet Park, High Street, E6	220
70.	Jewish Cemetery, Pound lane, NW10	220
71.	Jewish Cemetery, Rowan Road, SW16	221
72.	Jewish Cemetery, West Ham, Buckingham Road, E15	222
73.	Jewish Cemetery, Willesden, Glebe Road, NW10	223
74.	Kensal Green Cemetery & West London Crematorium, Harrow Road, W10	227
75.	Kensington Hanwell Cemetery, Uxbridge Road, W7	248
76.	Kingston Cemetery and Crematorium, Bonner Hill Road, Kingston	251
77.	Lambeth Cemetery and Crematorium, Blackshaw Road, SW17	253
78.	Lavender Hill and Strayfield Road Cemeteries, Cedar Road, Enfield	255
79.	Manor Park Cemetery and Crematorium, Sebert Road, E7	255

THE CEMETERIES

80.	Merton and Sutton Joint Cemetery, Garth Road, Morden, Surrey	256
81.	Mitcham Cemetery, Church Road, Mitcham	257
82.	Mitcham Cemetery, London Road, Mitcham	258
83.	Mortlake Old Cemetery, South Worple Way, SW14	258
84.	Mortlake Roman Catholic Cemetery, North Worple Way, SW14	260
85.	New Brentford Cemetery, Sutton Lane, Hounslow, Middx.	262
86.	North Sheen Cemetery, Lower Richmond Road, SW14	262
87.	Nunhead Cemetery, Linden Grove, SE15	263
88.	Paddington Cemetery, Mill Hill, Milespit Hill, NW7	273
89.	Paddington Cemetery, Willesden Lane, NW2	274
90.	Paines Lane Cemetery, Paines Lane, Pinner, Middx.	276
91.	Pinner Cemetery, Pinner Road, Pinner, Middx.	277
92.	Plaistow Cemetery, Burnt Ash Lane, Bromley, Kent	278
93.	Plumstead Cemetery, Wickham Lane, SE2	278
94.	Putney Lower Common Cemetery, Mill Hill Road, SW13	279
95.	Putney Vale Cemetery and Crematorium, Kingston Road, SW15	280
96.	Queen's Road Cemetery, Queen's Road, Croydon, Surrey	288
97.	Richmond Cemetery, Grove Road, Richmond, Surrey	290
98.	Rippleside Cemetery, Ripple Road, Barking, Essex	294
99.	Roding Lane North Cemetery, Roding Lane North, South Woodford, Essex	295
100.	Royal Hospital Chelsea Burial Ground, Royal Hospital Road, SW3	295
101.	Royal Hospital Greenwich Cemetery, Chevening Road, SE10	297
102.	St Marylebone Cemetery and Crematorium, East End Road, N3	298
103.	St Mary's Roman Catholic Cemetery, Kensal Green, Harrow Road, NW10	305
104.	St Pancras and Islington Cemetery and Crematorium, High Road, N2	310
105.	St Patrick's Roman Catholic Cemetery, Langthorne Road, E11	314
106.	Streatham Cemetery, Garratt Lane, SW17	315
107.	Streatham Park Cemetery & South London Crematorium, Rowan Road, SW16	316
108.	St Thomas's Roman Catholic Cemetery, Rylston Road, SW6	319
109.	Surbiton Cemetery, Lower Marsh Lane, Surbiton, Surrey	322
110.	Sutton Cemetery, Alcorn Close, Sutton, Surrey	322
111.	Teddington Cemetery, Shacklegate Lane, Teddington, Middx.	323
112.	Tottenham Cemetery, Prospect Place, N17	325
113.	Tottenham Park Cemetery, Montagu Road, N18	325
114.	Tower Hamlets Cemetery, Southern Grove, E3	327
115.	Trent Park Cemetery, Cockfoster Road, Cockfosters	331
116.	Twickenham Cemetery, Hospital Bridge Road, Twickenham	332
117.	Walthamstow Cemetery, Queen's Road, E17	333
118.	Wandsworth Cemetery, Magdalen Road, SW18	334
119.	West Ham Cemetery, Cemetery Road, E7	336
120.	Westminster Cemetery, Uxbridge Road, W7	337
121.	West Norwood Cemetery and Crematorium, Norwood High Street, SE24	339
122.	Willesden Cemetery, Franklyn Road, NW10	359
123.	Wimbledon Cemetery, Gap Road, SW19	360
124.	Woodgrange Park Cemetery, Romford Road, E7	361
125.	Wood Green Cemetery, Wolves Lane, N22	363
126.	Woolwich Cemeteries, King's Highway and Camdale Road, SE18	363

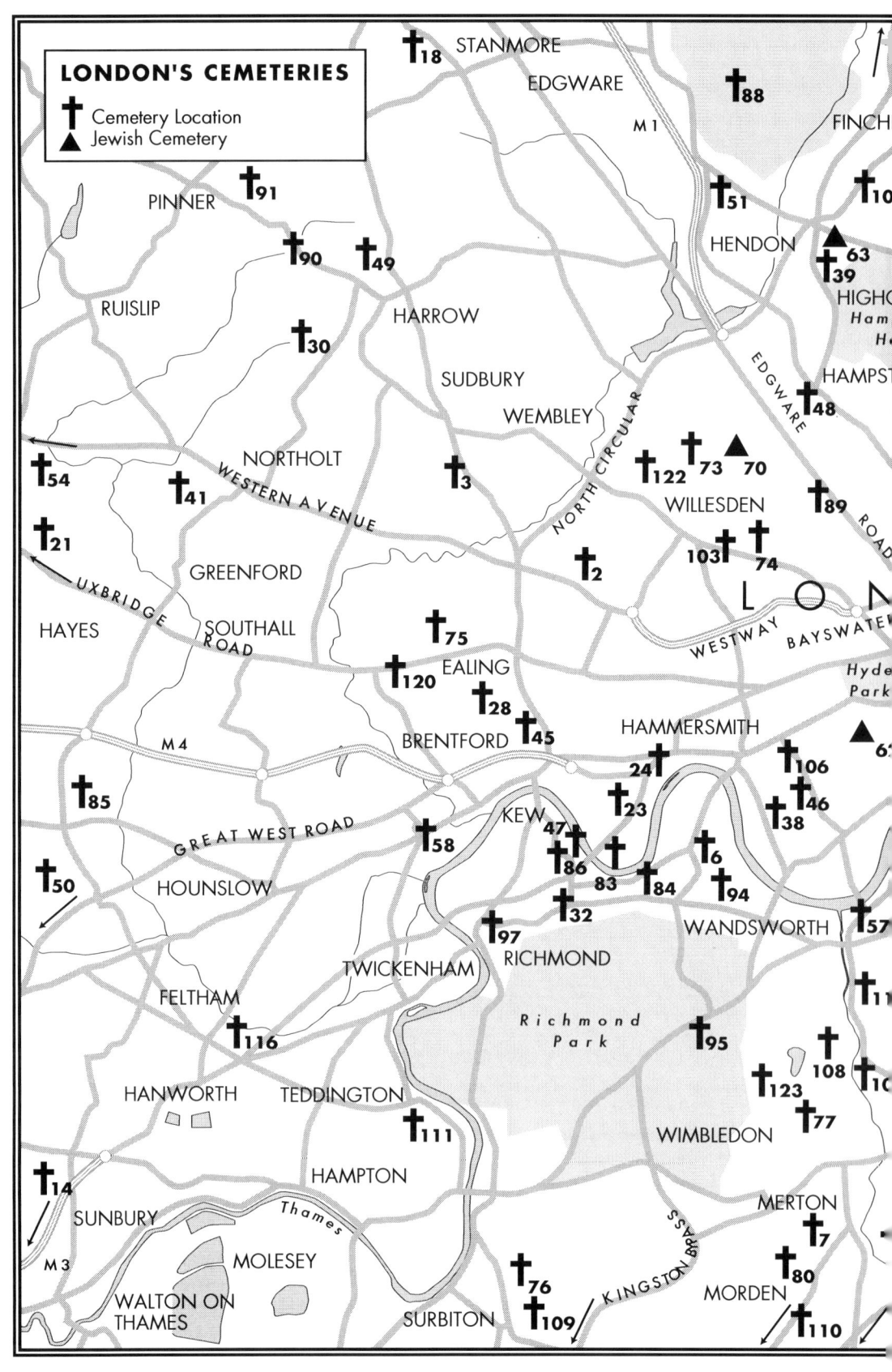

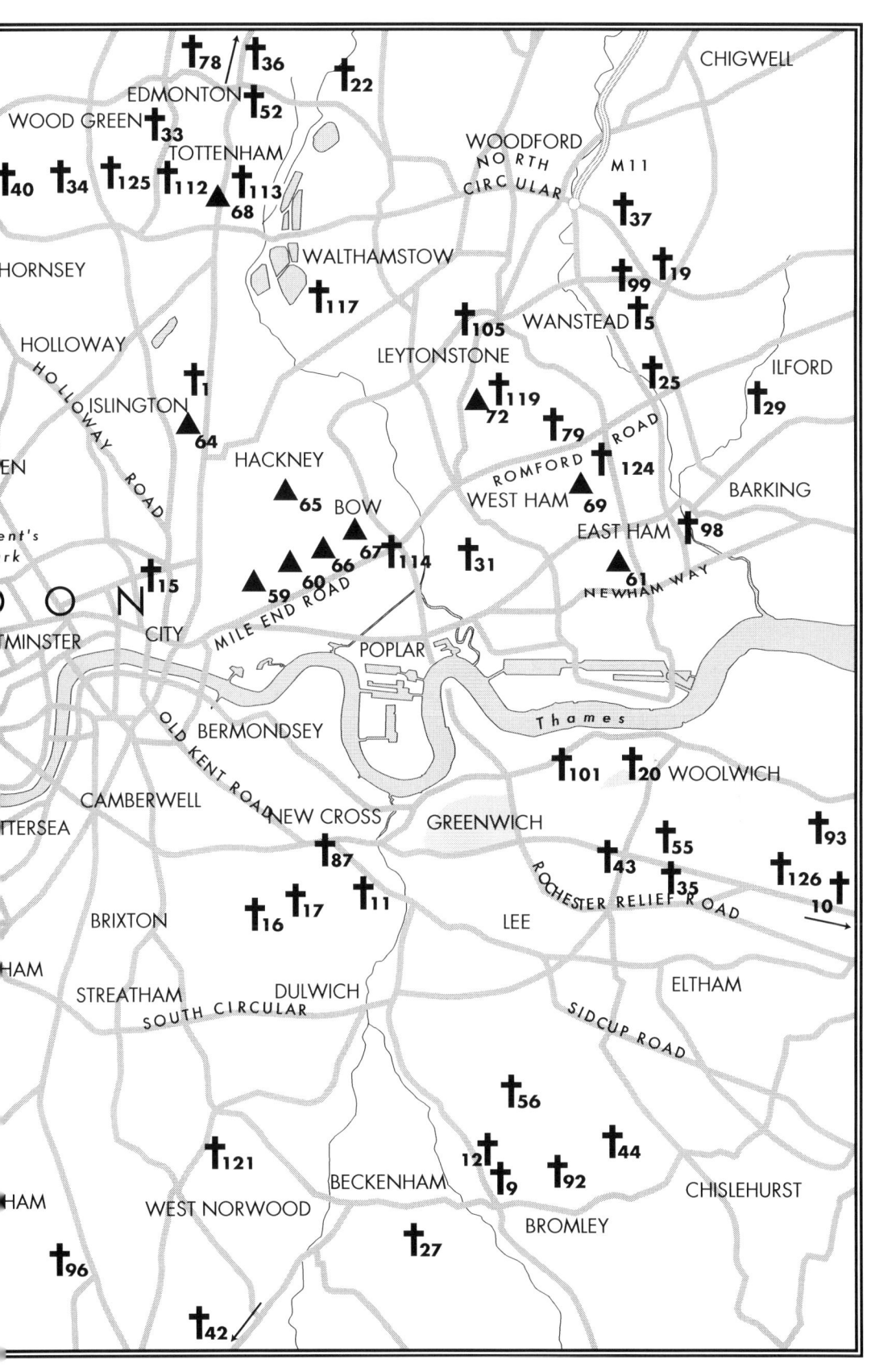

Illustrations

1. Cover image: Brompton Cemetery, 2006.
2. Frontispiece: Nunhead Cemetery: a fallen angel.
3. Wreath sellers in Islington.
4. A funeral procession at St Mary's R.C. Kensal Green (*c*. 1906).
5. Consecrated ground: illustration by Phiz for Dickens' *Bleak House (1852–53)*.
6. Victoria Park: following clearance in 1894 all that remains of the cemetery is the entrance, believed to be designed by Arthur Ashpitel. It is now called Meath Gardens.
7. Kensal Green: London's first garden cemetery: The tomb on the left commemorates Princess Sophia (1848).
8. The Pyramid: 'of Sepulchral magnificence unequalled in the world' . . . but never built. (By courtesy of Guildhall Library, City of London).
9. A coffin being loaded onto a train at the London Necropolis Station, Westminster Bridge Road, for the journey to Brookwood (*c*.1906).
10. Brookwood: A view of the proposed London Necropolis at Woking from *The Illustrated London News* (1852).
11. Golders Green: 'the world's foremost crematorium . . .'.
12. Kingsbury Lawn Cemetery; the abandoned chapel.
13. Forest Park: London's most recent cemetery and crematorium (2005).
14. Kensal Green: a view from the Anglican chapel in the early twentieth century.
15. Merton & Sutton: the twentieth century lawn cemetery concept.
16. Streatham Park: announcing the proposed cemetery from *The Undertakers' Journal* (September 1907).
17. Directors and shareholders of the Great Southern Cemetery, Crematorium and Land Company gather on the proposed site of the cemetery (*c*. 1909).
18. The City of London: 'one need only glimpse down one of the avenues . . .'
19. Monument to Dr Isaac Watts at Abney Park from *Modern Tombs Gleaned from the Public Cemeteries of London* by Arthur Hakewill (1851).
20. The premises of monumental masons, Henry Dunkley, adjacent to Abney Park Cemetery in Stoke Newington.
21. The Rothschild mausoleum at West Ham Jewish Cemetery by Sir Matthew Digby Wyatt (1866).
22. The Molyneux mausoleum at Kensal Green by John Gibson (1864)

23. The Berens sarcophagus at West Norwood by Edward Barry (1858) photographed in 1980.
24. Berens sarcophagus 2006.
25. Detail on a tile on the side of the Berens sarcophagus.
26. The Ralli family's Doric mortuary chapel at West Norwood by John Oldrid Scott (1872).
27. Kensal Green: 'an unparalleled folly' – the Ducrow mausoleum (1835).
28. Terracotta detail on the Doulton mausoleum at West Norwood (1897).
29. Alexander Gordon's Egyptian-style mausoleum at Putney Vale (1910).
30. An art deco monument in black granite.
31. A garden memorial; a typical design of the interwar period.
32. An empty chair in red granite at Pinner (1954).
33. Monoplane at Croydon in memory of Captain Leslie Thomas (1937).
34. The airman on the Bennett grave at Eltham (1938).
35. The life-size figure on the Lowndes memorial at Crystal Palace District Cemetery (1911). An identical but decapitated and toppled figure can be found at Camberwell Cemetery.
36. Two lions: Frank Bostock at Abney Park (1912) and on the Groves memorial at Streatham Park.
37. Brompton: Val Princep's Gothic sarcophagus, in Sienese marble (1904).
38. Mosaic on the Edwards grave (1918) at Chiswick Old.
39. Robed figure in bronze at Hendon on the King grave (1919).
40. Bronze memorial on the Boast grave (1895) by Aristide Fabbrucci at Hammersmith Old.
41. Brompton: Frederick Leyland's remarkable tomb – a unique example of 'Arts and Crafts' funerary design (1892).
42. West Norwood: The Gothic traceried Farrow tomb (1854) restored in 1999.
43. An unidentified iron grave surround.
44. A wooden graveboard at Hendon (1905).
45. The chapels at Battersea New by W.G. Poole (*The Building News* 1893). The scheme was changed when the North East Surrey Crematorium was created in 1958.
46. Exception to Gothic tradition: Renaissance chapels at Willesden (1891) by Charles Worley. Sadly, they were demolished in 1986 (courtesy of Brent Archive).
47. One of the pair of chapels at Streatham by William Newton-Dunn (1892)
48. The chapel at Rippleside by Charles Dawson (1886) who drew inspiration from St Margaret's church and the Curfew Tower in Barking for the design.
49. Hendon: The reredos by Cantagalli (1899) is a facsimile of Luca della Robbia's Resurrection in Florence Cathedral.
50. The mosaic reredos at Richmond's Grove Gardens Chapel (formerly the cemetery chapel).
51. Described as 'Hacienda deco' in style, Mortlake Crematorium was designed by the Hammersmith borough surveyor, F. Douglas Barton (1939).
52. West London Crematorium by G. Berkeley Willis (1939).
53. Demolished: One of the chapels at Camberwell by George Gilbert Scott photographed in 1969. (Courtesy of the City of London, London Metropolitan Archives).
54. Demolished: The chapel by England and Brown at Chingford Mount (1884) photographed in 1980.
55. Greenford Park: Both the original lodge (pictured here) and its replacement have disappeared.
56. The lodge at Westminster Hanwell (1854), the largest in London.
57. Hammersmith New: A brick gate pier with acorn finial in Portland stone (1926).

ILLUSTRATIONS   xv

58. West Norwood gates: 'this massive iron enceinte'.
59. Finial mitre design at Putney Lower Common.
60. City of London: Catacomb and columbarium for funerary ashes (1856) (entrance on the right).
61. Anchor at Richmond.
62. Angel at East Sheen.
63. Butterfly at East Sheen.
64. Dove at Fulham.
65. Gateway at East Sheen.
66. Hands clasped (of husband and wife) at Fulham.
67. Hourglass at Abney Park.
68. Lamp alight at Mortlake R.C.
69. Lily at Fulham.
70. Skull at Bunhill Fields.
71. Torch upturned at Highgate.
72. Tree, cut by the hand of God at Abney Park.
73. Urn, draped, at Brompton.
74. Weeping willow at Abney Park.
75. Epitaph at Putney Lower Common.
76. An iron grave marker at Walthamstow (1921).
77. The grave of Will Crooks M.P. (1921) at Tower Hamlets.
78. Edmonton: Grass cutting.
79. Highgate: Preparing flowers for planting on graves (1906).
80. Brompton: Pigeons.
81. Abney Park: The spread of vegetation (1980).
82. Abney Park: Ivy (1980).
83. Abney Park: the chapel (1840) in 1980. The growth of trees prevents this view being taken today.
84. Abney Park: Detail on a gate pier.
85. Abney Park: Indicative monument to John Jones, 'for many years a member of the South Hornsey Local Board.' (1883).
86. Acton: Trumpet on tomb of Edward Howard Reynolds (1898).
87. Battersea New: The poplar lined drive in 1910 when this photograph was taken. The chapels were converted into the North East Surrey Crematorium in 1958.
88. Battersea St Mary's: the chapels are perfect miniatures (1860).
89. Battersea St Mary's: the large flaming urn commemorates Kaikhoshru Puntheki (1890).
90. Brockley: Detail on the gate at the Ladywell entrance.
91. Brockley: The cemetery (1906); the chapels can be seen in the distance.
92. Bromley Hill: The Fuller memorial (1935).
93. Brompton: Gates to the catacombs.
94. Brompton: The chapel (1840).
95. Brompton: Italianate Baroque, the San Giorgi monument (1903).
96. Brompton: Robert Combes' monument with uniformed scullers, now defaced (1860).
97. Brompton: An imperious lion on John 'Gentleman' Jackson's tomb (1872) photographed in 1980. The urn has since disappeared.
98. Brompton: 'Courage: initiative: intrepidity.' The memorial to Flight Sub Lieut. Reginald Warneford (1915).

99. Brookwood: The Pelham Clinton-Memorial (*c.* 1898).
100. Brookwood: The Parsee section (1907).
101. Bunhill Fields.
102. Bunhill Fields: Tomb of Dame Mary Page (1728).
103. Bunhill Fields: John Bunyan's memorial erected in 1862.
104. Camberwell: The layout of the cemetery.
105. Camberwell: The statue on Lord Rodney's grave 'on guard' no longer.
106. Camberwell: The three chapels (demolished) and lodge.
107. Chadwell Heath: The front elevation of the chapel (1934).
108. Charlton: The layout of the cemetery as seen in *The Illustrated London News* (1857).
109. Charlton: Tomb of Jemima Ayley (1860). Further deterioration has taken place since this photograph was taken in 1980.
110. Charlton: Tomb of Thomas Murphy (1932).
111. Chingford Mount: The entrance and lodge (1844), now demolished.
112. Chingford Mount: Beehives on the Norwood vault (1872). A single beehive can also be found on the Norwood grave at Abney Park (1864).
113. Chiswick New: The 'Great West Road' style chapel designed by the borough surveyor, Joseph Musto (1933).
114. Chiswick Old: Bronze table tomb to James McNeill Whistler (1903). The corner statuettes are resin replacements.
115. Chiswick Old: The Resurrection by Edward Bainbridge Copnall on the grave of Sir Percy Harris (1952).
116. Chiswick Old: Memorial to James Hitch (1913).
117. City of London: The entrance gate *c.*1900. The Anglican chapel can be glimpsed in the background.
118. City of London: The Dissenters' chapel by William Haywood (*The Builder* 1856).
119. City of London: Memorial to piano teacher Gladys Spencer (1931).
120. City of London: The Vigiland memorial (1955).
121. Croydon: Memorial to headmaster John Drage (1900).
122. Crystal Palace District: Plans of the cemetery chapels (*The Builder* 1874).
123. Crystal Palace District: Memorial to the cricketer, W.G. Grace (1915).
124. Crystal Palace District Cemetery: The grave of Henry Lowndes can be seen on the right and the consecrated chapel (now demolished) is in the background.
125. Eastbrookend (then Ilford Park) advertisement from *The Undertakers' Journal* (1916).
126. East Sheen: 'The angel of Death . . .' The Lancaster bronze by Sydney March (1920).
127. East Sheen: The Rennie-O'Mahony memorial (1928).
128. Edmonton: The layout of the chapels from *The Building News* (1889).
129. Fulham Palace Road: The tympanum above the chapel door depicting the Resurrection.
130. Golders Green: The Philipson mausoleum by Sir Edwin Lutyens (1914).
131. Golders Green: The Smith mausoleum by Paul Phipps (1904–5).
132. Golders Green: Ghanshyamdas Birla (1983) looking towards the cloister.
133. Golders Green: The Watkins memorial in the cloister.
134. Golders Green: 'Into the Silent Land' by Henry Pegram (1924 and installed in 1937).
135. Great Northern: A view of the gates on Brunswick Park Road before relocation into the cemetery grounds.
136. Great Northern: The chapel designed by Alexander Spurr (1861). The spire is 150ft high.

ILLUSTRATIONS xvii

137. Grove Park: The date of the cemetery's opening in 1935 is noted on this Portland Stone drinking fountain in the form of an urn.
138. Gunnersbury: The Anglican chapel designed by Arthur Knapp Fisher (1937). It had a short life as it was destroyed after the Second World War.
139. Gunnersbury: The black obelisk of the Katyn memorial photographed in 1980.
140. Hammersmith Old: Detail on the memorial to gold digger Abe Smith (1923).
141 Hampstead: View of the cemetery *The Builder* (1876).
142. Hampstead: The Bianchi monument (c. 1938).
143. Hampstead: Church organ in memory of Charles Barritt (1929).
144. Hampstead: The Wilson sarcophagus, 'a respectable imitation of an Egyptian temple.'
145. Hampstead: The snake-entwined bronze urn on the Frankau grave (1904). It was stolen in 1997.
146. Hampstead: Tomb sculptured by Sir William Goscombe John (1923). It was stolen but has since been recovered.
147. Hendon: The entrance shortly after opening. The words '& Crematorium' were added to the stone lettering in 1922.
148. Hendon: The burial chapel *c.*1905.
149. Highgate: The catacombs. The Beer mausoleum now occupies a prominent position on the terrace.
150. Highgate: The Beer mausoleum.
151. Highgate: Karl Marx (1956).
152. Highgate: George Wombwell (1880) photographed in 1980 before the undergrowth was cleared.
153. Highgate The Egyptian Avenue photographed in 1980 and after restoration (Copyright the late John Gay).
154. Hillingdon: The entrance on Hillingdon Hill by Benjamin Ferrey (1855).
155. Hither Green: The chapel by Francis Thorne (1873).
156. Jewish: Willesden: the Rosenberg tombs (1904–35).
157. Jewish: Plashet: Consecrating a memorial from *Living London* (1906).
158. Kensal Green: The 'towering Gothic confection' tomb of John Gibson (1894).
159. Kensal Green: Sir William Casement's mausoleum (1844).
160. Kensal Green: Baroque angels over Mary Gibson's Corinthian temple monument (1870).
161. Kensal Green: Renaissance effigy on the Mulready tomb (1863).
162. Kensal Green: Rickett's tomb by William Burges (1867).
163. Kensal Green: The Sievier family monument (1865).
164. Kensal Green: The Cooke family monument (1866) by Thomas Milnes photographed in 1980.
165. Kensal Green: The Dissenters' Chapel, restored in 1997.
166. Kensington Hanwell: Memorial to Edgar Smith, conchologist (1916).
167. Kensington Hanwell: The entrance arch by Thomas Allom (1855).
168. Kingston: The bronze figure by Richard Goulden on the Burton grave (1908).
169. Lambeth: Perspective view of the cemetery from *The Builder* (1854).
170. Mortlake R.C.: Sir Richard Burton's stone "tent" (1890).
171. Nunhead: The chapel by Thomas Little (1840).
172. Nunhead: As above . . . and after restoration.
173. Nunhead: The restored terracotta Stearnes mausoleum (*c.* 1900).
174. Nunhead: Detail from the Stearnes mausoleum.

175. Nunhead: James Bunning's entrance gates.
176. Paddington: The chapels by Thomas Little (1855).
177. Putney Vale: The entrance (1900). The chapel was converted to a crematorium in 1938, badly burned by fire in 1946 and reopened in 1956.
178. Putney Vale: The Ismay memorial (1937).
179. Putney Vale: Reclining figure on the Marsh grave (1920).
180. Richmond: Detail on a grave (1902).
181. Richmond: The tomb of William Harvey, engraver (1866).
182. Richmond: Passion flowers and lilies.
183. St Marylebone: The consecration service from *The Illustrated London News* (1855).
184. St Marylebone: Tomb of Thomas Tate by F. Lynn Jenkins (1909).
185. St Marylebone: Tomb of Harry Ripley by Sir William Reid-Dick (1914).
186. St Marylebone: The memorial to Thomas Skarratt Hall (1903) showing the bronze angels which were stolen in 1989.
187. St Marylebone: The interior of the Glenesk mausoleum by Sir Arthur Blomfield (1908).
188. St Mary's R.C.: Bronze relief of the Holy Family on the Connolly grave (1933).
189. St Mary's R.C.: The Emmet Mausoleum.
190. St Mary's R.C.: The Campbell family's Byzantine mausoleum by C.H.B. Quennell (1904).
191. St Pancras & Islington: Percival Spencer – Aeronaut (1905). The balloon has been removed.
192. St Pancras & Islington: The lodge (1900). It was demolished in 1970.
192. St Pancras & Islington: Memorial commemorating Harry Gardner.
193. St Pancras & Islington: The grave of William French (1896).
194. St Pancras & Islington: The Mond mausoleum by Darcy Braddell (1909).
195. Streatham: "A garden job" on the Krall grave (1903).
196. St Patrick's R.C.: The Ferrari mausoleum (1965).
197. Streatham: The blue terracotta temple commemorating Henry Budden (1907).
198. Streatham Park: 'He lived as he died a cyclist' – Maurice Selback (1935).
199. Streatham Park: South London Crematorium which opened in 1936.
200. Sutton: The chapel (1900).
201. Teddington: 'Typically Victorian'.
202. Tottenham: The chapels by George Pritchett (1856) before enlargement of the cemetery.
203. Tottenham: The tunnel under the footpath dividing the cemetery.
204. Tower Hamlets: The Anglican chapel by Thomas Wyatt and David Brandon.
205. Tower Hamlets: . . . and the Nonconformist chapel. (The Illustrated London News 1849).
206. Twickenham: Francis Francis's tomb (1886) Regrettably the fishing rod is missing.
207. Walthamstow: The chapels (1872). Unusually, they are positioned at right angles.
208. Wandsworth: The entrance from Magdalen Road following enlargement of the cemetery in 1898–9. The chapels are on either side of the drive.
209. West Ham: West Ham: Memorial to Sub-Officer Henry Vickers and Fireman Frederick Sell who died in the Slivertoun explosion in 1917.
210. West Norwood: The entrance (1905). The lodge was demolished in 1936 and the current building dates from 1950.
211. West Norwood: Completed before his death in 1939, the mausoleum commemorates Edmund Distin Maddick.
212. West Norwood: The Anglican chapel, demolished 1960.

213. West Norwood: Contrasts. Rear, Sir William Tite's monument for the banker J.W. Gilbart (1866), foreground, millstone grit monolith by George Godwin for John Britton (1857).
214. West Norwood: Memorial to John Wimble (1851) on Ship Path.
215. West Norwood: Detail on the Brown memorial (1884).
216. Wimbledon: The Cooke Mausoleum (1885). It has been vandalised since this photograph was taken in 1980.
217. Woolwich: The lodge and chapel on the right have been demolished.
218. Woodgrange Park: Artist's impression of the chapel by W. Gillbee Scott from The Architect (1889).
219. Woodgrange Park: The chapel in 2005. It was demolished a year later.
220. Brompton: Notice to visitors
221. Sutton, sans peur.

Authors' note to the fourth edition

Since 1981 when the first edition of this book appeared, there has been a marked renewal in all aspects of the management and history of cemeteries. Prior to that date little had been written on the subject and even now it is only the 'magnificent seven' – Kensal Green, Norwood, Highgate, Nunhead, Abney Park, Brompton and Tower Hamlets – which have been well documented.[1]

This new edition seeks to provide a comprehensive guide to the cemeteries of London. In defining cemeteries churchyards have been excluded and the scope has been limited to burial grounds unattached to any one parish church or chapel. They are nearly always owned by a local authority or a private company, usually with a funerary building or buildings within the ground and not merely confined to any one religious denomination. (Jewish cemeteries are an exception.) Only existing and accessible grounds are included; not all are still in use but the long lost plague pits, hospital, 'private and promiscuous' grounds referred to in Mrs Holmes' pioneering book *The London Burial Grounds* (1896) are excluded. The first edition contained 100 entries; a further three cemeteries were added to the second and third. This new edition contains 126 cemeteries representing the majority in the London boroughs, as well as others within a nine mile radius of central London (or roughly the area covered by the A-Z map). Although well outside this boundary, but integral to the development of London's nineteenth century cemeteries, the vast Brookwood cemetery at Woking also has an entry.

A minor problem has been caused by the multiplicity of names by which some cemeteries are known. For examples, Hammersmith New cemetery is also known as Mortlake Cemetery, while Hammersmith Old Cemetery is known as Margravine Road Cemetery. Two changes of name have been made for this edition; Lee is now Hither Green, while 'West' has been prefixed to Norwood Cemetery. For cemeteries with a crematorium this too has been appended to the title.[2] The date of founding indicates when work commenced on preparing the cemetery grounds; it is not necessarily the date of the first burial.

Each cemetery includes a selection of notable persons buried or commemorated there adding up to over two thousand names in all. These were picked as far as possible for their historical importance or curiosity. Many of them are still familiar to us today. The names are indexed in a single alphabetical list at the end for ease of research. There is also a separate index of architects, artists and sculptors whose work is represented in the cemeteries.

In producing the book expert help has been acquired from many. Those who deserved a particular mention include the late Reg Broadhurst who cut the wood engravings, Mrs H.K.

Meller, Gwyneth Nott-Macaire and Mrs B.H.W. Parsons for heroically typing the manuscripts. Photographs were taken by the late Vera Collingwood, Tiggy Ruthven, Hugh Meller and Brian Parsons. Gratitude is expressed to the Friends of Highgate Cemetery Trust for permission to use one image taken by the late John Gay. Archive photographs, except where indicated, are from Brian Parsons' collection. The book would not have been possible without them.

Guidance from the librarians of London's local history libraries, cemetery officials and local historians has been of immense help. New information has always been welcome and when the second edition appeared in 1984 Dr. J.D. Pickles, Michael Robbins, Eric Robinson, Eric Smith and Peter Stickley supplied a great deal of new material. Similarly, for the third edition Jeffrey Hart, Julian Litten, Jo Mahoney, Jean Pateman, Bob Flanagan, Nicholas Reed, Michael Kerney and Gregory Drozdz were generous with information.

For the fourth edition the following have been of particular assistance: Roger Arber, David Solman, John Clarke, Robert Stephenson, Bob Flanagan, Bob Langford, Jean Pateman, Richard Quirk, John Gallehawk, Dr Ian Hussein, Dr Sharman Kadish, Charles Tucker, Richard Baldwin, Bob and Sheri Coates, Celia Smith and Ian Beeson. Particular thanks is extended to Nicholas Parsons.

Nevertheless despite their help, mistakes or omissions will have crept in and the authors would be grateful to readers who can advise of any inaccuracy or of additional information.

Hugh Meller
Devon

Brian Parsons
London
September 2007

Introduction

'The Angel of Death seems to be continuously hovering over London', began a short article by TW Wilkinson in 1906 entitled '*Burying London*'.

> While he may not visit a secluded village once in a year, he spreads his wings over some one of the myriad houses in the mighty city every six minutes, and bears away an immortal soul. Ten times hourly does a mortal spark return to its Maker, leaving its earthly tabernacle to descend to the dust from which it sprang. And it is in consequence of the frequency of this natural separation – due, of course, to the size of the Metropolis, and not to an exceptionally high rate of mortality – that death is a great, ever-present fact in the world's capital.

The author then warms to his thesis on the black trade, 'Patent in nearly all business thoroughfares is the industrial side of life's dissolution.' He describes the West End firms which 'can, on occasion, put ladies in black in twenty-four hours'; the Islington wreath makers 'on the beaten track to the great gardens of sleep at Highgate and Finchley'; the Euston Road stonemasons' shops 'looking like a transplanted slip of cemetery' and the heart of the 'black trade' in a huge establishment in the City, 'where one might find a vast stock of wood, such as would set up in business two or three timber merchants, and coffin furniture by the ton'. Above all there was 'the still more important Metropolitan business' of the cemeteries, 'burying proper', as Mr Wilkinson bluntly described it.[1]

From this description there can be no doubt that in 1906 disposal of the dead in London was still an occasion of solemn ceremony

Wreath sellers in Islington (1906)

A funeral procession at St Mary's R.C. Kensal Green (1906)

culminating in a lavish funeral procession to the chosen cemetery where a small fortune might be spent on a mausoleum. The cemetery companies themselves took immense pains to attract custom by providing a wide range of brick lined graves, vaults and catacombs in carefully landscaped surroundings. Mrs Stone, writing in 1896, enthusiastically described a visit to a London cemetery. 'I entered the cemetery; a more beautiful and luxurious garden it is impossible to conceive.'[2] Her reaction would not have been unusual; casual visitors to cemeteries were expected in the nineteenth century. Arboreta were planted, guides written and epitaphs discussed.

Such sentiments waned during the twentieth century as attitudes to death became more reserved and appreciation of Victorian values and achievements were neglected and unrecognised. During this period cemeteries suffered from neglect and vandalism. The move towards cremation reduced income; the decline in expenditure on maintenance of the landscape was all too apparent while chapels and lodges were demolished. Only in the last twenty-five years has interest revived. The 'Friends' movement, the statutory listing of memorials and buildings, practical conservation work and publications have raised the profile of cemeteries.

Within about a ten mile radius of central London there are over 120 cemeteries and 25 crematoria. Their total acreage is approximately 3,500; about the size of one of London's smaller boroughs. Some are vast – St Pancras and Islington Cemetery is one of the largest at 185 acres; a few cover less than an acre; most comprise twenty to forty. All cemeteries, of course, exhibit a variety of monuments while most have at least one chapel and a lodge. Some were designed by distinguished architects. In Norwood alone there are works by Thomas Allom, Edward Barry, William Burges, George Godwin, John Oldrid Scott, George Edmund Street and Sir William Tite. Most can boast the graves of figures of national distinction or at least of local importance. Patient research has revealed the tombs of over 650 famous men and women at Kensal Green. Together with other Victorian cemeteries, such as Brompton, Highgate and Norwood they provide a chapter in Victorian history, as well as a galaxy of Victorian funerary art.

ONE

History

In the history of the cemetery movement, London played a major but often insalubrious role until well after the founding of its first garden cemetery at Kensal Green in 1832.[1] Before that date the means of burial in London was either traditionally in the churchyard or in one of the recently founded private burial grounds and chapels. By the 1830s neither method was proving satisfactory. Some churchyards had been in use since the middle ages (St. Paul's had a continuous history of burial since the Romans), and they were now expected to cope with over 40,000 deaths annually, fuelled by cholera epidemics and a vast increase in the population. The City churchyards were, quite simply, filled to overflowing, a fact which did not escape the attention of many commentators who described their ghastly state in the most resounding Victorian prose.

The Builder was dramatic:

> This London, the centre of civilization, this condensation of wisdom and intelligence, this huge wedge and conglomerate of pride, buries – no it does not bury – but stores and piles up 50,000 of its dead to putrefy, to rot, to give out exhalations, to darken the air with vapours, faugh! It is loathsome to think of it; but it is strictly true, 50,000 desecrated corpses are every year stacked in some 150 limited pits of churchyards, burial grounds they are called, and one talks of decent and Christian burial . . .[2]

Dickens was sardonic:

> Such strange churchyards hide in the City of London; churchyards sometimes so entirely pressed upon by houses, so small, so rank, so silent, so forgotten except by the few people who ever look down into them from their smokey windows. As I stand peeping in through the iron gate and rails, I can peel the rusty metal off, like bark from an old tree. The illegible tombstones are all lopsided, the gravemounds lost their shape in the rains of a hundred years ago, the Lombardy Poplar or Plane-Tree that was once a drysalter's daughter and

Consecrated ground: illustration by Phiz for Dickens' book *Bleak House* (1852–53)

several common-councilmen, has withered like those worthies, and its departed leaves are dust beneath it. Contagion of slow ruin overhangs the place . . .[3]

He could also be horrific, as in *Bleak House*:

"There!" says Jo, pointing, "over yinder, among them pile of bones, and close to that there kitchin winder! They put him very nigh the top. They was obliged to stamp upon it to git it in. I could unkiver it for you with my broom, if the gate was open. That's why they locks it I s'pose," giving it a shake. "It's always locked. Look at the rat!" cries Jo, excited. "Hi! Look! There he goes! Ho! Into the ground!"[4]

The anonymous author of a poem called 'City Graves' treated the subject with macabre humour:

> I saw from out the earth peep forth
> The white and glistening bones,
> With jagged ends of coffin planks,
> That e'en the worm disowns;
> And once a smooth round skull rolled on,
> Like a football, on the stones.[5]

Others argued scientifically, but no less sensationally. Dr Lyon Playfair reckoned that 2,572,580 cubic feet of gases were emitted annually from London's graveyards – which would explain Dickens' remark that 'rot and mildew and dead citizens formed the uppermost scent'[6] in the City.

George Walker, a surgeon with a strong stomach and a dedication to burial reform, zealously visited about fifty London graveyards and in 1839 published his findings in a book, *Gatherings from Grave-Yards, Particularly those of London, with a concise History of the Modes of Interment among different Nations, from the earliest Periods: and a Detail of dangerous and fatal Results produced by the unwise and revolting Custom of inhuming the Dead in the midst of the Living*. He described the London malpractices at length: drunken gravediggers, second-hand coffins, illegal exhumation, fatal 'miasmas' and the sort of perils that sometimes attended funerals.

> In making a grave a body, partly decomposed, was dug up, and placed on the surface, at the side, slightly covered with earth; a mourner stepped upon it, the loosened skin peeled off, he slipped forward, and had nearly fallen into the grave.[7]

Walker was sternly critical of such appalling incidents which prevailed, more especially in the private burial grounds such as Victoria Park which opened in 1845 and was closed around forty years later.[8]

Victoria Park: following clearance in 1894 all that remains of the cemetery is the entrance, believed to be designed by Arthur Ashpitel. It is now called Meath Gardens

An indignant history of these dubious enterprises was written by Mrs Basil Holmes in 1896. The overcrowded churchyards in the late eighteenth century prompted 'some adventurers to start cemeteries as private speculations', she wrote. By 1835 she estimated, 'there must have been at least fourteen burial grounds in London carried on by private persons, besides some additional chapels with vaults under them conducted in the same way'. These speculations appear to have been managed by totally unscrupulous entrepreneurs who attracted business by undercutting the church's burial charges. Often the officiants were not ministers of religion at all and Mrs Holmes quotes the case of a shoemaker living near such a chapel who conducted funerals dressed in a surplice. Gravediggers were 'obliged to be half groggy to do it' in burial grounds that in one case measured under an acre but had admitted 14,000 bodies in only twenty years, some buried only 2ft deep. Bodies were burnt and mutilated, quicklime was used to hasten decomposition, gravestones were moved 'to give an impression of emptiness'. Bone stealing was common (they were ground down and sold as manure), coffin lead was also stolen and the timbers broken up for firewood.

> No doubt practices as vile, as unwholesome and as irreverent were carried on in many of the churchyards, but the overcrowding of the private grounds is so associated with the idea of a private gloating over private gains that is more repulsive.[9]

– said Mrs Holmes.

The most notorious of these places was Enon Chapel, Clements Lane, a dissenters' chapel opened in 1823, which Walker first described in 1839.

> Vast numbers of bodies have been placed here . . . soon after interments were made, a peculiarly long narrow black fly was observed to crawl out of many of the coffins; this insect, a product of the putrefaction of the bodies, was observed on the following season to be succeeded by another, which had the appearance of a common bug with wings. The children attending the Sunday School, held in this chapel in which these insects were seen to be crawling and flying, in vast numbers, during the summer months, called them "body bugs".[10]

Between the coffins and the chapel floor there was nothing but the boards, not even tongued and grooved. The 'effluvium' in the chapel became so intolerable that no one attended the services although the interments continued.[11] It was reports such as these that belatedly forced the Government to act.

In fact there had been several previous attempts to provide London with adequate burial grounds. Problems encountered as long ago as the plague in the seventeenth century and the opportunity provided by the Great Fire had stimulated plans for extra-mural cemeteries from John Evelyn and Sir Christopher Wren, neither of them implemented. In the early eighteenth century Sir John Vanburgh pleaded that new churches:

> Be free'd from that inhuman custome of being made burial places for the Dead; a custome in which there is something so very barbarous in itself besides the many ill consequences that attend it . . . there must therefore be cemitarys provided in the skirts of the Towne . . . Handsomely and regularly wall'd in, and planted with Trees.[12]

A few churches like St George's, Bloomsbury were provided with small detached churchyards and, after initial misgivings, they became popular but soon filled to capacity. There was also Bunhill Fields in the City which evolved from a seventeenth-century plague pit into the foremost dissenters' cemetery of the eighteenth century, but this was exceptional.

Meanwhile foreign cities in similar difficulties took the first steps towards providing large cemeteries independent of parish churches. British reformers were able to quote precedents in India, Turkey, Louisiana and especially France. Burial in city churchyards had been forbidden in France since 1804, the same year that the grandest of all European cemeteries was founded

Kensal Green: London's first garden cemetery. The tomb on the left commemorates Princess Sophia (1848)

at the Père-Lachaise in Paris. Dr John Strang, a pioneering enthusiast for Scottish cemeteries exhorted Glaswegians in his book *Necropolis Glasguensis* (1831) to imitate the French in the formation of a Scottish Père-Lachaise, and it was in the centres of nonconformity like Scotland and Ulster that British cemeteries came into being.[13]

The Rosary Cemetery in Norwich was licensed for 'burial of all denominations' in 1819, the first in England, followed four years later by the Liverpool Necropolis, a year after the barrister George Carden began his campaign for establishing public cemeteries in *The Penny Magazine of the Society for the Diffusion of Useful Knowledge*.[14]

In February 1830 Carden convened a meeting to consider the formation of a London cemetery and the London Cemetery Company was constituted. In January 1832 the first of a series of cholera epidemics hit London, proving once more how necessary it was to provide cemeteries. Many people in fact believed that the evil-smelling city graveyards were in some way responsible for the disease. In July 1832 the company obtained the right by Act of Parliament to open a cemetery at Kensal Green.

Below: A coffin being loaded onto a train at the London Necropolis station, Westminster Bridge Road, for the journey to Brookwood (c. 1906)

Above: The Pyramid: 'of Sepulchral magnificence unequalled in the world' . . . but never built. (By courtesy of Guildhall Library, City of London)

Brookwood: A view of the proposed London Necropolis at Woking from The *Illustrated London News* (1852)

It was a success, and very quickly other joint-stock companies were formed to provide a *cordon sanitaire* of seven private cemeteries around London. £400,000 was invested, 260 acres purchased and 3,336 burials coped with annually, according to Sir Edwin Chadwick, who produced a report for the Poor Law Commissioners, *On the Results of a Special Inquiry into the Practice of Interment in Towns* in 1843. Chadwick emphasised that cemeteries should not be the exclusive preserve of commercial companies, but that public cemeteries should be founded to cater for the poorer classes. He and others complained that burial in private cemeteries was becoming synonymous with luxury. The cheapest graves in Kensal Green cost thirty shillings and there was the additional expense of travelling there. Brick vaults cost as much as £50 and the huge mausolea could easily exceed £1,000. In contrast, burial at Enon Chapel had been bought for a mere twelve shillings. On another point Chadwick was adamant. Burial in towns should be 'entirely prohibited'.[15]

His advice was heeded by the 1850 Metropolitan Interments Act. It legislated that the Board of Health should have powers to lay out new cemeteries, advise on the closure of old churchyards in which further burials were forbidden and even to purchase compulsorily the private cemeteries. Brompton Cemetery was, in fact, acquired before the Act was repealed by the 1852 Burial Act, which empowered London vestries to form Burial Boards and provide new burial grounds of their own. This Act was the foundation of a spate of new Burial Acts that were only finally rationalised by the 1972 Local Government Act.

In 1850 a scheme for the two national cemeteries was proposed – one at Erith called the Great Eastern Metropolitan Cemetery and the equivalent in the west being an enlarged Kensal Green Cemetery.[16] Although these failed, the proposal for a large burial area, away from the populated area with room for future expansion, was realised in 1854 when the London Necropolis and National Mausoleum Company opened their vast Brookwood Cemetery at Woking. However, with the exception of pauper burials, the cemetery was not the success its directors had hoped

Golders Green: 'the world's foremost crematorium . . .'

for as competition increased from Burial Board cemeteries and also private companies who continued to be active in the second half of the nineteenth century. Chingford Mount (1884), Crystal Palace District (1880), East London (1872), Hendon (1899), Manor Park (1874) and Woodgrange Park (1888) all opened in this period.

One further important development in the history of London's cemeteries was a twentieth-century phenomenon although deeply rooted in the nineteenth century – cremation. There had been advocates of the practice for centuries, including, in the first half of the nineteenth century George Walker and John Loudon. There was support too from the general public according to information in *The Builder* in 1850.

> An association has been formed, at the City of London Mechanics Institution to promote the practice of decomposing the dead by the agency of fire. The members propose to burn, with becoming solemnity, such of their dead as shall have left their remains at the dispersal of the association.[17]

In 1874 Sir Henry Thompson, the Queen's surgeon, sensing the swing of public opinion in its favour, founded the Cremation Society whose supporters included Sir John Millais, Sir John Tenniel, Anthony Trollope, Charles Voysey and Sir Thomas Spencer Wells. The Society intended using land at the Great Northern Cemetery for building Britain's first crematorium, but it was thwarted by the Bishop of Rochester who refused to allow its construction on consecrated ground. In 1878, an acre of land was bought from the London Necropolis Company, whose Brookwood cemetery was nearby but despite building a cremator the following year, due to legal issues the first official cremation was delayed until March 1885.[18]

In the 1890s, Manchester, Glasgow and Liverpool built crematoria and again London was slow in following the example of the provinces. However, by 1900 the increase in the number of cremations at Woking persuaded the Cremation Society to establish a separate London Cremation Company which soon made up for earlier inadequacies. In 1902 the Golders Green Crematorium was opened by Sir Henry Thompson which was to become, in the Company's own words, 'the world's foremost crematorium.'[19] The City of London Crematorium opened within their cemetery at Ilford in 1904 but it was not until 1915 that south London was provided with a facility when the South Metropolitan Cemetery Company opened West Norwood Crematorium.

By 1900 there were approximately eighty-six cemeteries in the London area; thirty years later that had risen to 116. While the joint-stock company had initially led the way only to be competing against burial board cemeteries, private enterprise continued in the twentieth century. Organisations like the Great Southern Cemetery, Crematorium and Land Company established Streatham Park Cemetery in 1909 (and a crematorium in 1936), and the Abney Park Cemetery Company having four cemeteries and a crematorium, rivalled United Cemeteries Ltd for being the largest proprietary cemetery company in the UK.

Meanwhile, burial and cemeteries were increasingly under threat. The opening of five crematoria during the inter-war years was followed by a shift in the preference for cremation with burial being finally overtaken in 1967. Demand at the City of London was at such a level that a new crematorium was built in 1971. There are now twenty-five crematoria in London but the upward trend for cremation appears to have steadied with the rate static at around 71 per cent.

The low point for cemeteries appears to have peaked in the 1970s. Private cemetery companies – particularly those without the revenue from a crematorium – fared the worst. All possible land including the verges of main drives and pathways were used for burials, while spare acres were sold for housing, such as at Great Northern. Some cemeteries were sold to local authorities. One of the first such acquisitions was Hendon Cemetery and Crematorium in 1965 by the London Borough of Barnet. Lambeth purchased the South Metropolitan Cemetery at West Norwood the following year, while Nunhead went to Southwark, Chingford Mount to Waltham Forest, Abney Park to Hackney and Tower Hamlets to the Great London Council (now the London Borough of Tower Hamlets). But for local authorities, cemeteries – whether their own or those acquired – were not a high priority and many suffered from a lack of recognition and capital. In many cases maintenance was minimal and cemeteries started to face two threats.

Firstly, there was a policy of inaction by those responsible for the cemetery's maintenance. At some of the most significant – Abney Park, Highgate, Nunhead and Tower Hamlets, the undergrowth had become impenetrable with buildings allowed to decay. Chapels and lodges started to disappear and their removal invited vandalism. Almost everywhere monuments had been smashed and toppled from their plinths. It must be conceded that only unusual vigilance could prevent determined vandals, but in some instances even basic precautions have been ignored. Barnes Common cemetery for example has had its railings removed, Putney Vale has quite inadequate railings on the Wimbledon Common side, while Highgate and Nunhead were for years inadequately protected, all with predictable results.

Secondly, active damage was usually conducted in the name of economy. Rather than pursue a programme of gentle maintenance, brutal tactics with machines and sledgehammers have flattened acres of Nunhead, Streatham, Streatham Park and West Norwood. In some cases, it can be argued that neglect by former owners leaves burial authorities with no alternative.

None of these ploys, however, compare with the unprecedented solution devised by the City of Westminster. In 1987 the City sold its three cemeteries – Paddington Mill Hill, St Marylebone and Westminster Hanwell – to a private company at a token cost of fifteen pence. Tory councillors had been exasperated by the intractable responsibility of cemetery ownership and welcomed the chance to pass the £400,000 annual expense to someone else. Not surprisingly the plan backfired. Within twenty-four hours the three cemeteries were sold on again, the first of several ownership changes by property companies callously speculating on the profits to be made from the land and buildings without regard to the maintenance of the cemeteries themselves. Lodges were prime targets to be fenced off and sold leaving the cemeteries unguarded for long periods which inevitably encouraged vandals.

In 1988 complaints from relatives of the deceased were upheld by the Ombudsman who severely criticised the Council's manoeuvre and ruled it was obliged compulsorily to buy the cemeteries back. The price, however, was no longer fifteen pence but closer to £10 million, and the owner a Panamanian registered company with its headquarters in Switzerland. The City Council was in trouble until luckily the district auditor decided it had had no powers to sell the cemeteries and the original sale was void. In 1992, contrary to expectations, Westminster Council repossessed the three cemeteries, albeit minus thirteen acres of development land at Mill Hill. The case is therefore an important warning to local authorities and other cemetery owners who neglect their duties. One estimate concludes it cost Westminster ratepayers £4.5 million.

A more recent concern has been the safety of memorials. While some authorities have taken a gentle approach by erecting warning signs and supporting memorials with wooden stakes, the strategy of others has been more dramatic. Not only have angels, crosses and larger headstones been marked by metal bands, wrapped in yellow plastic sheeting and designated as unsafe, but they have been laid flat on the ground. This crude solution has provoked considerable outrage. A report by the Local Government Ombudsman (2006) deemed this a last resort over other methods of stabilising memorials.[20] In an effort to cope with the demand for burial space and preservation of memorials, the City of London Cemetery introduced a novel solution. Old graves with sufficient depth remaining for two or three burials have been resold along with the memorial which is then cleaned and the inscription removed or the base simply 'turned around.' A team of cemetery officials, heritage personnel and others recommend each memorial for such preservation.

Kingsbury Lawn Cemetery; the abandoned chapel

Despite these threats, burials have continued in many London cemeteries, as existing graves have been required for new interments in addition to the demand for more graves. Since 1945 a handful of new cemeteries have opened; Carpenders Park (1954), Forest Park (2005), Hatton (1974), Hillview (1985), Trent Park (1960) and Wood Green (1995) have all been established. Astonishingly, Kingsbury Lawn Cemetery was completed but abandoned before the first burial took place.[21] As the shortage of burial space becomes critical, cemeteries have embraced land that was once used for recreational, allotment or other purposes.[22] Extensions can be found at Camberwell New, Chadwell Heath, Cherry Lane, Chiswick and Teddington with preparations also being made at Greenford Park and Twickenham. At East London, St Mary's Roman Catholic, St Patrick's and Wandsworth, areas already containing graves have been banked up with soil and then used for new interments. Unfortunately, two local authorities – Hackney and Tower Hamlets – have no burial space. Many cemetery managers consider that the reuse of old graves will provide sufficient graves in the future, particularly if they adopt the 'lift and deepen' system of excavating the contents of graves, burying the remains at a lower level and then offering the space for new burials.[23] Following the 2002 *Environment, Transport and Regional Affairs Committee Report on Cemeteries*, consultation with cemetery managers and the Ministry of Justice publishing their *Burial Law and Policy in the 21st Century: The Way Forward*, the power to disturb human remains was given in the London Local Authorities Act 2007.

The *Cemeteries* report came following two decades of 'cemetery rediscovery'. Increased public awareness of the value of cemeteries as an environment for art, architecture, local heritage, fauna and flora has meant that many are now visited and appreciated. Much can be attributed to the efforts of 'Friends' groups. Starting with Highgate in 1975, their agenda has been to raise cemetery profiles through guided walks, publications, open days, assistance with maintenance, special projects and fund raising. Groups now exist at Abney Park, Brockley,

Forest Park: London's most recent cemetery and crematorium (2005)

Brompton, Brookwood, City of London, Hampstead, Highgate, Kensal Green, Nunhead, West Norwood and Woodgrange Park. At both Highgate and Kensal Green their efforts have been instrumental in renovating the chapels and other worthwhile projects.

There have also been an increasing number of publications covering aspects such as the history and development of cemeteries and those interred. English Heritage has listed many more buildings and monuments. Better still, while there are a few exceptions, the owners of cemeteries have worked hard to improve the standard of maintenance of the grounds and buildings. In some, such as Tower Hamlets and Highgate, efforts have been made not only to preserve the monuments, but the selective pruning and planting of flowers and trees has created a balanced ecology in a wildlife enclosure. Signage, accessibility to records (Richmond Council's cemetery records are searchable on the internet), literature and maps have contributed to raising the overall profile of London's cemeteries.

The results from all these endeavours should cater for a wide range of interests that are as valid now as they were in 1843 when *The Builder* sagely remarked:

> Cemeteries are scenes not only calculated to improve the morals and the taste, and by their botanical riches to cultivate the intellect, but they serve as historical records.[24]

TWO

Planning

After the undoubted need for cemeteries had been proved in the early nineteenth century, the next step was to consider appropriate places and methods for building them. The Victorians were practised in devising new types of building for their myriad inventions, be they railway stations, pumping stations, piers, prisons, bathhouses, workhouses or cemeteries, all were tackled with confidence. In the case of cemeteries that *folie de grandeur* apparent in so many Victorian building schemes was originally much in evidence but, alas, rarely built. Not the least dramatic cemetery plan was also the first, conceived by Francis Goodwin.

Goodwin was an ambitious architect with a successful church building practice who aspired to greater things through the medium of architectural competitions. In these he was dogged by failure and finally killed in 1835 by a 'crisis which had long been prepared by previous severe professional application'.[1] His plans for a very grand national cemetery had been submitted to the General Cemetery Company five years earlier. He intended 'to surpass the famous Parisian cemetery' of Père Lachaise with a formal plan covering 150 acres of Primrose Hill. Buildings at focal points were copies of well known classical models, thus combining a museum of architecture with the cemetery. . .

> those who are strangers will ramble there, with the gratification of seeing the city of the empire from one of its most favourable points of view, while the terraces and walks on which they are exercising will present matters much more in accordance with the decencies due to departed life than England and Englishmen have heretofore been accustomed to...three grand entrances, one a copy of the Propylea, and the others right and left after the famous Roman arches of Constantine and Septimius Severus: all these entrances are, by means of terraces, to conduct to the great feature of the place, a temple built on the model of the Parthenon . . . it will afford a most delightful Sunday morning ride. . .[2]

The cost was estimated at about £400,000 and regrettably but perhaps understandably, it was never built. It was not, however, the only cemetery scheme proposed for Primrose Hill.

In 1842 another architect, Thomas Willson, a member of the General Cemetery Company board, was inspired by the Egyptian pyramids to publish probably the most fantastic cemetery design ever seen. He had concocted this megalomaniac scheme eighteen years earlier in which he envisaged a brick and granite faced pyramid with a base area the size of Russell Square and a height

> considerably above that of St. Paul's' to be built on Primrose Hill. The pyramid would be on a scale commensurate with the necessities of the largest City in the World, embracing prospectively the demands of centuries; sufficiently capacious to receive five millions of the dead, where they may repose in perfect security.

– in 215,296 catacombs built on ninety-four stepped levels. With characteristic Victorian opportunism an observatory was planned for the top. 'The whole will form a *coup d'oeil* of sepulchral magnificence unequalled in the world'[3], it was undeniably claimed, but the £2,500,000 cost and the misgivings of the St. Pancras vestry prevented its erection.

An alternative and more practical school of thought advocated building cemeteries away from the centres of population altogether. A correspondent to *The Builder* in 1845 recommended the following:

> The whole of the city parishes would form one large and rich company, and if they purchased from 300 to 400 acres of land on the bank of the river Thames, might lay it out in serpentine walks, clumps and groves of trees, interspersed with the tombs, monuments, monumental statues etc. . . . with regard to the arrangements of the funerals, there should be a building for the reception of the corpse in some central situation close to the river . . . and as there will be many bodies each day, a large galley would be required.[4]

To complete the arrangements, 'a church in the form of a complete cathedral' was deemed necessary. Another correspondent in 1849 suggested the Isle of Dogs might be used for the

Kensal Green: A view from the Anglican Chapel in the early twentieth century

Merton & Sutton: The twentieth century lawn cemetery concept

purpose and in 1850 a Great Eastern Cemetery was actually considered by the Board of Health at Erith on the Thames. 'Receiving houses on the banks of the river would be established with steamers purposely fitted up to convey the dead to the new cemetery' where 'nearly two-thirds of the metropolitan dead would be buried'.[5] It was hoped this cemetery would supersede all others but once again the sheer magnitude of the enterprise defeated it. A similar plan for enlarging Kensal Green into a Great Western Cemetery also came to nothing. Eventually, the principle of a vast cemetery sited well away from the London suburbs was realised at Brookwood near Woking in 1854, served not by water transport but a branch railway line.

With uncanny foresight, the potential of Woking had been recognised in a short book published in 1843, titled *On the laying out, planting and managing of Cemeteries and on the improvement of Churchyards*. The author was a one-armed landscape gardener from Scotland named John Claudius Loudon. More than anyone else he influenced the planning of mid-nineteenth century cemeteries in a book full of detailed practical advice instead of improbable flights of fancy. Hard facts backed his recommendations: '1,361 graves to an acre' was enough, he reasoned, thus, 'estimating the deaths in a town population at 3% per annum, this acre would suffice for a population of 1,000 for forty-five years. Taking the population of London to be 1,500,000 this would require thirty-three acres per annum'.[6]

Loudon claimed to have seen 'all the more remarkable cemeteries on the continent from Stockholm to Naples, and all the large new cemeteries in Britain'. He was, therefore, in a position to criticise Kensal Green for its badly drained clay soil and its catacombs which were in 'bad taste'.[7] He was fascinated by gadgets and was impressed by the mechanical biers at Kensal Green and Norwood. The 'pleasure ground' style of Norwood however was objectionable and it was Loudon's main thesis that logically planned cemeteries, 'in an elevated and airy situation'[8] and well planted with dark coniferous trees were the ideal. The Abney Park arboretum received special praise. Above all, 'we would at all times keep every part of the cemetery in the highest order. The grass should be kept short and smooth by frequent mowing; the gravel free from weeds . . . the halls, chapel, lodge, gates, drains etc. kept in constant repair'.[9]

> All burial grounds . . . when once filled . . . should be shut up as burying grounds and a few years afterwards opened as public walks or gardens: the grave stones and all architectural or sculptural ornaments being kept in repair at the expense of the town or village; such trees, shrubs or plants being planted among the graves as the town council may determine.[10]

Certainly, whether Loudon's views were consciously accepted or not, London's early cemeteries were enjoyed in much the same way as its parks. The doubting residents of Highgate were quickly converted to the idea.

> The establishment of a cemetery at Highgate was strongly opposed by the inhabitants, but when its decorations with flowers and shrubs and trees and its quiet and seclusion were seen, applications were made for the keys, which conferred the privilege of walking in the cemetery at whatever time the purchaser pleased.[11]

Unfortunately the municipal cemeteries established after the 1852 Burial Act seldom emulated the same high standards. Despite this the Burial Boards endeavoured to locate suitable sites at a distance from the population yet accessible by public transport. Those in south east London, such as Greenwich, Woolwich and Plumstead with their undulating landscapes and views over the metropolis, and Battersea New with its impressive entrance and main avenue, showed that

IMPORTANT PRELIMINARY TRADE NOTICE.

A New London Cemetery

WITH GROUNDS RESERVED FOR

Church, Chapel, & Roman Catholic Interments.

Powers are also being taken to build, if found necessary, a Crematorium and Columbarium.

A NEW CEMETERY for the South and South-West of London, with no restrictions as to District, and moderate charges, has been so urgently needed for many years that it has at last become an imperative necessity.

A Deposit has been paid on a **FREEHOLD SITE** of about **82 ACRES** of most suitable land, well timbered, and in every way adapted for the purpose. It is near Three Stations and Tram and Bus Routes, and is situate about seven miles from London Bridge, in a south-westerly direction.

THE NECESSARY LICENCE HAS BEEN OBTAINED.

It is proposed to open only about 15 to 20 Acres for Cemetery purposes at present, as the remainder of the land is already **producing an income** (which can be greatly increased) from letting as Cricket, Tennis, and Sports Grounds, and can continue until required. **Ground Rents** can also be created, Houses built, and the Property profitably developed in many ways.

The Roman Catholic portion will no doubt be largely patronized, as there is no unrestricted ground for these interments in South London.

The Two First Directors have had over 25 years' experience of Funeral and Cemetery Business. Other Directors will be appointed.

The proposed Capital will be £40,000, but only £30,000 will be issued at present.

The Shares will be £1 each, payable **5s.** on application, **5s.** on allotment, and the balance in two calls of about three months each.

In order to give preference in the allotment of Shares to those in the Funeral Furnishing and Allied Trades applying for same, an early intimation of the number likely to be required will prevent the possibility of a disappointment. Such request will not incur any liability.

THE PROSPECTUS WILL SHORTLY BE ISSUED.

All communications and enquiries should be addressed to—

E. J. D. FIELD, Junr.,
35, Farringdon Street, London, E.C.

☛ NOTE.—This is a sound investment, and not a speculation.
A considerable number of Shares have been bespoken, and promises of support from the Trade have been received from all directions.

Streatham Park: Announcing the proposed cemetery from *The Undertakers' Journal* (September 1907)

Directors and Shareholders of the Great Southern Cemetery, Crematorium and Land Company gather on the proposed site of the cemetery (c. 1909).

the spirit for cemetery planning was continued despite responsibility for their development shifting from the architect to the local surveyor. Many were planned to enable future expansion. Wandsworth simply overtook neighbouring land in the late 1890s while Tottenham acquired land across a footpath in 1883 and, uniquely, provided a tunnel for access.

Demand for burial space continued in the early years of the twentieth century as new cemeteries were opened not only by local authorities but also private companies. The Great Southern Cemetery, Crematorium and Land Company Ltd which opened Streatham Park in 1909 provided a range of different types of graves in consecrated and unconsecrated well maintained grounds. Such was its popularity that by 1921 nearly 43,000 interments had taken place.

The interwar years saw the introduction of the cemetery managed on the lawn principles.[12] The model for this concept were the twentieth century war cemeteries containing disciplined memorials of immaculate design. The scheme for such uniformity was fully embraced at cemeteries like Merton and Sutton which opened in 1947. Landscaping was sacrificed to convenience and the motor mower became the chief agent of destruction as municipal authorities wage a continuous and unnecessarily severe war on grass. The regimented rows of tombstones permit a machine to accomplish in four hours what traditionally took one week to achieve with a scythe. However, the mixture of blue glass chippings, strange engraved headstones or heart-shaped slabs of marble in the municipal cemeteries are far removed from the war cemetery prototype. Such idiosyncrasies may have some appeal, but when concentrated in lines placed back to back among small ornamental trees they appear pathetically mean, any visions of a celebration of death dissipated.

One cemetery even went a step further to disguise death. At Greenlawn Memorial Park, which opened in 1938, commemoration was restricted to uniform sized bronze tablets laid flat on

The City of London: 'one need only glimpse down one of the avenues . . .'

the ground. As *The Times* stated, '. . . first consideration will be the preservation of the natural beauty of the scene. In place of the tombstones familiar in most cemeteries the trust will restrict memorials to tablets of bronze set flush with the turf, thus preserving the park-like appearance of the grounds.'[13] But while giving the impression of a well kept golf course, such regulations do little to serve the needs of the bereaved as they seek individual expression for their loss. Fortunately only two further cemeteries in the London area – Carpenders Park and Trent Park – have adopted this scheme.

In more recent years a number of cemeteries have relaxed their restrictions to offer a range of memorials. While stipulations on height and methods of fixing are enforced, burial authorities increasingly permit designs and expressions reflecting contemporary society. That is to be applauded but a tendency to stray into the realms of mawkish sentimentality is very prevalent. Today's cemetery designers and monumental masons could do worse than visit Highgate, the City of London or Brompton to appreciate the marvellous conjunction of artifice and nature which the Victorians contrived so well.

THREE

Monuments and Buildings

In 1851 a book called *Modern Tombs or Gleanings from the Public Cemeteries of London, measured drawn and etched by Arthur William Hakewill, architect* was published. Today this seems a strange immaterial topic but to the nineteenth century reader it was a subject of great importance. In his preface the author stated his purpose:

> In this book an endeavour has been attempted to draw the attention of the Public to a department of Fine Art which has of late years suffered much neglect in England viz. The designing of tombs and funeral memorials. These things have been, for the most part, left to the untutored taste of the mere Mason and mechanic . . .

Hakewill himself had undergone a rigorous classical training in the office of the Greek revival architect Decimus Burton, so it is hardly surprising he should write:

> Nothing can be more painful than a visit to the cemeteries of our metropolis; such tameness and insipidity, outrageous ugliness and vulgarity of sentiment are displayed in the heaps of stone and marble strewed over the surface of the ground in those establishments.

Classicists like Hakewill sought 'the grace of the Venus and the majesty of the Apollo' and were 'startled by the exaggerated pose of the clown, the silly smirk of the merry Andrew, the strained attitude of the harlequin . . .'[1]

In fact Hakewill's opinion was only one of many then current, for tomb design was a source of comment and controversy throughout the nineteenth century. Architects, clergymen, contributors to *The Builder* and *The Ecclesiologist* and *The Quarterly Review* all argued with enthusiasm. A matter-of-fact paragraph in *The Builder* of 1879 sums up the general attitude:

> The principles of proportion and of harmony of grace and form which are required by a well-dressed woman in her costume are equally applicable when she comes to choose a tombstone for her husband.[2]

In 1843 passions were aroused further when the case for the up and coming Gothic revival was put by the great A.W.N. Pugin in his *An Apology for the Revival of Christian Architecture in England*. The book ruthlessly criticised the classicists for using pagan symbols on tombs which Pugin regarded as inconsistent with the Christian faith. 'Surely,' he exclaimed, 'the cross must be the most appropriate emblem'.[3] He illustrated his point with a scathing cartoon of an 'entrance gateway for a new cemetery', depicted in a grotesque Egyptian style.

The debate was, of course, one which any mortal could join, and for the hundred years from 1830 to 1930, the various preferences materialised in infinite variety. The eighteenth century chest tombs and headstones with their rudimentary classical embellishments were replaced by an elaborate iconography of death and its attendant grief in an equal diversity of stone and metalwork. Monumental masons proliferated and where possible set up their workshops and showrooms near the cemetery gates. Two fine examples, built for John Cramb in the portentous Egyptian style, still exist in Hampstead and Paddington Old; the masonry firm of Dunkley, adjacent to Abney Park, Daniels at Nunhead and Farley, Garstin and Lander at Kensal Green were others.

Ironmongers were equally busy publishing catalogues depicting the popular chains and rails that so often encompassed the stonemason's creation. Although these have suffered badly from rust and wartime exigencies, good examples can be found at Brockley, Bromley, Kingston, Lewisham, London Road, Paines Lane and Queens Road, Croydon. Research shows that many were originally painted dark green. There is also a very rusted iron graveboard at Mitcham, Church Road, and iron grave markers at Paines Lane and Walthamstow.

In this confusion it is sometimes difficult to trace the changes in taste, let alone date monuments by their styles. Generally speaking, the monuments of

Monument to Sir Isaac Watts at Abney Park from *Modern Tombs Gleaned from the Public Cemeteries of London* by Arthur Hakewill (1851)

MONUMENTS AND BUILDINGS

The premises of monumental masons, Henry Dunkley, adjacent to Abney Park Cemetery in Stoke Newington

the 1830s and 40s tend to be simple headstones, shaped at the top in a manner suggestive of classical origins with a pediment, or 'ears' as on a sarcophagus. With the mounting impetus of the Gothic revival, ably promoted by Pugin in the 1840s, Gothic monuments became popular, headstones were pointed and the cross symbol proliferated. Around the 1860s the most notable change was an overall increase in size. Classicists, who were by no means eclipsed by the Gothic revivalists, began building entire temples. Ferdinand de Rothschild outstripped everything in sight at the West Ham Jewish Cemetery with his wife's tholos (1867). In West Norwood the Rallis constructed a Doric mortuary chapel (1872) and the mammoth Beer mausoleum at Highgate (1880) aped the lost original itself. The goths were equally bold. Towering mediaeval-style shrines were built in the City of London cemetery to mark the final resting place of remains moved from defunct City churchyards. At Kensal Green the Molyneux mausoleum (1864) is the largest of its genre (now decapitated) although the Berens sarcophagus at West Norwood (1858) is arguably the finest.

The Rothschild mausoleum at West Ham Jewish Cemetery by Sir Matthew Digby Wyatt (1866)

The Molyneux mausoleum at Kensal Green by John Gibson (1864)

The Egyptian style, which had enjoyed a brief architectural revival in the early nineteenth century, continued as an inspiration for sepulchral artists into the 1900s. The large mausolea in Brompton, Kensal Green, Putney Vale and St Mary's R.C. cemeteries are exceptional, but obelisks were built almost everywhere. The Ducrow mausoleum at Kensal Green (1835) is an unparalleled folly whereas the Wilson sarcophagus at Hampstead (1903) is a much smaller but respectable imitation of an Egyptian temple.

More exuberant Baroque style monuments, incorporating figure sculpture, although common enough in Italy, are rare in London. The nude male figure poised above a sarcophagus in Brompton (1903) in fact commemorates the Italian San Giorgi family. There are earlier examples. Mary Gibson's four gesturing angels above a little Corinthian temple in Kensal Green (1870) certainly qualify as Baroque, but the style's *tour de force* is a surprisingly late work. The Vigiland memorial in the City of London cemetery was sculpted in the early 1950s (in Italy) and is a near life-size tableau representing the Descent from the Cross.

MONUMENTS AND BUILDINGS

The Berens sarcophagus at West Norwood by Edward Barry (1858) photographed in 1980

Berens sarcophagus 2006

Detail on the side of the Berens sarcophagus

The Ralli family's Doric mortuary chapel at West Norwood by J.O. Scott (1858) photographed in 1980

Kensal Green: 'An unparalleled folly' – the Ducrow mausoleum (1835)

Terracotta detail on the Doulton mausoleum at West Norwood (1837)

There are no other easily defined nineteenth-century stylistic groups. The Romanesque Stearnes mausoleum at Nunhead is unique and at Kensal Green R.C. Cemetery, a few Byzantine mausolea are a surprise.

In the twentieth century, any visions of monumental design were soon snuffed out by the numbing reality of the Great War. In most of the London cemeteries the War Graves Commission was allocated a grave plot which was filled with headstones in a now familiar uniform design. Their height is two feet and eight inches and each bears details of the deceased, his service or regimental badge and an appropriate religious emblem. Many war cemeteries are also distinguished by the cross of sacrifice, designed by Sir Reginald Blomfield, and the Stone of Remembrance by Sir Edwin Lutyens.

In every other respect, the quality of the post-war cemetery art was desperately poor. The British Institute of Industrial Art was so concerned that it set up a committee of enquiry which reported in 1925:

> The existing situation of British monumental art in respect of design and the higher qualities of workmanship is so grave that we have little hope that it can be adequately met by any mere

Alexander Gordon's Egyptian-style mausoleum at Putney Vale (1910)

increase or improvement for the training of designers.[4]

The reasons were partly matters of taste and partly cost, but mainly the cemetery regulations, which placed restrictions on design and workmanship, and the stranglehold enjoyed by the white marble industry over the monumental masons. These shortcomings apply to this day. During the 1930s and 40s a few 'modern' designs were attempted but they are generally timid affairs; others gave the impression of recreating a suburban garden complete with a gate, patio, sundial and bird bath. Since the last war, polished black and white marble slabs are the rule, occasionally fashioned into 'mousetraps', as Barbara Jones heartlessly described the coy little hearts, teddy bears and gates that decorate the modern grave.[5]

These pitiable motifs are in fact the latest additions to the vast assortment of tomb symbols evolved in the last 150 years. Some are more personal than others, representing an attribute of the deceased. Coombes the sculler has a boat at Brompton (1860); Spencer the aeronaut, a balloon at St. Pancras & Islington (1913); Smith, the golddigger, a pick and shovel at Hammersmith Old (1923). Others worth seeking out include the empty chairs at Brockley (1924), Hammersmith Old (1924) and Pinner (1954); the monoplane for Captain Thomas at Croydon (1937), a dart board on the Gill memorial at East London (1990); a shell for Smith, a conchologist, at Kensington Hanwell (1916); an incised palette for the artist Harvey at Richmond (1866); and a helmet and kitbag on the Hull grave at Putney Vale (1916).

An art deco memorial in black granite

A garden memorial; a typical design of the interwar period

MONUMENTS AND BUILDINGS

An empty chair in red granite at Pinner (1954)

Monoplane at Croydon in memory of Captain Leslie Thomas (1937)

30   LONDON CEMETERIES

The airman on the Bennet grave at Eltham (1938)

Opposite top: The life-size figure on the Lowndes memorial at Crystal Palace District Cemetery (1911). An identical but decapitated and toppled figure can be found at Camberwell Cemetery

Opposite bottom: Two Lions: Frank Bostock at Abney Park and the Groves memorial at Streatham Park

   Representations of the deceased can also be found, such as Fuller (1935) at Bromley Hill, Ellis at Woolwich (1932), a scout on the Priestman grave at Hither Green (1929), the Rennie-O'Mahony soldier at East Sheen (1928), an airman at Eltham (1938) and on the Vassallo grave at East London (1981), while the figure of Alexander Lamond (1926) can be seen at St Pancras & Islington Cemetery. Near identical soldiers stand 'on guard' at Crystal Palace District on the Lowndes memorial (1911) and for Lord Rodney at Camberwell (although this has been toppled). At Chingford Mount and Abney Park beehives can be found on the Norwood graves (1872 & 1864).There are many examples of portraits sculpted in relief of the deceased including Pragley (1908) and Stanley (1909) at Crystal Palace District.
   Animals are well represented with at least five lions. They commemorate Wombwell the menagerist at Highgate (1850), Frank Bostock at Abney Park (1912), at Streatham Park, the Grove memorial, John Jackson at Brompton (1845) and on the Calvin grave at Lambeth (1897). Smaller examples of horses, dogs and cats can be found on many twentieth century memorials. Music and musical instruments are also represented; a piano can be found on the Thornton grave

at Highgate (1918) and Gladys Spencer is remebered by another at the City of London (1931). A full size organ commemorates Charles Barritt at Hampstead (1929) and a concertina appears on the Hobart (1927) grave at Highgate.

For the majority, however, who did not merit such distinction, one of the more usual symbols of death sufficed. Draped urns, broken columns and anchors stud the average nineteenth century cemetery in picturesque disarray. A brief guide to the most common, and their meaning, is listed at the end of this chapter.

As the nineteenth century progressed and the size of monuments increased, traditional Portland, Bath or York stone was superseded by more exotic materials, particularly marble and granite. Whereas it had been the custom to paint tombstones white, for preservative and decorative reasons, marble and especially granite are very hard-wearing and look good without continual maintenance. Their use increased as the nineteenth century railways linked up with the ports and remote hill quarries. The most popular granites came from Bodmin, Cornwall, a grey speckled stone with a salt and pepper appearance; Bessbrook, County Armagh, a dark grey and finely grained stone; Peterhead, Aberdeen, a pink stone and very hard wearing; Rubislaw, in Aberdeen itself, a fine grained greyish stone sometimes banded and with inclusions; and Shap, Cumbria a red stone with large felspar crystals. By the twentieth century red and black granite was also imported from Scandinavia.

Granite monuments can be found in all the nineteenth century cemeteries. It was especially favoured for Egyptian style mausolea, for example Keller at Westminster Hanwell and Courtoy at Brompton. One of the largest is just east of Putney Vale's chapel and contains Alexander Gordon, constructed in 1910. Obelisks, too, were favourite granite structures – that above Sir Richard Mayne's tomb in Kensal Green (1868) is one of the biggest. Transporting granite was expensive and the cost was even greater after it had been polished or hammer dressed. For those unable to afford such luxury, white Carrara or veined white 'Sicilian' marble was an equally respectable but cheaper material. This was imported in huge quantities after 1850, much of it pre-carved in Italy. Marble was often used for monuments deriving specifically from classical sources. Princess Sophia's sarcophagus at Kensal Green (1848) was sculpted from Carrara marble by Signor Bardi in *quattrocento* style. The Samuel family 'temple' at Willesden is an enclosure of marble Corinthian columns. The beautiful pink Sienese marble of Val Prinsep's raised Gothic sarcophagus at Brompton (1904) is very unusual. Unfortunately it also demonstrates marble's friable nature in the polluted London atmosphere, which soon became evident, and the traditional qualities of Portland and York stone were never totally ignored. Curiously, slate was not much in demand, being considered cold and unpleasing despite its durability and disposition to crisp lettering. The Smith *baldocchino* at Lambeth is exceptional and of fairly recent date (1932). In contrast very unsuitable sandstones were sometimes employed but they have worn badly. A classic case is the O'Brien mausoleum at Kensal Green (1895), resembling a small chapel and of considerable architectural interest, but totally impractical and now steadily crumbling into dust.

It is this diversity of materials that is so typical of Victorian tomb design, where several are often used in combination. Among the less common materials were the artificial stones which have survived well; the Mulready (1863), Casement (1894) and St. John Long (1834) tombs

Brompton: Val Prinsep's Gothic sarcophagus, in Sienese marble (1904)

Mosaic on the Edwards grave (1918) at Chiswick Old

Robed Figure in bronze at Hendon on the King grave (1919)

are all examples, near each other in Kensal Green. Terracotta also had its exponents, the best known mausoleum in this tough material being the pink Gothic tomb at West Norwood built for Sir Henry Doulton by his own firm (1897) and also for Stearne (1900) at Nunhead, (which has been restored). There is a fine terracotta kerb memorial on the Sullivan grave (1992) at Putney Vale and an obelisk to James Brown (1884) at West Norwood. Smaller terracotta memorials can be found at Lambeth and Brockley. There are also a number of glazed stone memorials such as Budden (1907) at Streatham, a similar design on the Carr grave (1911) at Wandsworth and an outstanding example by Doulton commemorating Harriett Shannon (1912) at Lambeth.

Tiles occasionally give extra colour as on the famous Berens tomb at West Norwood (1858) and also the Conybeare altar at Brompton (1871). Surprisingly vivid mosaics appear on memorials at Chiswick Old, East Sheen, Hendon and Putney Vale, West Norwood and in the Beer Mausoleum at Highgate. Brick is noticeably rare, although the Wren revival at the end of the nineteenth century ensured a few Queen Anne style specimens at Richmond and elsewhere, including the enormous Martin-Smith mausoleum at Golders Green (1905). More modern examples of brick mausolea can be found at Kensal Green, Westminster Hanwell and St Pancras and Islington along with the contemporary design for Ferrari at St Patrick's. Any more precious or fragile materials

Left: Bronze memorial on the Boast grave (1895) by Aristide Fabbrucci at Hammersmith Old
Right: Brompton: Frederick Leyland's remarkable tomb – a unique example of 'Arts and Crafts' funerary design (1892)

have suffered badly, often from vandalism, and survivors must now be hunted down in hidden overgrown corners.

Bronzes are rare and frequently despoiled (regrettable examples are the loss of four original corner statuettes stolen from the Whistler sarcophagus (1903) at Chiswick Old Cemetery; the bronze scout commemorating the Leysdown tragedy at Nunhead; Francis Francis's fishing rod at Twickenham and the Frankau urn at Hampstead). Bronze became more widely used in the late nineteenth and early twentieth centuries, sometimes with great dramatic effect, as in the Goscombe John statue at Hampstead (1923), the Burton angel at Kingston (1908), the figure entitled 'Into the Way of Peace' on the Pelham-Clinton grave at Brookwood (1898), 'Into the Silent Land' at Golders Green Crematorium (1937), the female robed figures at Hendon and St Marylebone (1914), the Tate bronze also at St Marylebone (1909), the striking cast bronze angel with sword at Hammersmith Old (1895) and the amazing Lancaster memorial at East Sheen (1920). More decorative is the magnificently restored bronze inlaid tomb chest of Frederick Leyland at Brompton (1892) which is unique. One of the most recent bronze installations is the

MONUMENTS AND BUILDINGS

West Norwood: the Gothic traceried Farrow tomb (1854) restored in 1999

An unidentified iron grave surround

A wooden graveboard at Hendon

figures by Francesco Nagni on the Manzi grave (1962) at St Pancras and Islington. Examples of bronze incorporated into stone memorials can be found in a number of cemeteries including Camberwell Old, East Sheen, Hampstead, Hendon, Kingston, Sutton, Twickenham and West Norwood.

Iron tombs are also scarce. They were most esteemed in the mid-nineteenth century and the finest is unquestionably the Gothic traceried Farrow tomb at West Norwood (1854), now restored. Stained glass was another nineteenth-century favourite, often fitted in the windows of mausolea, but these have been an easy target for vandals and not many are intact. Some of the best examples are at St Mary's, Kensal Green. The present vogue for coloured glass chippings is far removed from that tradition.

Finally, wood. With the availability of so many hardwearing materials, this was seldom used. The occasional deadboard can be found, such as the one at Harrow and above the Mallett grave at Hendon (1905) and for Pace (1896) at Brookwood. Sadly, the one designed by Mathews for his own grave at Abney Park has been partially destroyed. The disintegration of wooden paupers' crosses at Highgate, erected as recently as the 1940s, clearly demonstrates the reason for its rejection. The Victorians built their monuments to last. More recently, wooden cross 'grave markers' have appeared to mark the grave in the interval between the burial and erecting a memorial.

There is one other aspect of Victorian sepulchral art which distinguishes it from earlier forms, namely the use of leaded lettering. The traditional method of merely cutting and painting inscriptions on tombstones was impractical on marble, and anyway was too impermanent for Victorian taste. The new technique was introduced in 1853. An advertisement for Kensal Green monumental masons, Edward Lander, in an 1881 guide to the cemetery, offers:

> Imperishable Inscriptions in solid lead. Long has it been a distressing fact to surviving relatives that the PAINTED names of the dear departed soon fade away. Mr Edward James Physick, sculptor, discovered when in Italy, the successful plan adopted by the ancients.[6]

The results are easy to read but the commonly used sans serif letters are not attractive. On granite, carved letters were usually gilded or occasionally plugged with brass.

The cost of commemorating one's relatives in stone or metal was, of course, over and above the fees charged by the cemetery for the grave. The latter would be bought for a few pounds:

'£5 is perhaps the lowest sum for which a monument can be erected', reckoned *The Builder* in 1882, but:

> The prices of some of the more imposing ones would astonish anyone not acquainted with the costliness of this kind of work. As much as £7,000 or £8,000 is said to have been paid for some of the larger monuments in Kensal Green.[7]

In 1835 Andrew Ducrow paid £100 for the site of his family tomb and £40 more for the construction of the brick vault. The Egyptian style mausoleum cost £3,000 to build and he left another £500 to provide interest for its upkeep, altogether a large sum of money. In 1880 the Beer mausoleum at Highgate, designed by J.O. Scott and decorated with sculpture by Armstead and bronze doors by Farmer and Brindley, cost £5,000. Such vast sums reflect the great importance the Victorians attached to the 'celebration of death'.

CHAPELS

In the heady days of the early private cemetery companies, endowed with sufficient funds and spurred on by the stimulus of competition, chapels of size and quality were normal. From the start, a high standard was set at Kensal Green by J.W. Griffith's commanding Doric Anglican chapel with colonnades. The now restored Dissenters' chapel is of lesser standing but nevertheless a worthy complement (1832–37). In fact only Brompton, at least in conception, could improve on this, where Benjamin Baud's ambitious plan to build three classical style chapels linked by

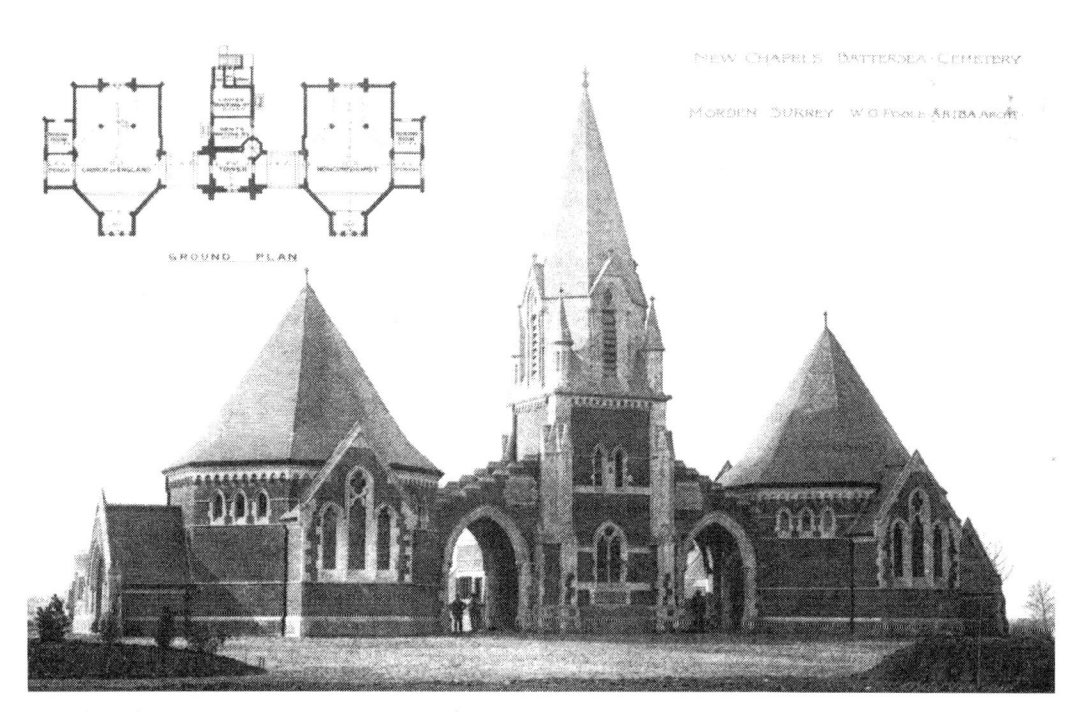

The chapels at Battersea New Cemetery by W.G. Poole (*The Building News* 1893). The scheme was changed when the North East Surrey Crematorium was created in 1958

Exception to Gothic tradition: Renaissance chapels at Willesden (1891) by Charles Worley. Sadly, they were demolished in 1986 (courtesy of Brent Archive)

colonnades was unfortunately pared down to just one (1844). Even Brompton was inconsiderable compared to the gigantic projects dreamed up by Francis Goodwin in 1830 or Thomas Willson in 1842 (Pages 13–14).

None of the above schemes involved a Gothic design but significantly, apart from these and Tower Hamlets' Byzantine chapel of 1849, London's cemetery chapels were all Gothic for the next forty years and even after that the only major exception was Charles Worley's gabled Renaissance chapels at Willesden of 1891. During the twentieth century, stripped classical and simplified Gothic chapels continued to be built, although during the inter-war years art deco made an appearance with distinctive chapels at Chadwell Heath, Chiswick, Gunnersbury (demolished) and Mortlake Crematorium.

Following Loudon's advice, most chapels are sited centrally in the cemetery, that is, both Anglican and nonconformist, but William Griffith's suggestion that, 'each chapel should be

One of the pair of chapels at Streatham by William Newton-Dunn (1892)

The chapel at Rippleside by Charles Dawson (1886) who drew inspiration from St Margaret's church and the Curfew Tower in Barking for the design

constructed in a different style' is largely ignored.[8] One reason for this was the practice of joining the two by a single *porte cochère*, on which a belfry was often built.

Although the *porte cochère* design dominated, the difference in overall size of the chapels is striking. Larger examples are at Acton, Beckenham, Edmonton, Hampstead, Highgate, Kingston, Queen's Road Croydon, Teddington, Tottenham and Walthamstow, while those at Putney Lower Common and St Mary's Battersea are perfect miniatures. Paddington, with two *portes cochères* is perhaps the grandest of this genre, while Beckenham has a three arched *portes cochère*, two being for pedestrians. Chapels not linked by this device can also be found; some are opposite each other or distanced by a flower bed, burial area or drive, such as at Brockley (demolished), Charlton, East London, Hillingdon, Lambeth, Lewisham, Streatham, Wandsworth, West Ham (demolished). Others are located further apart, such as the City of London, Greenwich, Lavender Hill, and Wimbledon.

Denominational requirements did not always necessitate the provision of two chapels and a number of cemeteries had only a single building. Examples can be found at Bexleyheath, Brompton, Hertford Road, Plumstead, Rippleside and Sutton. By attracting a specific denomination one chapel was considered sufficient at St Mary's, Kensal Green and St Patrick's, Leytonstone.

With the passing of the Burial Act in 1900 giving denominations the responsibility of financing the building of a chapel for their use, the trend for two chapels was effectively halted. Those opening in the period 1900–1940 such as Chadwell Heath, Chiswick, East Sheen, Eastcote, Eastbrookend, Eltham, Greenford Park, Grove Park, Hammersmith New, Merton & Sutton, New Brentford, North Sheen, Paddington Mill Hill, Pinner, Surbiton and Tottenham Park were only provided with a single building. However, two separate chapels appeared at Streatham Park and Gunnersbury while those at Alperton and Camberwell New show that the distinctive hallmark of cemetery chapels – the *porte cochère* – continued into the twentieth century. Curiously, Sir Aston Webb's substantial pair of chapels at Camberwell New did not use the area under the bell tower as a shelter for the hearse and mourners, entrance to each chapel is at the extremity of the building.

Nineteenth-century cemeteries without at least one chapel are rare; Edmonton and Southgate can be cited as the only example in London. In the twentieth century it was more commonplace to spare the authority the expense, so that cemeteries at Barkingside, Carpenders Park, Cherry Lane, Greenlawn, Hatton, Hillview, Wood Green have no chapel. Trent Park (1960) is unique in being a post-war cemetery with a chapel.

At Highgate, Kensal Green, St Mary's Kensal Green and West Norwood, a feature was a mechanical bier to lower coffins to the catacombs beneath the chapel (at Highgate this was to enable access to the ground across Swains Lane). However, chapel interiors tend to be modestly furnished. They compare with nineteenth-century Nonconformist chapels. Pews, a preaching box or pulpit for the minister and an altar were provided, but particularly in the smaller buildings there was scarcely room for more than twenty mourners. In some cases it was not intended for the coffin to be brought into the chapel for the reading of the *Order of the Burial of the Dead*. The coffin would wait on the hearse outside before the priest and mourners would be led to the grave for the committal. In many chapels and particularly those joined by the *porte cochère*, mourners entered and exited through the same doors. However, at Greenford, Streatham and Surbiton a sense of flow was created as mourners exited through a second door into the cemetery (At St Marylebone this has been bricked up). Collegiate style seating can be found at Camberwell New, East Sheen, Greenford Park, Surbiton and Tottenham Park.

Two exceptions to the absence of decoration can be found at Hendon, with its facsimile of Luca della Robbia's 'Resurrection' in Florence Cathedral, and the mosaic reredos in the sanctuary at Richmond.

A few interiors are enhanced by stained or plain coloured glass windows. There are good examples at Charlton, Crystal Palace District, East London, Kensal Green Anglican chapel and Rippleside. Those at Alperton, Manor Park, North Sheen and at Paddington Old are particularly striking. Municipal heraldry can be found in the windows at North East Surrey Crematorium and Westminster cemetery at Hanwell.

Cemeteries were also convenient places for mortuaries and these can still be found at Hammersmith Old, Isleworth and Teddington. Others at Fulham and Camberwell have disappeared, while at Walthamstow a mortuary and Coroner's court was built next to the cemetery lodge.

Hendon: The reredos by Cantagalli (1899) is a facsimile of Luca della Robbia's 'Resurrection' in Florence Cathedral

MONUMENTS AND BUILDINGS

The mosaic reredos at Richmond's Grove Gardens Chapel (formerly the cemetery chapel).

West Norwood Crematorium. The third crematorium to open in London, the crematory was added to the Nonconformist chapel in 1915

CREMATORIA

The development of cremation in the twentieth century gave a number of chapels a new lease of life as they were converted into crematoria. West Norwood predated this trend, as a crematorium was added to the Nonconformist chapel in 1915 (and due to war damage demolished and then replaced in 1956). In 1922, the crematorium at Hendon was built in the cloister adjoining the burial chapel. Putney Vale (1938) was one of the first in a series of conversions that was only interrupted by the War. During the 1950s, chapels at Battersea New, Crystal Palace District, East London, Manor Park and the Great Northern were converted into crematoria. They have not always been the most successful adaptations; confined space around the chapel with the problem of parking and future expansion, the addition of extensions to accommodate the crematory and the siting of a chimney (often in the bell tower) have detracted from the original concept. It is significant to note that in an attempt to remain solvent the majority of conversions were carried out in cemetery chapels owned by private companies.

Generally, London crematoria and their mandatory Gardens of Remembrance have been sited in existing cemeteries on unused burial ground or adjacent to cemeteries; there are plenty of examples, such as Croydon, Eltham, Kensal Green (West London Crematorium), Mortlake and St Marylebone. Only Golders Green (1902), South West Middlesex (1954) and Breakspear at Ruislip (1958) out of the twenty-five crematoria in London are in their own grounds. The cemetery at Enfield was opened some years after the crematorium and London's most recent crematorium at Forest Park (2005) incorporates a cemetery.

With the inauguration of Golders Green in 1902, Sir Ernest George successfully adapted the brick Lombardic style to create the Golders Green crematorium. Otherwise crematoria have followed an undistinguished course from limp classicism, through art deco – such as Mortlake

Described as 'Hacienda deco' in style, Mortlake Crematorium was designed by the Hammersmith borough surveyor, F. Douglas Barton (1939)

West London Crematorium by G. Berkeley Willis (1939)

Demolished: One of the chapels at Camberwell by George Gilbert Scott photographed in 1969. (Courtesy of the City of London, London Metropolitan Archives)

– and stripped Gothic, to the low slung glass and artificial stone of the City of London's 1971 model. The interior of some of these buildings is quite dreadful. Plastic and pine combine in a riot of mawkish vulgarity. One visit to Lewisham crematorium (1956) is sufficient to illustrate the type and the less said about it the better.

During the twentieth century, cemetery chapels have suffered on a number of counts. The declining preference for burial and therefore use of the chapel, the fortunes of private companies and the cost of maintaining the unused chapel of a pair, have resulted in a decline in repair and inevitably, demolition. While war damage claimed three at Brockley and both at West Norwood, chapels at the following cemeteries have disappeared: Barnes Common, all three at Camberwell Old, Chingford Mount, Crystal Palace District, Fulham, Gunnersbury, Hammersmith Old, Old Mortlake, Paines Lane, Nunhead, the Roman Catholic

Demolished: The chapel by England and Brown at Chingford Mount (1884) photographed in 1980

chapel at Streatham Park, both at Tower Hamlets, West Ham, Woodgrange Park and at Woolwich. Perhaps the most tragic loss has been the pair of Dutch Renaissance style chapels at Willesden which were demolished in 1986. Seldom or never used are those at Fulham, Hammersmith Old, Kensington Hanwell, Paddington Old, Putney Lower Common (which have been boarded up) St Mary's Battersea and Wimbledon.

Still standing but in a shocking state of repair are those at Abney Park, Greenwich, Isleworth, one at Lavender Hill and Hither Green, and both at Queen's Road Croydon. Tottenham Park is a disgrace.

At Beckenham, Hillingdon, Lambeth, Queen's Road, Teddington and Wimbledon, salvation for one of the pair has been found through use as a tool store and there have also been some positive developments. The chapels at the entrance to Highgate have been fully restored, while the one remaining at its sister cemetery, Nunhead, has been conserved but without the addition of a roof. The Dissenters' chapel at Kensal Green has also been magnificently restored along with replacement of the demolished colonnades. At Richmond, one chapel was sold and converted into a private residence, while the other (by Sir Arthur Blomfield) has been restored for community use. At Camberwell New, the cemetery and crematorium office now occupy one of the pair of chapels, an arrangement that can also be found at Bandon Hill and Streatham Park.

LODGES

In Loudon's view, gate lodges were another essential cemetery building with

> A room to serve as an office to contain the cemetery books, or at least, the order book and register, and the map book, where, from the system of squares being employed, such a book is rendered necessary.[9]

Many are large houses by contemporary standards, and when combined with an entrance arch, whether Gothic, as at the City of London Cemetery, Kensington Hanwell, Hillingdon, West Norwood, Plaistow, Plumstead or St Marylebone, mock Tudor at Hendon or a triumphal arch as at Kensal Green and Brompton, they form an impressive sight.

At Abney Park and Nunhead they are architecturally more interesting than their respective chapels. The Nunhead pair by Bunning (1840) are Soanian classical; one has now been repaired and is inhabited, but restoration of the other appears to have stalled. Hackney Council has recognised the rarity of Hosking and Bonomi's Egyptian lodges at Abney Park (1840) and has recently restored them. It is significant that where lodges have been uninhabited such as at Nunhead and Camberwell Old, the level of vandalism in the cemetery increases. Fortunately, the latter has been restored, but lodges too, like the chapels, have been victims of economies. Those at Barnes, Chingford Mount, Eastbrookend, Greenford (and its replacement), Harrow, Streatham Park, Woodgrange Park and Woolwich have disappeared. Some have been replaced with more contemporary but often quite bland structures – Bromley Hill, Charlton, Chingford Mount, Greenwich, Kingston, West Norwood, Plumstead, St Mary's Battersea and Twickenham are examples. Many of the twentieth century cemeteries were not provided with lodges, such as Chadwell Heath, Carpenders Park, Hatton, Greenlawn and Trent Park, although there are exceptions at Barkingside, Chiswick, Grove Park, Gunnersbury, Mitcham London Road, Mortlake,

Greenford Park: Both the original lodge (pictured here) and its replacement have disappeared

The Lodge at Westminster Hanwell (1854), the largest in London

MONUMENTS AND BUILDINGS

Hammersmith New: A brick gate pier with acorn finial in Portland stone (1926)

Pinner and Surbiton, They make ideal offices as demonstrated in the lodges at Battersea New, City of London, Crystal Palace District, East London, Lambeth, Manor Park, West Norwood and West Ham.

Elsewhere there are lodges that are empty, neglected and in some cases boarded up. Those at Fulham Palace Road, Greenwich, Hillingdon, Putney Lower Common, and Tottenham look particularly vulnerable to intruders and deterioration.

At Grove Park an impressive single storey office complete with ornamental stone urns (now a private residence) was opened opposite the lodge, while at Gunnersbury the smaller office inside the gates is in keeping with the chapel and toilet block. More functional administrative accommodation has been built at East Sheen, Great Northern, Putney Vale and St Pancras. At Cherry Lane this has been provided by an inelegant Portakabin. One further building found in some cemeteries is the shelter. At Richmond it is thatched; at Cherry Lane one on the boundary merges with the boundary trees, but both at Greenwich and Ladywell could easily have strayed from the Marine Parade at Brighton.

GATES AND RAILINGS

Proper enclosure of the cemetery is another vandal deterrent – the great black Victorian Gothic railings at Highgate and West Norwood are particularly splendid. The gates at Ladywell bear the cemetery's name and the emblem of the former authority while municipal coats of arms can be found on the gates at Eltham, Gunnersbury and St Marylebone. At Crystal Palace

West Norwood gates: 'this massive iron enciente'

District, Putney Lower Common, Teddington and others, the original railings with attractive designs remain. However, they are missing at Beckenham and in the case of Barnes Common were removed by the local authority, leaving the whole site vulnerable. At Chingford Mount the cemetery has now been replaced with a sturdy metal perimeter fence, more suited to a factory than a cemetery.

CATACOMBS

Finally there are catacombs. These were built in nine London cemeteries during the mid-nineteenth century – Brompton, West Norwood, City of London, Nunhead, Highgate, Abney Park, Kensal Green, St Mary's Roman Catholic and Tower Hamlets. The usual system was a brick vaulted passage, below ground level, equipped either with cells exposing only the end of the coffin

Finial mitre design at Putney Lower Common

City of London: Catacomb and columbarium for funerary ashes (entrance on the right)

or with shelves on which sumptuously decorated lead lined coffins were placed, often draped with velvet and enclosed with a grille or stone panel. At Westminster Hanwell and Brompton, Mural catacombs were set into a boundary wall. Mrs Stone, writing about a London cemetery in 1858, tells how she was charged one shilling to visit and admire them. The popularity of this grisly practice soon waned, the catacombs at the City of London cemetery were seldom used and plans to build them at the Great Northern in the 1860s were not completed. Space to accommodate coffins exists at Brompton, City of London and Kensal Green, while at the City of London a section was converted into a columbarium. Even the Victorians, the most unselfconscious people in matters of death, found catacombs rather too gloomy. Nevertheless, a new catacomb and mausoleum range has been built (and been well used) at Streatham Park by Italian families, and free-standing examples exist at Crystal Palace District, Putney Vale and Streatham.
The most common tombstone symbols:

MONUMENTS AND BUILDINGS 51

Anchor at Richmond

Angel at East Sheen

Butterfly at East Sheen

Dove at Fulham

52 LONDON CEMETERIES

Left: Gateway at East Sheen

Above: Hands clasped (of husband and wife) at Fulham

Below: Hourglass at Abney Park

MONUMENTS AND BUILDINGS 53

Lamp alight at Mortlake R.C.

Lily at Fulham

Skull at Bunhill Fields

Torch upturned at Highgate

Left: Tree, cut by the hand of God at Abney Park Centre: Urn, draped, at Brompton
Right: Weeping willow at Abney Park

Anchor:	'Hope' or 'At Rest'. An early Christian symbol.
Angel:	The agent of God, often pointing heavenwards; also the guardian of the dead.
Bed:	A deathbed, sometimes only a pillow.
Book:	Often with a cross lying on it, symbolising faith.
Butterfly:	The Resurrection.
Circle:	Eternity, usually incorporated into the Celtic cross.
Column:	The broken column traditionally signifies mortality, the support of life being broken.
Cross:	Has several meanings, but is above all the symbol of the Christian religion.
Crown:	The emblem of the Christian martyr who may expect reward in heaven.
Cypress tree:	Mourning and death on account of its dark colour and because once cut down it never grows again.
Dove:	The Holy Ghost or peace.
Gates:	Entry into Heaven.
Hands:	When clasped are a symbol of farewell. On Jewish tombs two outstretched hands with the thumbs touching symbolise a descendant of Aaron, the High Priest (nearly all named Cohen).
Heart:	Love and devotion.
Horse:	Strength, courage or the swiftness of the passage of time.
Hourglass:	The traditional symbol of Father Time, who also carries a scythe.
Ivy:	The evergreen, symbolising immortality or friendship.
Labyrinth:	In popular usage, symbolises eternity; used in esoteric tradition to represent the inward path.
Lamb:	Innocence, sometimes used on a child's grave.
Lamp:	Immortality, knowledge of God.

Laurel:	Fame, often of a literary or artistic figure.
Lily:	Purity and innocence.
Lion:	Courage, strength, the Resurrection.
Obelisk:	Eternal life, from the Egyptian sun-worshipping symbol.
Palm:	Triumph of a martyr over death.
Passion flower:	Christ's Passion, sacrifice and redemption.
Phoenix:	Christ's Resurrection
Rocks:	The Church or Christian steadfastness.
Rose:	Sinless, usually associated with the Virgin Mary or paradise.
Scythe or sickle:	The passage of time and death.
Shell:	Pilgrimage, the badge of pilgrims who travelled to Compostella in Spain.
Ship:	The Christian church, symbolically carrying the faithful through the world.
Skull:	Mortality.
Snake:	With its tail in its mouth, symbolises eternity.
Sundial:	Passage of time.
Sword:	Justice, constancy or fortitude.
Torch:	Immortality. Upturned symbolises life extinguished.
Tree:	Life, regeneration and immortality.
Urn:	Draped and empty, symbolises death, derived from classical cinerary urns. If flaming indicates new life.
Water:	A hand pouring water from a flagon may occur on Jewish tombs of the Levites whose duty in the synagogue is to pour water upon the hands of the priests.
Wheat:	Fruitfulness harvested.
Willow:	Grief and mourning.
Yew:	Mourning, on account of its dark colour and its association with churchyards.

FOUR

Epitaphs

The Victorians invented a whole new vocabulary for death, evading where possible any mention of its stark finality but relying on the comforting belief in an after-life instead. Metaphors abound. Many have botanical connotations, 'safely garnered' or 'cut down like a flower', for example. More extravagant versions are 'transplanted into God's garden', or 'the stem broke and the flower faded,' or 'a lily bud has dropped and died'. Best of all is a 1942 version at Lee: 'like a cruel untimely frost death touched this lovely flower'. More common euphemisms found in most cemeteries are 'enter into rest', 'called home', 'passed away', 'crossed the bar' and 'called hence'. Another category implies a direct passage to heaven such as 'translated to the heavenly life' or 'called to join the choir invisible'. Variations are legion. 'Fell asleep in Jesus' and 'promoted to higher service' are two Nonconformist favourites. Others include, 'God's finger touched him and he slept', 'an angel crossed over the bridge', 'the Great Shepherd took him home', 'called into the presence of the King himself' and even, 'passed into the keeping of the Great Architect of the Universe' (Plaistow 1938). A few defy classification: 'left her chair vacant' (Pinner 1954), 'fainted away in this vale of tears', (Brompton 1896), or 'though his body is under hatches his soul has gone aloft' (Lambeth 1874).

Epitaph anthologies are numerous but all have significantly few examples drawn from the later nineteenth century. *The Builder* of 1882 explained the reason:

> Elaborate epitaphs do not seem in accordance with modern taste . . . the day of 'uncouth rhymes' is nearly over . . . any verse or prose that might provoke a smile by its rugged originality or unconscious humour is sternly rejected by the cemetery authorities.

In the twentieth century 'the bald statement of the name and years of the departed'[1] was the custom and any additional text tends to lack originality. One rhyming version which has been in use for at least one hundred years is still a favourite:

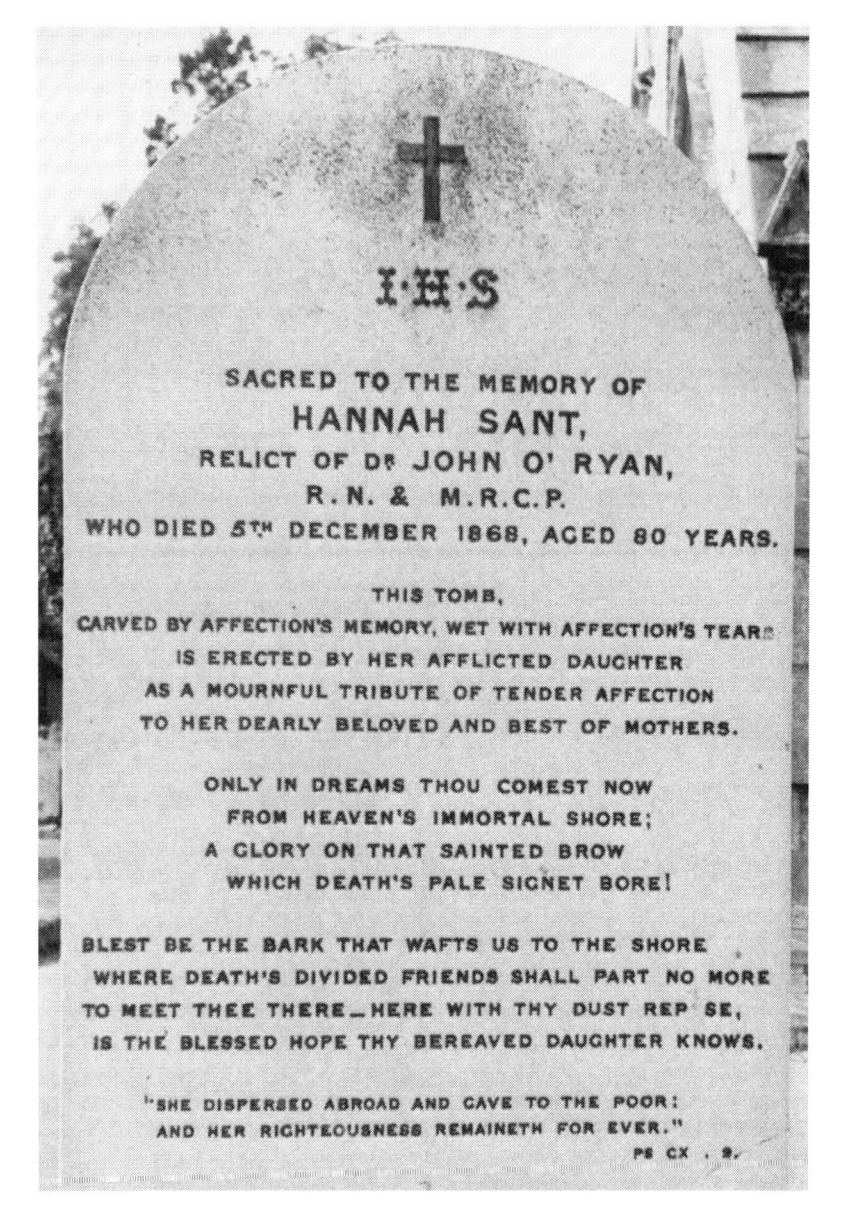

Epitaph at Putney Lower Common

> SACRED TO THE MEMORY OF
> **HANNAH SANT,**
> RELICT OF Dr JOHN O' RYAN,
> R.N. & M.R.C.P.
> WHO DIED 5TH DECEMBER 1868, AGED 80 YEARS.
>
> THIS TOMB,
> CARVED BY AFFECTION'S MEMORY, WET WITH AFFECTION'S TEARS
> IS ERECTED BY HER AFFLICTED DAUGHTER
> AS A MOURNFUL TRIBUTE OF TENDER AFFECTION
> TO HER DEARLY BELOVED AND BEST OF MOTHERS.
>
> ONLY IN DREAMS THOU COMEST NOW
> FROM HEAVEN'S IMMORTAL SHORE;
> A GLORY ON THAT SAINTED BROW
> WHICH DEATH'S PALE SIGNET BORE!
>
> BLEST BE THE BARK THAT WAFTS US TO THE SHORE
> WHERE DEATH'S DIVIDED FRIENDS SHALL PART NO MORE
> TO MEET THEE THERE — HERE WITH THY DUST REPOSE,
> IS THE BLESSED HOPE THY BEREAVED DAUGHTER KNOWS.
>
> "SHE DISPERSED ABROAD AND GAVE TO THE POOR:
> AND HER RIGHTEOUSNESS REMAINETH FOR EVER."
> PS CX . 9.

> A light from our household is gone
> A voice we loved is stilled
> A place is vacant in our home
> Which never can be filled.

Another regular runs as follows:

> The cup was bitter, the pain severe
> To part with one we loved so dear
> The trial is hard, we will not complain
> But trust in God we'll meet again

Perfectly scanning epitaphs are a rarity. A particularly excruciating example occurs at Charlton (1926):

> My anvil's worn my forge decayed
> My body in the dust is laid
> My coal is burnt my iron's run
> My last nail is in my work is done.

Sporting analogies are not uncommon, especially cricket. Tom Richardson, a Surrey and England cricketer, buried at Richmond, 'bowled his best but was himself bowled by the best' in 1912. However,

> Life's race well run
> Life's work well done
> Life's victory won
> Now cometh rest.

is the front runner among the sporting epitaphs.

The poetic imagination is inexplicably stronger in some areas rather than others, the remarkable flowering of epitaphs at Battersea St. Mary's is an example. The older cemeteries also disclose some extraordinarily potent lines revealing a strange mixture of Victorian morbidity and sensuality. Louisa Waklein was aged seventeen when she died in 1840 and is commemorated at Kensal Green with pre-Freudian innocence:

> She is mine and I must have her
> The coffin must be her bridal bed
> The winding sheet must wrap her head
> The whispering winds must o'er her sigh
> For soon in the grave the maid must lie
> The worm it will riot
> On heavenly diet
> When death has deflowered her eye.

James Bell was buried at Kensal Green in the same year but with all possible humility:

> Lord what was I? A worm dust vapour nothing
> What was my life? A dream, a daily dying
> What was my flesh? My soul's uneasy clothing
> What was my time? A minute's ever flying.
> My time, my flesh, my life, and I
> What were we, Lord, but vanity?

As was the dissenter, John Sears:

Who was born of sinful parents; born again of the Spirit of the kingdom of God; tasted of the promises of Jehovah's grace; longed for their consummation, and peacefully slept in Jesus on the 3rd May 1841, aged 23 years.

An iron grave marker at Walthamstow (1921)

Not all epitaphs are so humble. Justin McCarthy versified at length on the death of Sir Richard Burton, buried at Mortlake R.C. (1890):

Farewell dear friend, dead hero, the great life
is ended, the great perils the great joys
and he to whom adventures were as toys
who seemed to bear a charm against spear or knife
or bullet, now lies silent from all strife . . .

The eulogy on the tombstone of Henry Faudel (1863) in the Jewish cemetery, West Ham, evokes a man of superhuman stature:

A man of gentle nature of a refined and cultivated mind imbued with the loftiest sentiments of unostentatious charity unbounded generosity and a love for all that was truthful and just. Wisdom guided him, truth sustained him, practical in all he undertook, sensible in all he said, honourable in all he did with a thorough knowledge of human nature his life was a success.

Such veneration is in acute contrast to the bathos of the inscription on Edwin I. Edwin's headstone only a few yards away, 'who was killed in Holborn by the falling of a signboard' (1877). This is an example that is fairly common of the mundane circumstances of death recorded for posterity on the victim's tomb.

Reginald Witt at Teddington was 'killed by a ball while playing hockey in Bushey Park' (1893). A head prefect at Richmond was 'killed on a gateless level crossing North Wales 28 September 1925'. At Teddington, the grave of a meteorologist contains an occupational reference, 'Died 10.1.1983 when it was overcast, 50°, with a trace of rain.' Henry Mandeville at Charlton was 'struck by a motor car, and taken instantly to be with Christ April 26th 1912 while engaged in evangelistic work at Hartley Wintney Hants'. More dramatic was the death of Sgt Joseph Joyce, C.I.D., at Abney Park,

Who lost his life while arresting a thief at Charing Cross Road 20th June 1892 and although mortally wounded by two revolver shots he gallantly struggled with his prisoner until assistance arrived.

Allied to this category of faithfully recorded personal tragedies are the personal nicknames that can be quite startling discovered among the earnest tombstone verses and invocations. A random survey produced Snip, Noddy, Puggins, Doodles, Muz, Lizzie, Flash, Chickie, Little Ducks, Buddy, Skipper, Catty Poo, Corky, Jolly Jumbo and Golly.

It is refreshing, among such extremes, to chance upon a guileless verse like Robert Saddler's in the City of London cemetery:

> No marble column marks the spot
> Where he doth lie asleep
> We only know his resting place
> Is somewhere in the deep.

Saddler had been chief engineer on the S.S. Glencoe which foundered, with him aboard, in 1899. Death by drowning is a recurring feature commemorated in cemeteries whose catchment areas border the Thames. Typical, at Battersea, was the demise of Alfred Fell and Arthur Ronald, both aged nineteen, who drowned while boating on the Thames in 1873:

> Mark the brief story of a summer's day,
> At noon, in youth and health they launched away,
> Ere eve, death wrecked the bark and quenched the light;
> The parents' home was desolate at night . . .

These two were young enough, but infant mortality is the most distressing characteristic of nineteenth century epitaphs, sad proof of an average life expectancy that was less than forty years. Laman Blanchard's description of Kensal Green in 1842 devotes a section to the 'graves of the early nipp'd'.[2] A florid example reads:

> Enshrined within this narrow spot of earth
> Three beauteous babies rest, who at one birth
> Entered this lower world, but short their stay
> Celestial beings hastened them away
> To yonder glorious throne, where they now sing
> Seraphic strains to heaven's almighty King.

At Brompton the headstone of Egyptologist Joseph Bonomi refers not only to his own death but those of his four young children who all died in Easter week 1852. At Camberwell, five children of Georgina and William Waters died before reaching two years of age and the sixth was only twenty-two. The Victorians were very aware, as a West Ham epitaph of 1878 warned, that

> Dangers stand thick through all the ground
> To push us to the tomb
> And fierce diseases wait around
> To hurry mortals home.

They were therefore prepared for it. Thirteen year old Jessie Brown, buried in the City of London Cemetery in 1876, 'cruelly burned on board the steamboat "Sea Swallow" on the Thames by the carelessness of others', nevertheless thoughtfully composed 'her last words . . . I know that my Redeemer liveth'.

The fierce diseases included consumption and cholera. Almost side by side at Brompton are two casualties of inadequate medical treatment. Eliza Carmen was eighteen in 1857 when

> The pale consumption gave the lingering blow
> The stroke was final but the effect came slow
> With waiting pain death found me sore apprest
> Pitied my sighs and kindly gave me rest.

Jane Manning died in 1855 aged twenty-eight,

> From the effects of morphia which she had been induced to take in an unhappy moment in the afternoon of the preceding day.

Victims of traffic accidents become increasingly common in the twentieth century but they are not unknown in the nineteenth. One pathetic casualty was nine-year-old William Earnest, run over in 1885 and buried at Tower Hamlets:

> I am a little sparrow
> A bird of low degree
> My life is of little value
> But there is one who cares for me.

Despite such tragedies, it was difficult to resist an occasional cemetery joke. One child's jingle, which would have given little comfort to the parents of William Earnest, ran as follows:

> My son Augustus in the street one day
> Was feeling quite exceptionally merry.
> A stranger asked him, 'Can you show me, pray,
> The quickest way to Brompton Cemetery?'
> 'The quickest way? You bet I can,' said Gus,
> And pushed the fellow underneath a bus.[3]

Finally, an enigmatic inscription at Great Northern 'ABN Born 16.12.1938 Died: Never.'

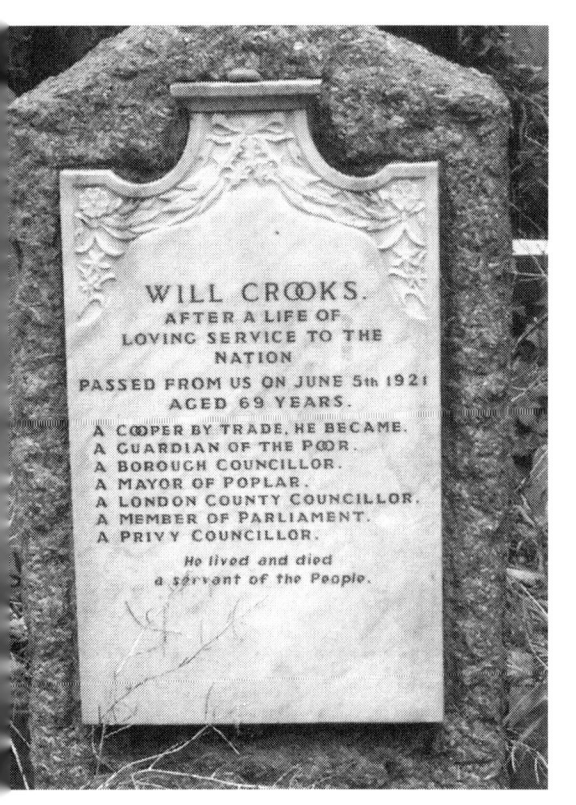

The grave of Will Crooks M.P. (1921) at Tower Hamlets

FIVE

Flora and Fauna

John Claudius Loudon, the most influential writer on the landscaping and planting of cemeteries, wrote in 1843:

> A general cemetery in the neighbourhood of a town, properly designed, laid out, ornamented with tombs, planted with trees, shrubs and herbaceous plants all named, and the whole properly kept, might become a school of instruction in architecture, sculpture, landscape-gardening, arboriculture, botany, and in those important parts of general gardening, neatness, order and high keeping.[1]

These were extravagant claims. For most people who had endured 'the misery of attending a funeral in the damp and dreary, and in many respects, noxious burial places of London',[2] fresh air was what they really needed. Loudon quotes the case of the sculptor Sir Francis Chantrey who built a splendid vault for himself in Westminster Abbey and offered space within it to his friend, the art historian Allan Cunningham. The offer was declined: 'No, no, I'll not be built over when I'm dead. I'll lie where the wind blow over and the daisy grow upon my grave'.[3]

Cunningham chose Kensal Green which a few years previously had been rapturously described in a guidebook for visitors by Benjamin Clark:

> The cemetery at Kensal Green adorned as it is with such a goodly variety of beautiful flowers and freshest evergreens, presents a smiling countenance as well amidst the gloomy winter as in the sunny days of blooming summer, and, unlike the desolate, pent up burial grounds of the crowded metropolis, instead of repelling our approach but when positive duty commands, allures us to enter its sacred precincts, both by the floral charms within, and the view afforded thence of the extensive and pleasing scenery without.[4]

Among the older, and especially the privately owned cemeteries, a lavish scale of planting was the norm. With typical confidence in the permanence and large scale of their projects, the

Victorians planted 'the lofty oak, the beech that wreathes its old fantastic roots so high; the rustling pine and the drooping willow'.[5] At Brompton, 'trees and shrubs have been allowed to arrive at maturity' noted *The Builder* which described an awakening interest in the cemetery's floral decoration.[6] At Brookwood the largest trees in the world – Sequoias – were deemed appropriate for what was then the largest cemetery in the world. Monkey puzzles were another favourite, planted at Brookwood as well as Edmonton, Hillingdon and St Pancras and Islington while cedars and yew were always popular.

Abney Park was famed as 'a complete arboretum' with 2,500 varieties and a rosarium with 1,029 species. At the end of the century its sister cemetery at Hendon was planted with thousands of trees but by then, more colourful and exotic, often deciduous species were replacing the sombre monochrome evergreens. A 1903 prospectus catalogues them at length:

> Avenues of Lombardy poplars, oaks, elms, maples, planes, and rose acacias border the roads, and there are footwalks between avenues of common acacias, thorns, limes and laburnums, which before long should have very striking and unusual beauty. Clumps of trees dot the meadows in which contrasts and harmonies have been studied, for in them we see such different forms and colours as are given by wild cherry, copper beech, mespilus, white poplar, Persian plum, ilex, thorn, chestnut maple and yew.[7]

Complementing these was an understorey of flowers representing only native species which were allowed to grow naturally, implying that Hendon was ahead of its time. A list refers to

> 'briar roses, flags, teazles, barberries and others'. Pools were stocked with 'waterlilies, kingcups, Japanese flags' and 'creepers . . . adorn the walls, poppies cover waste heaps and bedding annuals, bulbs and herbaceous plants break in upon the stretches of grass'.[8]

More often the planting of many Burial Board cemeteries mimicked that displayed in the public parks. The cherry tree – a fond favourite of the municipal gardener – along with beech were planted in many cemeteries, particularly those of the inter- and post-war years such as Chiswick (1933), Grove Park (1935) and Merton and Sutton (1947). Most private cemeteries had a horticultural department as T.W. Wilkinson found in 1906:

> Go behind the scenes at Highgate. You are in a maze of beds and glass-houses, working in and about which is a regular staff of twenty-eight gardeners. Merely for bedding-out some 250,000 to 300,000 plants are raised every year.[9]

To save on the expense of purchasing stock, similar buildings were also erected at Kensal Green and Streatham Park, but staffing was always the key to maintenance. Despite efforts to sustain a well-kept landscape, by the end of the nineteenth century it was apparent that some burial grounds were experiencing difficulties. In 1896 Mrs Holmes reported that at Tower Hamlets Cemetery '. . . parts of the grounds are very untidy.'[10]

As the twentieth century progressed the original permanent planting in the Victorian cemeteries matured with trees providing a splendid backdrop to the cemetery monuments. Exceptionally varied evergreen and deciduous specimens in the City of London cemetery, Greenford Park and Willesden provide year round interest. At Battersea New an avenue of tall poplars effect a dignified approach to the chapels, London planes provide a similar service at Chingford Mount as do evergreens at Teddington.

FLORA AND FAUNA 65

Edmonton: Grass cutting

Highgate: Preparing flowers for planting on graves (1906)

In some cemeteries, however, the ground became overgrown with private companies often faring the worst. A decline in burial revenue mirrored expenditure on maintenance which, in the post Second World War years was minimal. One solution was to adopt a ruthless lawn cemetery regime, another was to do nothing but condone a jungle interior beyond a few token flowerbeds to greet visitors at the entrance. By the 1960s large areas of significant cemeteries like Abney Park, Chingford Mount, The Great Northern, Highgate, Nunhead, Tower Hamlets and others had become impenetrable. Ash, and more commonly sycamore, capable of robbing the soil of its fertility, flourished in many cemeteries to the extent that memorials became dislodged, while brambles, bindweed and grasses encroached allowing only tough shade-resistant plants to thrive, such as ground elder, laurel, snowberry and especially ivy. Sometimes the rampant horsetail, well known for growing on compacted, badly drained soil, eradicated all other ground cover, as in parts of Highgate's east cemetery.

For those administering such cemeteries this presented a dilemma – whether to clear the ground or choose the increasingly popular option of working with nature by maintaining a managed woodland or, as one report at St Pancras and Islington put it, adopting 'a policy of informed indifference.' Gardening at Highgate on that basis began in the early 1970s and by 1978 the Friends could report:

> Already in less than three years there is promise; there are clusters of wood anenome, bluebells and oxlip, woodland violets, lesser celandine, wild arum, wild garlic, hart's tongue fern, teazle and foxglove...[11]

By the twenty-first century some 100 species of wild flowers had been noted, and documentation had extended beyond the familiar to the cemetery's lesser-known species such as snails and spiders. Other cemeteries to favour this compromise approach are Hampstead and St Pancras and Islington which attract a host of wild flowers more usually found in rural hedgerows and woodland boundaries. Elder, cow parsley, hogweed, white bryony, garlic mustard and bugle are among them. At Battersea New Cemetery an 'ecological management plan' supports the 256 invertebrate species and 110 species of wild flowers and grasses, which include the only green winged orchids in London. Paddington Old and Tower Hamlets each have a 'nature reserve' while Barnes Common, by default, forms part of a 'wildlife conservation area' of the common land.

Brompton: Pigeons

Indeed cemetery websites now take pride in publicising the diversity of their natural world – an enterprise that encourages visitors, in marked contrast to the barren and dusty compounds created by the drastic use of chemical weedkillers at Chingford Mount, St Patrick's R.C. and many of the Jewish cemeteries.

Unlike any of the above, there is one cemetery with a unique range of flora and that is Brompton. Its origins as a market garden have had unusual consequences since wild cabbage, asparagus, garlic, radishes and mushrooms now sprout among its graves. They grow in tandem with trees which number some sixty species, including the unusual Indian horse chestnut.[12]

Ferns, mosses and especially lichens have always favoured churchyards where ancient undisturbed stones provide an ideal habitat. Cemeteries have the added advantage of a wider range of materials that support an equally wide variety of lichens. At Abney Park for example, thirty-eight species have been identified. Fungi too enjoy the cemeteries' undisturbed ground. At Nunhead for instance, numerous species have been detected and at Abney Park rarities include the earthstar, red lead roundhead and artist's fungus.

The diversity of birds found in cemeteries is dependant on the habitats that the range of plants confer. Thus the benign nature conservation policy at Highgate has had its reward with over fifty species now observed. Both Kensal Green and Nunhead claim eighty-five species and at Abney Park they include the less common bullfinch, firecrest, goldfinch, kestrel, long tailed tit, tawny owl, woodcock and the greater and lesser spotted woodpeckers. Woodgrange Park, which offers little of architectural interest, compensates by offering 'one of the best sites for birds in the borough.'[13]

Cemeteries with ponds attract particular species. At Carpenders Park and the City of London, ducks, herons and moorhens are predictable inhabitants but the kingfishers at the former are a rare sight in London. In 2002 the British Trust for Ornithology calculated the average number of bird species in over forty cemeteries was sixteen, the most common being the blue tit followed by the blackbird, robin and wood pigeon.

Butterflies are another species that are increasingly common in London's cemeteries. At Nunhead a small book has been published describing them (pairing another on the cemetery's

Abney Park: The spread of vegetation

68 LONDON CEMETERIES

Abney Park: Ivy

trees). Tower Hamlets claims twenty-six species and twenty-one have been recorded at Abney Park, including some, like the speckled wood, more frequently seen in woodland. Moths of course are far more numerous – Brompton merits an impressive 200 species. Invertebrates are also encouraged at Eastbrookend, where the management has allowed an apiary to be sited within the cemetery, and at Brompton where fourteen species of wasp are on record.

The mammal population of cemeteries is more difficult to evaluate but any regular visitor can expect to see bats, foxes (there is a colony at Highgate), hedgehogs, mice, rabbits, rats, grey squirrels and voles. Badgers, deer and weasels are not uncommon. In the City of London cemetery a remarkable list of eleven different mammal species has been compiled to add to an already comprehensive species catalogue of 500 insects, 92 flowering plants, 87 beetles, 47 birds, 31 spiders, 22 fungi and 16 trees!

There can be no doubt that the benefits of the conservation approach to cemetery management is now appreciated and the totally neglected ground is in the minority, but there is another option. Both private and local authority owners have worked hard on improving the standard of maintenance over the last 200 years. One outstanding example of what can be achieved is the spring display of croci at Golders Green which is unrivalled anywhere. The extraordinary rock garden and waterfall at Crystal Palace District is another unusual cemetery feature but the failure of Grove Park to match the suburban dream of neat terraces and formal pond confirms how labour intensive such schemes have become.

It may also be argued that the 'Britain in Bloom' style of hanging baskets, manicured lawns and flower beds filled with vibrant standard roses are not to everyone's taste but more suited to tidy civic parks. Equally, the more undisciplined character of a cemetery, coupled with the need for contemplation and tranquility inspires a more natural approach to planting. This was a sentiment that Loudon advocated well over 150 years ago when he criticised those cemeteries that 'Bear too great a resemblance to pleasure grounds.' Even the planting of ornamental flowers was contrary to his opinion. 'A state of quiet and repose'[14] was the objective, and surely that is still true.

Abney Park: The chapel (1840) in 1980. The growth of trees prevents this view being taken today

Gazetteer

ABNEY PARK CEMETERY
STOKE NEWINGTON HIGH STREET, N16

Founded: 1840
Owner: London Borough of Hackney
Acreage: 32

'The *campo santo* of the English nonconformists'[1] declared a 1903 brochure of the Abney Park Cemetery Company. The cemetery had been opened by the Lord Mayor of London in 1840, after Bunhill Fields, the foremost burial ground for Dissenters since 1665, was judged 'filled to repletion'. To replace it the Company had fortuitously secured the Abney estate in Stoke Newington, a district at the heart of Nonconformity in London. Abney House, built in 1700, had been the home of the dissenter Sir Thomas Abney (1640–1722). All but the southern gates were demolished in the 1840s but the grounds, described as 'well timbered with varieties of forest trees that pleasantly shaded the many walks' were absorbed into the cemetery plan and provided the nucleus for 'one of the most complete arboretums in the neighbourhood of London'[2] and were highly praised by Loudon.[3] A list of plants compiled by the company's secretary, names 2,500 varieties of shrubs and trees and 1,029 varieties of rose bushes growing in the exceptionally fertile ground. There were American oak, chestnuts, elms, evergreens, planes, silver birch, tulip trees and a huge cedar reputedly 200 years old with a scythe embedded in it. The man responsible for this planting was a celebrated Victorian nurseryman, George Loddiges of Hackney.

At the centre of the ground the brick chapel was built, near the site of the old house. Originally the customary two chapels were planned, but in view of the company's policy to leave the chapel unconsecrated, and therefore open to all religious denominations, it was decided one was sufficient. The Reverend Barker, the first chaplain attached to the cemetery, wrote:

> Every portion of this cemetery is accessible to all parties without distinction or preference . . . no breath of envy lives in this hallowed spot. How pleasing to God! How delightful to angels![4]

He was probably not aware that the chapel was also the first non-denominational cemetery chapel in Europe.

The architect was William Hosking, who had been educated in Australia and travelled in France and Italy before becoming Professor in the 'Art of Construction' at King's College, London. As an engineer he had successfully constructed a road over the Grand Junction Canal which in turn was raised over the railway at Kensal Green. As an architect, however, his work is curiously insubstantial. The chapel's (ritual) west front borrows elements from Beverley Minster, but one would need a wild imagination to equate the twin towers and ogee portals of the two buildings. The spire is a more exact copy of the magnificent fourteenth-century example at Bloxham, Oxfordshire. South of the chapel is a small catacomb once entered through a Romanesque style door. Barker described it as a 'cold and stony death place . . . the chilliness is awful and repulsive'.[5] In 1920 the War Graves Commission built over it to create a platform for the Cross of Sacrifice. South again on the same axial path is the finest of the cemetery's monuments, a nine foot high statue of Isaac Watts by Edward Baily R.A., a highly successful sculptor trained under Flaxman. Watts is in fact buried at Bunhill Fields, but he knew Abney House well and died there in 1748. A small mound, which has been reinstated in the north east corner of the cemetery, is still marked as his 'favourite retirement'.

The main east entrance lodge, office and gate piers are the best of Abney Park's buildings.[6] They were a pioneer design in the suitably funereal Egyptian style by Hosking advised by Joseph Bonomi junior, a distinguished Egyptologist who became curator of Sir John Soane's museum. A genuine hieroglyphic inscription in the concave cornice of the office was devised by him. Translated it reads, 'The gates of the abode of the mortal part of man'. Loudon thought the gates were very grand but they were exactly the sort of thing that Pugin, the Gothic purist, deplored.

The one serious shortcoming in Abney Park is the lack of first rate monuments of the calibre found in Norwood or Kensal Green. Just north of the chapel is the tomb of John Spreat (died 1865) the only known design in the cemetery by a great Victorian architect, Alfred Waterhouse. Otherwise there is the occasional ensemble lining the main paths and near the south entrance which are impressive, but that is all. The thrifty habits of the dissenters are surely responsible for this deficiency. The draped urn is probably the most recurring symbol. There is some compensation

Abney Park: Detail on a gate pier

Abney Park: Indicative monument to John Jones, 'for many years a member of the South Hornsey Local Board.' (1883)

in the imagery of the pointing finger on top of several of the obelisks and in melancholy epitaphs like that of the Tod grave:

> 'Passing stranger call not this a place of dreary gloom; I love to linger near this spot, it is my parent's tomb'.

Graves of note at Abney Park include the shrine with a sculpted relief portrait to Henry Richard M.P. (1888), the Rogers family mausoleum, the Bostock lion (1912), the baroque sarcophagus to John Jay (1872), the female figure on the Mechi grave (1845), the massive granite Celtic cross commemorating Andrew Reed (1892), the ornate Devereaux grave and the beehive on the Norwood memorial (1864) which replicates one at Chingford Mount.

In contrast there was a funeral at Abney Park in 1861 which even by Victorian standards was an epic event. Mr Braidwood, superintendent of the London Fire Brigade had been killed in a burning warehouse while leading his men at the biggest London fire since 1666. His hearse was followed by fifteen mourning coaches and representatives of all the London fire brigades, the London rifle brigade, the Tower Hamlets Volunteers and the police. The procession was over a mile long, shops and streets were closed and every church en route save St Paul's rang a funeral peal. Funerals of this scale were expensive and exceptional. In 1896 Messrs Dunkley, monumental masons, whose premises adjoined the Abney Park gates, advertised a more modest range of services. For £28 10s 0d. they could provide a '1st Class funeral' which included a hearse and four horses, two coaches with pairs, feathers, velvets, attendants, porters, pages, lead coffin and an elm case covered with black cloth. Alternatively four guineas bought a 'carriage funeral'[7] consisting of a hearse and one horse, a mourning coach with one horse, an elm coffin and bearers. (Henry Dunkley was buried in the cemetery in 1900.)

Abney Park was a popular cemetery, perhaps too popular. Within fifteen years of its opening, the ground was described as a 'mass of corruption underneath'.[8] Writing in 1896 Mrs Holmes said, 'The tombstones are crowded together as closely knit as it seems possible and yet they are being constantly added to, although the greater part of this cemetery is already over full'.[9] In 1882 the original Nonconformist enterprise had been assimilated into the Abney Park cemetery Company, but its income was negligible, because as the Reverend Barker put it, 'The bodies for the most part sleep in freehold' and its fortunes suffered.[10] By 1939 maintenance was minimal and by 1974 the company had been declared bankrupt. The lodge and office were burned out by arsonists, who also destroyed company records. The chapel was wrecked. In 1974 a number of local residents formed the Save Abney Park Cemetery Committee which helped persuade

Hackney to purchase the cemetery for a nominal sum and take steps to preserve what was left. In 1992 The Abney Park Cemetery Trust was founded and the cemetery is now a designated local nature reserve and conservation area. Today only the occasional 'discretionary' burial takes place.

It is a major task to clear the prolific growth of sycamore and ash saplings, remove the dead elms and poplars and restore the buildings and major monuments. Several proposals have been submitted since 1974 which have distinguished those areas best left undeveloped and those that could provide more obvious public amenities. Although a start has been made at implementing these recommendations, more ambitious plans have sadly not been fulfilled and they remain daunting objectives. The chapel is stripped of everything back to its brickwork, and iron railings now replace the doors. The undergrowth is dense, although this offers a certain degree of protection from vandalism of memorials. Positive developments which have taken place include improvements to the entrance courtyard and part of the south lodge now converted into a visitor centre. A temporary classroom was added next to the north lodge in the late 1990s, the lodge itself has been used for stone masonry training courses and some monuments have been repaired.

For a full history see the second edition of *A Guide to Abney Park Cemetery* by Paul Joyce published in 1994 and available from the Cemetery.

THOMAS BINNEY 1798–1874
Eloquent Nonconformist preacher and writer sometimes called the 'Archbishop of Nonconformity'.

BRAMWELL BOOTH 1856–1929
Son of William Booth. 'General' of the Salvation Army 1912–29.

CATHERINE BOOTH (NÉE MUMFORD) 1829–90
Preacher, 'Mother of the Salvation Army' and wife of William Booth.

GENERAL WILLIAM BOOTH 1829–1912
Founder of the Salvation Army in 1878.

FRANK BOSTOCK 1866–1912
Menagerist.

JAMES BRAIDWOOD 1800–61
Superintendent of the London Fire Engine Establishment 1832–61. Killed by a falling wall in a fire at Cotton's Wharf, Tooley Street, his body was recovered two days later while the fire raged for a month and caused £2 million worth of damage.

REV. AARON BUZACOTT 1829–81
Congregationalist minister and secretary of the Anti-Slavery Society.

EDWARD CALVERT 1799–1883
Landscape painter and wood engraver, he was a disciple of William Blake.

Thomas Caulker 1846–59
Described as 'son of the King of Bompey', in West Africa, sent to England to acquire a Christian education.

Josiah Conder 1789–1855
Bookseller and author. A champion of Nonconformity, he edited *The Patriot* for twenty-three years. Wrote *The Modern Traveller* in thirty volumes, despite the fact he never went abroad.

Joseph Corfield 1809–88
An admirer of nineteenth-century radical reformers, he erected the Reformers' Memorial in Kensal Green Cemetery inscribed with the names of eighty-five 'men and women who have generously given their time and means to improve the conditions and enlarge the happiness of all classes'.

Rev. William Ellis 1795–1872
Missionary in the South Seas and Madagascar. Translated the Bible into Malagasy and wrote the histories of Madagascar and the London Missionary Society.

Rev. Alexander Fletcher 1787–1860
Presbyterian divine 'The Prince of Preachers to children', for thirty-five years minister of Finsbury Circus Chapel, the largest in London.

Matthew Habershon 1789–1852
Architect, he completed St James' Cathedral, Jerusalem, in 1842. Author of *The Ancient Half Timbered Houses of England* (1836).

John Hall 1774–1860
Bookseller and author of the *Sinner's Friend* which reached its 356th edition before his death.

Tommy Hall –1949
Record breaking cyclist. Broke the world motor paced record in 1903.

Rev. Dr John Harris 1802–56
Congregationalist preacher. He 'blazed like a meteor upon the religious world' with his publication of *Mammon*.

Rev. Ebenezer Henderson 1784–1858
For many years agent of the British and Foreign Bible Society in Scandinavia and Russia.

James Hibberd 1825–90
Horticulturalist, editor of the *Gardener's Magazine* 1875–90.

Mary Hillum 1759–1864
'Of Church Street, Stoke Newington, who died in the 105th year of her age. She died in the same house in which she was born, scarcely ever slept out of the house in the whole of her life, never travelled either by omnibus or railway and was never more than 15 miles from home'.

William Hone 1780–1842
Bookseller and writer, prosecuted for blasphemy in his *Political Litany* and acquitted. £3,000 was raised for him by public subscription as a result. Dickens attended his funeral.

Rev. Edwin Hood 1820–85
Congregationalist minister and biographer of Oliver Cromwell, Isaac Watts and William Wordsworth.

Sir Walter Johnson 1845–1910
Mayor of Hackney 1901–2 and member of the first L.C.C.

Enoch Bassett Keeling 1837–86
Architect, he was an original exponent of the High Victorian Gothic style.

Theodore Kitching 1866–1930
Salvation Army Commissioner and secretary to General Booth.

George Leybourne 1842–84
Music hall artiste known as 'Champagne Charlie'.

Conrad Loddiges 1821–65
Hackney horticulturalist, son of George Loddiges who first planted the cemetery.

Rev. Robert Mather 1808–77
For forty years a missionary in India, translated the Bible into Hindustani.

Rev. Walter Medhurst 1796–1857
For forty years a missionary in China, author of a Chinese-English dictionary and translated the Bible into Mandarin.

John Mills 1798–1879
A Congregationalist millionaire silk manufacturer and one of the wealthiest commoners in England. M.P. for Wycombe 1862–68.

Rev. John Morison 1791–1859
Nonconformist minister and author, he wrote *Counsels to a New Wedded Pair*.

Samuel Morley 1809–86
Hosiery manufacturer, M.P. for Nottingham and Bristol, worked for dissenters' emancipation, endowed Morley College for adult education.

James O'Brien 1797–1864
Irish born radical, journalist and leader of the Chartist movement.

George Offor 1787–1864
Editor and biographer of Bunyan, his library was burned in a fire at Sotheby's in 1865.

Sir Hugh Owen 1804–81
Philanthropist and a founder of the University College of Wales at Aberystwyth.

Dr Robert Philip 1791–1858
Congregationalist minister and biographer of John Bunyan and George Whitefield.

Rev. Andrew Reed 1787–1862
Founded a number of orphanages and the Royal Hospital for Incurables 1855. The Celtic cross was by the O'Shea brothers of Kilkenny.

Sir Charles Reed 1819–81
Hackney's first M.P. 1868–74, printer, typefounder and antiquary. Chairman of the London School Board 1873–81.

Talbot Baines Reed 1852–93
Honorary secretary of the Bibliographical Society, author of numerous books for boys.

Henry Richard 1812–1888
Congregationalist minister, secretary to the Society for Promoting Permanent and Universal Peace and M.P. 1868–1888 for Merthyr Tydfil.

Thomas Robertson 1829–71
Dramatic playwright and actor.

Nathanial Rogers 1808–84
A doctor and donor of stained glass windows to St Paul's Cathedral and elsewhere. He is buried in the only mausoleum in the cemetery.

Samuel Sharpe 1799–1881
Banker and Egyptologist, he translated numerous Hebrew texts into English.

Sir Edward Sieveking 1816–1904
Physician extraordinary to Edward VII and author of medical works.

John Pye Smith 1774–1851
Nonconformist theologian. The first dissenting Fellow of the Royal Society.

Rev. Dr James Spence 1821–74
Congregationalist minister, editor of the *Evangelical Magazine*.

John Swan 1787–1869
Invented the steamship screw propeller (1824) and the self acting chain messenger (1831) but failed to patent either so 'never received the slightest remuneration'.

Henry Vincent 1813–78
Militant Chartist leader, his imprisonment in 1839 led to fierce rioting. Subsequently a successful lecturer on political and social subjects in England and America.

Thomas Wilson 1764–1843
Wealthy nonconformist benefactor, he built and repaired numerous chapels throughout the country. A founder member on the Council of University College, London.

There seems to be no foundation to the theory that Bridget Fleetwood, d.1662, daughter of Oliver Cromwell and wife of General Charles Fleetwood, was ever buried in Abney Park's chapel. There is, however, evidence that she was buried in St. Anne's, Blackfriars, since demolished.

ACTON CEMETERY
Park Royal Road, NW10

Founded: 1895
Owner: London Borough of Ealing
Acreage: 16½

At a glance this cemetery appears to offer little of interest. The ground is almost bereft of planting and is cut in two by a railway line. The chapels are sober Early English Gothic by the Borough's surveyor, Daniel Ebbetts, and clustered round them are the graves of long forgotten civic dignitaries. Further afield, however, are a few monuments with considerable curiosity value. A granite cross emerges from a seaborne lifebelt to commemorate Albert Perry, one of over 1000 passengers drowned in the *Lusitania* in 1915; a dove flutters over George Temple's monument, the first British airman to fly upside-down. What is the significance of the trumpet carved on the Howard Reynolds tomb? And what ill luck struck Robert John, killed by a Zeppelin air raid over London in June 1917!

Acton: Trumpet on tomb of Edward Howard Reynolds (1898)

Sir William Champness 1873–1956
City solicitor and antiquary.

John Leech 1857–1942
A judge in Northern Ireland.

Sir Samuel Lewis 1843–1903
Chief Justice of Sierra Leone, he took a leading part in the affairs of the colony.

John Manning 1829–1908
The last constable of Chester Castle and governor of Chester, Wakefield and Pentonville Prisons.

Albert Perry –1915
American drowned with 194 others when the *Lusitania* was torpedoed by a German submarine.

George Temple 1892–1914
The first British airman to fly upside down, killed at Hendon aerodrome.

Sir George Wright 1848–1927
A J.P. and for thirty-eight years a member of Middlesex County Council.

ALPERTON (WEMBLEY) CEMETERY
Clifford Road, Wembley, Middx.

Founded: 1914
Owner: London Borough of Brent
Acreage: 10

Alperton is a typical municipal creation. Gate piers with laurel wreath decorations precede the main drive to the pair of chapels. A simple *porte cochère* links the two which are built of red brick with white painted dressings in the perpendicular style. They were constructed in 1937 at a cost of £4,700 and the budget for the burial chapel was stretched to allow for stained glass depicting a fortressed hilltop city. A columbarium was opened in the other chapel which was dedicated in May 1942. The designer was the borough engineer and surveyor Cecil R.W. Chapman with modifications by his successor C.S. Trapp. The lodge, also in red brick with Portland stone dressings, is north of the entrance. A ground floor extension in keeping with the building acts as the office for the Brent cemeteries service. All buildings are maintained to a high standard.

The ground, divided into small numbered plots including a children's section, is well maintained with several flower beds and that favourite of municipal gardeners, flowering cherry trees. If only some of the care lavished on a cemetery like this could be diverted to more deserving causes like Abney Park and Nunhead. This is twentieth century commuter country where death is treated with sanitised detachment rather than Victorian drama. The attitude is neatly illustrated by one remarkable monument, the figure of a scrubbed, uniformed 1928 schoolboy, Gordon Nott, and, beneath, the epitaph: 'With a kindly smile and a wave of the hand he has wandered into a better land.' He died after a road accident on his brand new bicycle. The statue was stolen but recovered in 1996; the original is now displayed in the burial chapel.

BANDON HILL CEMETERY
Plough Lane, Wallington, Surrey

Founded: 1900
Owner: Bandon Hill Cemetery Joint Committee
Acreage: 14

Situated behind a thick hedge off a busy road, Bandon Hill complements its suburban surroundings. It is maintained to a high level but regrettably there is little of interest for cemetery enthusiasts.

Passing the lodge the main drive gently rises to a pair of red brick chapels designed by R.M. Chart.[1] Unusually, the chapels are linked by a white painted wooden framed *porte cochère*, topped with a copper fleche and weather vane. Common to both are the unadorned lancet windows interposed by buttresses. The sanctuary to the Anglican chapel is apse ended. Both chapels have basements and one now serves as the cemetery office. At the back of the cemetery is a redundant coroner's mortuary complete with large glass skylight and neighbouring brown-tiled cold room.

With a few exceptions, the memorials play safe. In front of the chapels is the immaculately maintained white *pietà* on the Pazzi grave, while to the south of the cemetery there is a winged angel with head bowed in sorrow over a distinctly classical podium. A 1920s monument incorporates a headstone with a pair of winged angels, an ensemble rather spoiled by the crazy paving over the grave.

Charles Alfred Barnard –1935
Editor of the *Era*.

Samuel Coleridge-Taylor 1875–1912
Composer. The memorial has an inscription by Alfred Noyes and includes four bars from his *Hiawatha*.

Thomas Cook –1937
Geologist.

Sir Charles Hose 1863–1929
A member of the Supreme Council of Sarawak, author and naturalist. The Hose's Palm Civet is named after him.

Joseph Peter Kegan (Joe Elvin) 1862–1935
Music hall comedian. Founder member of the Grand Order of Water Rats in 1889.

Andrew Wilson Murray 1845–1930
Secretary to Field Marshal the Duke of Connaught and Strathearn for thirty-eight years.

Eugeen Stratton 1861–1918
Music Hall star, buried next to this friend   Joe Elvin (see above).

BARKINGSIDE CEMETERIES
LONGWOOD GARDENS, ILFORD, ESSEX

Founded: East, 1923; West, 1954
Owner: London Borough of Redbridge
Acreage: East, 8; West, 13½

The cemetery is split into two by the road. The eastern section is now full and although well maintained it represents a sorry departure from the exuberance of Victorian cemetery planning. The ground is flat, the tombstones feeble, planting is scant and buildings nil. A centrepiece has been formed by an ugly brick structure that resembles a wishing well but actually houses a dripping tap. Dull anonymity prevails. On the north east side a small hedged-in plot has been reserved for deceased members of a Dr Barnardo's home.

Over the road, the western section is an excellent example of a modern cemetery. At the gate a rose garden absorbs ashes of the cremated, beyond, acres of black and white marble slabs chequer the ground. They are set bolt upright in sunken concrete kerbs aligned to allow sufficient room for the motor mower. Ornamental trees and one prominent weeping willow are also uniformly spaced.

There is no chapel, only a waiting room and lavatories. Functionalism reigns supreme in a world that the Victorians would find hard to recognise.

REV. PAUL LEVERTOFF 1878–1954 (E)
Hebrew scholar and author on religious subjects.

BARNES COMMON CEMETERY
OFF ROCKS LANE, SW13

Founded: 1854
Owner: London Borough of Richmond upon Thames
Acreage: 2

These two acres of sandy ground were originally purchased by the Church authorities for £10 and a further £1,400 was spent on providing a chapel and landscaping. The cemetery was closed in 1954 and acquired by the Borough from the church in 1966 with the intention of turning it into a lawn cemetery. As a first step the chapel and lodge were demolished and the boundary railings removed, making it fair game for all manner of unsavoury happenings and many headstones were smashed.[1] The vandals may have been encouraged by Barnes' sinister reputation that preceded the 1970s. Stories of murder and hauntings include that of a ghostly nun who is said to hover over the place where the body of an unfortunate Mrs Thomas was once exhumed.

By 1971 a councillor was quoted as saying, 'I've seen burial grounds at Flanders marched over by scores of troops – but even they did not look as bad as the Barnes cemetery'. Some clearing up was done soon after but the cemetery is in an appalling state and continues to suffer from neglect and vandalism despite the number of distinguished Victorians buried here. Fortunately, the exceptional Hedgman monument, commemorating a family of local benefactors, has defeated the vandals' onslaught, probably on account of its size. Nearby is a classical monument supporting a near life-size female figure casting a floral tribute over perhaps an urn or portrait bust – the image is long gone and only an empty niche remains, invaded by moss and ivy.

The inscription over the Pickersgill memorial recording Jeanette Caroline Pickersgill – the daughter-in-law of Henry Pickersgill RA – notes 'Who was cremated'. She was the first person to be cremated at Woking Crematorium in Surrey in March 1885 although her ashes are in fact in the catacomb at Kensal Green Cemetery.[2]

Baron de Sampayo 1794–1860
Served in the Portuguese Embassy in London.

Alexander Finberg 1866–1939
Artist and art historian, authority on J.M.W. Turner, adviser to the Inland Revenue on picture valuations and founder of the Walpole Society.

James Heywood 1810–97
M.P. for North Lancashire 1847–57 and a pioneer of the free library movement, he maintained a free library at Notting Hill at his own cost.

Charles Innes 1825–1907
Architect, he designed St Michael's, Barnes and rebuilt much of the parish church.

Augustus Mayhew 1826–75
Writer of popular novels, sometimes collaborating with his brother Henry.

Francis Palgrave 1824–97
Professor of poetry at Oxford and compiler of the *Golden Treasury*.

Henry Pickersgill 1782–1875
Portrait painter who painted many of the celebrated people of his time.

Lt.Gen.Sir Alfred Wilde 1819–78
Took an active part against the Indian Mutiny, led the party which captured the Begum's palace in Delhi, A.D.C. to the Queen and member of the Council of India.

Edward Williams 1782–1855
Landscape artist, known as 'Moonlight Williams' from his use of moonlight effects. Senior member of a large family of artists.

Henry J. Williams 1811–65
Landscape artist, son of the above.

BATTERSEA NEW CEMETERY (MORDEN) AND NORTH EAST SURREY CREMATORIUM

Lower Morden Lane, Morden, Surrey

Founded: 1891
Owner: London Borough of Wandsworth
Acreage: 70

The approach is impressive: spiky Gothic gates, an agreeable lodge in the half timbered style, and the vista of a drive running straight between an avenue of poplars, like a road in France but here leading to the chapels. Separated by a *porte cochère* and a central spire, the twin chapels with Bath stone dressings in the Early English style were designed by William C. Poole for the Battersea Burial Board and cost £16,545. The land was formerly Hobbald's Farm, Morden.[1]

In 1958 the right hand chapel was converted into the North East Surrey Crematorium. The *porte cochère* were enclosed with the area behind the central spire extended to accommodate the cremators. It was opened by the Earl of Verulam, president of the Crematorium Society of Great Britain on 1 May 1958. The scheme was planned by the firm of E. Guy Dawber, Fox and Robinson who were also responsible for Enfield and Lambeth crematoria.

In 2005 the burial chapel was also converted for cremation services and a new Hall of Memory constructed on land to the right of the chapel adjacent to the Gardens of Remembrance.

The monuments are less evocative but the ground is well kept and in spring brightened up by cowslips and primroses. A stream, the Pyl Brook, flows through a corner. One cenotaph bears this legend:

Battersea New: The poplar lined drive in 1910 when this photograph was taken. The chapels were converted into the North East Surrey Crematorium in 1958

Erected in gratitude by the London Medical Schools to commemorate those who generously bequeathed their bodies to assist in the progress of medical education and research.

MAJ.GEN. SIR FRANCIS CLERY 1838–1926
Professor of tactics at Sandhurst. He served in many nineteenth century African campaigns.

WILLIAM HENDY –1960
Sculptor and artist, for many years a contributor to *Punch*.

JOHN SINNOTT 1829–1896
Won the V.C. during the Indian Mutiny.

EDWARD THOMAS 1878–1917
Poet and writer about the countryside of southern England. Killed in action.

ALEXANDER THOMSON –1905
'For many years conductor of the famous Pullman Ltd train between Victoria and Brighton.'

BATTERSEA ST MARY'S CEMETERY
BOLINGBROKE GROVE, SW11

Founded: 1860
Owner: London Borough of Wandworth
Acreage: 8½

In a heavily built up area of Clapham this small L-shaped cemetery is the proverbial green oasis bordered by busy roads and panel beaters. It is also typical in having iron gates decorated with appropriate religious motifs, a lodge (newly rebuilt), a pair of tiny Gothic style chapels and the more extravagant monuments clustered round them. The architect was Charles Lee of Golden Square, Westminster and the builders Messrs Adamsons & Sons of Putney. The total cost of establishing the cemetery was £8,000.

Battersea St Mary's: The chapels are perfect miniatures (1860).

Battersea St Mary's: The large flaming urn commemorates Kaikhoshru Puntheki (1890).

Plane trees and poplars line the cemetery paths but the effects of vandalism and a council policy of flattening unstable tombstones have thinned out the ground. All this is predictable but St Mary's is nevertheless worthy of a visit for its unique anthology of rhyming epitaphs, emanating it seems from a local school of poets.

A record of railway deaths at Clapham Junction is not unexpected here; a 1950 inscription states simply that the deceased was 'killed whilst shunting at Clapham Junction Goods Yard'. How much more descriptive is the partly obliterated stone commemorating an engine driver in 1876 on which a steam engine is carved above the following lines:

> When to his work he went
> he little thought of death
> Or that his noble engine
> would chuse him to lose his breath
> His heart on duty bent no thought of danger near
> When launched into eternity to the grief of friends so dear.

There are many others, for example Rose Pavitt who died in 1881:

> The cup is bitter and the wound severe
> To part with those we love so dear
> Tis the Almighty's will it should be so
> And when He's ready we all must go.

Or twenty-three year old Samson Traylen who died in 1894:

> Reader this silent grave contains
> A much loved son's dear remains
> Death like a frost, has nipped his bloom
> And sent him early to his tomb.

Samson was one of many who died young in Clapham around the turn of the century, spurring the local poet(s) to dizzy heights of pathos. The schoolboy Horace Montford's bronze plaque of 1910 depicts science books overprinted thus:

> From him of the loveliest and the best
> That from his vintage rolling time hath prest
> Alas how soon life's brimming cup was snatched.

Henry Blunden, killed in 1871 aged twenty-two cautions:

> All you that come my grave to see
> Oh think of death and remember me
> Just in my prime and fully skilled
> When on the railway I was killed
> Take warning, hear, and do not weep
> But early learn thy grave to seek.

Alfred Fell and Arthur Ronald were both aged nineteen when they drowned in the Thames in 1873.

> Mark the brief story of a summer's day
> At noon, in youth and health they launched away,
> Ere eve, death wrecked the bark and quenched the light,
> The parents' home was desolate at night.

There is, in contrast, a world weary message from John Goodman's tomb of 1916:

> Farewell, vain world I've had enough of thee
> And now am careless what thou say's to me.

The design of the Battersea tombstones is less interesting. A fine red and grey granite confection erected by the Evans family closes the end of the northern path and a large flaming urn commemorates a Parsee lawyer, Kaikhoshru Puntheki from Bombay (1890).[1]

WILLIAM BISHOP 1903–61
'Medical historian', responsible for establishing the Wellcome Historical Library in 1949. Wrote several books on medical history including a Dictionary of Medical Biography.

JOHN BREESE 1817–89
Sergeant Major of H.M.Bodyguard. 'Formerly of the 11th Hussars and one of the Balaclava six hundred.'

RT.HON.JOHN BURNS 1858–1943
Liberal politician, president of the Board of Trade 1914, M.P. for Battersea 1892–1914.

ARTHUR HARDWICK –1922
'Late wireless operator of the ex Egypt.' The *Egypt* sank off Ushant with over £1 million on board in gold and silver bullion and coins, with the loss of ninety-six lives.

ARCHIBALD MADDEN 1864–1928
British Consul in Morocco 1907–14.

HENRY MEYER 1797–1865
Ornithologist, he produced *Illustrations of British Birds* 1835–41.

JOHN NICHOLS 1800–67
Editor of *Zion's Trumpet*.

SIR WILLIAM ROSE 1820–81
Paint merchant. Lord Mayor of London and M.P. for Southampton 1862–65

BECKENHAM CEMETERY
LONDON ROAD, BROMLEY, KENT

Founded: 1877
Owner: London Borough of Bromley
Acreage: 5

A small but intact Victorian cemetery that still boasts a complete ensemble of decorative iron gates, (although the boundary railings have disappeared), mortuary and twin chapels joined by a three-arched *porte cochère*. The matching lodge has been completely rebuilt. The architect was George Truefitt whose design was selected in competition with others. During his career he was chiefly concerned with housing on the Tufnell Park estate but here proved himself equally competent at designing Gothic buildings with the added flourish of large French-inspired crocket capitals. The chapels are now dwarfed by large trees.

The cemetery is immaculately kept and although the monuments themselves are nothing special three are worth observing. These are the large multi-coloured granite column erected for William Digby in 1901 and two adjacent sarcophagi, one in grey and pink granite commemorating the Johnson family and the Tweedy memorial in white marble which still retains its original iron railings.

MAJ.GEN.HENRY BABBAGE 1825–1918
Served in India for many years and spoke fluent Hindi. Among his publications were several on the calculating machine invented by his father in the 1820s.

HORACE, EARL FARQUHAR, 1844–1923
Master of the household of Edward VII, Lord Steward 1915–22.

SIR RALPH FORSTER 1850–1930
Deputy Lieutenant for Surrey.

WALTER HAZELL 1843–1919
M.P. for Leicester 1894–1900. Member of many committees concerned with social reform – he ran a farm for the unemployed.

THOMAS LYLE 1845–1931
Historian.

Sir Edward Scott 1842–83
Banker, sheriff of Kent 1878.

Maj.Gen.William Welman 1827–1906
Veteran of the Zulu War during which he commanded the 99th Regiment.

BEXLEYHEATH CEMETERY
Banks Lane, Broadway, Bexleyheath, Kent

Founded: 1876
Owner: London Borough of Bexley
Acreage: 5¼

Tucked away behind a busy shopping street and a new lodge building, the south side of the cemetery is a little Victorian backwater. Evergreen hollies and yews are thick on the ground and the cemetery is well cared for. There is a tiny chapel in the early fourteenth-century style by E. Hodgkinson with a large bell in the fleche. Behind the chapel is a memorial garden opened in 2001 for the burial of ashes.

Significant memorials are lacking although unusually well-sculpted angelic figures stand above the Littlehales, Forsaith and Burr Butler graves. Near the latter is a cannon carved into the memorial to Bombardier Frederick H. Binskin. The sarcophagus to Cromwell Fleetwood Varley who died in 1883 contains a fine portrait sculptured in relief. Colin Bullen who was buried in 1968 is represented by figures of a suited young man and an angel standing either side of a cross.

Surprisingly, many of the iron tomb railings have somehow survived, although the introduction of a policy to test the stability of memorials has left many memorials staked at the rear. Towards the north of the cemetery and at the rear of the lawn grave section is a large bronze ledger commemorating thirty-three local residents who died in World War Two including four unidentified women and one man.

Pressure on burial space led to graves being sited in all parts of the cemetery including a single line down each side of the entrance from Church Road and today Bexleyheath does not accept new burials.

Surg. Gen.Henry Kendall 1821–90
Served throughout the Crimean War and the Indian Mutiny.

Cromwell Varley 1828–83
Electrical engineer and pioneer in the use of submarine cables.

BROCKLEY AND LADYWELL CEMETERY
BROCKLEY ROAD, SE4

Founded: *1858*
Owner: *London Borough of Lewisham*
Acreage: *21*

Until 1948 Brockley comprised two cemeteries, Deptford to the west and Ladywell to the east, founded within a month of each other. Local government reorganisation prompted amalgamation by which time Deptford's Victorian chapels had been destroyed by bombs. These were both two Gothic buildings joined by a *porte cochère* and slender spire. Nearby was another chapel with a rose window and bellcote; the foundations are still visible. A grassed ridge now marks the line of the old dividing wall. The Ladywell chapel which is in the decorated style by architects Morphew and Green survives. Although seldom used it is in a very good state of repair, but both windows and doors have been protected with grilles. In 2006 an area against the boundary wall in Ladywell cemetery was cleared to accommodate new graves, marked by small pedimented boxes faced in black marble that resemble television sets. A feature at Ladywell – and not dissimilar to those at Greenwich cemetery – are the green painted wood 'bus' type shelters.

The best approach is through the Ladywell entrance with its fine iron gates which manage to incorporate the words 'Ladywell Cemetery' as a decorative motif. Past the substantial lodge and the ground is packed with monuments through which the paths curl as if part of a maze. Among the familiar granite and marble the use of slate in 1868 for Hannah Rachel is very striking, and worth seeking out is the empty chair on the Steemson grave (1924). In the old Deptford section the number of tombs thins and some suitably lugubrious evergreens and poplars have flourished. Near the Deptford gates the best monuments are a series of large granite examples bordering an L-shaped avenue.

Overall, however, there is little in Brockley that is very grand and its interest tends to be local. Adjacent to one of the several raised areas of ground is an isolated arched iron gate which does not appear to mark a specific area. The Vancaillie memorial (1887) comprising an angel clutching a cross stands prominently on a chest tomb but as on so many similar memorials, the iron chains have, regrettably, disappeared. As Deptford's dockyards are just two miles away it is not surprising to find many sailors commemorated here, several having

Brockley: Detail on the gate at the Ladywell entrance

Brockley: The cemetery (1906) – the chapels can be seen in the distance

drowned. Another peculiar sailing hazard is described by the inscription on the monument to midshipman William Rivers of HMS *Sapphire*, 'killed by falling from her maintop at Hobart Town November 5th 1877 age 19'. The sense of Victorian lower middle class respectability is also epitomised in characteristic epitaphs like John Harris's of 1882, 'for many years connected with the South Eastern Railway Company, this monument is erected by the Station Masters of the above railway in memory of their late superintendent', or Matthew Bromley's, a licensed victualler who died in 1881, 'respected by those who knew him'.

The seamier side of life is also represented by the monument erected by public subscription for Jane Clouson. On a plinth crouches the image of a pathetic waif and beneath the sorry explanation: 'A motherless girl who was murdered in Kidbrooke Lane Eltham age 17 in 1871. Her last words were, "Oh, let me die".' The case became a Victorian *cause célèbre* when it was discovered that the girl was pregnant and had recently been dismissed by her employer, Ebenezer Pook, on account of her intimacy with his son Edmund. There was overwhelming evidence against Edmund but despite that he was acquitted at his trial.

However it is the names picked at random from the tombs that above all seem so eminently Victorian. The following selection are all within 100 yards of the Deptford gates: Crisp Beddingfield, Alberta Codbolt, Absalom Dandridge, Charlotte Glock, Lydia Goody, Amelia Gossage, Horace Lermit, Alice Pyefinch, Philadelphia Sampson and Benjamin Sloss.

The successor to Brockley is Grove Park cemetery which opened in 1935.

Ernest Dowson 1867–1900
Fin de siècle poet who died of tuberculosis six years after his parents committed suicide.

Sir William Eames 1821–1910
Marine engineer.

Sir John Gilbert 1817–97
Illustrator, he drew 30,000 woodblocks for the *Illustrated London News* and designed a cover for *Punch*.

Sir George Grove 1820–1900
Civil engineer and lighthouse keeper before becoming first director of the Royal College of Music in 1882 and author of the *Dictionary of Music and Musicians*.

Sir William Hardy 1807–87
Deputy Keeper of Public Records 1878–86.

Sir Alexander Nisbet 1812–92
Inspector General of the Royal Navy and honorary physician to the Queen.

William Stephens 1817–71
Grand Warden of the Grand Lodge of England.

BROMLEY HILL CEMETERY
Bromley Hill, Bromley, Kent

Founded: 1905
Owner: London Borough of Bromley
Acreage: 6¼

A run-of-the-mill suburban cemetery offering little chance of repose on account of the busy main road that skirts its longer side. The chapel is by Evelyn Hellicar, a local church architect, who was stylistically up to date with his Perpendicular Gothic brick and stone dressed design. His lodge has gone, replaced by a modern council house.

The cemetery is well planted with a wide variety of 'cemetery trees': cedar and other firs, silver birch, copper beech and ornamental fruit trees. One monument is worth a mention, the white marble Fuller sculpture of 1935 depicting the deceased standing in his best suit as an angel guides him, presumably, to heaven.

Sir Edward Campbell 1879–1945
Conservative M.P. for Bromley 1930–45.

Albert Dimes 1915–72
Soho gangleader and bookmaker known as 'Italian Albert'. A cortege of fifty-nine cars attended his funeral.

Bromley Hill: The Fuller memorial (1935)

P/O ROY MARCHAND 1918−40
Battle of Britain pilot, his photograph was used on R.A.F. recruiting posters. Originally a large memorial marked his grave but it was moved to the London Air Museum in 1971.

DEBORAH SIBREE, JAMES SIBREE, MARY SIBREE
Died 1920, 1919, and 1926 they were missionaries in Madagascar for forty-five, fifty-two and thirty-four years respectively.

SIR ALFRED TYLER 1870−1936
Printer and publisher.

BROMPTON CEMETERY
OLD BROMPTON ROAD, SW10

Founded: 1840
Owner: Department of Culture, Media and Sport (managed by The Royal Parks)
Acreage: 39

Otherwise known as the West London and Westminster Cemetery, Brompton ranks among the finest of London's cemeteries. It is large, has some splendid architecture and is crammed with magnificent tombs. Quite rightly, it is now included in English Heritage's Register of Parks and Gardens and is a conservation area.

Brompton's history is unusual because, in the over-ambitious effort to create a very grand cemetery, the original owners, The West of London & Westminster Cemetery Company, ran into all sorts of difficulties. The Company was formed in 1836 and appointed Stephen Geary, a member of the London Cemetery Company, as architect, while a former market garden site was bought from Lord Kensington. A contemporary critic wrote, 'The site has no natural attraction whatever ... not a tree and scarcely a shrub adorn the place'.[1] This was explained by the brick-

Brompton: Gates to the Catacombs

making activities also formerly here, but nothing daunted, a competition was announced for a cemetery design.

Headed by Sir Jeffry Wyatville, the 'Committee of Taste' judged the winner to be Benjamin Baud, who conceived a magnificent formal design. (Geary, who had been eligible for the competition, was asked to resign, promptly sued the company and lost.) Baud's previous work had displayed his talents with mediaeval-style buildings. He had assisted with improvements to Windsor Castle and had submitted an unsuccessful design in the competition for the new Houses of Parliament in 1835. Surprisingly, his scheme for Brompton was a very different classical conception. He intended the cemetery to be walled around with catacombs incorporated in the western wall beyond which was the Kensington canal (now the route of a railway). A large section of the wall catacombs were removed after bomb damage during World War Two. The main entrance was built in the form of a triumphal arch, not unlike Kensal Green's. Access to Fulham Road was only gained in 1846 when a small portion of land was purchased from the Equitable Gas Company. From the main entrance a long tree-lined avenue terminates, as at St Peter's in Rome, in a circular colonnade of Bath stone culminating in the domed Anglican chapel with the cemetery office within its wings. Beneath the colonnades, catacombs were fashioned, entered by cast iron doors decorated with various symbols of death, particularly the snake. All this survives, but it is regrettable that an even grander scheme that included Roman Catholic and Nonconformist chapels on either side of the Great Circle, each with a matching bell tower was never achieved.

While Baud worked on this plan, the company employed Isaac Finnemore, a landscape gardener, and the resourceful J.C. Loudon as consultant, for laying out the grounds. Messrs. Veitch supplied the plants. It is no wonder therefore that the directors soon found themselves in financial trouble. Baud's designs were altered, building specifications skimped and Finnemore resigned. By 1844 building defects became apparent and Baud was sacked. Ruinous litigation followed from which Baud's architectural practice never recovered.

Meanwhile the whole principle of cemeteries operated as a commercial concern was being scrutinised in Parliament. In 1850 the Metropolitan Interments Act was passed granting the Government powers to purchase private cemeteries. Before the Act was repealed in 1852, Brompton had been compulsorily purchased by the Board of Health for £74,921 14s,

Brompton: The Chapel (1840)

Brompton: Italian Baroque, the San Giorgi monument (1903)

considerably less than the £166,762 12s 8d asked for by the company.

Due to these vicissitudes, Brompton had a slow start before gaining popularity. The first burial in 1840 was of Emma Shaw whose grave is marked by a flat stone slab without an inscription. But by 1889 Mrs Holmes described the cemetery as crowded, containing 155,000 bodies. A total of 211,000 burials have now taken place and the cemetery continues to accept interments in new graves. Maintenance is at a high level but vandalism and theft have been a problem and it is unfortunate that the monuments which suffer most are usually the most interesting. Thus the uniformed scullers at the corners of Robert Coombes' monument (1860, near the south entrance) are defaced and several bronzes have, as usual, been stolen.

Tombs generally are not quite in the same class as the best at Kensal Green or Norwood. The earliest are south of the chapel and resemble eighteenth century headstones. Mausolea are concentrated either side of the main axial path or at ronds points, where the rectangular system of paths cross each other. Of note are those for James McDonald (1915) and Hannah Courtoy (1854). Just west of the main path is Frederick Leyland's remarkable tomb (1902) by Edward Burne-Jones. It resembles a Romanesque shrine sheathed in copper arabesques and is a unique example of 'Arts and Crafts' funerary design. Near it is Val Prinsep's charming carved marble sarcophagus (1904), rather like a Gothic window box.

Quite different from these intricate works are the granite cannonballs above Gen. Alexander Anderson's grave (1877) on the opposite side of the main path, and the imperious lion sprawled upon John 'Gentleman' Jackson's tomb (1845) to the east. In 1872 *The Builder* wrote of the

> handsome but rather too pretentious marble mausoleum, with a figure of 'Hope' at the top . . . recently erected by a Mr Henry France, of Wardour Street, to the memory of his wife, which must have cost a very large sum indeed.

The article also referred enigmatically to

> the grave of Sydney Lady Morgan, upon which rests an effigy of an Irish harp, above which are two volumes, inscribed 'Wild Irish Girl' and 'France'.[2]

Unfortunately, the harp and books are now missing.

The early twentieth century fashion for reproducing sculpted likenesses of deceased children is represented by a solemn brother and sister above the Todd grave 1927/28 near the north entrance. (Both were stolen, but have been recovered although not refixed) Rather less solemn is Isabella David's epitaph (1954), which reads simply, 'Have a good sleep dear'.

A distinguishing feature of Brompton is the large number of soldiers' tombs. The proximity of Chelsea Hospital is the reason, and there is a granite obelisk erected in memory of 2,625 pensioners in a plot specially acquired by the hospital for use between 1855 and 1893. Another separate enclosure contains only military graves, including a massive memorial to the Brigade of Guards, erected in 1889. Remarkably, there are 12 VC holders buried in the cemetery.

ANTONY, METROPOLITAN OF SOUROZH 1914–2003
Founder and first head of the Diocese of Sourozh, the diocese of the Russian Orthodox chuch in Britain.

MILNOJ ARACIC 1891–1951
Former member of the Royal Yugoslav government.

ACTON AYRTON 1811–86
Lawyer and Liberal M.P. for Tower Hamlets 1857–74. For many years he was first Commissioner of Works with a reputation for economy.

Brompton: Robert Coombes' monument with uniformed scullers, now defaced (1860)

Brompton: An imperious lion on John 'Gentleman' Jackson's tomb (1872) photographed in 1980. The urn has since disappeared

PRINCE ALEXANDRE BAGRATION 1877–1955
Russian prince.

SIR SQUIRE BANCROFT 1841–1926
Actor-manager responsible for introducing the drawing room comedy to the London stage. With his wife (Marie Wilton 1840–1921), also buried here, they converted the old Queen's Theatre, known as 'the dust bowl' into the fashionable Prince of Wales. The mausoleum was badly damaged during World War Two although the front façade survives.

WILLIAM BANTING 1797–1878
The Royal undertaker, he made Wellington's funeral car in 1852; also a practitioner of and author on dieting.

JOSEPH BONOMI 1796–1878
Egyptologist, he spent several years in Egypt and illustrated books on Egyptian art and architecture. Curator of the Soane Museum.

GEORGE BORROW 1803–81
Author, philologist and for many years agent of the British and Foreign Bible Society; he described his travels in several books, including the semi-autobiographical *Lavengro* in 1851.

ELEANOR FORTESQUE-BRICKDALE 1872–1945
Third generation Pre-Raphaelite painter and designer of stained glass.

FANNY BRAWNE 1800–65
Fiancée of John Keates.

FRANCIS BUCKLAND 1826–80
Naturalist, author and inspector of salmon fisheries for England and Wales.

HENRY BYRON 1834–84
Prolific dramatist and author.

GEN WILLIAM CAFÉ 1826–1906
Won the V.C. during the Indian Mutiny.

SIR WILLIAM CAIRNS 1828–88
Colonial administrator, governor of South Australia 1877.

MARCHESA CASATI 1881–1957
Italian born art collector and extravagant dresser, she was buried wearing leopard skin and false eyelashes.

THOMAS CHENERY 1826–84
Barrister, professor of Arabic at Oxford, editor of *The Times* 1877–84.

Henry Chorley 1808–72
Music critic, librettist and unsuccessful novelist.

Sir Campbell Clarke 1835–1902
Librarian at the British Museum 1852–70, journalist, translator and librettist.

Sir Henry Cole 1808–82
An assistant keeper in the Record Office which he helped to set up in Fetter Lane, first director of the South Kensington Museum (now the Victoria and Albert) opened in 1857. He helped found the Royal College of Music.

Charles Collins 1828–73
Pre-Raphaelite painter and novelist, he married one of Charles Dickens' daughters. Brother of novelist, Wilkie Collins.

Thomas Cooke 1786–1864
Served under Nelson at the battle of St. Vincent, later a successful actor.

Robert Coombes 1808–60
Champion Thames sculler 1846–52, he died in a lunatic asylum. The memorial was erected by his friends.

Lt.Gen. Sir Sydney Cotton 1792–1874
Indian Army Officer and governor of the Royal Hospital, Chelsea 1872–74.

Joseph Crocker 1834–69
Christy minstrel, one of thirty-five performers who appeared as the Ethiopian troupe at St. James' Hall, Piccadilly for many years.

Sir Samuel Cunard 1787–1865
American born, he founded the Cunard Steam Packet Company in 1840.

Thomas Cundy III 1820–95
London architect and surveyor to the Duke of Westminster, he was responsible for designing parts of Belgravia.

James Davison 1813–85
Music critic for The Times 1850–78.

Thomas Donaldson 1795–1885
Architect and founder member of the R.I.B.A.

L/Cpl. Joseph Farmer 1854–1930
Won the V.C. at Majuba, South Africa, in 1881. The boulder on his gravestone is from Majuba.

Sir John Fowler 1817–98
Railway engineer, he built the first sections of the Metropolitan railway from Kings Cross 1853–63 and collaborated on the building of the Forth Bridge 1883–90. President of the Institution of Civil Engineers 1866–67.

William Fox 1786–1864
Unitarian preacher, politician, man of letters and M.P. for Oldham 1847–63.

Tom Foy 1866–1917
Music hall comedian known as 'The Yorkshire Lad' he used to appear on stage with a donkey. He collapsed while playing The Argyle, Birkenhead and died shortly afterwards.

Adm. Sir Charles Fremantle 1800–69
Founded Fremantle, Australia, 1829.

Brian Glover 1934–97
Wrestler, teacher and actor.

George Godwin 1815–88
Architect and editor of *The Builder* 1842–63.

Sir George Goldie 1846–1925
'Founder of Nigeria', he established the National African Company in 1879 which subsequently enjoyed wide administrative and commercial privileges in West Africa. President of the Royal Geographical Society 1905.

Benjamin Golding 1793–1863
Doctor and founder director of the Charing Cross Hospital in 1831.

Gen. Sir Thomas Gordon 1832–1914
Served in India and Persia, he wrote of his experiences in the Himalayas and the Near East.

Frederick Hafner –1907
Director of continental journeys for Edward VII.

F.M. Sir Frederick Haines 1819–1909
Commander in Chief, Indian Army 1876–81.

Sir Augustus Harris 1852–96
Theatre manager at Drury Lane and Covent Garden, renowned for his spectacular pantomime and operatic productions.

Sir James Hay 1839–1924
Governor of Sierra Leone 1888–92, governor of Barbados 1892–1900.

George Henty 1832–1902
Prolific writer of stories for boys based on his experiences as a war correspondent. A keen yachtsman, he died on board his boat.

John Jackson 1769–1845
Pugilist known as Gentleman Jackson, champion of England 1795–1803. Subsequently proprietor of a boxing school in Bond Street attended by Byron. His monument by Timothy Butler, was raised by public subscription and described as 'hideous' by *The Builder* in 1872.

Louis Campbell-Johnson 1862–1929
Founder of the British Humane Society.

John Jones 1800–82
Made a fortune as a tailor; he retired from business aged fifty to concentrate on his art collection, left to the Victoria and Albert Museum on his death.

Joseph Kanné –1888
Queen Victoria's courier and director of continental journeys for forty years.

Sir James Kay-Shuttleworth 1804–77
Manchester doctor, assistant poor law Commissioner and educationalist dedicated to promoting popular education.

Robert Keeley 1793–1869
Comic actor, he was only 5ft 2ins tall.

Constant Lambert 1905–51
Composer and conductor.

Percy Lambert 1881–1913
The first man to drive over 100 miles in an hour, killed at Brooklands, 'whilst attempting other records'.

Nat Langham 1820–71
Middleweight bare fist boxing champion, he lost only one fight in a ten-year career.

Bernard Levin 1928–2004
Writer and critic.

Frederick Leyland 1831–1892
Shipowner and patron of the Pre-Raphaelites. The Peacock Room created by J.M. Whistler at his house in Prince's Gate is now in Washington, D.C.

Princess Violette Lobanov-Rostovsky 1893–1932
Russian princess.

Archibald Low 1888–1956
Electrical engineer, author and inventor, he designed a guided missile system in 1917.

Blanche Macchetta (née Roosevelt) 1858–98
Singer and biographer of Gustave Doré.

Maj.Gen.Sir William MacPherson 1858–1927
Deputy General of the Army Medical Service; edited a medical history of the Great War.

John McCulloch 1789–1864
Statistician and political economist, the first professor of political economics at London University 1828–32.

Gen.Frederick Maude 1821–87
Won the V.C. in the Crimea in 1857.

Henry Mears 1873–1912
Building contractor, he founded Chelsea Football Club at Stamford Bridge in 1905.

Alfred Mellon 1820–67
Violinist and conductor.

Sir Edward Merewether 1858–1938
Colonial administrator and governor of Sierra Leone 1911–15 and the Leeward Islands 1915–21.

Herman Merivale 1806–74
Lawyer, Under Secretary for India, Oxford economist and author.

John Mole 1815–86
Watercolour painter, chiefly of landscapes.

Sir John Monckton 1832–1902
Town Clerk of London 1873.

Lionel Monckton 1862–1924
Composer and music critic of the *Daily Telegraph*.

Sydney, Lady Morgan 1783–1859
Irish born actress and successful authoress. Her tomb is by James Westmacott.

Sir Roderick Murchison 1792–1871
Geologist, he discovered the Silurian system in 1835, twice president of the Geological Society and president of the Royal Geographical Society between 1843 and 1871.

Lilian Neilson 1848–80
Yorkshire millhand who became a celebrated Shakespearian actress.

FRANCIS NICHOLSON 1753–1844
Watercolour painter and author.

F.M. LORD WILLIAM NICHOLSON 1845–1918
Chief of the Imperial General Staff 1908–12, responsible for a reorganisation of the Army resulting in the creation of the territorial force.

RENTON NICHOLSON 1809–61
Variously a pawnbroker, journalist, publican, impresario, authority on boxing and a bankrupt.

JOSEPH NIGHTINGALE 1827–82
Dramatist.

MATTHEW NOBLE 1818–76
Sculptor, Thomas Hood's memorial at Kensal Green is by him. Probably his best known work is the statue of the Prince Consort in the Albert Memorial, Manchester.

F.M. SIR HENRY NORMAN 1826–1904
Indian Army officer, governor of Jamaica 1883–86, Queensland 1889–93 and Chelsea Hospital 1901–04.

SIR WILLIAM PALLISER 1830–82
Inventor of an improved type of rifled gun and cast iron 'Palliser Shot'. Conservative M.P. for Taunton 1880–82.

EMMELINE PANKHURST 1858–1928
Militant leader of the suffragettes.

GEN. SIR JOHN PENNEFATHER 1800–72
The hero of the battle of Inkerman in the Crimea War, governor of Chelsea Hospital 1870–72.

STEPHEN PENTON 1793–1873
Traveller and authority on South America.

THOMAS PETTIGREW 1791–1865
Surgeon, he was the first to vaccinate Queen Victoria; gave up his profession in 1854 to pursue his antiquarian interests, particularly on the subject of Egyptian mummies. Published a book on embalming.

HENRY PETTITT 1848–1893
Successful dramatist, died of typhoid fever.

VALENTINE PRINSEP 1838–1904
Printer, artist and associate of the Pre-Raphaelites.

Sir Robert Rawlinson 1810-98
Civil and sanitary engineer, president of the Institute of Engineers 1894.

William Rendle 1820-81
Horticulturalist, aquarium entrepreneur, Brighton hotelier and banker.

Henry Richards 1819-85
Composer, pianist, director of the Royal Academy of Music and a friend of Chopin. In 1862 he composed 'God Bless the Prince Of Wales'.

James Rogers 1823-63
Comedian, Blondin carried him on his shoulders at the Crystal Palace.

John, Lord Romilly of Barry 1802-74
Liberal M.P. for Bridport 1832-35 and Devonport 1847-52. Master of the Rolls 1851-73.

Adm. Lord Edward Russell 1805-87
M.P. for Tavistock 1841-47, racehorse owner.

Milosh St Bobisch 1886-1951
Former member of the Royal Yugoslav government.

Vladimir Saponjic 1896-1952
Former member of the Royal Yugoslav government.

Archbishop Sawa 1898-1951
Bishop of the Polish Orthodox Church, driven from Poland by the Nazis in 1943. He was head of the Polish church in exile in England.

Samuel Smiles 1812-1904
Journalist, biographer, historian of the Huguenots, secretary of the Leeds and Thirsk, and the South Eastern railways, author of *Self Help*, 1859.

Albert Smith 1816-60
Doctor, journalist, contributor to *Punch* and impresario at the Egyptian Hall, Piccadilly.

Sir Francis Smith 1808-74
Inventor of the 4-bladed screw propellor for steamships, first demonstrated by the *Archimedes* in 1838.

Adm. William Smith 1799-1892
Naval officer, he escorted Napoleon to St Helena in 1815.

John Snow 1813-58
Anaesthetist, pioneer in the use of ether and chloroform, he administered chloroform to the Queen at the births of Prince Leopold in 1853 and Princess Beatrice in 1857. He also discovered the cause of cholera.

Samuel Sotheby 1805–61
Auctioneer, antiquary and author on printing history, drowned in the River Dart.

Sir Thomas Spencer Wells 1818–97
Surgeon to Queen Victoria who pioneered the oviarotomy. A member of the Council of the Cremation Society of Great Britain, his ashes were buried in the grave.

F.M.Sir Donald Stewart 1824–1900
Indian Army officer and governor of Chelsea Hospital 1895–1900.

Richard Tauber 1891–1948
Austrian born tenor singer of light opera and conductor.

Tom Taylor 1817–80
Professor of English at London University 1845, journalist, prolific dramatist, art critic and editor of *Punch* 1874–80.

William Terriss 1847–97
Sheep farmer in the Falkland Islands, successful actor of melodramas, known as 'Breezy Bill', murdered outside the Adelphi Theatre by a madman.

Alfred Thesiger 1838–80
Appointed a Lord Justice of Appeal aged only thirty-nine, died of blood poisoning.

Brandon Thomas 1850–1914
Actor and playwright, he wrote *Charley's Aunt*.

William Thoms 1803–85
Antiquary, clerk and deputy librarian to the House of Lords, founder editor of *Notes and Queries*, secretary of the Camden Society 1838–73, introduced the term 'folklore' into the English language.

Jonathan Holt Titcombe, Bishop 1819–87
First bishop of Rangoon.

James Veitch 1815–69
Orchid collector and nurseryman with establishments at Chelsea and Coombe Wood. Brompton itself was planted by the Veitch nursery.

Maj.Richard Wadeson 1826–85
Won the V.C. during the Indian Mutiny. Lieutenant governor of the Royal Hospital, Chelsea, 1881–5.

Edward Wadsworth 1889–1949
Painter and engraver, influenced by the vorticists and cubists, experimented with dazzle camouflage on ships during the Great War.

Brompton 'Courage: initiative: intrepidity.' The memorial to Flight Sub-Lieut. Reginald Warneford (1915)

MACKENZIE WALCOTT 1821–80
Antiquary and ecclesiologist, he published numerous works on mediaeval architecture.

REGINALD WARNEFORD 1891–1915
Awarded the V.C. for being the first airman to shoot down a zeppelin from an aeroplane. Killed in a flying accident. His monument was funded by donations from readers of the *Daily Express*.

SIR ANDREW WAUGH 1810–78
Astronomer and surveyor general in North India, he surveyed and named Mount Everest after his former colleague Sir George Everest.

BENJAMIN WEBSTER 1797–1882
Actor-manager and musician.

CHARLES WESTHALL –1868
Athlete, he walked twenty-one miles in three hours in 1858.

Gen. Sir William Williams 1800–83
Successful commander in the Crimean War, captured at the siege of Kars, governor of Gibraltar 1870–76, constable of the Tower of London 1881.

John Wilson 1788–1870
Honorary physician to the Queen and an authority on tropical diseases.

John Wisden 1826–84
Sussex and England cricketer and founder of *Wisden's Cricketers' Almanack*. The headstone was erected on the hundredth anniversary of his death.

Bennet Woodcroft 1803–79
Inventor of the pitch screw propellor for steamships in 1832, clerk to the Commissioners of Patents 1864, largely responsible for establishing the Patent Office Library and Museum.

George Wyness –1882
For thirty-two years head gardener at Buckingham Palace.

BROOKWOOD CEMETERY
Cemetery Pales, Brookwood, Woking, Surrey

Founded: 1852
Owner: Brookwood Cemetery Ltd
Acreage: c. 450

As chapter one (History) noted, a number of schemes for burying the dead away from the metropolis were proposed in the mid-nineteenth century. The only one to be realised was Brookwood.[1]

The London Necropolis and National Mausoleum Company acquired 2,200 acres of heathland at Woking from Lord Onslow and engaged the London architect Sydney Smirke to lay out the 500 acres which opened in November 1854. Smirke also designed the non-conformist and Anglican chapels. A Roman Catholic chapel was built in 1899 and a new Anglican chapel around 1910. Both were designed by Cyril Tubbs and Arthur Messer.

As the cemetery was twenty-three miles from London, the most convenient form of transport was by rail, and the London and South Western Railway was engaged to convey coffins and mourners from a private station in York Street at Waterloo. At the cemetery the funeral trains ran along a private track either to the North Station adjacent to the Nonconformist chapel or the South Station beside the Anglican chapel. In 1902 a new station opened at 121 Westminster Bridge Road but after sustaining major damage in 1941 the funeral trains ceased, although the station entrance survives.[2]

Landscaping was shared by Smirke, the landscape gardener William Broderick Thomas (1811–1898), and the nurseryman Robert Donald (c.1826–1866). The original plan involved the use of giant sequoias planted among bold avenues of monkey puzzle, cedar, bay, laurel and rhododendron. Over time the landscape has developed to include elements of deciduous park-like planting, a lawn cemetery (in the military sections), and a forest cemetery (in the Glades of Remembrance). Overall, Brookwood has a funereal landscape of great variety, spaciousness and grandeur.

Brookwood: The Pelham-Clinton memorial (c. 1898)

Plots were reserved by London parishes and also other groups, such as Parsees and the Royal Hospital Chelsea. There are several plots containing reburials from city churches, such as St Clement Danes and St Mary-le-Strand. In the sandy soil at Brookwood, Dr Seymour Francis Haden encouraged burial in *pâpier mâché* coffins to facilitate quick decomposition and future re-use of the ground.

The extensive military cemeteries were laid out in 1917–18 and are now administered by the Commonwealth War Graves Commission. The Brookwood Memorial was inaugurated by the Queen in October 1958. There are also sections for American, Belgian, Canadian, Czechoslovakian, French, Italian and Polish war dead.

Plans to build a crematorium in the cemetery have twice been prepared and failed, although a mausoleum was converted into a columbarium in 1910, and the Glades of Remembrance, designed by Edward White for burying ashes, was completed in 1950.

There are many memorials of interest. In addition to thirty mausolea, and three memorials designed by Eric Gill, the most dramatic work is the unattributed bronze sculpture group on the Pelham-Clinton grave (c.1898; listed Grade II*). Other notable monuments include the incongruous henge to Charles Warne (c.1887), the huge headstone-style memorial to Henry Douglas Freshfield by Edward Onslow Ford (c.1892), the terracotta pedestal with a relief portrait on the Van Laun grave by Emmeline Halse, (c.1896), the memorial to Guilio Salviati with four separate mosaic panels by the firm (c.1898), a bronze angel and portrait by Lillian Wade commemorating Lieut. Rex Moir (c.1915), the memorial to William de Morgan designed by his widow and carved by Sir George Frampton (c.1919), the American Memorial Chapel (completed in 1929 to designs by Egerton Swartwout, John Pope and Harry Cresswell), the three mausolea in the Parsee section (one by Gilbert Bayes, 1931–32), the Vickers family tomb by Sir Edwin Lutyens (c.1937), the RAF memorial and shelter (1947) and the Canadian records and reception building (1946) both by Sir Edward Maufe.

The passage of time has seen many changes at Brookwood. The fine bust of Charles Bradlaugh (Francis Verheyden, 1893) was stolen in 1938. The Anglican chapels are now home to the St Edward Brotherhood (along with the tenth century relics of St Edward the Martyr), while the Najmee Baag burial ground occupies the area around the North Station and the Nonconformist chapel. The Gothic Bent memorial (1859) in Bath Stone has badly eroded, but is listed Grade II, along with nineteen other structures.

Brookwood: The Parsee section (1907)

Brookwood remains privately owned but is in desperate need of major external funding support to assist maintenance work in what is Britain's largest cemetery. The majority of burials today are Moslem, meaning that in time Brookwood will evolve into the country's largest Moslem burial ground.

Sir John Wolfe Barry 1836–1918
Civil engineer. His best known work is London's Tower Bridge.

Charles Bradlaugh 1833–91
Radical Liberal M.P., atheist and republican.

Sir Joseph William Chitty 1828–99
Master of the Rolls, Oxford M.P. and athlete. He gained an Oxford blue for rowing and cricket.

William de Morgan 1839–1917
Potter and designer of stained glass and ceramics.

Caroll Gibbons 1903–54
Musician and dance band leader.

Dr Robert Knox 1791–1862
Edinburgh anatomist associated with Burke and Hare who supplied him with corpses.

Edward William Mountford 1855–1908
Architect who specialised in Edwardian baroque buildings including the Old Bailey central criminal courts.

Lord Edward Pelham-Clinton 1836–1907
Son of the 5th Duke of Newcastle, soldier and M.P for North Nottinghamshire.

SIR OWEN WILLANS RICHARDSON 1879–1959
Physicist and Nobel prize winner in 1901.

SIR F.M. WILLIAM ROBERTSON 1860–1933
Field Marshal, the only man who rose to that rank from private.

SHAPURJI SAKLATVALA c.1874–1936
Businessman; Britain's first communist MP (for North Battersea).

GIULIO SALVIATI c.1843–98
Venetian glass and mosaic merchant. The family firm of Salviati, Jesuram & Co. undertook mosaic work on the Albert Memorial chapel and Albert Memorial.

JOHN SINGER SARGENT 1856–1925
American artist, the most successful portrait painter of his time.

DANIEL CHARLES SOLANDER 1733–82
Swedish Botanist who accompanied Joseph Banks on Captain Cook's voyage in the *Endeavour*.

EDITH THOMPSON 1893–1923
Executed at Holloway Prison (see also the entry for the City of London Cemetery) for the murder of her husband.

RAVUAMA VUNIVALU 1921–64
Fijian patriot and parliamentarian.

DAME REBECCA WEST 1892–1983
Feminist novelist and journalist.

EDWARD WHITE c.1872–1952
Landscape architect.

SIR ALLEN WILLIAM YOUNG 1827–1915
Arctic explorer.

BUNHILL FIELDS
CITY ROAD, EC1

Founded: c.1665
Owner: *The Corporation of London*
Acreage: 5

Two hundred years ago London was peppered with tiny Nonconformist burial grounds, so many in fact that no one ever counted them all. Since then the majority have been grassed or built over but the most interesting, Bunhill Fields, survives. It is the only cemetery still in the City of London

Bunhill Fields

and because of its antiquity and the fame of many of the dissenters buried here, its long history is well documented.[1]

The ground it occupies was originally part of a prebendal estate attached to St Paul's Cathedral. In the fourteenth century the land was leased to the Mayor and Aldermen of the City who, by the sixteenth century, were permitting its use as a depository for bones from the charnel house of the old cathedral. The name 'Bunhill' probably derives from 'Bonehill', the name given to it about this time. In 1665 it was 'set apart and consecrated as a common cemetery for the interment of such corpses as could not have room in their parochial burial grounds in that dreadful year of pestilence. However, it not being made use of on that occasion . . .' a Mr Tindale 'converted it into a Burial Ground for the Use of Dissenters'.[2]

A tombstone dated 1623 is an isolated example, there are no others with such an early date and it seems likely that it marks the spot of a reinterment. The next stone in date order is 'Joannes Seaman, natus 6 Feb 1665 ob. Juli 23 1665'. So great was the number of burials thereafter, including a vast number of dissenting divines, that the ground was extended in 1700. By 1852 more than 120,000 burials had taken place and it became necessary for an Order in Council to close the cemetery. The last recorded burial is however on 5 January 1884 when no doubt an old vault was opened to accommodate the coffin of Elizabeth Oliver, aged fifteen. In 1867 the old prebendal estate became the property of the Ecclesiastical Commissioners who considered exploiting its development value had not an Act of Parliament prevented this by transferring the ground into the care of the City. A restoration programme was undertaken and in 1869 the ground was reopened to the public.

Bunhill is now overshadowed by office blocks but the wall piers are still easily recognisable inscribed with names of the most famous Dissenters buried here. There are two mistakes. 'Samuel

Wesley' should read 'Susannah Wesley' and 'John Horne Tooke' should not be here; he was buried in Ealing churchyard. Inside the ground, south of the main path, the monuments are closely packed. Almost all are shaped headstones or chest tombs built usually with Portland stone or occasionally slate. Ornament is almost entirely of classical origin. There is virtually no use of granite or metalwork and the lettering is cut in the stone without lead filling. The contrast with the average Victorian cemetery is marked. Bunhill as near as possible maintains the appearance of the cramped city churchyards whose condition so shocked the nineteenth century reformers.

A few monuments for some of the more distinguished Nonconformists were built anew in the nineteenth century with fulsome threnodies engraved, but eighteenth-century epitaphs are worth seeking out. The most peculiar is also the most visible. On the side panels of a large chest tomb, it reads:

> Here lies Dame Mary Page relict of Sir Gregory Page Bart. She
> departed this life March 11th 1728 in the 56th year of her age. In 67
> months she was tap'd 66 times had taken away 240 gallons of water
> without ever repining at her case or ever fearing the operation.

At one time there was a separate Quaker burial ground on Roscoe Street near Bunhill, also dating from the 1660s. It was closed in 1855 and part is now a recreation ground laid out in 1965 and part overrun by road widening. Some 5,000 bodies were reinterred, with carbolic acid, in Bunhill. The Quakers were never much concerned with tombstones and only George Fox's grave was marked by a small stone. This attracted so many visitors that an over-zealous Friend had it removed.

Following wartime bomb damage the cemetery was restored in 1960 by the eminent landscape architect Sir Peter Shepherd. It is now maintained to a high standard by the Corporation of London. An attendant is on duty at most times and information on those buried is displayed in the kiosk.

Bunhill Fields: Tomb of Mary Jane Page (1728)

Bunhill Fields: John Bunyan's memorial erected in 1862

THOMAS BAYES 1701–61
Clergyman and statistician.

WILLIAM BLAKE 1757–1827
Poet, mystic and artist, together with his wife Catherine 1762–1831. (The monument does not mark their grave, the location of which is unknown).

THOMAS BRADBURY 1677–1759
Congregational minister and author of religious and political works. He refused the bribe of a bishopric.

JOHN BUNYAN 1628–88
Preacher and author of sixty books, including *Pilgrim's Progress*. His recumbent effigy was erected here in 1862.

GEORGE BURDER 1752–1832
Congregationalist minister; began his career as an engraver, founder member of the Religious Tract Society and the British and Foreign Bible Society.

JOHN CONDER 1714–81
Congregationalist minister, president of Homerton College. His epitaph concludes 'Peccavi. Resipui. Confidi. Amavi. Requiesco. Resurgam. Et ex gratia Christi et ut indignu, Regnabo'.

Henry, 1658–1711, Hannah, 1653–1732 and William Cromwell
Grandson, (memorial only), granddaughter-in-law and great-grandson of Oliver Cromwell. There are eleven other members of the Cromwell family buried here.

Daniel Defoe 1661–1731
Journalist and novelist, he published over 250 works including *Robinson Crusoe* (1719). The marble obelisk over his grave was erected in 1870.

Thomas Doolittle 1632–1707
Pastor of St Alphage, London Wall until ordained a Presbyterian, after which he was constantly preaching in defiance of the law and narrowly escaped being shot by troops in his pulpit.

Henry Fauntleroy 1785–1824
Banker and forger, he allegedly mis-appropriated £¼ million from his bank, squandering it on women and gambling. Executed at Newgate although it was rumoured he escaped death by insertion of a silver tube in his throat.

Charles Fleetwood c.1618–92
Cromwellian general, he married Cromwell's eldest daughter Bridget. After the restoration he retired to Stoke Newington. His monument was discovered seven feet below the ground in 1869.

Theophilus Gale 1628–78
Nonconformist teacher and author of *The Court of the Gentiles, or a Discourse Touching the Original of Humane Literature* (1669).

Andrew Gifford 1700–84
Baptist minister and numismatist, his coin collection was bought by George II.

Thomas Goodwin 1600–80
Independent preacher, he attended Cromwell on his deathbed.

Thomas Hardy 1752–1832
Piccadilly bootmaker and radical politician, tried for high treason in 1794 having advocated parliamentary reform, but acquitted.

Joseph Hart 1712–68
Hymn writer, 20,000 people attended his funeral.

William Jenkyn 1613–85
Presbyterian minister, imprisoned in Newgate for refusing to take the Oxford Oath, where he died.

William Kiffin 1616–1701
Wool merchant and influential campaigning Baptist.

Andrew Kippis 1725–95
Nonconformist minister and biographer. He produced the second edition of the *Biographica Brittanica* 1778–93.

Hanserd Knollys 1599?–1691
Separatist minister, he held several offices in Cromwell's government. Author of *Flaming Fire in Zion*.

Nathaniel Lardner 1684–1768
Biblical scholar, he was the leading authority in his day on early Christian literature.

John Lettsom 1744–1815
Quaker physician. He made a small fortune in the West Indies and was active in numerous charitable organisations, founder member of the Royal Humane Society. Introduced the mangle wurzle into Britain.

David Nasmith 1799–1839
Scottish originator of city missions which he founded in Britain and America, he organised the London City Mission 1835. Died a pauper.

Daniel Neal 1678–1743
Historian, published four volumes of the *History of the Puritans* 1733–38.

Thomas Newcomen 1663–1729
Designer of the first practicable steam engine for industrial use.

John Owen 1616–83
Theologian, appointed vice-chancellor of Oxford University by Cromwell, author of eighty books.

Thankful Owen 1620–81
Independent divine and president of St John's College, Oxford, 1650–60.

Vavasour Powell 1617–70
Nonconformist preacher in Wales, arrested at the Restoration spending most of his remaining years in prison where he died.

Richard Price 1723–91
Nonconformist minister and writer on morals, politics and economics, he supported American independence and was a friend of Benjamin Franklin.

Hugh Pugh 1812–40
Welsh harpist and guide on Cader Idris.

Daniel Quare 1648–1724
London clockmaker, he invented repeating watches and possibly the concentric minute hand. He made a clock for William III that needed winding only once per year.

ABRAHAM REES 1743–1825
Welsh Nonconformist minister and author of forty-five volumes of *The New Cyclopaedia* 1802–19.

JOHN RIPPON 1751–1836
Baptist minister, he collected eleven volumes of manuscript material on the history of Bunhill Fields and copied all the grave inscriptions, now in the Guildhall library.

JOSEPH RITSON 1752–1803
Antiquarian, barrister, collector of ballads, and eccentric, he lived most of his life on a diet of vegetables and milk.

THOMAS STOTHARD 1755–1834
Painter and illustrator. He illustrated works by Milton, Pope, Shakespeare, Chaucer, etc. and decorated the grand staircase at Burghley House.

ROBERT TILLING –1760
Executed at Tyburn for murdering his master.

JOHN TOWNSEND 1757–1826
Founder of the London Asylum for the deaf and dumb and joint founder of the London Missionary Society.

ISAAC WATTS 1674–1748
Hymn writer, he wrote about 600 including 'O God our help in ages past'. He died at Abney Park where a memorial to him stands in the cemetery.

SUSANNAH WESLEY 1670–1742
Wife of Samuel Wesley and mother of John and Charles and seventeen other children. The present tombstone was erected in 1936.

GEORGE WHITEHEAD 1636?–1723
Quaker preacher. He was frequently imprisoned for publishing numerous controversial works.

DANIEL WILLIAMS 1643?–1716
Nonconformist minister. He left some £50,000 to charitable uses and an endowment to house his library, now at No.14 Gordon Square.

CAMBERWELL CEMETERY
Forest Hill Road, SE22

Founded: 1856
Owner: London Borough of Southwark
Acreage: 29½

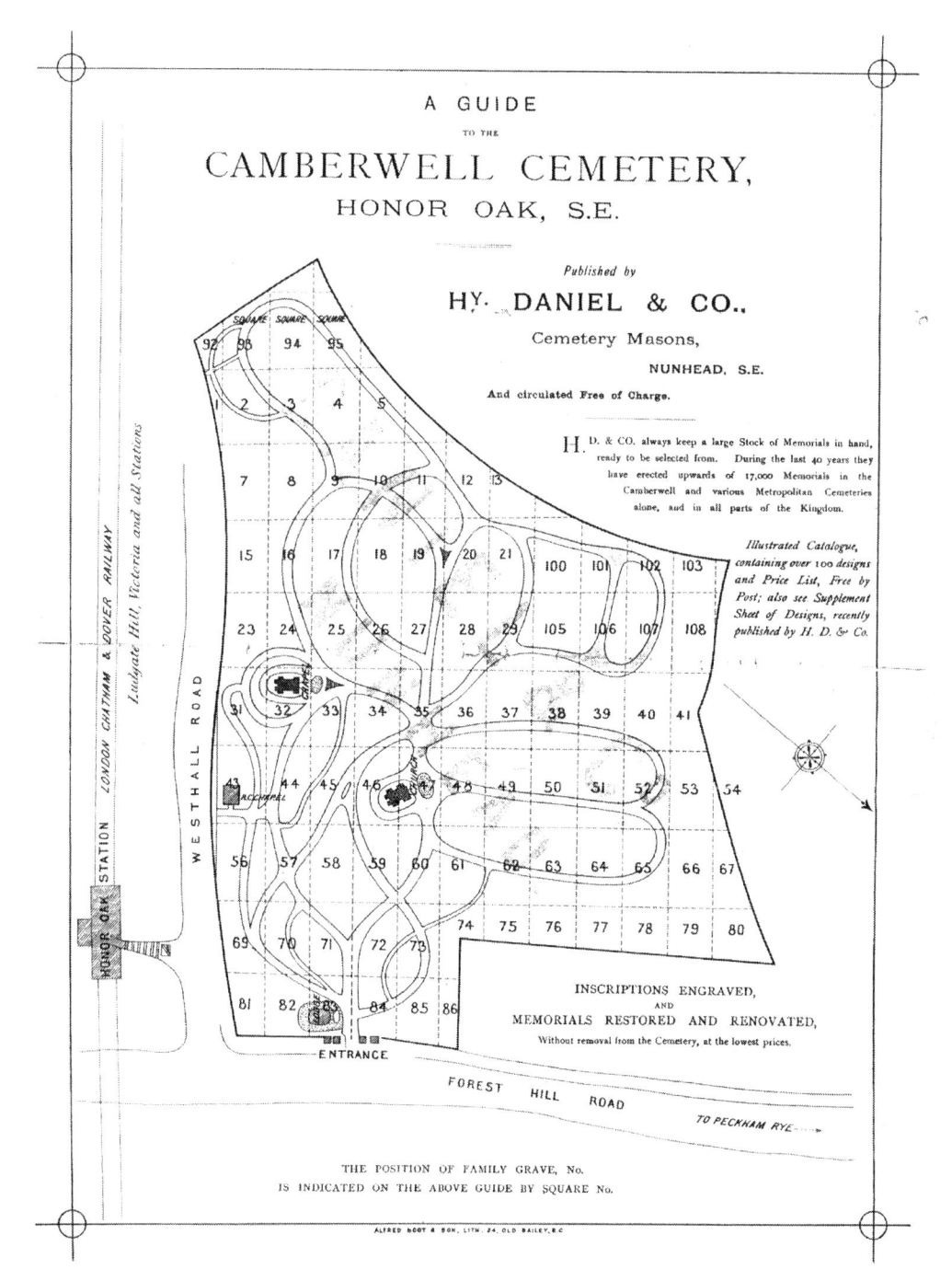

Camberwell: The layout of the cemetery.

Shortly after the Metropolitan Interment Act of 1852, the Camberwell Vestry set about buying land and laying out their cemetery at a total cost of £17,200. They did it in style. Unusually for a cemetery of this size three chapels were built, Church of England, Nonconformist and Roman Catholic, the first two designed by one of the foremost architects of the day, George Gilbert Scott. In 1842 Scott had designed Camberwell's Parish Church of St Giles, by 1856 his career was in its prime. He employed a large staff and had a vast practice. He was surveyor of Westminster Abbey and was in the throes of designing what he considered his best church at All Souls, Haley Hill and he had embarked on one of his greatest works, the Whitehall Government Offices. Like these other new designs, the Camberwell chapels were Decorated Gothic and apparently 'almost identical in construction'.[1] Each had a gabled polygonal angular apse and an asymetrically placed octagonal tower and spire. Most unusually, they had an end gallery and some fine stained glass. They were demolished in the 1960s, while the Catholic chapel survived into the 1970s. The large Gothic lodge has been restored since 1994, although a green painted wooden shelter at the entrance has disappeared.[2]

These losses were not the first misfortune to affect Camberwell. When it opened it was regarded as 'eminently picturesque'[3] but by the 1890s the local newspapers were full of complaints that it had 'degenerated . . . into one of the most disorderly and uncared for'[4] cemeteries in London. Whereas it had been built especially for the 'middle, artisan and poorer classes' who had 'experienced considerable difficulty in burying their dead' due to the closure of churchyards, a correspondent to the *South London Press* in 1892 had witnessed 'the poor tumbled into holes like so many dogs. . . in consequence of the stench arising from the cemetery (it) is swarming with rats'.[5] Up to forty bodies were consigned to common graves that were left open for weeks on end and children in the neighbourhood were alleged to be suffering from sore throats. Responsibility for the scandal appears to have lain with a new superintendent who shortly afterwards resigned.

A few monuments of note are near the junction of the two main axial paths and recent memorials to members of the Irish community demonstrate that sepulchural tableaux are still being commissioned. Popular features include lavish use of polished marble, religious sculpture, photographs of the deceased and innumerable gold lettered texts.

Camberwell: The statue on Lord Rodney's grave 'on guard' no longer

THE NEW CEMETERY AT FOREST HILL.

Camberwell: The three chapels (demolished) and lodge

Further into the cemetery a life-size soldier stood 'On Guard' above Lord Rodney's grave – until it was toppled and decapitated in 1980. The figure is identical to one at Crystal Palace District Cemetery. Beneath an urn lies William Waters in 'peace, perfect peace', predeceased by his wife and six children, five before reaching their second birthday. There is also a fine granite replica of the Cenotaph on the Watson grave and a similar example in Portland stone commemorating Walter Brooker.

Among a collection of war memorials in the cemetery's north east corner is one dedicated to members of the borough killed by German bombs dropped from a zeppelin during the Great War.

Efforts have recently been made to reclaim part of the cemetery from dense undergrowth, but acres of it on the north side are still barely visible through trees and brambles. Elsewhere, over zealous clearance has spared neither monuments nor trees and ground is once again being used for new burials. This is a cemetery to visit in autumn when conkers and blackberries are plentiful.

For a longer list of those buried in the cemetery see Ron Woolacott's *Camberwell Old Cemetery: London's Forgotten Valhalla*.[6]

James Berkley 1819–62
Trained by Robert Stephenson. Chief Engineer of railways in Western India, he built the first railway line in India. £3,000 was raised by public subscription for his monument.

Rebekah Horniman –1895
Wife of F.J. Horniman, tea merchant and founder of the Horniman Museum.

Able Seaman Albert Mackenzie 1898–1918
Won the V.C. at Zeebrugge in 1918 when aged nineteen. He died in the 'flu pandemic seven months later.

EDWARD SEALE −1867
Proprietor of *The Sunday Times* 1858–67.

RICHARD WALLIS
For sixty-three years clerk to Camden Chapel, Peckham.

CHARLES WATERS 1839–1910
Founder of the International Bible Reading Association 1882; manager of the London and County Bank, King's Cross for twenty-five years.

GEORGE YANNI −1903
Convicted of murdering three Armenians, also buried here, in 1903, as part of the political intrigue involving the Armenian club in Peckham Rye, which was a front for a secret Society dedicated to freeing Armenia from Turkish rule.

CAMBERWELL NEW CEMETERY AND HONOR OAK CREMATORIUM
BRENCHLEY GARDENS, SE23

Founded: 1927
Owner: London Borough of Southwark
Acreage: 61

The cemetery sprawls along the ridge of a hill which offers a splendid site for the largest of London's cemetery chapels by the architects Aston Webb and Sons. Sir Aston Webb had enjoyed a huge and prestigious practice at the turn of the century with a penchant for the Baroque revival style.[1] He redesigned the Victoria and Albert Museum and laid out the Mall. At Brenchley Gardens, Pevsner describes the buildings as 'quite impressively neo-gothic'.[2] Passing the matching former office and shelter immediately inside the entrance gates, complete with borough arms, the main drive rises to the twin chapels which are divided by a big central tower and octagon supported by flying buttresses. One chapel now serves as the cemetery and crematorium office, the other remains in use as the burial chapel. Its period furnishings including small dark oak pews are spoilt by a modern light wood altar.

Regrettably the tombstones do not compare with the grandeur of the buildings. A depressingly large number are greying marble headstones but there is evidence too of the new fashion for black marble. This leaves scope for sandblasting designs on the highly polished surface. The figure of a boxer and a large car in this medium (near the chapels) should not be missed.

A portion of land beyond the chapels has already been reclaimed for burials. It remains to be seen how much longer Honor Oak 'Rec' survives as playing fields.

To the east of the cemetery is Honor Oak Crematorium, opened in 1939 by that staunch advocate of cremation, Lord Horder. The architects were Maurice Webb, son of Sir Aston, and William Bell, the borough architect, who chose an Italianate style in brick, with a chimney that resembles St Mark's campanile in Venice.[3] When opened in March 1939, the *Camberwell and Peckham Times* declared,

Our reporter rubbed his eyes when he beheld Honor Oak Crematorium. . . For these were obvious differences between the finished building and the architect's drawing. . . There are four more loopholes in the tower of the actual building, its keystone is more elaborate than the architect's original conception, two circular windows . . . on the frontage of the main building are replaced by conventional rectangular ones, the real steeple is steeper and a low brink wall surrounds a forecourt in front of the tower.

Reassuringly, the reporter concluded, 'But none of the alterations detract from the dignity and efficiency of this latest example of civic dignity.' Inside, the catafalque descends leaving a bronze shield on the floor of the chapel beneath which extends the crematory.

The usual cloister, with over 6,000 tablets and two gated columbaria, are south of the chapel and the garden of remembrance meanders among six acres of rose beds and the ever popular willows and silver birch. A new free-standing columbarium on both sides of the drive approaching the chapel is unnecessarily intrusive. Similarly, the over-provision of memorial benches in the Gardens of Remembrance shows a lack of control – at one point they form an almost continuous boundary of seating.

GEORGE CORNELL C. 1928–1966
Criminal murdered by Ronnie Kray in the Blind Beggar pub.

GEN. FREDERICK COUTTS 1899–1986
General in the Salvation Army 1963–69.

GEN. WILFRED KITCHING 1893–1977
General in the Salvation Army 1954–63.

FREDDIE MILLS 1919–65
World light heavyweight boxing champion 1948–50. He died by his own hand.

WILLIAM PULLUM 1887–1960
'a pillar of strength', he was a world weightlifting champion.

JOHNNY TRUNLEY 1898–1944
'The fat boy', he weighed thirty-three stone at the age of eighteen and appeared on the stage with Fred Karno.

CARPENDERS PARK CEMETERY
OXHEY LANE, WATFORD, HERTS

Owner: *London Borough of Brent*
Founded: *1954*
Acreage : *14 acres*

The drive into the cemetery looks promising enhanced as it is by the Hartsbourne stream running through the wooded area to the right, but then the gently undulating site opens out to a lawn devoid of any substantial planting. There is no chapel and the only building is a heavily fortified brick office. Bronze tablets level with the ground give the impression that few burials have taken place. In fact, there have been nearly 9,000, including many Muslims. There is a section devoted to woodland burials.

James Hanratty who was hanged in 1962 for the notorious murder of Michael Gregsten on the A6 was exhumed from Bedford Prison and reburied at Carpenders Park in 1966.

CHADWELL HEATH CEMETERY
WHALEBONE LANE, MARK'S GATE, ESSEX

Owner: *London Borough of Barking and Dagenham*
Founded: *1934*
Acreage: *11 acres (currently being extended by 8 acres)*

Chadwell Heath flaunts civic pride in a cemetery typical of its period which is more Gaumont than God's Acre. It was designed by the borough engineer and surveyor, Thomas Philip Francis on an elevated site, once isolated from London's urban sprawl.

The entrance sets the tone, announced by plain brick piers embellished with the monogram of Dagenham Urban District Council and supporting iron gates and railings in art deco style. Directly ahead is the austere brick bulk of the chapel, provided with apse end, steep gabled red tiled roof and a massive west tower. Stone dressings to the windows and wall tops are developed further at the west door which is surrounded by stone cladding that rises in a flourish to the parapet incorporating a Celtic cross on route. A tympanum of coloured glass over the door provides the setting for a symbolic casket.

Chadwell Heath: the front elevation of the chapel (1934)

All paths radiate from the chapel, one leading to the only other building in the cemetery – a rectangular brick shelter with sinuous iron grilles in the openings. That and the chapel, however, are the only distinctive features in a cemetery which has no planting or memorials of interest. Civic pride too has now surrendered before the requirements of lawn cemetery planning. Despite that the original eleven acres are filled and a further eight are being reclaimed to provide burial space for the next fifty years.

CHARLTON CEMETERY
CEMETERY LANE, SE7

Founded: 1855
Owner: London Borough of Greenwich
Acreage: 14½

When Charlton was founded it was an exclusive eight acre 'Gentleman's Cemetery' in the County of Kent, carved out of land formerly part of Sir Thomas Wilson's estate. The high cost of burial fees ensured only the wealthy could afford to be buried here. Today, despite the loss of its original lodge and the addition of seven acres in the twentieth century, the Victorian nucleus remains, still recognisable from an 1857 drawing in the *Illustrated London News*.[1] There are two small compact chapels, Early English style for the Church of England and Decorated for the Catholics (no longer in use) which were designed by Mr S. Hewitt of Southwark. The former is unusual in having a stained glass west window depicting the entombment, presented by the local vicar in 1865. All around the chapel are the typical grey granite monuments of the empire builders, soldiers and sailors who lived in Greenwich and Woolwich during the nineteenth century. There are more than the average number of deaths recorded that occurred from drowning, fever or war wounds. One appalling Caribbean disaster in July 1861 is commemorated by an urn supported on a large plinth inscribed with the names of fifty-two men and boys who died of yellow fever aboard HMS *Firebrand*.

A most unusual but now very weathered tomb commemorates Jemima Ayley, to the right of the gates. She lies in effigy, mediaeval style, beneath a little domed canopy. The precise minute of her death in 1860 is recorded on the inscription and the story goes that her sister died in Norfolk on the same day. Apparently the vault beneath the monument is 22 ft deep and houses a table and chair, originally used by mourning relatives.

Charlton: The layout of the cemetery as seen in *The Illustrated London News* (1857)

There are two other inscriptions at Charlton which are similarly pre-occupied with the minutiae of death. Henry Mandeville was 'struck by a motor car, and taken instantly to be with Christ April 26th 1912 while engaged in evangelistic work at Hartley Wintney Hants'. And there is Albert Inigo 'the third and beloved son of Lt.Col. W.J.B. Graham who was drowned on Sept. 7th 1881 in his 19th year from the ship 'Collingwood' bound for Melbourne, Australia during a heavy gale in Lat. 41° 18' S: Long. 34° E'. Two more typical epitaphs, and classics of their kind, appear on the tombstones respectively of Mr Gradidge who died in 1926:

> When the one great scorer writes the score against his name,
> He will put not what he won or lost but how he played the game.

and Jabez White, a blacksmith who died in 1926:

> My anvil's worn, my forge decayed
> My body in the dust is laid
> My coal is burnt my iron's run
> My last nail is in my work is done.

Finally, in the newer southern half of the cemetery, there is a splendid monument built for Thomas Murphy in 1932, erstwhile owner of Charlton greyhound track. Two life-size stone greyhounds keep watch for their master at the foot of three large Corinthian columns.

Charlton is very well cared for. Some fifty years ago an enterprising superintendent sensibly planted his own choice of trees including monkey puzzle and larch instead of the usual ornamental cherries which overrun so many council owned cemeteries. They are ideal traditional cemetery evergreens which blend well with a few mature holm oaks. Some of the memorials have been classified as unsafe, but they have been fenced or decorated with a warning badge rather than drastically laid flat as often happens elsewhere.

BARING BARING-GOULD 1843–1917
Secretary of the Church Missionary Society.

PETER BARLOW 1776–1862
Mathematician and pioneer in magnetism, he invented a method to compensate compass errors in ships.

WILLIAM BARLOW 1812–1902
Engineer, he designed the St Pancras train shed and the Tay Bridge.

Charlton: Tomb of Jemima Ayley (1860) Further deterioration has occured since this photograph was taken in 1980

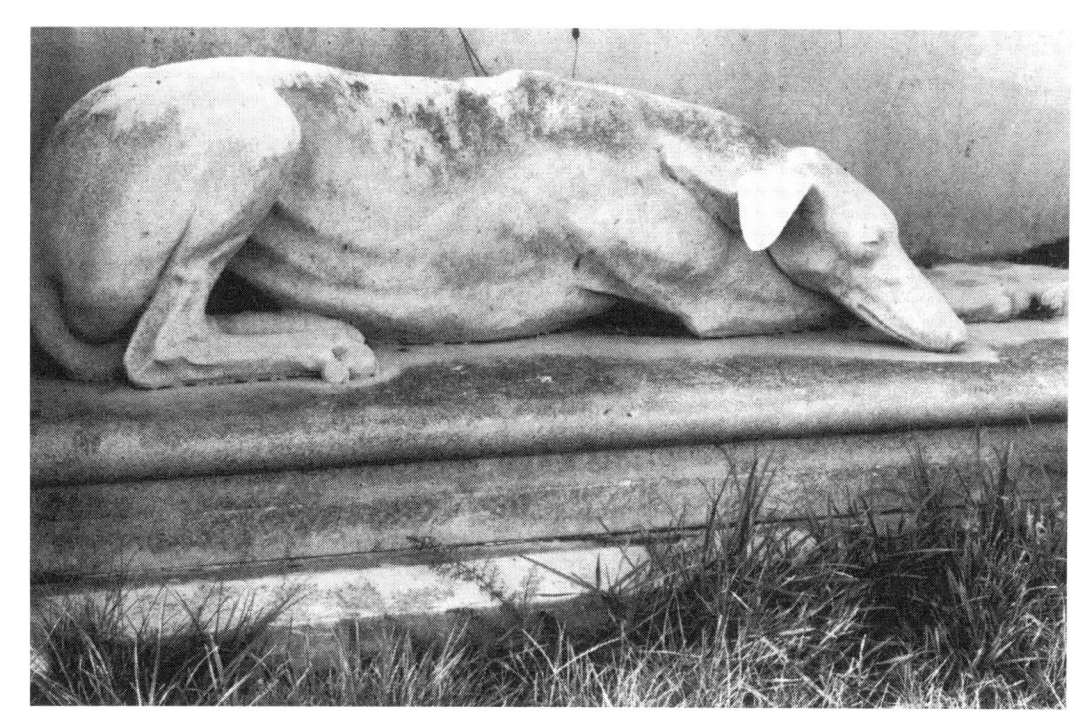

Charlton: Tomb of Thomas Murphy (1932)

Gen. Sir Robert Biddulph 1835–1918
High Commissioner in Cyprus 1874–86, governor of Gibraltar 1893–1900, where he organised the rebuilding of the fortress and docks.

Adm. Sir Crawford Caffin 1812–83
After a distinguished naval career as director-general of naval artillery, he retired to found a religious centre at Blackheath 'of very pronounced views'.

Sir Geoffrey Callender 1875–1945
First director of the National Maritime Museum, 1934, he was instrumental in saving H.M.S. *Victory* as a museum.

Gen. Sir Frederick Campbell 1819–93
Superintendent of the Royal Gun factories 1863–75.

Sir James Cooper 1868–1936
Accountant and industrialist.

William Cowie 1849–1910
'By his instrumentality 31,000 square metres of territory in British North Borneo were added to the British Empire.'

Sir Thomas Crawford 1824–95
Director general Army Medical Department 1882–1889, honorary surgeon to Queen Victoria.

SIR WILLIAM DALYELL 1784–1865
Fought in the Napoleonic War and imprisoned in France 1805–14. Exhumed from the Greenwich Royal Hospital where he was commander 1840–65.

GEN. SIR WILLIAM DOBBIE 1879–1964
Governor of Malta during the siege 1940–42.

GEN. SIR HENRY GEARY 1837–1918
Governor of Bermuda 1902–04.

ARTHUR HARRIS –1931
Trade unionist.

THOMAS HILDYARD 1821–88
South Nottinghamshire M.P. for twenty-five years and builder of Flintham Hall, Notts.

RODERICK MACDONALD 1840–94
H.M. Coroner for London and Middlesex, 1888–1894.

SIR JOHN MACDOUGALL 1844–1917
Chairman of the L.C.C.

SIR JOHN MARYON-WILSON 1802–76
Lord of the Manor of Hampstead and instrumental in preserving Hampstead Heath for the nation.

FRANK MILES 1889–1912
Drowned in the *Titanic* 15 April 1912.

THOMAS MILWARD 1826–74
Superintendent Royal Laboratory, Woolwich. Inventor of light mountain guns used in the Abyssinian campaign and elsewhere.

SIR WILLIAM MUIR 1818–85
Director general Army Medical Department 1874–82, honorary physician to Queen Victoria.

GEN. SIR CHARLES NAIRNE 1836–99
Commander-in-Chief, India, 1898.

GEN. JOHN ORMSBY 1810–69
Commandant Royal Military Academy, Woolwich, 1867–69.

JAMES PARRATT –1878
Inspector general of army hospitals.

ADM. SIR WATKIN PELL 1788–1869
Served under Nelson and lost a leg in battle in 1800, commissioner of Greenwich Hospital.

ADM. GEORGE PERCEVAL, 6th EARL OF EGMONT 1794–1874
Served as a midshipman at the battle of Trafalgar 1805.

GEN. PETER SCRATCHLEY 1835–85
Military engineer to the Australian colonies, H.M. Commissioner in New Guinea. (Memorial only).

SIR WILLIAM SMITH 1850–1932
Founder president of the British Institute of Public Health and professor of forensic medicine at London University.

EDWARD WARD-ASHTON –1880
Friend of Empress Eugenie who placed a wreath on his grave.

MAJ. GEN. ORDE WINGATE 1903–44
Chindit leader in Burma during the 2nd World War, killed in a plane crash in India. (Monument only, his remains were buried in Arlington Cemetery, Washington D.C.).

CHERRY LANE CEMETERY
SHEPISTON LANE, WEST DRAYTON, MIDDX.

Founded: 1937
Owner: London Borough of Hillingdon
Acreage: 60

The boundary of this cemetery, marked by iron railings and tightly packed mature evergreen trees, runs alongside a busy road near the M4 north of Heathrow Airport. Cherry trees planted near the entrance are a welcome contrast to these grim surroundings, especially in the spring.

There is a no chapel, only a wooden shelter and a central maintenance compound including a Portakabin. Two unusual features are the attractive pitched and tiled watering can racks, and a pond which attracts flocks of Canada geese. Next to it is an area for the burial of cremated remains and children's graves. There is also a Muslim section.

The cemetery has been considerably extended and a stone inscription records that 'the landscape and improvement work in this area were made possible and carried out by the London Borough of Hillingdon and Tarmac working in partnership for the community. September 1996.' In the centre of this section is a circular shelter which could easily be mistaken for a bandstand; a smaller one is located near the pond. Lawn graves of regulation dimension have started to fill the extension.

The one memorial of note records the death of thirty-seven workers' from the Gramophone Company who were killed by a flying bomb at the Hayes factory in 1944. The stone was erected by fellow workers and the Company.

CHINGFORD MOUNT CEMETERY
OLD CHURCH ROAD, E4

Founded: 1884
Owner: London Borough of Waltham Forest
Acreage: 41½

The cemetery stands on the brow of a hill leading from a busy suburban high street. It was formed from land known as 'Caroline Mount' (named after its owner, an admiral's wife) with 'wise and commendable forethought' to provide for nonconformist burials after Abney Park (the company's first of four cemeteries) had become congested. In a stirring opening address the Revd. Dr. Bevan emphasised the cemetery's role in providing a Christian burial for all, including 'the unbaptised, the suicide, the heretic and the excommunicate'.[1] The first burial took place in May 1884.

Despite these altruistic objectives, the company's revenue declined in the twentieth century and in 1975 new owners proposed building houses on part of the unused ground. Fortunately the plan failed but subsequently the cemetery was left to rot. Vandals succeeded in gutting both the red brick lodges, one of which had enjoyed notoriety as the scene of poltergeist happenings, and set fire to the ragstone chapel (designed by architects Messrs England and Brown), destroying most of the records in the process. Pressure from local residents and relatives of those buried in the cemetery persuaded the owners to give the consecrated ground to the Council in 1976, but by then the lodges were past saving and had to be demolished along with both the chapels.

Since then Chingford's fortunes have improved considerably. A feasibility plan revealed that only three quarters of the ground has been used since 1884 and room was available for a further 100,000 burials. The scheme encouraged conservation of the best trees which might appear more at home in a country park than a suburban cemetery. Some of them are magnificent, especially the great avenue of planes that follows the curve of the central drive. The cemetery now has a

Chingford Mount: The entrance and lodge 1884, now demolished

Chingford Mount: Beehives on the Norwood vault (1872). A single beehive can also be found on the Norwood grave at Abney Park (1864).

secure perimeter fence, there is clear sign posting and a new lodge and office have been built at the main entrance. In addition, significant clearance of the dense vegetation has taken place.

Apart from the partly draped granite beehives (identical to another at Chingford's former sister cemetery, Abney Park) of the Norwood family tombs, there are none of any distinction. Chingford was, and is, a modest suburb and for the most part the tombs and their epitaphs reflect this.

Two interments are exceptional. First there are the remains of those formerly buried in the eighteenth-century Whitefield Tabernacle ground, a Nonconformist burial plot in the Tottenham Court Road. Two hundred lead coffins, numerous wooden coffins and one iron coffin 'quite intact except for rust' were removed to Chingford in 1898 after the graveyard had become a site of 'constant rioting and disorder.'[2] Only the Rev. Augustus Toplady's coffin was allowed to remain behind on account of its great depth in the ground. Secondly there are remains from Ram's Chapel, Homerton. This was built in 1723 by Stephen Ram, a banker, after he had failed to obtain exclusive use of pew number thirteen for himself and his family in Hackney parish church. The chapel survived until 1933 when a dwindling congregation and unstable fabric forced its demolition and transfer of the churchyard remains to Chingford Mount.

John Bacon 1740–99
Sculptor, several of his memorials can be seen in Westminster Abbey and St Paul's. (Removed from Whitefield Chapel).

Ernest Dobbs 1901–27
A member of the R.A.F. parachute test section known as the parachute king, killed while balloon jumping. 'In science he leaped to fame and in the cause he met his death.'

Rev. John Eyre 1754–1803
Evangelical minister at Ram's chapel, a founder of the London Missionary Society 1795. Also his wife Ann, 'few equalled, none excelled her'.

Charlie Kray 1927–2000
Gangster sentenced to ten years imprisonment for involvement in the murder of Charlie Cornell (q.v.) and Jack 'the hat' McVitie.

Frances Kray 1944–67
Wife of the gangster Reggie Kray, she committed suicide and was buried in her wedding dress.

Reggie Kray 1933–2000
With his twin brother, Ronnie (1933–95), sentenced to life for the murder of Charlie Cornell (q.v.) and Jack 'the hat' McVitie.

Violet Kray 1910–82
Mother of Charles, Reggie and Ronnie.

William Nutter 1759–1802
Engraver. (Removed from Whitefield Chapel).

Robert Overton 1854–1924
Poet, dramatist, journalist and lecturer on literary and philosophical subjects.

Matthew Pearce –1775
Architect and builder of the original Whitefield Chapel. (Removed from Whitefield Chapel).

Benjamin Pollock 1856–1937
Builder of toy theatres and owner of the famous Pollock's toy shop in Hoxton, now in Scala Street.

William Powley 1818–96
Superintendent of the General Post Office and founder of the Post Office Orphans Home.

Rev. Stephen Ram –1746
Banker and founder of Ram's Episcopal church at Homerton.

George Smith –1784
Governor of Tothill Fields, Bridewell. 'He was so much respected and loved by the prisoners . . . that on his decease, it was stated they wept for their friend.' (Removed from Whitefield Chapel).

Margaret Smith –1815
'For many years attached to the household of H.R.H. Princess Amelia, second daughter of George III.' (Removed from Whitefield Chapel).

James Spicer 1807–88
Founder of the paper merchants of that name. Active supporter of nonconformist causes, he financed the building of several chapels in Essex.

Elizabeth Whitefield 1704–68
Wife of the evangelist George Whitefield, described by a contemporary as a 'ferret'. Her coffin was 'solid cast lead half an inch thick with the handles and plates soldered on'.

CHISWICK NEW CEMETERY
Staveley Road, W4

Founded: 1933
Owner: London Borough of Hounslow
Acreage: 15

This is not one of London's most appealing cemeteries and must be the noisiest, set down in a water meadow sandwiched between an arterial road and a suburban railway line. The planners probably realised the site was not ideal for residential development, but would not have anticipated the additional roar of aeroplanes that now regularly fly overhead to Heathrow. However, the dead don't complain and the cemetery remains in regular use. A further six acres to the west, formerly used by allotment holders, were absorbed in 1989.

The chapel is a characteristic brick and Portland stone building in 1930s Great West Road style. Designed by Joseph R. Musto of Brentford Council surveyor's department it cost £5,000 to build and was never consecrated, to allow for interdenominational services. The design is not dissimilar to the now demolished Anglican chapel in the nearby Gunnersbury Cemetery.[1] An unexpectedly exotic element in Chiswick is the surprising number of Russians and Poles buried here. There has been a Russian community in the Chiswick area for years and the distinctive Russian crosses with names like Woronzow and Count Soumarokoff have a distinctly pre-revolutionary flavour.

Ralph Bates 1940–1991
Actor, best known for his role in the British sitcom, *Dear John* (1986)

Chiswick New: The 'Great West Road' style chapel designed by the borough surveyor, Joseph Musto (1933)

CHISWICK OLD CEMETERY
Corney Road, W4

Founded: 1888
Owner: London Borough of Hounslow
Acreage: 9

The cemetery is unusual because it is really an extension of the old graveyard to St Nicholas Parish Church with which it merges. Both are now maintained by Hounslow, but strictly speaking the area adjacent to the church and two extensions to it, donated by the Duke of Devonshire in 1838 and 1871, are still the churchyard although separated from the cemetery only by a slight change in ground level. Among those buried in the former are William Hogarth, (1764), Philip de Loutherbourg (1812) and Ugo Foscolo (1827).

The cemetery is not an attractive place; flat, virtually treeless and gradually recovering from a heavy dose of weedkiller. There is no chapel, burial services being conducted in the church. Monuments worth looking for are James McNeill Whistler's bronze table tomb (against the north wall) in Renaissance style with resin corner statuettes replacing bronze originals that were stolen, Frederick Hitch's granite tomb, sculpted draped with a Union Jack on which sits a pith helmet, the memorial to Sir Percy Harris with a scene of the Resurrection designed by Edward Bainbridge Copnall, president of the Royal Society of British Sculptors 1961–66, and the granite headstone of the Schram family carved with a strange emblematic and sinuous relief.

Chiswick Old: Bronze table tomb to James McNeill Whistler (1903). The corner statuettes are resin replacements

Chiswick Old: The Resurrection by Edward Bainbridge Copnall on the grave of Sir Percy Harris (1952)

Chiswick Old: Memorial to Frederick Hitch (1913)

ARTHUR BURDEN 1890–1915
Assistant purser on the *Lusitania*, sunk off the Irish coast.

MONTAGU CHAMBERS 1799–1886
M.P. for Greenwich and Devonport and editor of the *Law Journal Reports* 1835–86.

SIR ARTHUR ELLIS 1883–1966
Canadian born pathologist, a specialist on renal diseases, he was Regius Professor of Medicine at Oxford University.

SIR PERCY HARRIS 1876–1952
Deputy chairman of the L.C.C. and Liberal M.P. for twenty-five years, deputy leader Liberal Party 1940–45. Wrote *London and its Government*, a standard work in its day.

FREDERICK HITCH 1856–1913
A private in the South Wales Borderers, he won a V.C. in defence of Rorkes' Drift during the Zulu War in 1879.

Henry Joy 1819–93
'Staff trumpeter to General the Earl of Lucan, sounded the memorable charge of the Light Brigade.' His monument was erected by officers of the 17th Lancers and his family.

James Kelly 1886–1920
A police officer shot while on duty in Gunnersbury Lane. His killer was never caught.

James MacLean 1835–1906
President of the Institute of Journalists, proprietor of the Bombay Gazette, the first Conservative M.P. for Cardiff in forty years 1895–1900, published works on Indian politics.

Frank Loughborough Pearson 1864–1947
Architect son of John Loughborough Pearson whose work at Truro and Brisbane cathedrals he completed. His own practice included several new churches.

Adm. Sir Robert Smart 1796–1874
Commander in Chief Mediterranean Fleet 1863–66.

James McNeill Whistler 1834–1903
American born artist, after studying in Paris, moved to London in 1859. Painted pictures, advanced for their time, in which he explored the juxtaposition of related tones and colours.

THE CITY OF LONDON CEMETERY AND CREMATORIUM
Aldersbrook Road, E12

Founded: 1856
Owner: The City of London Corporation
Acreage: 200

In a book published on London's cemeteries (in Belgium), Guy Vaes considered that the City of London cemetery *'est l'ultime efflorescence d'un âge d'or funéraire'*.[1] Certainly it is a cemetery that has everything, built shortly after the first wave of public cemeteries was completed which advantageously supplied the City commissioners with ideas for their own enterprise. Unlike so many cemeteries, the City's buildings are still well preserved and the grounds maintained to a high standard (it has won a number of awards), no mean feat for the UK's largest municipal cemetery. The site's historical significance has been recognised by English Heritage's decision in 2004 to upgrade the cemetery's status on the Register of Parks and gardens of Special Historic Interest from Grade II to Grade II* (there are none graded higher).

In fact, to gain an impression of a cemetery such as the Victorians would have recognised, one need only glimpse down one of the avenues that leads to the *rond point* occupied by the Anglican chapel. Magnificent chestnuts, now at their mature best, shade prominent granite tombs that survive polished and upright as befits the City worthies who lie beneath them, while the vista is closed by the large Gothic chapel with its crocketed spire.

The mastermind behind this beautifully organised plan was William Haywood, surveyor and engineer to the London Commissioners of Sewers, with the assistance of the landscape gardner, Robert Davidson. More of an engineer than architect, Haywood is comparatively unknown today.

City of London: The entrance gate c. 1900. The Anglican chapel can be glimpsed in the background

He had trained with the engineer/architect George Aitchison and worked with Joseph Bazalgette on the Abbey Mills pumping station and with James Bunning on the Holborn viaduct.

Haywood's masterpiece, however, is the City of London cemetery, where his ashes now rest in a Gothic mausoleum near the entrance gates. His involvement with the project began in 1849 when he reported to the Commissioners that 'the number of churchyards within the city was eighty-eight and their total superficial area about eight and a half acres'.[2] Estimating that 'the population of the City, about 130,000 persons, has been dying during these five years at the rate of about 24 per 1000 per year', the situation had become a 'crying evil'.[3] The state of some of these churchyards has been described in chapter two and the Commissioners were justifiably concerned. With some difficulty they found what was needed in 1853, namely 200 acres of farmland near Epping Forest which was bought for £30,721 from Lord Wellesley. The farm house was demolished, a large fishpond drained, (now the site of the catacomb valley) and the building of the cemetery began immediately.

The Commissioners' intentions were quite clear:

> We have regarded the City of London cemetery as a work for posterity as well as the present Generation's and considered that the required Buildings and other works should be substantial.[4]

In this they succeeded, eventually spending some £45,450, about £26,000 more than the original estimates. On completion Haywood published *Plans and Views* of the cemetery together with a short description:

> The principal entrance is . . . in the Pointed style, as are all the buildings throughout, with ornamental iron gates, and has on one side the superintendent's house, and on the

City of London: The Dissenters' chapel by William Haywood (*The Builder*, 1856)

other the porter's lodge. . . Directly upon entering the principal gates the Dissenting and Episcopal chapels, although 700 ft apart from each other, are both in view, the roads to each being in direct lines from the entrance. The plan of the ground was designed in reference to the surface configuration, and other conditions, and is composed partly of straight and partly serpentine roads.[5]

In addition a railway siding and special station had been projected, linked to the Eastern Counties Railway, but this depended on other parishes sharing the cost, which, it transpired, they were not prepared to do.

All save the catacombs was complete by the end of 1855, when a tiresome snag prevented the consecration. *The Builder* expounded:

The Commissioners of Sewers have laid out a cemetery for the whole City, which comprises more than a hundred parishes, to nearly the whole of which parishes there are district clergymen and other officers, and as the consent of the whole of these vestries is requisite to fees and other respects, it must be seen what difficulties lie in the way of a comfortable adjustment of the affair.[6]

After much argument the Burial Acts Amendment Bill was enacted which unravelled the problem and the cemetery was belatedly consecrated in November 1857. The first burial had already taken place after the gates had opened on 24 July 1856. Straight away the cemetery became so popular that Haywood commented:

> There is no instance upon record of a place of sepulture, which has been so much used within so short a space of time.[7]

In 1858, 2,681 interments took place and over half a million have occurred since.

All buildings including both cemetery chapels, the old crematorium and the catacombs are still used. Of 275 cells available in the latter, only a third have been sold in 120 years. One wing has been converted into a columbarium for ashes. The crematorium was built at a cost of £7,000 and opened on 25 October 1904 in the presence of Sir Henry Thompson of the Cremation Society of England.[8] The first cremation took place a year later. London's second crematorium was designed by an engineer, D.J. Ross, who provided it with two coke fired furnaces and an eighty feet high perforated chimney, all disguised within a Gothic framework. Since the construction of the new crematorium in 1971, to the designs of E.G. Chandler, the old building was decommissioned before recently being brought back into use for services with cremations taking place at the new facility. The new crematorium has two chapels and four cremators in the basement area that can cope with over forty funerals a day. 2,967 cremations were performed in 2005.

One result of cremation's popularity (approximately three quarters of the population now choose – or have chosen for them – this method of disposal), has been the practice of commemorating the deceased by planting trees, flowers and shrubs. In 1937 a Garden of Rest was constructed and a series of Memorial Gardens followed. These now cover over thirty-two acres and have been planted with the staggering number of over 20,000 rose bushes along with a range of more contemporary memorials. Perhaps Haywood might have approved, but he would surely have condemned the monotonous lawn cemetery policy adopted since 1951 for coffin burial, which ignores any pretence at landscaping. It should be realised that the cemetery's attraction lies in the undulating ground with prospects revealed down great avenues of trees and among spreading cedars, banks of rhododendrons and granite monuments.

Among the monuments are some of unusual size erected over the remains removed here from City churchyards, in a few cases, it is said, incorporating features taken from churches demolished following the 1860 Union of Benefices Act. Haywood himself designed the largest, erected in 1871 over the reinterred lead coffins from the churchyards of St Andrew, Holborn and St Sepulchre. Other communal graves are the contents of plague pits, the reinterred remains from Christ's Hospital burial ground Newgate Street, redeveloped by the Post Office in 1903, and the remains from Newgate prison burial ground, demolished in 1900 to make way for the Old Bailey. According to Mrs Holmes, that ground consisted of:

> A passage in the prison used for the interment of those who are executed; 10 feet wide and 85 feet long.[9]

A Gothic screen memorial commemorates children from the Royal Orphanage, Wanstead and a granite rock the ground for the Hospital for poor French Protestants which was in Bath Street in the City.

Individual monuments are less striking. They are more effective when seen deployed in echelon along some of the seven miles of the cemetery's roads; only occasionally does one stand out. Examples are the tall Cheetham memorial of 1913 and the Tregurtha sundial with

136   LONDON CEMETERIES

City of London: Memorial to piano teacher Gladys Spencer (1931)

City of London: The Vigiland Memorial (1955)

details of the family births and deaths neatly filling the columns provided. But worth searching for is Gladys Spencer's memorial who died aged thirty-four in 1931. She was a popular trainer of children dancers and performers at the Classical Academy of Music and Dancing in Manor Park, and above her grave is carved a grand piano over which sprawls an anguished figure. Surpassing all is the Vigiland white marble representation of the Descent from the Cross, claimed to weigh fifty tons. It is an extraordinary Baroque flourish and would be more at home in an Italian cemetery than here. It was carved in a studio in Pietrasanta in Italy and was dedicated in May 1955. The memorial was thoroughly cleaned in 2003. The contrast between this traditional memorial and a temple sheltering a colourful statue of the Hindu god Shiva is striking.

Despite the size of the cemetery, the City of London is approaching capacity and the Corporation has been pioneering the reuse of graves. This involves identifying graves with sufficient burial space remaining, cleaning the memorial and then offering both for purchase. The headstone or part of the memorials with the original inscription is simply 'turned around' giving the opportunity for a new one to be added and visible from the path side.

SIR GEORGE BARCLAY 1862–1921
Diplomat, British ambassador to Romania.

GEORGE BINKS 1793–1872
Inventor of wire ropes.

LIEUT. GEORGE DREWRY 1894–1918
As a midshipman won a V.C. at the Dardanelles landing in 1915.

CATHERINE EDDOWES 1842–88
Fourth victim of Jack the Ripper, one of five prostitutes murdered by him in 1888.

ELIZABETH EVEREST –1895
Nanny to Sir Winston Churchill, who contributed to the erection of the memorial and attended her funeral.

GEORGE FOOTE 1850–1915
First editor of *The Freethinker* 1881, imprisoned for blasphemy 1882, president of the National Secular Society 1890–1915.

BENJAMIN GARDNER 1865–1948
Labour M.P. for West Ham for fourteen years.

WILLIAM HAYWOOD 1821–94
Surveyor and engineer to the Commissioners of Sewers for London 1845–94.

ROBERT HOOKE 1635–1703
Natural philosopher, scientist and architectural assistant to Sir Christopher Wren.

ROBERT HUNTER 1823–97
Theological college tutor and 'author of humorous works besides the Encyclopaedic Dictionary, a monument of industrious scholarship' in seven volumes.

JOHN JOHNSON 1661–1701
Glazier to William III (reinterred from St Mary Somerset).

REV. ALEXANDER MCCAUL 1799–1863
Professor of Divinity and Ecclesiastical History at London University, rector of three City churches, he declined several offers of a bishopric.

GEORGE MICKLEWRIGHT 1817–76
Conservationist, through his efforts, and those of others, Epping Forest was preserved from being built over.

BOBBY MOORE 1941–91
Captain of England's World Cup Football Team 1966. Cremated here.

DAME ANNA NEAGLE 1904–86
Actress and singer.

SIR JAMES ROLL 1846–1927
Worked for fifty years with Pearl Assurance, Lord Mayor of London 1920–21.

WILLIAM SAUNDERS 1825–1901
Medical Officer of Health for the City of London.

JOHN SIMS –1881
Won the V.C. during the Crimea War in 1855. He received his medal from Queen Victoria. Plaque erected 2003.

REV. BOWMAN STEPHENSON 1839–1912
Methodist minister, founder of the National Children's Home and Orphanage.

AARON STERN 1820–85
German-born Anglican missionary to the Jews in the Near East and Abyssinia, where he was imprisoned and tortured by King Theodore.

PERCY THOMPSON –1922
Husband of Edith Thompson, who, with her lover Frederick Bywaters, was hanged for his murder. (See Brookwood).

SGTS. CHARLES TUCKER AND ROBERT BENTLEY –1910
They and another policeman were shot dead by Russian anarchists attempting a jewel robbery; two of the anarchists were later cornered and died in the Sidney Street siege.

SIR HERBERT WILCOX 1892–1977
Film producer, several of his most successful films starred his wife, Anna Neagle. (q.v.).

SIR WALTER WILKIN 1842–1922.
Barrister, Lord Mayor of London 1895–96.

THERE ARE REINTERMENTS FROM THE BURIAL GROUNDS OF THE FOLLOWING CITY CHURCHES:

All Hallows, Bread Street
The church was demolished in 1878, following unification of the parish with St Mary-le-Bow.

All Hallows, Lombard Street
A Wren church, demolished in 1939.

All Hallows, Staining
The church was demolished in 1870.

Holy Trinity the Less, Trinity Lane
The church was destroyed in 1666 and the churchyard cleared in 1872 following the construction of the Mansion House station.

Holy Trinity, Minories
The church was destroyed in 1940. Burials include ancestors of George Washington.

St Alban, Wood Street
The church, save for the tower, was destroyed in 1940.

St Alphage, London Wall
The eighteenth century church was demolished, with the exception of the fourteenth century tower, in 1924. Several seventeenth and eighteenth century tomb slabs are preserved with the monument.

St Andrew, Holborn
The churchyard was acquired for the Holborn Viaduct in 1866, William Haywood designed the monument.

St Antholin, Watling Street
A Wren church demolished in 1875 because, the memorial inscription states, it was 'impossible to provide fit congregations to worship in the church'.

St Benet, Gracechurch Street
A Wren church, demolished in 1867 on the widening of Fenchurch Street.

St Botolph, Aldgate
The remains of 2,500 persons were moved here from the north part of the churchyard in 1965.

St Dionis, Backchurch
A Wren church demolished in 1879.

St Helen, Bishopsgate
Reinterment from the churchyard in 1892.

St James, Duke's Place
The church was demolished in 1874.

St John the Evangelist, Watling Street
The church was destroyed in 1666 and the churchyard cleared in 1954.

St John Zachary
The church was destroyed in 1666.

St Katherine, Coleman Street
An eighteenth century church demolished in 1925.

St Leonard, Eastcheap
Reinterment from the churchyard in Fish Street Hill in 1882 on the construction of the District Line. The church had been burned down in 1666 and was never replaced.

St Martin, Outwich
An eighteenth century church, demolished in 1874.

St Martin, Pomeroy
The church was destroyed in 1666.

St Martin, Vintry Street
The church was destroyed in 1666.

St Mary, Aldermanbury
A Wren church bombed in 1940 and removed to America in 1965.

St Mary, Colechurch
The church was destroyed in 1666 and the churchyard cleared to make way for Old Jewry.

St Mary Magdalen, Old Fish Street.
A Wren church destroyed in 1886.

St Mary, Somerset
A Wren church demolished in 1871.

St Mary, Woolchurch
The church was destroyed in 1666, part of the churchyard was built on by the Mansion House. Reinterment 1892.

St Mary, Woolnoth
The remains in the crypt were moved here following construction of Bank station.

St Matthew, Friday Street
A Wren church demolished in 1884.

ST MICHAEL, CORNHILL
Reinterment from the churchyard.

ST MICHAEL, QUEENHITHE
A Wren church demolished in 1876, reinterment 1969.

ST MILDRED, POULTRY
The church was demolished in 1872.

ST OLAVE, OLD JEWRY
A Wren church demolished, save the tower, in 1888.

ST PETER LE POER, OLD BROAD STREET
A mainly eighteenth century church demolished in 1908, replaced by housing.

ST PETER, PAUL'S WHARF
The church was destroyed in the Great Fire, Reinterment 1961.

ST SEPULCHRE, HOLBORN VIADUCT
The churchyard was acquired for the Holborn Viaduct in 1866, the monument is shared with St Andrew, Holborn.

CROYDON CEMETERY AND CREMATORIUM
MITCHAM ROAD, CROYDON, SURREY

Founded: 1897
Owner: London Borough of Croydon
Acreage: 43

The cemetery plan is a curious three-legged affair on account of its enlargement in 1935 and again with the building of the crematorium in 1937. The main entrance in Mitcham Road leads into a monotonous field of grey stone monuments in which the cross symbol dominates. There is a good late nineteenth century tile hung lodge, a less interesting brick Gothic chapel and no more, but the cemetery is remarkable for the high standard of garden maintenance. In the newer ground one is overwhelmed by the variety of formal flower beds and lily ponds. Roses, as usual, dominate.

The centrepiece is the Borough's crematorium designed by the Borough engineer and surveyor, C.E. Boast. The larger east chapel was opened in 1962. Both buildings rise above the customary low standard of crematorium architecture, especially the earlier version in an austerely simple Gothic design. Individual taste is allowed to flourish in the cloisters where pink and green onyx memorial tablets have sprouted like a nasty rash. Opposite the crematorium is a modern office building.

Near the Thornton Road entrance there are the usual monuments to long forgotten civic dignitaries and a trio of unusual examples. A large paved area with a raised flower bed and black granite cross is a dignified memorial to the thirty-four boys and two masters from Lanfranc School

Croydon: Memorial to Headmaster John Drage (1900)

who lost their lives in 1961 in an air crash off the Norwegian coast. Across the drive the stone model of a 1937 monoplane has landed on the tomb of Captain Leslie Thomas, and a metal relief commemorates John Drage 'Headmaster for over 50 years of the Croydon Boys British Schools'

Derek Bentley 1934–53
Executed in prison for his part in the murder of a policeman. His remains were removed to Croydon in 1966 but his father's wish to have the words 'A victim of English justice' inscribed on the tombstone was refused.

Sir Charles Flynn 1884–1938
Deputy chairman of Customs and Excise.

William Hurlstone 1876–1906
'One of the most promising young composers of his period', on the staff at the Royal College of Music.

CRYSTAL PALACE DISTRICT CEMETERY AND BECKENHAM CREMATORIUM
Elmers End Road, SE20

Founded: 1880
Owner: The Crematorium Company
Acreage: 30

Although sandwiched between a railway line, a sewage works and the A214, this cemetery remains popular and surprisingly rural in character. The boundary railings remain intact and have a most attractive finial similar to a pine cone.

Inside the main entrance is a large Edwardian lodge which has been extended to the side and rear. The old part of the cemetery is nearer the main entrance, but here maintenance is minimal and by midsummer a thick layer of undergrowth hides all but the tops of many monuments. The cemetery originally had two chapels designed in the fourteenth century style by Alexander Hennell of Bedford Row.[1] The consecrated chapel was demolished in the 1960s following damage in the Second World War. The survivor was extensively altered when converted into a crematorium in 1956 and furnished with an attractive stained glass window. An uncoordinated group of buildings beyond the east end accommodates the crematory; a *porte cochère* has been added outside the chapel doors and a stone semi-circular waiting-room at the rear. A building in sympathy with the chapel has been built nearby to accommodate the Book of Remembrance.

West of the chapel is a unique feature among London's cemeteries, a large ornamental rock waterfall and behind it a network of pergolae which join up with the neatly landscaped rose garden. Here the roses are carefully graded by colour and size and are very splendid indeed. Hedges separate the gardens from the remainder of the cemetery.

For some reason, perhaps because of Sydenham's healthy reputation as a spa, there is an extraordinary number of doctors buried here, but no very exceptional monuments, the best as usual being close to the main drive. The fine chest memorial for Dr Henry Prangley (1908) is enlivened by a portrait sculpted in relief as is William Ford Stanley (1909) and the MacDonald grave (1895). Near the chapel is the Watts grave (1915) supporting a shell, (now damaged). There is an immaculate white angel on the Birdseye grave (1995) and on the main drive a recently erected freestanding catacomb range in black granite. Beyond that are two new single coffin height mausolea.

An unidentified memorial cross dedicated in 1894 was designed by J.L. Pearson, architect of Truro Cathedral. Elsewhere a stone commemorates twenty-one members of Beckenham's fire service, killed on duty on 19 and 20 April, 1941, the night of one of London's heaviest air raids. Near the north boundary there is an eerie full size military figure standing 'on guard' over a soldier's grave, in this case, Henry Lowndes, a hero of the Crimea and the Indian Mutiny. It is almost identical to the soldier above Lord Rodney's grave at Camberwell Old Cemetery. Happily, the graves of Lord Stamp and W.G. Grace have recently been cleaned and a memorial marking the resting place of Frederick Wolseley was erected in 1988 for the 'Australian bicentennial by Wolseley enthusiasts worldwide.'

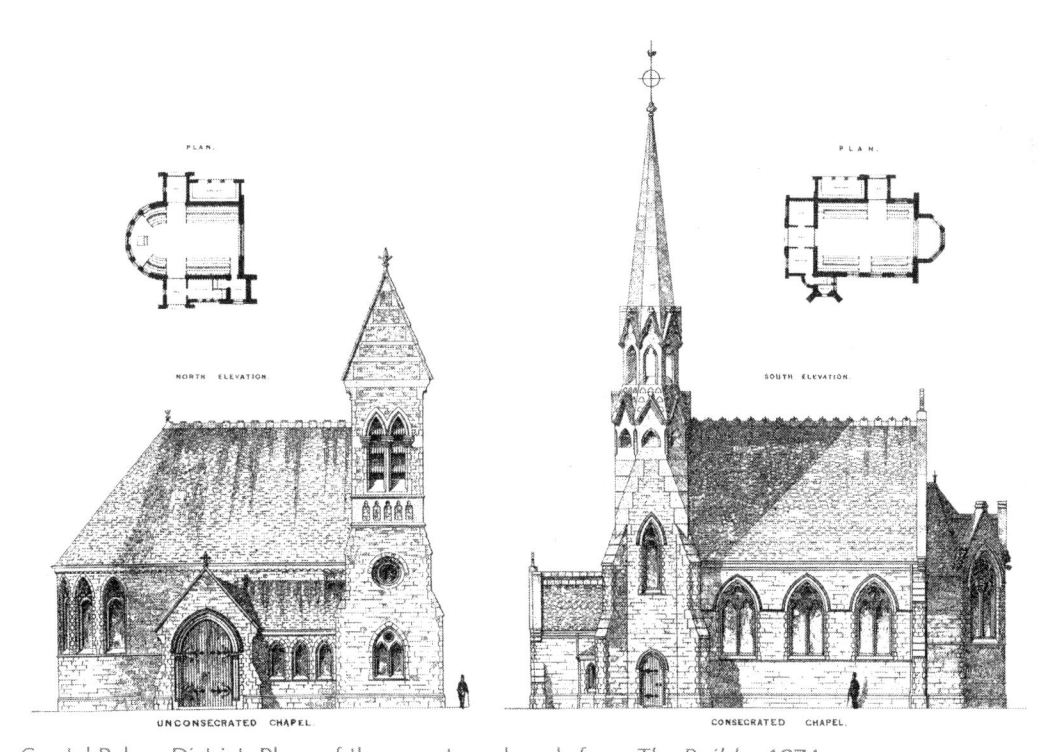

Crystal Palace District: Plans of the cemetery chapels from *The Builder* 1874

Frank Bourne −1945
The last survivor in the defence of Rorke's Drift, Natal, where during the Zulu war in 1879, 120 British troops fought off an attack by 4,000 Zulus.

Sir John Drughorn 1862−1943
Shipowner.

William Grace 1848−1915
'W.G.' Doctor and cricketer, his cricketing career spanned forty-three years during which time he scored 126 centuries. His last job was cricket manager at Crystal Palace.

Albert Saunders 1863−93
Chief constructor H.M. dockyard, Chatham.

Josiah, 1st Lord Stamp of Shortlands 1880−1941
Economic advisor to the government, a director of the Bank of England and I.C.I. and president of numerous organisations including the Geographical Society, the Institute of Transport, the Advertising Association, the Society of Genealogists and the L.M.S. railway.

William Walker 1869−1918
Liverpudlian deep sea diver who, single handed, underpinned the retrochoir of Winchester Cathedral working in total darkness for over five years.

Frederick Wolseley 1837−99
Went out to Australia where he invented a sheep shearing machine. On his return to Birmingham he successfully manufactured the machine and, in the 1890s, diversified with the aid of an employee, Herbert Austin, into building the Wolseley car.

Crystal Palace District : Memorial to the cricketer, W.G. Grace (1915)

Crystal Palace District: The grave of Henry Lowndes can be seen on the right and the consecrated chapel (now demolished) is in the background.

EALING AND OLD BRENTFORD (SOUTH EALING) CEMETERY
SOUTH EALING ROAD, W5

Founded: 1861
Owner: London Borough of Ealing
Acreage: 24

A visit should be made in the spring when this cemetery's magnificent magnolia trees are in bloom. The cemetery is divided by a public footpath with the older part to the west. Here are two chapels, designed by Charles Jones, the borough engineer, in the Decorated style, surrounded by yew trees. Unusually, a gong replaced the bell in the fleche. Everything is well maintained and on a small scale, which gives the cemetery the air of a country churchyard. The larger of the two lodges has been sensitively converted into flats and sold.

There are no very grand monuments but one deserves a special mention. Mr Lucas, director of the Brilliant Sign Company, is immortalised by the company's own product, his name emblazoned in gold leaf behind glass (1953).

Beyond the footpath the new cemetery comprises the usual acres of white marble, now confined to regulation sizes. Included is a large Polish section, characteristic of this part of West London.

ASPLAN BELDAM 1841–1912
First president of the Institute of Marine Engineers. All his seven children, buried nearby, died before reaching two years of age.

SURG.GEN.LEWIS BRUCE 1831–99
Served in Persia, the Indian Mutiny and the Afghan War.

JOHN DIXEY –1853
'Privy chamberlain of the cape and sword.'

GEORGE EVANS 1876–1937
Major in the Manchester Regiment. Winner of the last V.C. to be awarded in the Great War.

REV.WILLIAM JACKSON 1811–95
Bishop of Antigua 1860–95.

SIR BRYAN ROBINSON 1808–87
A judge of the Supreme Court, Newfoundland, he supported projects for opening up the interior of the colony.

LT.GEN.SIR ALEXANDER ROSS 1840–1910
Spent most of his military career in the north west frontier region of India, serving with the 1st Sikh Infantry Punjab frontier force in every grade to command, 1861–92.

SIR STEPHEN WALCOTT 1806–87
Chief colonial land and emigration commissioner in Canada.

RT.HON.SPENCER WALPOLE 1806–98
Conservative M.P. for Cambridge University, for several years Secretary of State for the Home Office during the 1850s and 60s.

LIONEL WALTER, 29TH EARL OF MAR 1891–1965
Premier earl of Scotland for twenty-three years.

EASTBROOKEND CEMETERY
THE CHASE, OFF DAGENHAM ROAD, DAGENHAM, ESSEX

Founded: 1914
Owner: London Borough of Barking and Dagenham
Acreage: 11

Eastbrookend Cemetery is situated at the eastern end of the vast London County Council Becontree estate, where 25,000 houses were built between 1912 and 1932. Eastbrookend was an example of provision before need. Encouraged by directors from the Great Southern Cemetery, Crematorium and Land Company at Streatham, a local enquiry was held into the siting of the cemetery in 1912 which was first known as Becontree Park, then Ilford Park, before settling on Eastbrookend Cemetery. The single chapel, lodge and other works were completed by September 1914.[1] Four acres were consecrated by the Bishop of Barking on 7 April 1923.

By the 1920s this cemetery and Tottenham Park were both owned by United Cemeteries Ltd who eventually also owned both Highgate and Nunhead Cemeteries. Today, it is surrounded by Eastbrookend Country Park and, unique in London, an apiary is passed on the driveway into the cemetery.

Apart from cherry trees, the site is largely devoid of planting. The lodge has been demolished but the surviving chapel, a functional looking building of rendered brick, has a large cross set into the pink tiled roof. The architect was probably John Bannen.

There are no distinctive memorials.

Eastbrookend (then Ilford Park) advertisement from *The Undertakers' Journal* (1916)

EASTCOTE LANE CEMETERY
EASTCOTE LANE, SOUTH HARROW, MIDDX.

Founded: 1900
Owner: London Borough of Harrow
Acreage: 3½

There is little to be said for poor Eastcote Lane, it is small, modest and dull. A small brick chapel of indeterminate style incorporates the office and lavatories within its compass. It has not been improved by vandals who have smashed the coloured glass windows while side doors and windows have been boarded up. Its one remaining feature is a cordon of dracaena palms. Beyond it is a central driveway with a conveniently positioned turning circle for funeral vehicles. Four lonely flowering cherry trees complete the bleak picture.

The cemetery is only used for the reopening of graves, although a section for the burial of cremated remains has been allocated near the chapel. Many of the memorials are straight from the monumental masons' brochures of the interwar years. Only one merits a second glance, carved with a square rigger on the rock commemorating Thomas Holmes, late R.N. (1939). Several members of the Salvation Army have been buried here.

EAST LONDON CEMETERY AND CREMATORIUM
GRANGE ROAD, E13

Founded: 1872
Owner: The East London Cemetery Company
Acreage: 35

Located in a quiet residential area of East London the cemetery continues to be owned by the founding private company. Its boundaries comprise the 'Greenway' walk to one side which effectively covers the Northern Outfall Sewer heading towards Beckton and sports fields to the other. Lack of imaginative planting and the flat terrain make it scenically dull. The paths are laid out symmetrically, bordered by avenues of trees. To the east beyond the office is a vast expanse of memorial rose bushes all of a uniform height. At the centre of the cemetery is a pair of simple Gothic style chapels. The crematorium chapel to the west, the sixty-ninth to open in the UK, was converted to plans drawn up by Douglas W. Rowntree F.R.I.B.A. at a cost of £12,500 and opened in 1954.[1] The other chapel, which is consecrated and dedicated to St Michael and All Angels, remains in use for burial services. Its best features are the west windows designed by Archibald John Davies, believed to date from 1930–32, depicting angels in striking colours of gold, pink and blue. Below is a tablet recording the fifty-three years of service given by the company secretary and director who died in 1996. The tapestry hanging above the altar is a reproduction of William Morris's 'Vine and Acanthus' of 1879 (the original hangs at Kelmscott Manor). Single story buildings have been added to the end of both buildings; one contains the crematory, the other beyond the burial chapel, houses the Book of Remembrance.

There are only a few exceptional monuments among the acres of simple slabs, many of recent date and a number erected for bomb victims of the last war including three war memorials. On the main drive is a life-size figure on the Vassallo (1981) grave while opposite the entrance is the monument to those who died when viewing platforms collapsed at the launching of HMS *Albion* in 1898. It is distinguished by a large ship's anchor. Another boating tragedy is commemorated by the tomb of George Davis, his wife and four children, victims with 700 others who drowned in 1878 when the paddle steamer *Princess Alice* sank in the Thames after colliding with another boat.[2] Their granite monument is a reminder of the worst civilian disaster in British history. Unusually, the cemetery also includes three calvaries including one in terracotta.

On the west side of the cemetery another granite monument was erected in 1927 'in memory of the Chinese who have died in England', this being a traditional burial ground for both Chinese and Japanese. In *Burying London*, T.W. Wilkinson (1906) describes an early twentieth-century Chinese funeral here.

> By a yawning hole lies a coffin on which the almond-eyed mourners proceed to place fish, flesh and fowl. The fish is unrecognizable, the flesh a joint of pork, the fowl a veteran cock, cooked in its entirety, with head, neck, etc. intact. Basins of rice, on top of which are laid chopsticks, are also deposited on the coffin, as well as a bottle of gin and some tea. Meanwhile the mourners have lit their pipes and been laughing uproariously as if the whole proceeding were an excellent jest ...[3]

LILIAN BAYLIS 1874–1937
Manager of the Old Vic and Sadlers Wells theatres. Her ashes were scattered here.

EAST SHEEN CEMETERY
SHEEN ROAD, RICHMOND, SURREY

Founded: 1906
Owner: London Borough of Richmond upon Thames
Acreage: 16

Turn off the main road past a pair of brick gate piers and one approaches the cemetery thorough an avenue of plane trees. It resembles the entrance to a country house with a lodge, luxuriant cedars and pampas grass clumps beyond.

East Sheen: 'the angel of Death . . . ' The Lancaster bronze by Sydney March (1920)

The chapel, designed in 1906 by Reginald Rowell, a local architect who is buried here, is thirteenth-century Gothic in style with a slender flèche.[1] Its foundation stone in the porch, listing the dignitaries present at the event, is typical of many cemeteries, as is the Second World War air raid shelter excavated near the boundary.

Several memorials transcend the average. Not far from the chapel is the marble figure of a soldier on the Rennie-O'Mahony (1928) grave. To the north a silver coloured dolphin leaps from its plinth and in the far corner is a half-size representation of Christ as the Good Shepherd accompanied by three lambs. There is more Christian imagery on a now illegible headstone framing an unusual mosaic depicting St Francis and Mary Magdalene. It is in total contrast to the aircraft carved on the memorial to Pilot Officer Denis Power (1931), the maritime imagery on the Hervey grave (1917) and a bronze panel by Alfred Buxton of a woman in a classical musician on the Buxton memorial (1927). More unusual is the beautifully maintained miniature walled garden bordering the main drive. It commemorates Louise Espinosa and her husband. However, everything in the cemetery is eclipsed by the immensely powerful figure of a bronze angel that mourns over the Lancaster tomb. Identified as the work of Sydney March and dating from the 1920s it is arguably the most dramatic sculpture in any of London's cemeteries. The Lancaster's were a north-country family who made their money in coal mining. March was one of a remarkable family of seven brothers and a sister, all of them accomplished artists, based in Kent. Together in 1939 they created their masterpiece, the Canadian National Memorial in Ottawa. Sydney March died in 1967 aged 92.

Robert, Lord Chalmers 1858–1938
Chairman, Board of Inland Revenue 1907–11, governor of Ceylon 1913–16, Under-Secretary for Ireland 1916, Master of Peterhouse 1924–31.

Gen.Sir O'Moore Creagh 1848–1923
Won the VC in Afghanistan in 1879. He later wrote a history of the V.C. and D.S.O. and was Commander in Chief, India, 1909–13.

Sir Miles de Montmorency 1893–1963
Portrait painter and author of *A Short History of Painting in England*, 1934.

Grp.Capt. Arthur Donaldson 1915–80
From a famous family of fighter pilots, his mother attended decoration ceremonies at Buckingham Palace thirteen times.

Edouard Espinosa 1871–1950
Founder, with his wife Louise (died 1943) of the British ballet organisation in 1930.

Quazim Kastrati 1908–74
Private secretary to King Zog of Albania in exile, for many years worked to promote Anglo-Albanian cooperation.

Roy Kinnear 1934–88
Character actor.

Fulton MacKay 1922–87
Actor.

Sir Alec Martin 1884–1971
Chairman of Christies 1940–58, chairman of the Wallace Collection and governor of the Foundling Hospital.

Sir John Martin-Harvey 1863–1944
Actor-manager and an early advocate for a national theatre.

Sir Ralph Moor 1860–1909
First high commissioner to Southern Nigeria 1900. He committed suicide.

East Sheen: The Rennie-O'Mahony Memorial (1928)

SIR BENJAMIN MORGAN 1874–1937
Engineer and economist, he served on numerous committees concerned with trade and the empire.

MAJ.GEN.WILLIAM OFFICER 1903–1988
Army doctor, honorary surgeon to the Queen 1961–63.

SIR FREDERICK PAINTER 1844–1926
Sheriff of the City of London 1913–14.

WILLIAM ELLSWORTH ROBINSON 1861–1918
Magician known as 'Chung Ling Soo' who caught bullets in his mouth. He was mortally wounded on stage when the trick went wrong.

MAJ.GEN.DOUGLAS SCOTT 1848–1924
Railway engineer in India and the Sudan.

GEORGE SUTCLIFFE 1878–1943
Artist and craftsman.

LT.GEN.SIR MICHAEL TIGHE 1864–1925
Had an active military career serving in Burma, China and Africa; a big game hunter.

SIR FREDERICK WIGAN 1827–1907
High sheriff of Surrey 1894, hop merchant and church benefactor, he took a leading role in the formation of Southwark diocese.

EDMONTON CEMETERY
CHURCH STREET, N9

Founded: 1884
Owner: London Borough of Enfield
Acreage: 30

The visitor enters the cemetery through iron gates, with appropriately floral embellishments, and a drive in the grand Victorian manner. He is surrounded by an ambuscade of sombre evergreen shrubs and spreading cedars beyond which are twin Kentish rag chapels set about with mature monkey puzzles, the single *porte cochère* topped by a neat belfry and flèche.[1] Unusually, the buildings for storing equipment tucked away to the side of the cemetery are of a similar design. All this augurs well, but west of the chapels the cemetery fans out into a thickly planted but otherwise disappointing landscape. Its chief distinction is the number of massive polished granite monuments in traditional style erected only in the last twenty years or so. Well-to-do families in Edmonton still like to commemorate their relatives with panache, particularly those from the Greek community. Elsewhere airborne deaths are the occasion for two large monuments. A granite monolith recalls local residents killed during the Blitz and a stone screen is inscribed with the twelve names of those killed at nearby Dunholme Road on 4 September 1938 when an aeroplane crashed into the street.

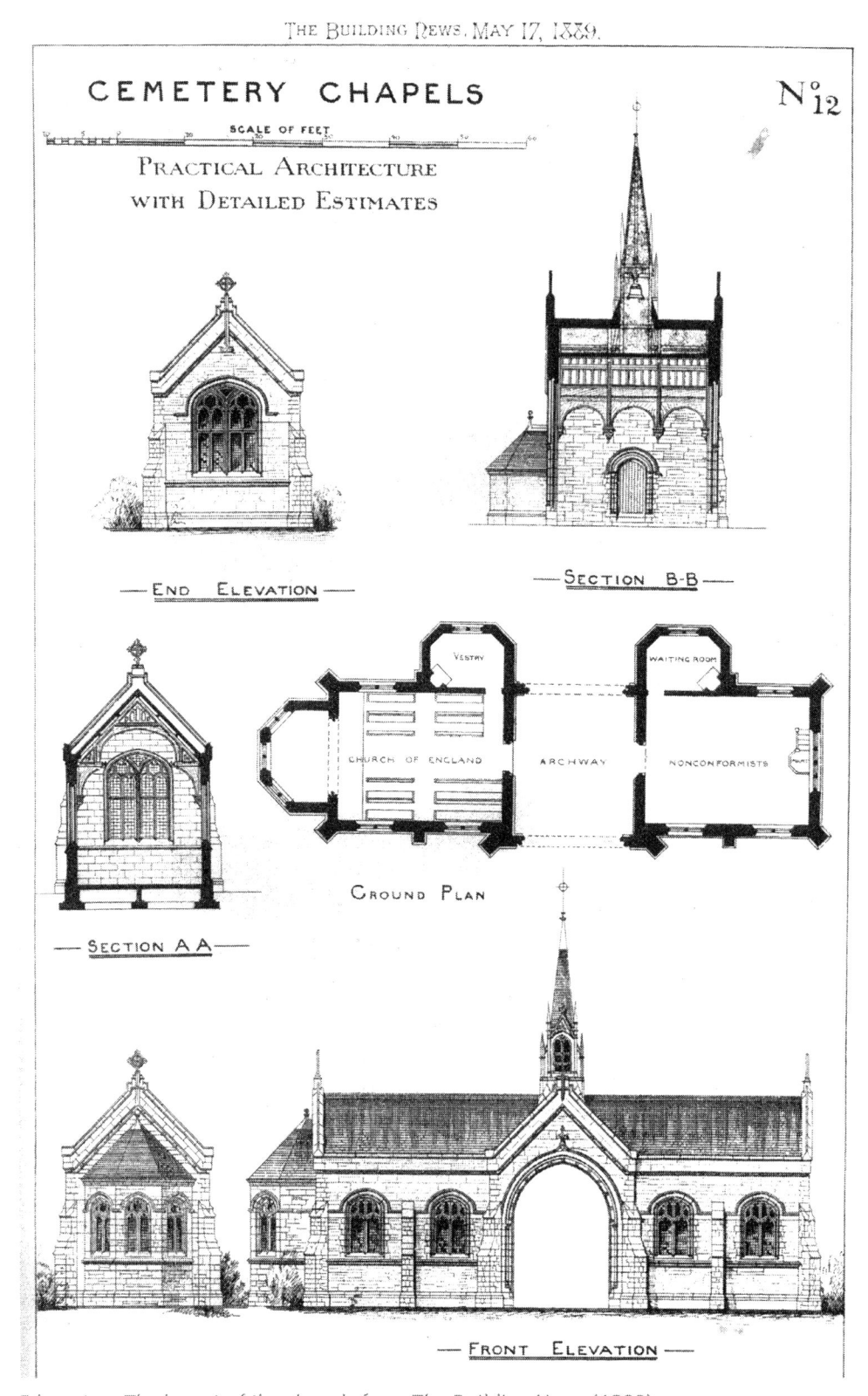

Edmonton: The layout of the chapels from *The Building News* (1889).

The cemetery office at the north east corner is an earlier Victorian villa, dating from the days when Edmonton was a rural Middlesex village and the cemetery land was a field belonging to the Church Commissioners.

JAMES ORD HUME 1864–1932
Composer and bandmaster.

EDMONTON AND SOUTHGATE CEMETERY

WATERFALL ROAD, N11

Founded: 1880
Owner: London Borough of Enfield
Acreage: 11

Here is a rare example of a cemetery without a chapel, mainly on account of Sir Gilbert Scott's parish church conveniently placed just up the road with its splendid array of Pre-Raphaelite glass. In comparison the cemetery is a dull place, with its ornate Gothic railings the only redeeming feature. The paths are organised on a gridiron pattern and the only building is a box-like lodge built in 1953 and now vandalised. Otherwise the cemetery appears to have escaped unscathed as most of the angels are intact save the medieval looking figure kneeling next to a shield, which has lost both arms and whatever it was carrying. The new fashion for the mown lawn cemetery has caught on here: each memorial stone of uniform size has it own pruned rose bush. They seem entirely in keeping with the suburban bungalows outside the gates and their carefully groomed front gardens. There are no outstanding monuments.

ELTHAM CEMETERY AND CREMATORIUM

ROCHESTER WAY, SE9

Founded: 1935
Owner: London Borough of Greenwich
Acreage: 27½

A prim suburban cemetery devoid of mystery. It was built to the specification of the borough engineer, H.W. Tee, on a flat site that enabled him to plan a grid pattern of plots for easy grave identification. Trees are relegated to the paths and edges of the ground, including a copse of oak, so far unused for burial. The chapel is tidy brick Gothic without surprises, but its bell tower has been truncated. Only one monument is of interest – a half size figure dressed in flying gear, commemorating an airman killed in 1938.

To the east the crematorium dates from 1956 and more recently, a remembrance chapel has been built resembling a tiny version of Liverpool's Roman Catholic Cathedral, but spoiled by lumpy stained glass windows in abstract designs. Around both buildings are walls with memorial plaques and the fussy flower beds habitual to crematoria, including the apparently compulsory rose garden.

MAJOR FRANCIS BEECH 1885–1969
Solicitor, M.P. for West Woolwich 1943–45 and mayor of the borough 1955–56.

RICHMAL CROMPTON 1890–1969
Author of the *Just William* books. She was cremated here.

GEN. ERNEST STOCKLEY 1872–1946
A much decorated figure in the Great War.

ENFIELD CREMATORIUM AND CEMETERY
GREAT CAMBRIDGE ROAD, ENFIELD, MIDDX.

Founded: 1938 (Cemetery in 1961)
Owner: London Borough of Haringey
Acreage: 40

Situated off a busy dual carriageway, Enfield is unique in being a crematorium with a cemetery opening at a later date. The forty-fourth to open in the UK it was designed by Sir Guy Dawber and A.R. Fox and opened by the mayor of Tottenham in 1938.[1] Dawber was essentially a country house architect, but he had been an assistant to Sir Ernest George who designed Golders Green Crematorium. His firm was also responsible for crematoria at Lambeth and North East Surrey. The scheme at Enfield has few parallels with its more distinguished counterpart, although it is of a higher standard than many post-war facilities.

Passing a gate lodge, the approach to the buildings is impressive. A broad drive is aligned straight to the center of a brick and pantiled cloister. Rising behind it a brick tower combines the crematorium chimney stack and clock tower and in front is a large three tiered fountain. The notion of symmetry is emphasised by the identical gabled chapels at each end of the cloister. These are now partly hidden by the planting along the drive – a sweet chestnut avenue that provides a backdrop to a hedge and a line of palms and topiary planted in the broad grass verges.

The style of architecture is diluted Lombardic, influenced perhaps by Golders Green. An attempt was made to match the quality of the exterior with the internal fittings. A contemporary description mentions the Indian silver greywood panelling in the north chapel and the oak equivalent in the south. Both had '. . . ceilings of special design and a moderate use of stained glass . . . the catafalques are built in Clipsham stone with a bronze rim.' It is unfortunate that the later addition of a mean and badly detailed columbarium and the accumulated clutter of memorial plaques to the rear of Dawber's buildings have spoiled his original concept.

Burials commenced in 1961 adopting the lawn principles. This has severely restricted individuality, although aided maintenance. More recently a section has been provided for the burial of children.

FOREST PARK CEMETERY AND CREMATORIUM
Forest Road, Hainault, Essex

Founded: 2005
Owner: The Westerleigh Group PLC
Acreage: 18

London's newest cemetery and crematorium was opened, not surprisingly, on the edge of the metropolitan area. Located away from the suburban inter-war housing that followed the building of the Central Line, Forest Park occupies a prominent site adjacent to Hainault country park.

The entrance leads directly to the chapel, beyond which is separate office accommodation. Both are built of pale brick and stained timber, in the same style as a modern petrol station or supermarket. The decoration of the chapel is sparse and comprises bare brick and white paint with a curtained proscenium arch. Cultural and religious symbols are kept to a minimum and are inter-changeable.

Many of the design faults of early crematoria or those in converted cemetery chapels have been eliminated at Forest Park. The building is spacious, light, has good access and a sense of 'flow' as mourners move and gather under the *porte cochère* and enter the chapel by the main entrance. After the service they leave through a side door into a covered flower-viewing area.

Opposite the crematorium chapel is the Garden of Remembrance with an array of memorials, dedicated flowers bed, miniature kerb memorials, a few benches and 'Sanctum' vaults for caskets of ashes. The positioning of these modern *memento mori* looks somewhat random. Beyond is the cemetery accommodating both lawn and full memorials in a variety of stone.

Planting is gradually developing at Forest Park. The banks built-up around the crematorium and car park have been generously stocked (with over 11,000 plants and shrubs) and elsewhere trees such as red oak, silver birch, ornamental 'Chanticleer' pear and, appropriately, London planes, may in time soften the landscape of this exposed site which, despite limitations, provides much needed burial space for this corner of north east London.

FULHAM CEMETERY
Fulham Palace Road, SW6

Founded: 1865
Owner: London Borough of Hammersmith and Fulham
Acreage: 13

A neat rectangle of land with an extra tongue that extends to Munster Road added in 1874, and a further addition in 1880. The cemetery was designed by John Hall (while a pupil of A.W. Blomfield), who built the now uninhabited lodge, dated 1865, and the chapels, both in Gothic style. The latter is distinguished by a hefty bellcote over the west end and a scene of the Resurrection carved in the tympanum. There was also a Dissenter's chapel, but this has been demolished as has the mortuary designed by R. Cox in 1880.

The cemetery was consecrated on 3 August 1865 and the first interment later in the day was of a child. Astonishingly for the 1860s, the thirteenth interment was that of a centenarian from the Fulham Union Workhouse.

Fulham Palace Road: The tympanum above the chapel door depicting the Resurrection

The best tombs are to the north of the surviving chapel, but none are very special and all are threatened. A night attack in the 1980s by vandals caused the decapitation of about thirty tombs, and the Council is now pursuing a policy of grassing over all graves older than fifty years. This has allowed for easy maintenance, which is of a comparatively high standard, and reopened space for a 'garden of rest', but it has destroyed all traces of the traditional nineteenth-century cemetery. A more sympathetic and selective policy is required before modest reminders of Fulham's past, such as the tomb 'erected by intimate friends in memory of the sad death of James Croft who was killed on the District Railway on October 2nd 1890', are lost.

WILLIAM BLAKELEY 1830–97
Comic actor well known as a 'mugger' on account of the comic faces he pulled on stage.

LIEUT.GEN.SIR BURKE CUPPAGE 1794–1877
Governor of Jersey, 1863–68.

ROBERT DALZELL, 15TH EARL OF CARNWATH 1847–1910
A member of one of the oldest Scottish families and a representative peer for Scotland.

GOLDERS GREEN CREMATORIUM
Hoop Lane, NW11

Founded: 1902
Owner: The London Cremation Company
Acreage: 12

In 1900, after years of battling against public prejudice, the Cremation Society of England was sufficiently encouraged by the slow but steady national increase in the number of cremations to launch the London Cremation Society.[1] Since 1885, Londoners wishing to be cremated had been transported by rail from the London Necropolis Station in Westminster Bridge Road to Woking in Surrey where the first crematorium had been built. It was, however, an inconvenient journey and London was lagging behind six northern towns which already had crematoria of their own. The new Society's 'idea of establishing a crematorium within easy driving distance of central London' was realised by the purchase of land at Golders Green for £6,000 and Sir Ernest George with his partner Alfred Yeates were employed to design the buildings. William Robinson, a member of the Cremation Society Council and prolific gardening writer and horticulturalist, laid out the gardens. Golders Green was finally opened in 1902 by Sir Henry Thompson, Queen Victoria's surgeon and founder president of the Cremation Society.

Sir Ernest George was the architect of several large neo-Georgian country houses as well as Claridges Hotel, but his crematorium design is very different. He envisaged a range of red brick buildings in Lombardic style linked by a 240ft long south cloister. In fact construction was piecemeal as money became available. Among the earliest buildings was the spacious and dignified west chapel, which set the standard for later additions, mercifully free of most of the coy fripperies that disfigure so many of the recent crematoria. It is empty of monuments save a fine bust of Sir Henry Thompson, who died in 1904, and a plaque to the Maharajah of Cooch Behar and his family (see below).

Another early building was the Ernest George mausoleum, which runs parallel to the cloisters with a pavilion tower at each end. A central apse is decorated with a brilliantly coloured mosaic and along the walls are spaces for 1,700 cinerary urns and caskets. These are elaborately designed in metalwork, alabaster and ceramics. Sigmund Freud's ashes are contained in a Greek vase. In 1911 the large columbarium was built on five levels with small niches masking every wall filled with an urn or casket. The Duke of Bedford's chapel was built in the same year. The 9th Duke had helped finance the Woking crematorium and built a small crematory there which was first used for his own cremation in 1891. The 11th Duke was responsible for the Bedford chapel and his interest in cremation was such that in 1934 he became president of the Cremation Society.

At first there were four gas furnaces which produced a heat of '2,000° Fahr., something near the melting point of silver'. *The Building News* described the process:

> The furnace is ready for cremation as soon as the cremating chambers glow with a bright orange colour. The body to be cremated can then be introduced, and after about an hour the process is completed and the remains are by means of an asbestos brush pushed into the hopper, falling hence, without being touched by human hands, into the urn which has previously been placed underneath.[2]

The cloister was completed in 1914, the smaller columbarium in 1916, the east chapel by Mitchell and Bridgewater in 1938 and the chapel of memory in 1939. Other buildings have been added to the complex and include a small tea room.

In contrast to this impressive architectural ensemble there is barely a tomb in sight although two mighty mausolea on the east side of the ground compensate for this by their quality. The Martin Smith mausoleum is a large brick building in the style of Wren dated 1905. Near it is the extraordinary Philipson mausoleum dating from 1914–16, designed by Sir Edwin Lutyens. It resembles a small circular temple with an additional concentric Portland stone skin in lattice form. The space between the inner and outer walls was intended to be planted with roses. Inside, two ceramic urns rest on a pedestal opposite the door. One freestanding monument of note is a charming bronze sculpture of a girl being lifted heavenwards by a mysterious draped figure 'Into the Silent Land'. The bronze, by Henry Pegram, was a gift to the crematorium from the Royal Society of Arts in 1937. Another bronze statue commemorates the industrial magnate Ghanshyamdas Birla. The war memorial was designed by Edward Maufe.

On almost every wall at Golders Green there are commemorative tablets. The earlier ones are set in the cloister walls, representative of a wide variety of designs. Several are circular glazed terracotta plaques in the style of the della Robbia family. More recently, simple rectangular slabs in stone or Westmoreland slate have been used. Very effective too is the custom of planting croci in the ash strewn remembrance lawn. In spring the huge display of purple and white flowers is unrivalled in London.

By the 1930s over one quarter of all cremations in Britain were performed at Golders Green. However, the competition of newer municipal crematoria in London, (the City of London also opened in 1902, Hendon in 1922, a further eight in the 1930s and eight more in the 1950s), has had its effect. The number of cremations at Golders Green reached a peak of about 7,500

Golders Green: The Philipson mausoleum by Sir Edward Lutyens (1914).

Golders Green: The Smith mausoleum by Paul Phipps (1904–5).

Golders Green: Ghanshyamdas Birla (1983) looking towards the cloister.

Golders Green: The Watkins memorial in the cloister

Golders Green: 'into the silent land' by Henry Pegram (1924 and installed in 1937)

per year in the 1950s but has now fallen to an average of about 2,000. Nevertheless, over 314,000 cremations have been performed here since 1902, far more than at any other British crematorium.

The full story of the crematorium can be found in *Golders Green Crematorium 1902–2002: A London Centenary in Context* by Peter C. Jupp and Hilary J. Grainger available from the crematorium.

The following have been cremated at Golders Green and are commemorated by a plaque or casket. (Many other celebrated people have been cremated here but are not represented by any monument).

WILLIAM ALLEN 1888–1958
Railwayman, chief of establishment and staff, British Transport Commission.

EDWARD ARMSTRONG 1878–1945
Scientist and chairman of the Royal Society of Arts 1943–45.

SIR JAMES BAILLIE 1873–1951
Philosopher and Vice Chancellor of Leeds University 1943–45.

ERNEST BEVIN 1881–1951
Trade unionist leader known as 'the Dockers' K.C.' Labour M.P. for Wandsworth 1940–50 and East Woolwich 1950–51, wartime Minister of Labour and Foreign Secretary 1945–51.

WILLIAM, LORD BIRKETT OF ULVERSTON, 1883–1962
One of the judges at the Nuremberg war trials and a Lord Justice of Appeal 1950–57.

THOMAS BURKE 1886–1943
Writer of many books on the history of London.

SIR PHILIP BURNE-JONES 1861–1926
Artist. Son of Sir Edward, the Pre-Raphaelite.

NEVILLE CHAMBERLAIN 1869–1940
A Birmingham Conservative M.P. 1918–40, Prime Minister 1937–40. His ashes are buried in Westminster Abbey.

ERIC COATES 1886–1957
Composer and conductor, his best known work is 'The Dam Busters March'.

LIONEL, LORD COHEN OF WALMER 1888–1973
Lord of Appeal 1951–60.

H.H. THE MAHARAJAH SIR NRIPENDRA OF COOCH-BEHAR 1862–1911
Honorary A.D.C. to Edward VII, Grand Senior Warden of England and big game hunter.

EDWARD, LORD DALTON OF FOREST AND FIRTH, 1887–1962
Lawyer, economist and Labour M.P. for Camberwell 1924–29 and Bishop Auckland 1935–59, he held several ministerial positions including Chancellorship of the Exchequer 1945–47.

SIR CHARLES DAVIS 1873–1938
The first Under-Secretary of State for Dominion Affairs 1925–30.

SIR GUY DAWBER 1861–1938
Architect, he specialised in the design of country houses, the first chairman of the Council for Protection of Rural England.

SIR JAMES DEWAR 1842–1943
Natural philosopher and inventor of the thermos flask.

CHARLES DOUGHTY 1843–1926
'Poet, patriot, explorer'; he wrote *Travels in Arabia Deserta* (1888), describing his journeys in Arabia, sometimes disguised as an arab.

KATHLEEN FERRIER 1912–53
Contralto singer.

SIR ALEXANDER FLEMING 1881–1955
Bacteriologist and discoverer of penicillin in 1928, awarded the Nobel Prize for medicine 1945. His ashes are buried in St Paul's.

ERIC FOGG 1903–39
Composer and music director of the BBC empire service 1934–39.

SIR JOHN FOX 1874–1944
Government chemist.

SIR GEORGE FRAMPTON 1860–1928
Sculptor in the Arts and Crafts movement. 'Peter Pan' (1912) in Kensington Gardens is his best known work.

SIGMUND FREUD 1856–1939
Austrian born pioneer of psychoanalysis, together with his wife. His ashes repose in a Greek urn given to him by Princess Marie Bonaparte.

SIR FORREST FULTON 1846–1925
Lawyer, Recorder of London 1900–22.

HUGH GAITSKELL 1906–63
Labour politician and economist, M.P. for Leeds South from 1945, leader of the Labour Party 1955–63.

SIR WILLIAM GARSTIN 1849–1925
Engineer, took part in building the Aswan Dam. A director of the Suez Canal Company.

ADELINE GENÉE-ISITT 1878–1970
Founder president of the Royal Academy of Dancing 1920–54.

SIR ERNEST GEORGE 1839–1922
Successful country house architect, his London buildings include Golders Green crematorium and Claridges Hotel.

ELINOR GLYN 1864–1943
Authoress of romantic novels, Hollywood script-writer and *femme fatale*.

ARTHUR GREENWOOD 1880–1954
Labour politician, M.P. for Nelson and Colne 1922–31 and Wakefield 1932–54, deputy leader of the party 1935–42.

SIR ROBERT HAY-DRUMMOND 1840–1926
Diplomat and Arabist.

EMANUEL HEDMONDT 1857–1940
American tenor, 'Interpreter of Wagner'.

ARTHUR HENDERSON 1863–1935
Trade unionist and Labour politician, the party's first Home Secretary 1924, Foreign Secretary 1929–31, winner of the Nobel Peace Prize 1934.

GEORGE JACK 1855–1931
Architect and craftsman. He worked for William Morris and wrote a manual on wood carving.

JESSIE JACOB 1890–1933
Stained glass artist.

HERBERT JOLOWICZ 1890–1954
Professor of Roman law, London University 1941, professor of civil law, Oxford University 1948.

RUDYARD KIPLING 1865–1936
Author and traveller, active on the War Graves Commission. The 'Last Post' is sounded at The Menin Gate by his endowment.

SIR MERVYN MACCARTNEY 1853–1932
Architect in the neo-classical tradition, editor of the *Architectural Review*.

SIR JAMES MACKENZIE 1853–1925
Physician at the London Hospital, he specialised in diseases of the heart.

TOM MANN 1856–1941
Trade unionist, first president of the Dockers' Union and a founder member of the British Communist Party 1920.

SIMON, LORD MARKS OF BROUGHTON 1888–1964
Managing director of Marks and Spencer which he established with Israel Sieff (see below).

SID MITRA 1856–1925
Indian scholar and journalist, he 'introduced Hindu medicine into Europe'.

BENNO MOISEIWITCH 1890–1963
Russian born concert pianist.

PRINCE HYDER WAHID OF MYSORE 1837–1923
Of the old Hindu reigning family of Mysore.

CONSTANTINE NABOKOFF 1871–1927
Chargé d'Affaires at the Russian Imperial Embassy.

RICHARD NORTHCOTT 1871–1931
Music critic and archivist of the Royal Opera Company.

IVOR NOVELLO 1893–1951
Actor, composer and playwright, his matinee idol status attracted tens of thousands of mourners to his funeral.

NORMAN O'NEILL 1875–1934
Composer, particularly of ballets and songs.

SIR ALEXANDER ONSLOW 1842–1908
Chief Justice of Western Australia 1883–1901.

PRINCESS OSTAFMEDJY –1934
A 'great artist'.

ANNA PAVLOVA 1881–1928
Russian born ballerina, she excelled in classical roles such as 'Giselle' and 'Swan Lake'.

SIR ISAAC PITMAN 1813–97
Inventor of a very successful system of shorthand based on phonetic spelling (cremated at Woking).

HARRY POLLITT 1890–1966
Chairman and a founder member of the British Communist Party.

ADM. SIR ROBERT PRENDERGAST 1864–1946
A.D.C. to George V.

H.H. THE RAJAH OF PUDUKOTA 1875–1928
Of Madras together with his wife, the Ranee.

SIR WILLIAM REYNOLDS-STEPHENS 1862–1943
Sculptor and president of the Royal Society of British Sculptors 1931–33.

WILLIAM ROBINSON 1838–1935
Gardener and writer. He campaigned against the artificial elements in Victorian gardening and was a keen advocate of cremation.

VICE ADM. SIR CHARLES ROYDS 1876–1931
Deputy Commissioner of the Metropolitan Police.

SIR FELIX SEMON 1849–1921
Laryngologist and physician to Edward VII.

SIR ALFRED SHARPE 1853–1935
First governor of Nyasaland 1907–1910.

GEORGE, LORD SHEPHERD OF SPALDING, 1881–1954
Labour Party national agent 1929–46, chief whip in the House of Lords 1949–54.

ISRAEL, LORD SIEFF 1890–1972
Managing director of Marks and Spencer 1916, vice-president of the World Jewish Congress, farmer and horticulturalist.

MARTIN SMITH –1905
First chairman of the London Cremation Society.

WILLIAM STEKEL 1868–1940
An Austrian psychologist and 'Founder of active psychoanalysis'.

WILHELMINA STITCH 1888–1936
Authoress.

BRAM STOKER 1847–1912
Irish author of *Dracula* and associate of Henry Irving in managing the Lyceum theatre.

MARIE STOPES 1880–1958
Pioneer advocate of birth control, her book *Married Love* was published in 1918.

JOHN SWINBURNE-HANHAM 1860–1935
Vice-president of the Cremation Society of England, director of Golders Green Crematorium 1900–34.

CHARLES, LORD SWINFEN OF CHERTSEY, 1851–1919
Master of the Rolls, 1918–19.

SIR HENRY THOMPSON 1820–1904
Founder president of the Cremation Society, physician, artist, author and astronomer.

DMITRI TZOKOV –1926
Bulgarian ambassador to Britain.

RALPH VAUGHAN WILLIAMS 1872–1958
Composer, he wrote nine symphonies besides choral works, ballet and chamber music. Much of his work was inspired by traditional English music.

CHARLES VOYSEY 1857–1941
Architect and designer, often regarded as a pioneer of the modern movement.

COL. THOMAS WATSON 1867–1917
Won the V.C. in the Mohmand Campaign, India, 1897.

SIR CUTHBERT WHITAKER 1873–1950
Editor of *Whitaker's Almanac*.

JOSEPH WOODWARD 1872–1945
An authority on sea lions. Employed by the Navy for training them to track down submarines in the Great War.

THE GREAT NORTHERN CEMETERY (NEW SOUTHGATE CREMATORIUM)
BRUNSWICK PARK ROAD, N11

Founded: 1861
Owner: The Westerleigh Group PLC
Acreage: 60

Following the campaign in the 1840s to clear up London's overflowing graveyards, a number of new private cemetery companies were formed. One of the most ambitious was the Great Northern Cemetery Company which employed an architect, Alexander Spurr, to design a cemetery originally intended to cover some 200 acres planned around a series of concentric paths. At the hub of the plan a chapel was built in Early English lancet style capped by an imposing broach spire 150 feet tall. It is one of London's finest cemetery chapels, even though the intended catacomb crypt was never completed and in the 1950s the interior was radically altered by its conversion into a crematorium. As it happened this development at long last fulfilled the efforts of the infant Cremation Society of England, launched in 1874, when the cemetery might have witnessed history if the Society had had its way.[1] In that year the Great Northern directors offered the Society land on which to build the country's first crematorium, but it was unable to achieve its purpose after the Bishop of Rochester intervened forbidding it from using consecrated ground. The Society was forced to wait four years before finding a more suitable site at Woking.

At one time mourners could travel to the Great Northern via a branch line of the Great Northern railway. *The Builder* described the process:

> . . . a station . . . where is a reception room, where the bodies of persons belonging to families in straitened circumstances may be deposited until the appointed day of sepulture . . .[2] One doorway leads to an apartment, and in the centre of this hall is a space for the reception of coffins: then by means of a machine, worked by hydraulic power, the remains of the dead are lowered, slowly and silently, to a place below, which communicates with the mortuary, when necessary, or with the platform of the Railway station. . .[3] By this accommodation the dead may be at once removed from among the living. The time occupied in transit from the York Road Station (at Kings Cross) to Colney Hatch is about fifteen minutes. At the latter station a siding nearly a mile in length is made to the private cemetery station of The Company, but parallel to the main line. . .[4] Each coffin is placed upon a bier, which moves upon wheels, followed by friends.'[5]

The service was not well patronised and only ran from 1861 until 1863. No trace of the railway buildings remain which were in a section of the cemetery on the other side of East Barnet Lane (now Brunswick Park Road). Those buried in that area were exhumed in 1971 and reburied in the main cemetery.

The Great Northern is now only entered through elaborate gargoyled Gothic gatepiers. Adjacent is the lodge which has been sold and some of its doorways bricked up but it is well maintained. The view from the main entrance is one of a heavily planted landscape and rhododendron drives. This effectively camouflages all the tombstones. The trees are now a mature size including some large yews that the Victorians would have appreciated. Despite a low level of maintenance the south west part of the cemetery remains one of the most attractive rural spots in north London.

The north east is less well preserved. In the 1960s the Hendon Reform Synagogue Cemetery and columbarium were built there. Around this site the Gardens of Remembrance have been developed with the usual assortment of commemorative paraphanalia. Beyond is a very large section for Greek burials and further ground is being reclaimed. There appears to be a *laissez-faire* policy towards memorial regulations and every conceivable design and material (including fibreglass) can be found. Overlooking it all is a large statue of the Virgin Mary beneath a canopy supported on five slim Doric columns – all highly polished.

As expected of a large and old established cemetery, the Great Northern has a number of unusual monuments including several marking communal graves. The earliest commemorates the reinterred dead removed from the Savoy Chapel in the Strand following a fire there in 1864. Another monument refers to '29 coffins and 197 boxes of human remains from St Michael Bassishaw', a City church designed by Wren and demolished in 1900. The site includes some eighteenth-century tomb slabs. Remains from the churchyard of the City church, St Mary Mounthaw, destroyed in 1666, were moved here in 1868 on the building of Queen Victoria Street. There are also remains from St Andrew by the Wardrobe, St Nicholas Cole Abbey and the former St Nicholas Olave, destroyed in 1666. In 1880, construction of the Thames embankment led to the destruction of the German Lutheran Church in the Savoy and the transfer of the graveyard contents here.

Towards the end of the nineteenth century, the Society of Friends erected a huge obelisk in an unconsecrated area of the cemetery. It was intended that deceased Quakers would be buried in the immediate vicinity. The obelisk, although now stripped of its bronze plaques and surrounded by tombs, remains an impressive landmark. Nearby a more modest stone slab bears a German inscription. It records the names of fifty-one German civilians who died at Alexandra Palace while interned there during the Great War.

There are a number of large memorials hidden behind the hedge which screens the crematorium car park from the cemetery, including one to the Beauclear family complete with iron railings. Nearby is an anonymous slender octagonal gothic column surmounted by a bronze cross. A more recent memorial in white marble states emphatically: 'Born 16.12.1838, Died: Never'.

Great Northern: A view of the gates on Brunswick Park Road before relocation into the cemetery grounds

One monument in the cemetery, however, eclipses all others. Set in a walled flower garden is a massive marble column. It supports a Corinthian capital and a golden eagle standing on a globe. The inscription simply says, 'Shogi Effendi', the name of the leader of the Baha'i faith who died on a visit to London. The Great Northern was chosen for his tomb because it fulfilled the requirement of the faith that burial should take place within one hour's journey of the place of death. The grave is regarded by followers of the Baha'i faith as 'the most sacred spot in the West'. It was the good fortune of the National Spiritual Assembly of the Baha'i's that the gatepiers which stood on land now sold for housing, have been relocated near the chapel. They act as an impressive entrance to this section of the cemetery.

RICHARD BETHELL, 1ST LORD WESTBURY, 1800–73
Barrister, his annual income in the 1840s was estimated to exceed £20,000. Liberal M.P. for Aylesbury and Wolverhampton, Solicitor General 1851–56, Attorney General 1856, Lord Chancellor 1861–65.

SHOGI EFFENDI 1896–1957
Grandson of the founder of the Baha'i Faith, he assumed leadership of the Faith from the age of twenty-four until his death. Among his many written works was a history of the Faith.

ALFRED BARING GARROD 1819–1907
Physician who helped discover the cause of gout.

ALAN ROSS MCWHIRTER 1925–75
Known as Ross McWhirter, with his twin brother, Norris McWhirter they co-founded the *Guiness Book of Records.*

ALEXANDER SPURR –1873
Architect of the cemetery chapel and superintendent of the cemetery.

BALDASSARE VISCARDINI 1830–96
A veteran of Garibaldi's liberating campaign in Italy.

Great Northern: The chapel designed by Andrew Spurr (1861). The spire is 150 ft high

GREENFORD PARK CEMETERY
Windmill Lane, Greenford, Middx.

Founded: 1901
Owner: London Borough of Ealing
Acreage: 32

Set back in a dip off the busy Greenford Road, this was the last of the four cemeteries opened by the Abney Park Cemetery Company, owners of Abney Park, Chingford Mount and Hendon Park. The original gate piers have disappeared along with the lodge and its 1970s replacement. The main drive rises to a substantial symmetrically planned Art and Crafts style chapel with a hint of Gothic Tudor. A pair of oversized castellated porches dominate each end and, above them, are five light mullion and transom windows, a pattern repeated in the gabled bays each side of the chapel. The building materials are brick and tile but the detailing is emphasised by the use of white paint. Inside, the pew seating is organised in collegiate style. Dedicated in July 1931, the chapel stands prominently among mature deciduous trees and well-maintained flower beds.

Plans in the mid 1960s to build a crematorium at Greenford Park came to nothing and finally, in 1966, the cemetery was acquired by the borough from its original owners. Land adjoining has been reclaimed and prepared for burials.

There are no significant memorials.

Wilf Slack 1953–89
England Test cricketer, died playing cricket and is buried with his bat.

GREENLAWN MEMORIAL PARK
Chelsham Road, Warlingham, Surrey

Founded: 1938
Owner: London Borough of Croydon
Acreage: 6½

Greenlawn was one of a new breed of burial grounds to open in the twentieth century in stark contrast to those developed by the Victorian pioneers one hundred years earlier. Here, as *The Times* so well expressed, the, '... first consideration will be the preservation of the natural beauty of the scene. In place of the tombstones familiar in most cemeteries the trust will restrict memorials to tablets of bronze set flush with the turf, thus preserving the park-like appearance of the grounds.'[1]

First impressions of this cemetery are promising. Its rural location on the outskirts of the borough is reminiscent of the cemeteries at Plaistow or Hendon and its brick gatehouse, through which the driveway passes, looks smart and practical. Beyond it the drive divides and thereafter initial expectations become horridly unfulfilled. On one side is a rose garden, with the usual bird bath, surrounded by a mosaic of bronze tablets marking the graves. On the other are 'Sanctum Vaults' for cremated ashes. Everywhere floral tributes struggle to survive. 'Natural beauty' is now an ironic description for a landscape that resembles a nasty rash of botanical measles.

The T-shaped site then opens out. A narrow boundary road provides access to the lawns where burials take place. Planting is minimal and unfortunately native forest trees have been sacrificed for ornamentals which are haphazardly dotted about in what could be mistaken for a golf course fairway. Beyond a hedge at the cemetery's south end is a Muslim burial section.

Although no permanent unauthorised memorials are evident, it is clear the rigid restrictions do little to satisfy the need to mark informally the burial plots as flower pots, planters and hanging lamps proliferate in chaotic disarray.

There is no chapel and the memorial park has been managed by the London Borough of Croydon since 1947.

GREENWICH CEMETERY
WELL HALL ROAD, SE9

Founded: 1856
Owner: London Borough of Greenwich
Acreage: 22½

A hill site was the dream of the early cemetery planners who achieved dramatic results in such circumstances at Highgate and Père Lachaise. The elevated site at Greenwich is certainly spectacular with a huge panorama of London below it, but the cemetery itself is a more modest creation.

It is set back from the main road beyond a green sward. A large boarded-up lodge bears the date 1922. The main path then follows the contour near the hilltop beside which were built two large but lumpish Gothic chapels. From the end of the path 'The Great War Heroes' Corner' commands views of Crystal Palace, the City and Canary Wharf. The corner incorporates the usual cross of sacrifice and hundreds of names on bronze plaques of those killed in the war. Nearby is a small characteristically neat Commonwealth burial ground. This otherwise noble concept is ruined by the proximity of a preposterous bus shelter type building of which there are three in the cemetery.

Greenwich has few monuments of interest. A little crescendo of larger ones surrounds the Church of England chapel but most are simple pointed headstones. A few coffin shaped stones are also in evidence, a rare design in London cemeteries, including the Parsons vault with a short flight of steps leading to a substantial padlocked door. Unique are the large horizontal incised slabs erected for Henry Smith (died 1923) and his family with heraldic devices, and elsewhere a glass 'headstone' engraved with details of the deceased is dated about 1928 but now, predictably, is smashed and indecipherable.

Two special sections of the cemetery have been set aside, one for Norwegians who died in England as refugees during the last war, and another for children, recognisable by the rows of diminutive headstones.

Finally there are the unusual circumstances surrounding the remains of Nicholas Ogareff who died in Russia in 1877. Eighty-nine years later his body was exhumed, cremated and transported to Greenwich for reburial.

GEN. SIR ARTHUR HOLLAND 1862–1927
Conservative M.P. for Northampton 1924–27, commandant of the Royal Military Academy, Woolwich.

Surg.Gen.James Jameson 1837–1904
Director general army medical services during the Boer War and commander of a British ambulance division in the Franco-Prussian war.

Sir William Poland 1797–1884
Doctor and Sheriff of London and Middlesex 1831.

Christopher Rowland 1929–67
Labour M.P. for Meriden 1964–67.

Sir Andrew Scott 1857–1939
Lawyer and secretary of Lloyds Register of Shipping.

Capt.Walter Stone 1891–1917
V.C., awarded posthumously following a heroic rearguard action at Cambrai.

GROVE PARK CEMETERY
Marvels Lane, SE12

Founded: 1935
Owner: London Borough of Lewisham
Acreage: 33

Grove Park was a brave attempt to create the 1930s version of a well planned cemetery that Loudon had envisaged almost a hundred years previously. It enjoys a splendid hill site and was ambitiously and imaginatively designed. A smart office (now a private residence) and lodge either side of the main entrance gate is a prelude to an expansive drive bordered by thickets of ornamental shrubs and trees. Civic pride in the venture is commemorated by a Portland stone drinking fountain incorporating an urn inscribed with the information that the Metropolitan Borough of Deptford engineer, H. Morley Lawson designed the cemetery and that it was opened by the Mayor in June 1935. It became the property of the London Borough of Lewisham upon amalgamation of the Boroughs of Lewisham and Deptford in 1965.

To the west the hillside was landscaped with paved terraces incorporating scenic viewpoints with seats and an ornamental pool constructed of fashionably white painted concrete. Surrounded by Torbay palms, the timber chapel

Grove Park: The date of the cemetery's opening in 1935 is noted on this Portland stone drinking fountain in the form of an urn

more than faintly resembles a Bisley shooting lodge, but nevertheless has pointed windows and is a serviceable building. To the north a weathered headstone in neo-Georgian style records the death of Charles Terry on 17 September 1935 and the fact that he was the first to be buried in the new cemetery.

But there the civic vision ends. The headstone is cracked and stands alone, the terraces are unkempt, and the pool is now a flower bed. The reason is simple: a more economical form of commemoration has been discovered. White marble tombs in serried ranks are now creeping down the hillside devoid of any pretence towards landscaping. The lawn cemetery technique has superseded the 30s blueprint and sadly wastes the potential so carefully planned.

HELMUTH BARTH 1906-46
Circus horse trainer with Sangers Circus, killed at Romford.

GUNNERSBURY CEMETERY
GUNNERSBURY AVENUE, W4

Founded: 1929
Owner: Royal Borough of Kensington and Chelsea
Acreage: 22

The cemetery is built on land originally part of the Rothschilds' Gunnersbury Park estate, but there is nothing of architectural significance here. The present cemetery buildings, including the chapel are simple brick structures without stylistic pretensions. The original scheme comprised two chapels designed by Arthur Knapp-Fisher, the winner of a competition in 1937.[1] The Anglican chapel was typical of its period – a monumental brick block punctuated by tall unadorned arched windows. It was buttressed north and south by a single storey mortuary and vestry, by a porch to the west and a tall east apse. To add emphasis to their height, each elevation was slightly battered. It was an unusually fine building for a cemetery and its loss after the Second World War is regretted. The Nonconformist chapel remains in use and credit must be given to the Royal Borough on the standard of maintenance lavished on the cemetery.

The monuments too tend towards the plain although some have beautifully lettered inscriptions. The one exceptional sculpture of Nereo Cescott playing his accordion has been smashed by vandals. Recently a few flashy exceptions have appeared in the glossiest of polished marble embellished with gold lettering, complemented by the fashion of a colour photograph of the deceased inset in the headstone.

But all pales in comparison with the great black obelisk of the Katyn memorial designed by Louis Fitzgibbon and Count Stefan Zamoyski. This was dedicated on 18 September 1976, amid great controversy, 'In remembrance of 14,500 Polish prisoners of war who disappeared in 1940 from camps at Kozielsk, Stavobielsk and Ostaszkow of whom 4,500 were later identified in mass graves at Katyn near Smolensk'. Two panels added at the foot of the obelisk states 'Murdered by the Soviet Secret Police on Stalin's orders 1940', and 'Finally admitted in April 1990 by the U.S.S.R. after 50 years shameful denial of the truth.' Soil from the graves is interred in a casket under the memorial. The monument stands on the site of the former Anglican chapel and is a focus for the large Polish community in Ealing and elsewhere.

Polish tombs, together with most other East European nationalities dominate the Roman Catholic, southern half of the cemetery. White Russians are especially numerous, some from very grand origins like the Romanoff Vsevolod, Prince of Russia. Others are more modest. One slab lists five names and the inscription, 'Here rests the Bodies of Cossacks'. In this company English names and occupations appear more than usually prosaic save one who 'Fell to her death on Mount Popocatepetl Mexico'.

Denzil Batchelor 1906–69
Writer, broadcaster, sporting journalist on *Picture Post* and *bon viveur*.

Rear Adm. William Beresford Whyte, 1863–1932.
Paymaster of the Fleet.

Gen. Tadeusz Bór-Komorowski 1895–1966
Commander of the Polish resistance 1943–44. In August 1944 he ordered the Warsaw uprising and was appointed Commander in Chief of the Polish forces in the West.

William, Lord Broughshane of Kensington, 1872–1953
Mayor, 1913–19, and Conservative M.P. for Kensington 1918–45. During the Great War he raised and equipped three battalions at his own expense.

Hugh Burden 1913–1985
Television and radio actor.

George, Lord Cole –1979
Chairman of Unilever 1960–70 and Rolls Royce 1970–72.

Ernestine Costa Bertolt –1959
Actress, pupil of Max Reinhardt and friend of Brecht.

Thomas Croft-Fraser –1956
Laird of Inverallochy, 'Choir Sacristan and Chief Master of Ceremonies of the Vatican Basilica'.

Rt. Rev. Charles Dowse 1862–1934
Bishop of Cork, 1912–33.

Sir Gerald Henderson 1886–1963
High Court judge in India.

Sir George Humphreys 1863–1945
Chief engineer L.C.C. 1912–24.

Rev. Arthur Ingram –1934
Royal chaplain at Hampton Court 1894–1926.

Gunnersbury: The Anglican Chapel designed by Arthur Knapp-Fisher (1937). It had a short life as it was destroyed after the Second World War

ADM. SIR FREDERICK LEARMONTH 1866–1941
Hydrographer to the Navy 1919–24.

SYDNEY LEE 1866–1949
Painter and engraver.

JULIUS LEPIANKIEWICZ 1910–73
Polish pianist.

CAPT. KENNETH MCCALLUM 1891–1963
For twenty years managing director of Trust Houses.

NICHOLAS MCCASKIE 1881–1967
Judge of the Court of Admiralty, recorder of Sheffield, 1941–57.

RT. REV. MGR. ALEXANDER MALYNOWSKI 1888–1957
Papal prelate, Vicar General for Ukrainian catholics.

AIR MARSHAL SIR HAROLD MARTIN 1918–88
Australian born bomber pilot. He took part in the 'Dambusters' raid on the Ruhr in 1943. In 1947 he set a new speed record for flying from London to Cape Town.

Gunnersbury: The black obelisk of the Katyn memorial photographed in 1980

ALFRED MESSINA, 1900–63, GUISEPPE MESSINA, 1879–1946
Maltese-born vice racketeers in post-war Soho.

CHARLES MORGAN 1894–1958
Novelist and drama critic for *The Times*.

SIR DESMOND MORTON 1891–1971
A.D.C. to Earl Haig 1917, civil servant, personal assistant to Sir Winston Churchill, 1940–46.

JOHN OGDON 1937–1989
Virtuoso pianist and composer.

GEN. A.A. ONOPRIENKO 1874–1922
Commander of the 16th Cavalry Division of the Russian Imperial Army.

VERA PAGE 1920–31
The subject of a cause célèbre following her murder in Kensington. Despite incriminating evidence, the chief suspect at the inquest was never charged with the offence.

SIR CAROL REED 1906–76
Film director. His masterpiece was *The Third Man* filmed in 1950.

KAZIMIERZ SABBAT 1913–1989
For ten years prime minister of the Polish government in exile and fifth president of the Polish republic in exile 1986–89.

GEOFFREY SHUTE 1892–1951
Colonial administrator in Nigeria 1915–39.

SIR MATTHEW SMITH 1879–1959
Artist, much influenced by the French fauves.

GEN. JOZEF SMOLENSKI 1894–1978
Polish cavalry officer, wrote the history of the 7th Lancers, after 1945 involved in many exiled Polish organisations.

EDMUND SOBOLEWSKI 1884–1974
Polish delegate to the United Nations.

AIR MARSHAL SIR HERBERT SPRECKLEY, 1904–63
Director General of Technical Services and controller of engineering and equipment at the Air Ministry.

ARCHBP. BESSAK TOUMAYAN 1912–81
Apostolic delegate and prelate of the Armenian church in London.

MARDA VANNE 1896–1970
Actress who specialised in 'parts of odd querulous or combative women'.

PRINCE VSEVOLOD 1914–73
'Prince of Russia', great-great-grandson of Czar Nicholas I and cousin of Nicholas II, last of the Russian emperors.

ADM. ARTHUR WAYMOUTH 1864–1936
Gunnery officer who invented the Waymouth Cooke range finder.

SIR ASTON WEBB 1849–1930
Architect, his practice at the turn of the century was the largest in England.

GREVILLE WYNNE 1919–90
Businessman and British intelligence agent in eastern Europe. Imprisoned in Russia for eighteen months on spying charges.

HAMMERSMITH CEMETERY
MARGRAVINE ROAD, W6

Founded: 1869
Owner: London Borough of Hammersmith and Fulham
Acreage: 17

Although no longer in normal use for burials, the cemetery offers a popular short cut between Barons Court tube and Fulham. It was laid out by George Saunders, a local architect who designed the Gothic style lodge and two chapels. The larger of the two, at the end of the main drive, was demolished in 1939 and only a shrubbery and CCTV camera mast mark the site. The remaining chapel, less its spire, stands boarded-up. Lodges at all three entrances are retained, although one has now been sold. An unusual building that survives in good condition, but as a toolshed, is the octagonal brick mortuary. The cost of purchasing the land and erecting the buildings was £15,104. Near the mortuary, shaded by several large trees, is a poignant group of little tombstones re-erected together to form 'Angels' Corner'. They mark the graves of infants who died in the 1920s and 30s.

The cemetery is maintained to a high standard. Neatly clipped hedges mark the boundary of the paths at the Barons Court end, but the pursuit of tidiness has led to the clearance of many memorials along with an impressive avenue of trees along the main drive.

Of the 83,197 recorded burials, a few, flnking the main drive, were commemorated by unusual tombs. Here are the throne and Corinthian column of the Fletcher family (1924), the pillowed bed of Sextus Van Os and his wife (1918), and the cello propped against a cross of Tom Brown, the bandmaster. Inside the main entrance and adjacent to the war memorial is a vulnerable terracotta mausoleum. Only one of its attractive stained glass panels remains. Sadly the figure of thirteen-year-old Jack Pierce dressed in scout uniform (1925) has been stolen. There is a magnificent cast bronze angel with sword on the memorial to George Boast (1895) by the local sculptor Aristide Fabbrucci, and the touching vignette of 'Abe' Smith, died 1923 'for many years gold digger Mount Browne N.S.W.'. A relief sculpture depicts him in his digger's hut beneath the epitaph:

> A kindly and a cheerful heart
> A smile for young and old
> A mind content, a cheery word
> A heart of purest gold.

SIR WILLIAM BULL 1863–1931
Maltravers Herald Extraordinary, solicitor and Conservative M.P. for Hammersmith 1900–29.

ROY BYFORD 1873–1939
Stage actor.

Hammersmith Old: Detail on the memorial to Abe Smith (1923)

HAMMERSMITH NEW CEMETERY & MORTLAKE CREMATORIUM
CLIFFORD AVENUE, SW14

Founded: 1926
Owner: London Borough of Hammersmith and Fulham/Mortlake Crematorium Board
Acreage: 20

Also known as Mortlake Cemetery, it was designed on a grandiose scale. Two sets of fanciful gate piers with acorn finials set the scene but the money ran out before both chapels could be completed. The survivor is a pleasant brick Gothic building designed by R. Hampton Clucas, the borough engineer and surveyor.[1] Planting was lavish and extraordinarily varied and maintenance is at a high standard. Monuments however are very pedestrian, and not likely to improve now that a lawn cemetery policy has been introduced. Greenhouses adjoining Mortlake Crematorium have been demolished to provide additional burial space, but these are soon to be filled.

Mortlake Crematorium was built to the north in 1939, a dour brick and tile building, by the Hammersmith borough engineer F. Douglas Barton, who had no architectural qualifications. The forty-eighth in the UK, it was opened by Lord Horder. The crematorium has been described as, '"Hacienda deco" in style, it looks as if it belongs more in New Mexico than Mortlake. Its wealth of deco features include a wonderful chapel, iron grilles, subtle brickwork and entrance pillars and gates.'[2]

JAMES COLLINS 1869–1934
Secretary to the Treasury in Australia 1916–26, his signature appears on all paper money issued in Australia between 1910 and 1926. Financial adviser to Australia in London 1926–33.

ARTHUR HAYNES 1914–66
Television comedian, probably the highest paid British artiste of his day. In 1961 was elected T.V. personality of the year.

HAMPSTEAD CEMETERY
FORTUNE GREEN ROAD, NW6

Founded: 1876
Owner: London Borough of Camden
Acreage: 37

The Hampstead environs have attracted the wealthy and famous for years and this distinction is reflected in the Hampstead cemetery. The standard is set at the entrance noticeable not so much for the Gothic lodge but the astonishing premises across the road built for John Cramb the monumental mason in 1886. Recently redecorated, its design is a bastard Egyptian style, short on vertical lines but rich in formalised lotus flower decoration. Also restored is the large lodge, with funding from the National Lottery, which has the unusual attribute of an elegant blue clock facing down the drive.

Returning to the iron cemetery gates, the broad main drive cuts a straight course through rows of impressive monuments, across a public footpath that bisects the cemetery and up to the *porte cochère* of the twin chapels. These were designed by Charles Bell (who is buried in the cemetery) in the Decorated style, each with an eastern apse.[1] The keystone in the *porte cochère* bears the date 1876. Bell was the winner of a design competition that also included two chapels and a lodge designed by Henry S. Legg.[2] Seen from the far end of the drive the central spire provides the appropriate accent pointing heavenwards. Only one of the chapels is now in use, its interior enriched in 1903 by three stained glass windows by the local artist J. Dudley Forsyth, and roof timbers resting on corbels, carved, according to *The Builder*, to represent the wild flowers of the neighbourhood. An unusual detail is the granite water fountain attached to the outer wall. The cemetery was extended by five acres in 1901.

It cost £2,500 to plant and lay out the grounds, work which was carried out by Joseph Fyfe Meston. Originally thirty gardeners kept the cemetery in trim, and despite reduced resources, a pleasant garden atmosphere is maintained with a good variety of trees including a large cedar and a mulberry. The best of the old monuments are generally near the main paths, most new graves having to find a place in the furthest corners. Aside from those bearing famous names there are some fine and eccentric works. The Bianchi monument proves that the stupendous in cemetery art did not end with the Victorians. A huge stone gateway, over which hovers an effigy of the deceased, was erected by the Italian chef at the Café Royal in the 1930s to commemorate the death of his opera singer wife in childbirth. The memorial was carved in Italy and constructed by the Kensal Green masonry firm of Farley.

Nearby is a complete stone organ, with music and stool (once stolen but now replaced), built in 1929 in memory of Charles Barritt. On the main drive was the extraordinary snake-entwined bronze urn marking the grave of the poet Arthur Frankau (1904). It was stolen in 1997. A further important work that disappeared but fortunately has been retrieved is the life-size bronze figure sculpted in 1923 by Sir William Goscombe John on his wife's tomb, later also his own. Among other memorials worth noting are the pink granite Egyptian temple to James 'Pasha' Wilson; the cluster of three angels on the Mordaunt Gwynne grave and the splendid memorial to the Fletcher family near the chapels.[3] Everywhere there are massive Celtic crosses, probably because so many of the dead are of Scottish origin.

Such extravagance is now hardly possible. Aside from expense, any design straying from the norm would incur official censure, although here at Hampstead individualism continues to flourish; two granite armchairs marking the memorial garden of the Kashni-Sepanji family (1989) can be found near the entrance. This is despite a cemetery regulation of 1934 that dictated the constraints, 'Headstones must not be less than three inches in thickness, in the front row next to any path they must not exceed five feet and in any other part of the ground five feet six inches in height.' Sepulchral art cannot flourish on those terms.

For a more extensive list of those buried at Hampstead see *The Good Grave Guide to Hampstead Cemetery* by Marianne Colloms and Dick Weindling.

FRED ARCHER 1857–86
Champion jockey, five times winner of the Derby, severe slimming ruined his health and he shot himself.

THOMAS BAYNES 1823–87
Editor of *The Edinburgh Guardian* and professor of logic, metaphysics and English literature at St Andrews University.

Hampstead: View of the cemetery in *The Builder* (1876)

Hampstead: The Bianchi monument (c. 1938)

SIR ROBERT BLAIR 1859–1935
First education officer for London.

DENNIS BRAIN 1921–57
Virtuoso French horn player, killed in a car accident.

JOHN BROWN 1830–1922
Congregational minister and biographer of John Bunyan.

DAME GLADYS COOPER 1888–1971
Gaiety girl and actress, she continued working up to her eighty-second year.

SIR WILLIAM CREMER 1838–1908
Trade unionist, politician and winner of the Nobel Peace Prize in 1903 for his efforts to promote international arbitration.

PHILIP DAWSON 1825–90
Secretary to the Railway Clearing House. He was buried in the presence of 1,200 clerks.

SEBASTIAN DE FERRANTI 1864–1930
Electrical engineer and inventor, he pioneered the use of long distance transmission of high power electrical currents.

SIR JOHN ERICHSEN 1818–96
Surgeon Extraordinary to Queen Victoria, professor of surgery at University College, London, president of the Royal College of Surgeons 1880.

Hampstead: Church organ in memory of Charles Barritt (1929)

ANDREW FISHER 1862–1928
Prime Minister of Australia 1908–9, 1910–13, 1914–15. Australian High Commissioner in London, 1916–21.

HARRY FISCHER 1907–77
Viennese born art dealer, publisher and bookseller.

SIR BANISTER FLETCHER 1833–99
Architect and author of *A History of Architecture on the Comparative Method*. The monument was designed by his son.

Hampstead: The Wilson sarcophagus, 'a respectable imitation of an Egyptian temple.'

Hampstead: The snake entwined bronze urn on the Frankau grave (1904). It was stolen in 1997

ARTHUR FRANKAU 1849–04
Poet, together with his wife, Julia, a novelist.

PAMELA FRANKAU 1908–67
Popular novelist and grand-daughter of Arthur.

KATE GREENAWAY 1846–1901
Painter and illustrator of children's books.

JOHN HARGRAVE 1894–1982
Artist and writer, founder of the Kibbo Kift, later the Social Credit Party: 'The Green Shirts'.

FREDERICK HENGLER 1820–87
Circus proprietor and riding instructor to the Royal family.

HENRY IRVING 1870–1919
Actor and barrister, son of Sir Henry Irving.

SIR WILLIAM GOSCOMBE JOHN 1860–1952
Welsh sculptor who worked in the 1890s under Rodin in Paris.

JOHN KENSIT 1853–1902
Religious agitator killed in a Liverpool riot.

CAPT. SIR BERTRAM LIMA 1886–1919
Chairman of the Daily Mirror and other newspaper companies.

JOSEPH, LORD LISTER 1827–1912
First exponent of antiseptic surgery.

MARIE LLOYD 1870–1922
Cockney music hall singer, 'The Queen of the Halls', rated by Max Beerbohm one of the three most memorable women of the age.

DWIN LONG 1829–91
Artist, specialising in oriental subjects.

JOSEPH MAAS 1847–86
Tenor opera singer. 'A great singer and a good man'.

JUSTIN MCCARTHY 1830–1912
Irish novelist, journalist and M.P. Chairman of the Irish anti-Parnell Party.

SIR GEORGE MACFARREN 1813–87
Composer and conductor, professor of music at Cambridge 1875–1887.

HENRY STACY MARKS 1829–98
Artist, specialising in natural history subjects.

SIR HENRY MIERS 1858–1942
Professor of mineralogy at Oxford, principal of London University 1908–15, vice chancellor of Manchester University 1915–26. Claimed he never slept more than four hours a night.

GRAND DUKE MIKHAIL MIKHAILOVICH 1861 1929
Exiled from Russia following his morganatic marriage to Sophie, Countess de Torby, 1868–1927, buried beside him.

DAVID MORGAN 1862–1937
X-ray pioneer and reformer of medical services at sea.

Hampstead: tomb sculpted by Sir William Goscombe John (1923). It was stolen but has since been recovered

SIR TOM O'BRIEN 1900–70
Twice president of the T.U.C., Nottingham Labour M.P. 1945–59.

REV. JOSEPH PARKER 1830–1902
Congregationalist preacher and writer.

JOSEPH PARRY 1841–1903
Welsh composer, he wrote 400 hymn tunes.

SIR ARTHUR PEARSON 1866–1921
President of the National Institute for the Blind and author of books on blindness.

ARTHUR PRINCE 1881–1948
Ventriloquist, buried with his dummy, the first to use the routine of drinking while his doll chattered on. Appeared at the first Royal Command Performance 1912.

SIR RICHARD QUAIN 1816–98
Chest specialist and Physician Extraordinary to Queen Victoria 1890.

EDWARD SEARLE 1809–87
Boat builder to Queen Victoria, the Emperors of Russia and Austria, and Oxford and Cambridge Universities. He patented the sliding seat in 1871.

ALBERT SHORT 1875–1932
Brother of Horace Short (q.v.). Developed the design of sea planes, died in the cockpit of one of his planes while landing.

HORACE SHORT 1872–1917
World traveller, captured and worshipped as a king by cannibals in the South Sea Islands, later wrote about his experiences. Became an aircraft designer and experimented with folding wings and torpedo carrying planes.

HENRY SMART 1813–79
Composer, organist and organ builder.

SIR ALLAN SMITH –1941
Engineer, solicitor and M.P. for Croydon South 1919–23.

FRED TERRY 1863–1933
Actor and brother of Ellen Terry, he specialised in Shakespearian roles.

FLORENCE UPTON 1873–1922
Children's author famous for the Golliwogg books first published in 1895.

HARROW CEMETERY
PINNER ROAD, HARROW, MIDDX.

Founded: 1888
Owner: London Borough of Harrow
Acreage: 7

Although by no means exceptional by London standards, this little cemetery provides unmistakeable evidence of Harrow's middle class history. Almost all the monuments are unassuming in size and design, so that a beautifully carved timber deadboard to a priest and a scaled down version of the Whitehall cenotaph are noticeable. Many belong to families connected with the army, the church and local government. The now redundant chapel is a functional red brick Perpendicular style building joined by a bridge to the office. At the cemetery entrance a spacious lodge was built of brick and tile hung in the fashionable late nineteenth-century style of Norman Shaw's suburban villas. It was designed by the Harrow Burial Board Surveyor, Frederick Cowell, but foolishly demolished in 1985.

It is distressing to witness the cemetery's current decay. Vandals have entered unchecked from the next door recreation ground and smashed tombs. The decapitated figure of ten-year-old 'Peter' near the chapel is typical of the destruction. The cemetery urgently needs attention, or at least recording, before these references to Harrow's past disappear.

SIR REGINALD BLAIR 1881–1962
Accountant, Conservative M.P. for Hendon 1935–45 and chairman of the Racehorse Betting Control Board.

HATTON CEMETERY
FAGGS ROAD, FELTHAM

Founded: 1974
Owner: London Borough of Hounslow
Acreage: 10 acres (and 12 in reserve)

Occupying a flat site beyond some enormous greenhouses, this cemetery must be one of the noisiest in London. Being immediately below the flight path into Heathrow airport, it gives the impression of almost forming part of the runway. There is no chapel and the majority of burials so far have been for Muslims. No attempt has been made at planting with the exception of a few hedges and trees. Thanks to the reserve acres, Hatton is likely to be the resting – but far from peaceful – place for many living in the Borough in the years to come.

HENDON CEMETERY AND CREMATORIUM
HOLDER'S HILL ROAD, NW4

Founded: 1899
Owner: London Borough of Barnet
Acreage: 40

The cemetery was founded by the Abney Park Cemetery Company which had been established at Stoke Newington in 1840. The Company had also opened Chingford Mount Cemetery in 1884 and established their last cemetery at Greenford in 1900. Land that comprised Dollis Farm was secretly purchased in 1899, much to the indignation of the local residents.[1] Although the matter had also been kept from the local council, Home Office approval was obtained and by August the cemetery had been planned by the Company Secretary, Arthur Clark. Daily interments (except Sundays) were advertised and interment cost 10s for adults, 5s for children while a family grave cost 48s and a purchased grave 25s. Initially, services were held in a temporary chapel of the 'tin tabernacle' variety.

Company pride is proclaimed at the gatehouse by Gothic letters several feet high announcing the cemetery's name although this has deteriorated. After suffering fire damage the lodge has been rebuilt but is unoccupied. Its architectural style, repeated in the chapel, is a curious mixture of knapped flint Perpendicular and black and white Tudor, inspired, according to a 1903 brochure, by 'old Hertfordshire churches.'[2] The chapel was designed by Alfred A. Bonella, a London architect. The climax to the burial chapel, however, is inside, where a large white and blue painted reredos by Cantagalli is a facsimile of Luca della Robbia's *Resurrection* in Florence Cathedral. Adjoining cloisters were divided from the chapel by a drive. The building was opened on the 7 July 1903 at which the Revd Dr Horton of Hampstead spoke of the role of the cemetery chaplain and urged that, '. . . mourners feel that in entering cemetery chapels they are not coming into a region of gloom, but treading on the very doorstep of the Kingdom of Heaven.'[3].

Within these cloisters a crematorium was created which opened on 1 March 1922.[4] It was the fifteenth to open in the country and the fourth in London. The architectural style was in keeping with that of the chapel with the chimney incorporated into the existing tower. In more recent years the burial chapel has been reordered to become a second crematorium chapel. The cloister around the chapel contains a columbarium.

The cemetery ground is unusually rural, traversed by a stream with several rustic bridges. The 1903 brochure described in detail the trees and shrubs originally planted by the company in their thousands. Around the cemetery boundary was,

> . . . a row of evergreen firs, pine, ilexes and hollies and another row of black poplars alternating with oaks, elms, maples, ashes and other deciduous trees.

There were 'Avenues of Lombardy poplars, oaks, elms, maples, planes and rose acacias. . . ' bordering the roads and a host of flowers and creepers disguising every wall and waste heap.[5] Those that have survived are now very big.

There are no especially remarkable monuments but a few are worth mentioning. The slender robed figure in bronze on the King grave (1919) is regrettably unsigned but not dissimilar to that on the Ripley grave at St Marylebone Cemetery. Below the portrait of Harry Lay (1923) the inscription contains a line of melody, and nearby is a curious marble tree stump memorial.

For its age (1905), the Arts and Crafts style graveboard commemorating Charles Mallett is in very good condition; it was carved by William Lock of Hendon. It is a feature of Hendon that several plots are devoted to particular nationalities.

The Greeks who bought a plot after the earlier Greek cemetery in Norwood became full. This contains several mausolea including two slablike stone vaults enlivened by mosaic panels in the Greek tradition. These depict the Resurrection and other Biblical subjects. So far they have survived the elements and are an unusually colourful contribution to cemetery art. A Swiss monument inscribed 'Union Helvetia' which refers to a Swiss Hotel Employees' Benefit Society founded in 1886, and a large Japanese enclosure in the form of the traditional Japanese garden planted with firs and cherry trees.

The cemetery and crematorium were acquired by the London Borough of Barnet in 1956.

SIR FREDERICK BOLTON 1851–1920
Shipowner and chairman of Lloyds of London.

GUNNER ISAAC LODGE 1866–1923
Won the V.C. during the Boer War in an attempt to rescue trapped guns at Bloemfontein.

EDWIN MULLINS 1848–1907
Sculptor, he executed the sculpture on the Fine Art Society building in Bond Street.

CHARLES SWAN –1923
Founder of the first Royal Flying Corps hospital.

Hendon: The entrance shortly after opening. The words '& crematorium' were added to the stone lettering in 1922

Hendon: The burial chapel c.1905.

FAU KUANG TAO –1976
Co-founder with his wife, Su Ying, of the Chinese church in London in 1951.

JOSEPH WILSON 1858–1929
Founder and president of the National Union of Seamen. Labour M.P. for Middlesborough and South Shields.

SIR EDWARD WOOD 1854–1930
Engineer and ironfounder, high sheriff of Lancashire 1915–16.

HERTFORD ROAD CEMETERY
HERTFORD ROAD, ENFIELD

Founded 1881
Owner: London Borough of Enfield
Acreage: 11

The cemetery is inactive apart from burial of ashes in a garden of rest adjacent to the now derelict chapel. The cemetery adjoins the churchyard of St James' and is sandwiched between this and a recreation ground. Beyond the chapel the drive and pathways are lined by crudely pollarded cherry trees. There are no memorials of note except an urn-topped granite column erected, surprisingly, in 1945.

HIGHGATE CEMETERY
SWAINS LANE, N6

Founded: 1839
Managed by: The Friends of Highgate Cemetery Trust
Acreage: 37

In many ways Highgate is exceptional. Although not the oldest or the biggest of London's cemeteries it is by far the best known and probably the most visited.[1] Until recently it suffered from rampant decay but owes its renaissance to the dedicated work of the Friends of Highgate Cemetery, a voluntary body with delegated management responsibility of the cemetery in place of the now defunct United Cemetery Company. Highgate's attractions are manifold. The site is of rare ecological importance near central London, the catacombs are unique and as a Victorian Valhalla, only Kensal Green and Norwood can compete. The Friends have worked to conserve this extraordinary place since 1975.

Highgate's story began in 1836 when an Act of Parliament was passed 'for establishing cemeteries for the Interment of the Dead, Northward, Southward and Eastward of the Metropolis by a Company to be called The London Cemetery Company'.[2] Inspired by its architect, Stephen Geary, the company founded Highgate to the north and Nunhead to the south which would, said the company chairman, amid cheers, 'not only rival all other cemeteries in their public utility, but . . . will prove most interesting ornaments to the suburbs of this great metropolis, and be an honour to the country'.[3]

Geary was an entrepreneur with eclectic interests. His first major work, in 1830, was an enormous statue of George IV at King's Cross set on an octagonal pedestal which doubled as a police station and later a pub. He is also reputed to have designed London's first gin palace and taken out patents for artificial fuel, paving streets, water supplies and other inventions. He would be forgotten today but for his greatest talent – designing cemeteries. In 1854 he ended his days, unobtrusively buried at Highgate.

In 1838 the company chose a site for their new northern speculation which was to establish the cemetery's reputation from that day to this. For nearly 150 years the southern slopes of Highgate had formed the garden and park of Ashurst Manor, a late seventeenth century house. In 1830 the Manor had been demolished to make way for Lewis Vulliamy's St Michael's Church which provided an appropriate backdrop for the twenty acres of land to the south, purchased by the company for £3,500. This was landscaped to brilliant effect by a gardener, David Ramsay, with 'circuitous roads winding about the acclivity' of the well-planted hillside. Nowhere was the Victorian habit of strolling in cemeteries better rewarded than here especially if the rambler was equipped with William Justyne's *Guide to Highgate Cemetery* which extols its charms in purple prose.

> No cemetery near London can boast so many natural beauties. The irregularity of the ground, rising in terraces, the winding paths leading through long avenues of cool shrubbery and marble monuments, and the groups of majestic trees casting broad shadows below, contribute many natural charms to this solemn region. In the genial summer time, when the birds are singing blithely in their leafy recesses, and the well-cared-for graves are dazzling with the varied hues of beautiful flowers, there is a holy loveliness upon this place of death, as the kind angels hovered about it, and quickened fair Nature with their presence, in love for the good souls whose tenantless bodies repose there.[4]

Likewise a marvellous, if sooty, view of London was commended:

> There spread out like a broad map, is the great metropolis of the world with its countless spires of every shape and almost every age – some of the design of zealous monks in the far away past, and some light workmanship of modern piety, all more or less dimly depicted in the grey film of smoke which curtains the mighty city by day.[5]

At the entrance to the cemetery Geary built two chapels. These are brick Tudor Gothic, contemporaries with that other experimental Gothic revival building, the Houses of Parliament. Like them, classical symmetry and Gothic detail are linked, but there the similarity ends. John Lloyd, writing in 1888 was not being over critical when he described the building as 'Undertakers Gothic but it is fitted with simple good taste'.[6] It needed Justyne's imagination to wonder:

> How many tears, consecrated by charity and love, have bedewed these formal pews! To what stirring dramas, to what strange vicissitudes, has this chapel been the closing scene.[7]

On a more practical level he mentions the hydraulic bier which silently lowered coffins from the chancel of the south chapel to a tunnel communicating with the east cemetery. This unfortunately is long gone. The chapels were listed in 1972, and restoration completed in 1989 to provide an office accommodation for the cemetery and Friends.

Northeast of the chapels is the original cemetery office, in similar style, and to the west, the colonnade which acts as a retaining wall for higher ground beyond. From this point on the landscape has changed radically from its mid-nineteenth-century appearance. The eastern boundary wall and western Gothic railings are hidden by vegetation which has also covered smaller paths and narrowed the width of the sunken roads, gently inclined for horse drawn hearses. Where the landscape was once dominated by a scattering of huge granite monuments, regularly embellished by flowers from the company's own greenhouses, there is now in Professor Girouard's words, 'a vast army of Victorian merchants, officers, widows and judges gently crumbling into anonymity beneath ivy and saplings and lushly sinister mare's tails'.[8] Nowhere is the Gothic gloom more sinister than in the Egyptian Avenue and the catacombs.

The inner circle was built first, Egyptian style, around a cedar tree that predates the cemetery by some 150 years. In 1839 James Bunstone Bunning (himself now lying in Highgate) was appointed surveyor to the company and he designed the Gothic terrace catacombs that abut the churchyard on the north boundary and the classical catacombs that are set into the outer bank of the eastern road. In the 1870s new classical style catacombs were built on the outside of the Lebanon circle, either side of the plot acquired by Julius Beer for his family mausoleum. At the same time repairs were made to the Egyptian catacombs, but in Portland cement rather than expensive stone, which has barely survived the intervening 100 years. When Justyne saw them he commented:

> As we enter the massive portals, and hear the echo of our footsteps intruding on the awful silence of this cold, stony death-palace, we might almost fancy ourselves treading through the mysterious corridors of an Egyptian temple.[9]

The Victorians loved it. The first burial was on 26 May 1839 of Elizabeth Jackson from Golden Square, aged thirty-six. Nearly all the 204 burials during the first year of business were of Londoners whose average age was under thirty-five. But soon the cemetery attracted a more varied clientele, not only on account of its natural advantages but also because the high cost of

Highgate: The catacombs. The Beer Mausoleum now occupies a prominent position on the terrace

vault and catacomb burial made it relatively exclusive. In the 1850s, terrace catacombs might be purchased in perpetuity from between £10 and £94, depending upon the number of coffin spaces required, a brick grave accommodating twelve coffins cost £21 or £15 15s. for six, even a common grave cost over £2 representing a considerable investment to a working class family. The company prospered and following the 1852 ban on churchyard burials in London it was decided to open a nineteen acre extension south of Swain's Lane. (This lacks the distinction of its neighbour, and, since the demolition of a lodge which stood at the south entrance, has no buildings of its own). To date there have been over 168,000 burials in 52,000 graves.

The one disappointment at Highgate is the moderate quality and variety of its monuments, which seldom compare with the best at Kensal Green or Norwood. As early as 1859 a writer in *The Builder* remarked on the 'unusual number of pillars broken, at various heights', which showed 'a great lack of invention'. The number of draped urns also caught his attention. 'We can trace the fashion of covering the vases to different degrees until at last the object supposed to be covered presents a shapeless and unsightly mass'.[10]

Among these conventional symbols one stupendous mausoleum stands out, erected in the 1880s for Julius Beer. The architect was John Oldrid Scott, who took as his model the original Mausoleum at Halicarnassus, one of the seven wonders of the world. (It was restored in 1993.) Other Highgate favourites are George Wombwell's sleepy lion, John Atcheler's horse, described, perhaps unfairly, by Lloyd as 'a monstrosity which surpasses the usual level of cemetery art'[11] and Tom Sayers' dog, which played a prominent part at his master's funeral.[12] Decked out in a black crepe collar, it sat alone in a carriage at the head of a long cortège. One monument, much admired in its day, was a seven feet high figure representing 'Religion' on the grave of Mrs Vaughan, sculpted in 1866 by Joseph Edwards.

Entering the east cemetery one first encounters a number of seemingly indestructible early twentieth century polished granite mausolea before coming face to face with the gigantic bronze bust of Karl Marx. His remains, and those of his family, were removed to the present grave in 1954 from a site 100 yards to the south.

A more dramatic exhumation at Highgate occurred one night in 1869. Seven years after Elizabeth Siddal's death, Dante Gabriel Rossetti retrieved a manuscript of some poems he had placed in her coffin. By the light of a bonfire the coffin was opened and the book removed from among the golden tresses of his wife's remains. A further notable exhumation took place in December 1907 when the coffin containing Thomas Charles Druce was examined in the belief that he was the fifth Duke of Portland.

Epitaphs at Highgate are inclined, not surprisingly, towards the eulogistic. A typical example appears on Gilbert Abbott A'Beckett's tomb. He died in 1856,

> Endowed with a genial, manly spirit, gifted with subtlest powers of
> wit and humour. They were exercised to the healthiest and most
> innocent purposes.

In more simple prose is a 1912 version: 'He went about doing good'. It is refreshing occasionally to chance upon something rather different, such as:

> Life's like a winter day,
> Some only breakfast and away;
> Others to dinner stay, and are full fed,
> The older ones but sup and go to bed.

> Wretched is he that lingers out his day;
> He that does soonest has the least to pay.

Or on the tomb of Professor Clifford, an atheist:

> I was not and was conceived.
> I loved, and did a little work.
> I am not, and grieve not.

After the last war the profits of the London Cemetery Company began to decline seriously. Peripheral buildings and land were sold and paupers' graves opened in every available space, marked only by small wooden crosses. Maintenance was minimal. In 1960 the company was absorbed into the larger United Cemeteries Company but to no avail. The west cemetery was closed in 1975 and the Friends of Highgate Cemetery was launched the same year. Since then considerable work has taken place in what is now a Grade II* listed park. In addition to restoration of the chapels, the Beer Mausoleum and other memorials, work has been completed on the terrace catacombs and the colonnade. Conservation of the Egyptian Avenue and Lebanon Circle has also taken place. More recently, repairs to drains and the resurfacing of some roads have been undertaken along with paving of the forecourt. Landscaping projects are continuous while repairs are currently taking place to boundary walls. There are also plans to restore the Dissenters' catacombs. Much of the work has been financed by the Friends together with assistance from English Heritage. The cemetery is not underpinned financially by any public body and relies on income from burials and donations from visitors to meet the annual current

Highgate: George Wombwell (1880) photographed in 1980 before the undergrowth was cleared

Highgate: The Beer mausoleum

running costs of around £270,000. It has been an enormous but immensely worthwhile endeavour which has inspired the Friends and supporters of other cemeteries.

Special thanks are due to the FOHC for permission to use the fruits of their research in helping to compile the following.

BURIED IN THE EASTERN CEMETERY

ANDREW BAIRD 1842–1908
Pioneer of modern techniques for observing tides; deputy surveyor-general of India.

SIR ALBERT BARRATT 1860–1941
Director of Barratt & Co., sweet manufacturers.

FARZAD BAZOFT 1958–90
British journalist executed in Iraq on account of his alleged spying activities.

WILLIAM BETTY 1791–1874
Child actor who inspired 'Bettymania' in the audiences who flocked to see him.

CATHERINE BOOTH-CLIBBORN 1858–1955
Eldest daughter of William Booth, founder of the Salvation Army in France and Switzerland.

HENRY BRIDGEMAN 1845–98
Architect, he patented the street watering post adopted in London.

SIR FREDERICK BROOME 1842–96
Colonial governor, he secured Western Australia's constitution in 1890.

SIR GEORGE BARCLAY BRUCE 1821–1908
Engineer who designed railways in India, Germany, Spain, South Africa and Argentina.

SIR THOMAS LAUDER BRUNTON 1844–1916
Successful surgeon who pioneered drug therapy for heart disorders.

JOHN BRYDON 1840–1901
Architect of the English Baroque revival style. He designed Chelsea Town Hall in 1885.

SIR JAMES CAIRD 1816–92
Agricultural reformer, author of *Our Daily Food* (1868).

SHURA CHERKASSKY 1911–95
Russian pianist residing in London.

MARTIN COLNAGHI 1821–1908
Picture dealer and collector.

George Critchett 1817–82
Eye surgeon at Moorfields, president of the 1872 International Congress of Opthalmology.

Yusef Mohammed Dadoo 1909–83
President, South African Indian Congress.

Davison Dalziel, Lord Dalziel of Wooler 1854–1928
Director of the Pullman Car and Inter-national Sleeping Car Companies. Chairman of the General Motor-cab Company, he introduced the first large motor cab company into London in 1907.

Lewis F. Day 1845–1910
Master of the Art Workers' Guild, designer and author of books on the arts and crafts, he helped arrange the collections of the Victoria and Albert Museum.

Francis Elgar 1845–1909
Naval architect and director of dockyards in Glasgow.

George Eliot 1819–80
Novelist, her friend George Lewes 1854–78 and husband, John Cross, 1840–1924, are also buried here.

William Foyle 1885–1963
Founder of the Charing Cross Road bookshop.

William Friese-Greene 1855–1921
Inventor of cinematography. His first film was shown in 1890 but he died penniless.

George Fripp 1813–96
Water colourist, he painted a series of pictures of Balmoral for Queen Victoria.

Highgate: The Egyptian Avenue photographed in 1980. (Copyright the late John Gay)

Richard Garnett 1835–1906
Keeper of printed books at the British Museum, 1890–99. Author of *The Twilight of the Gods*.

Charles Green 1785–1870
Balloonist. In 1838 he reached an uncomfortable record height of 27,146 feet.

John Groom 1845–1919
Philanthropist who founded John Groom's Crippleage at Clerkenwell.

Reginald Harrison 1837–1908
Liverpool surgeon, he introduced the system of street ambulances to Britain.

Sir William Herdman 1858–1924
Marine biologist, oyster expert, president of the Linnean Society.

William Henry –1928
Founder of the Royal Life Saving Society.

Gen. Sir Henry Holden 1856–1937
Chairman of the R.A.C. from 1905, president of the Radio Society of Great Britain from 1927, director of Mechanical Transport at the War Office 1914–16.

George Holyoake 1817–1906
Radical propagandist for the co-operative movement, imprisoned for blasphemy in 1842, wrote his autobiography *Sixty Years of an Agitator's Life*.

James Kennedy 1803–68
Authority on cholera, advocated the quarantine of foreign shipping during the epidemic of 1831.

William Kennedy 1839–85
Commander of the Canadian boatmen who guided Wolseley's boats up the Nile to relieve General Gordon. Died of smallpox.

George Kingsley 1827–92
Brother of Charles and father of Mary. Travelled with the Earl of Pembroke to Polynesia and wrote of his experiences in 'South Sea Bubbles'.

Joseph Knight 1829–1907
Drama critic, contributor to the D.N.B., editor of *Notes and Queries* 1883–1907.

Gen. Sir William Knollys 1797–1883
Military adviser to Prince Albert, founder of the camp at Aldershot.

John Lash Latey 1808–91
Editor of the *Illustrated London News* 1858–90.

LEONE LEVI 1821–88
Commercial law reformer and advocate of metrication.

JOHN WESTLAND MARSTON 1819–90
Poet, critic and playwright, author of successful poetic tragedies, together with his son Philip Marston 1850–87, a poet blind from childhood.

KARL MARX 1818–83
Leader of the Communist League. Wrote the *Communist Manifesto* with Engels (1848) and *Capital*. His daughter Eleanor 1855–1898, a trades union supporter, committed suicide and is buried with him. The bust, by Lawrence Bradshaw, was completed in 1956.

FRANK MATCHAM 1854–1920
The most successful of late Victorian and Edwardian theatre architects. At least twenty London theatres are his.

CARL MAYER 1894–1944
German film maker, co-author of the screenplay *The Cabinet of Dr Caligari* (1919).

JAMES BUDGETT MEAKIN 1866–1906
Dressed as a Moroccan he travelled in North Africa using his experiences to write *The Moorish Empire* (1899) and *The Moors* (1902).

WILLIAM HENRY MONK 1823–89
Organist and musical editor of *Hymns Ancient and Modern*, composed 'Abide With Me'.

SIR SIGISMUND NEWMANN 1857–1916
Bavarian born diamond merchant and racehorse owner.

SIR SIDNEY ROBERT NOLAN 1917–92
Australian artist.

WYATT PAPWORTH 1822–94
Curator of the Soane Museum and editor of the *Dictionary of Architecture*.

PAUL FALCONER POOLE 1807–79
Artist, enjoyed temporary fame with his 'Solomon Eagle' (1843) then regarded as the greatest history painting by an English artist.

JONES QUAIN 1796–1865
Professor of anatomy and physiology at University College, London; his *Elements of Anatomy* continued selling into this century.

SIR RALPH RICHARDSON 1902–83
Actor in the classical tradition. Director of the Old Vic in 1944 and National Theatre, 1975. Appeared in many films.

Highgate: Karl Marx (1956).

GEORGE RICHMOND 1809–96
Artist, he specialised in portraiture.

HENRY CRABB ROBINSON 1775–1867
Lawyer and scholar, lived for a while in Germany where he met Goethe and Schiller, *The Times* correspondent in the Peninsular war, a founder of the Athenaeum and University College, London.

SIR EYRE MASSEY SHAW 1830–1908
Superintendent of the London Fire Brigade 1861–91, dealt with over 55,000 fires.

DONALD SMITH, 1ST LORD STRATHCONA AND MOUNT ROYAL 1820–1914
Canadian financier, governor of the Hudson's Bay Company, director of the Canadian Pacific Railway, drove in the last spike on the railway in 1885. M.P. for Winnipeg and from 1890 was High Commissioner for Canada in London.

RICHARD SMITH 1836–1900
Patented the process for manufacturing Hovis bread.

HERBERT SPENCER 1820–1903
Philosopher, evolutionary theorist and sociologist, coined the phrase 'survival of the fittest' and the word 'evolution' in the modern sense.

SIR LESLIE STEPHEN 1832–1904
Scholar and first editor of the *Dictionary of National Biography*. Father of Virginia Woolf and Vanessa Bell.

SIR IAIN JOHNSTONE SUTHERLAND 1925–86
Diplomat. UK Ambassador in Greece 1978–82 and Soviet Union 1982–85

SIR ANDREW TAYLOR 1850–1937
Architect practising in Canada, designed McGill University. Mayor of Hampstead 1922.

JAMES THOMSON 1834–82
Poet, referred to as 'The Laureate of Pessimism' on account of his poem *The City of Dreadful Night*. Died of dipsomania.

HARRY THORNTON –1918
Classical pianist and entertainer of the troops during the Great War. Died in the 1918 'flu epidemic.

Feliks Topolski 1907–89
Painter and illustrator.

Edward Truelove 1809–99
Publisher, tried in 1877 for publishing birth control literature but acquitted.

Max Wall 1908–90
Comedian and actor.

Sir Lawrence Weaver 1876–1930
Architectural historian, director general of the Land Department 1920–22.

Capt. John Wood 1813–71
Explored Afghanistan for the East India Company, discovered the source of the River Oxus.

Patrick Wymark (A.K.A. Cheeseman) 1926–70
Actor and producer.

Lady Ruth Sasha Young 1930–93
Broadcaster and novelist. An accomplished painter, sculptor and poet.

BURIED IN THE WESTERN CEMETERY

Gilbert Abbott A'Beckett 1811–56
A Poor Law commissioner, author of comic histories and a founder of *Punch*.

Edward Baily 1788–1867
Sculptor, he carved the statue of Nelson on the Trafalgar column.

Valentine Bartholomew 1799–1879
Flower painter to Queen Victoria. Also his wife Anne, 1800–62, poet and flower painter.

Sir Herbert Bartlett 1842–1921
Contractor and yachtsman, he endowed London University's Bartlett School of Architecture.

Julius Beer 1836–1880
German-born financier, proprietor of the *Observer*. The mausoleum cost £5,000 to build in addition to £800 for the plot. Its restoration began in 1993.

Lady Diana Belcher 1806–90
Wrote *The Mutineers of the Bounty* (1870) in which she exonerated her step-father, Peter Heywood (see below), for his part in the Mutiny.

George Bell 1814–1890
Publisher, he founded George Bell & Sons.

EDWARD BLORE 1787–1879
Architect of country houses, Lambeth Palace and the east wing of Buckingham Palace.

JOHN BRINSMEAD 1836–1921
Piano manufacturer.

BERNARD BRODHURST 1822–90
Orthopaedic surgeon, published *The Deformities of the Human Body* (1871).

JACOB BRONOWSKI 1908–74
Scientist and broadcaster, he presented the T.V. series 'The Ascent of Man'.

JAMES BUNSTONE BUNNING 1802–63
Architect to the City of London and London Cemetery Company. His finest work, the Coal Exchange, was demolished in 1962.

FREDERICK CANSICK 1828–1918
Collector of epitaphs in the St Pancras area, including those at Highgate.

EDWARD, VISCOUNT CARDWELL 1813–66
Politician, as Secretary of War he carried out many reforms at the War Office.

RICHARD CROMWELL CARPENTER 1812–55
Architect of the Gothic revival with a large ecclesiastical practice.

WILLIAM BENJAMIN CARPENTER 1813–85
Marine biologist and registrar of London University, he proposed the modern theory of ocean circulation.

ALFRED EDWARD CHALON 1781–1860
Water colour artist, he was the first to paint Queen Victoria's portrait after her accession.

THOMAS CHIPP 1793–1890
Harpist, he was a member of all the principal London orchestras for over fifty years.

CHARLES CHUBB 1779–1845
Locksmith, he founded the security firm named after him.

WILLIAM COLLARD 1776–1866
Piano manufacturer with the firm Collard and Collard.

CECIL (JAMES H) COLLINS 1908–89
The great outsider of modern painting specialising in angels, fools, spirits often in glowing colours.

JOHN SINGLETON COPLEY, LORD LYNDHURST, 1772–1863
Son of the famous painter who persuaded him to become a lawyer. He prosecuted Queen Caroline in 1820 and was three times Lord Chancellor.

SIR CHARLES COWPER 1807–75
Five times premier of New South Wales.

GEORGE CRAWKEY 1833–19
Railway Contractor, he built railways throughout Europe and Mexico.

CHARLES CRUFT 1852–1938
Began his career working for James Spratt the dog food manufacturer. Founded his own dog show in 1886.

JAMES CUTBUSH 1827–1885
Nurseryman who specialised in the bulb trade. His son, Herbert (died 1918) is also here.

GEORGE DALZIEL 1815–1902, EDWARD DALZIEL 1817–1905 AND THOMAS DALZIEL 1823–1906 (WESTERN CEMETERY)
Engravers and book illustrators.

DAVID DEVANT 1868–1941
Conjuror, the first to attempt the Indian rope trick on a European stage.

CATHERINE DICKENS 1815–70
Wife of Charles Dickens, their daughter Dora is also buried here.

SIR PIERSON DIXON 1904–1965
Private secretary to Anthony Eden and Ernest Bevin, British representative at the UN 1954–60, ambassador to France 1960–64.

WILLIAM HEPWORTH DIXON 1821–79
Journalist and travel writer, an organiser of the 1851 Great Exhibition. Died due to strenuous overnight proofreading.

FREDERICK DOVE 1830–1923
A director of the Victorian building firm Dove Brothers, he supervised restoration of St. Bartholomew the Great, Smithfield.

THOMAS DRUCE 1793–1864
Furniture dealer. In 1896 his widow claimed he had been the famous recluse, the 5th Duke of Portland. She was removed to an asylum but his son G.H. Druce pursued the claim in court. The grave was opened in 1907 but Druce's body, not the predicted lead weights, were discovered.

MARIA DULCKEN 1811–50
Pianist to Queen Victoria.

HENRY EATON, LORD CHEYLESMORE 1816–91
Silk merchant, owner of White's Club, and M.P. for Coventry for twenty-one years. Died in Warsaw.

PIERCE EGAN 1772–1849
Sporting journalist, novelist and dramatist. His *Life in London*, (1820), featured the adventures of two Regency bucks, Tom and Jerry.

MICHAEL FARADAY 1791–1867
Chemist and natural philosopher. The first man to liquify gases, and pioneer the use of electricity.

SIR CHARLES FELLOWS 1799–1860
Mountaineer and traveller, he brought the Nereid Tomb from Xanthos to Britain.

WILLIAM FERGUSSON 1773–1846
Army surgeon, he proved malaria was not dependent on rotting vegetation, as had been previously argued.

EDWARD FITZGIBBON 1803–57
Angler, his writing and experiments with improved fishing tackle increased public interest in the sport.

JAMES FOGGO 1790–1860, GEORGE FOGGO 1793–1867,
Painters, they compiled the first catalogue of the National Gallery.

JOHN FOWLER-DIXON 1850–1943
Record breaking athlete; a founder of the Amateur Athletic Association and four times judge at the Olympics.

JOHN GALSWORTHY 1867–1933
Novelist and playwright, awarded the Nobel Prize for literature. Memorial only, his ashes were scattered over the Sussex Downs.

STEPHEN GEARY 1797–1854
Architect to the London Cemetery Company, responsible for the initial design of Highgate Cemetery.

HENRY GRAVES 1808–92
Printseller, a founder of the *Art Journal* and the *Illustrated London News*.

JOSEPH GREEN 1791–1863
Founded the department of anatomy at Kings College, London. President of the General Medical Council 1860 and executor of Coleridge.

SIR JOHN GURNEY 1768–1845
Lawyer and Baron of the Exchequer from 1832.

RADCLYFFE HALL 1880–1943
Poet and novelist, she wrote *The Well of Loneliness* (1928), declared obscene for its treatment of lesbianism. She is buried with her first lover Mabel Batten (died 1915). Her second lover Una, Lady Troubridge should have been buried with her but died in Rome and was buried there.

PHILIP HARBEN 1906–70
Cook and television personality.

SIR CHARLES HARTLEY 1825–1915
Engineer, he was responsible for making the Danube navigable and worked on the Suez Canal.

SIR BENJAMIN HAWES 1797–1862
Deputy Secretary for war during the Crimean War. Originator of the Fine Arts Commission, he promoted legislation to open the British Museum on public holidays.

JOSEPH HAYDEN 1786–1856
Edited Lewis's *Topographical Dictionary* (1842–47) and compiler of *The Dictionary of Dates* (1841). Died a pauper and buried in a common grave.

PETER HEYWOOD 1773–1831
Midshipman on board the *Bounty*, sentenced to death for his part in the mutiny but pardoned.

ROBERT GARDINER HILL 1811–1878
Lincoln psychiatrist, the first to abolish the use of strait jackets on lunatics.

SIR ROWLAND HILL 1795–1879
Founder of universal penny post (memorial only, buried in Westminster Abbey).

FRANK HOLL 1845–88
Artist, he painted scenes of social realism with great success, dying from overwork.

JAMES HOLMAN 1786–1857
Went blind aged twenty-five, spent the rest of his life travelling, writing up his experiences in four volumes.

WILLIAM HOSKING 1800–61
Professor of architecture and civil engineering at King's College, London; he was the designer of Abney Park Cemetery.

ROBERT HOVENDEN 1830–1908
Hairdresser's sundriesman, founded the trade's first newspaper, became Master of the Barbers' Mediaeval Guild, antiquarian.

DAVID EDWARD HUGHES 1830–1900
Inventor, electrician, musician. Invented a new microphone and type-printing telegraph, conducted early research of radiowaves.

CHARLES HULLMANDEL 1789–1850
Lithographer and co-inventor of lithotint.

LESLIE HUTCHINSON 1900–69
'Hutch', cabaret singer.
SIR JOHN HUTTON 1841–1903
Chairman of the L.C.C. 1892, proprietor of *Sporting Life*.

SIR WILLIAM JAMES 1807–81
Lord Justice of Appeal, privy councillor, wrote a history of British rule in India.

GEORGE JONES 1786–1869
President of the Royal Academy 1845–50, executor of Turner and Chantrey, and artist, drawing his subject matter from the Napoleonic wars, in which he had served.

SIR FITZROY KELLY 1796–1880
Earned £25,000 a year in the 1840s in his practice as a lawyer. Chief Baron of the Exchequer 1866.

JOHN LANDSEER 1769–1852
Engraver to George III. Father of artists Charles 1799–1879, Thomas 1795–1880 (both buried here) and Sir Edwin Landseer.

SIR PETER LAURIE 1779–1861
Made a fortune as a contractor for the Indian Army, Lord Mayor of London 1823–24.

HENRY LEE 1817–98
Surgeon at St George's Hospital where he promoted the merits of ventilation by keeping the windows open.

ELIZABETH LILLEY –1882
Midwife to Queen Victoria. She delivered Princess Victoria and, in 1841, the future Edward VII.

FREDERICK LILLYWHITE 1792–1854
Cricketer, 'a name to be remembered as long as the national game of England'; introduced round arm bowling. His monument erected by public subscription.

ROBERT LISTON 1794–1847
Surgeon, before the use of anaesthetics when speed was essential, he could amputate a leg in less than thirty seconds. In 1846 became the first surgeon to perform an operation using ether.

SAMUEL LUCAS 1811–65
Manchester economist and founder of the Emancipation Society; with his wife Margaret 1818–90, sister of John Bright and president of the Women's Temperance Association.

FREDERICK MACKENZIE 1787–1854
Architectural illustrator for Britton and Pugin among others. Died in poverty after photography superseded his work.

Gen. Sir Archibald MacLaine 1773–1861
Hero of the Peninsular war, held Matagorda with 155 men against 8,000 Frenchmen. Buried with several bullets still in his body.

John Maple 1815–1900
Founder of the furniture business in Tottenham Court Road.

Frederick Denison Maurice 1805–72
Anglican convert and theologian. Organised the Christian Socialist movement and was expelled from his professorship in London for his heretical views.

William Mellish –1834
Millionaire shipowner, he survived an assassination attempt by one of his captains eighteen months before he died. Exhumed from Wapping Church.

Sir Charles Mills 1825–95
The first agent general for Cape Colony.

Atkinson Morley 1781–1858
Studied medicine but followed a career as a hotel proprietor. He left £100,000 for the foundation of the Atkinson Morley Hospital, Wimbledon.

Walter Neurath 1903–67
Austrian born publisher, founded the firm of Thames and Hudson.

Rear Adm. Sherard Osborn 1822–75
Arctic explorer, took part in the search for Franklin.

Gen. Sir Loftus Otway 1774–1854
Cavalry officer in the Peninsular war and commander of three Portuguese Legions at Albuera.

John W. Parker 1792–1870
Cambridge University publisher of philosophic and religious works.

Frederick Pavy 1829–1911
Physician who specialised in the treatment of diabetes.

Joseph Payne 1808–78
First professor of education in England.

William Payne 1804–61
Actor, the 'King of Pantomime'.

Rear Adm. Frederick Pelham 1808–61
Lord Commissioner of the Admiralty, captain of the Baltic fleet during the Crimean war.

William Haseldine Pepys 1775–1856
A founder of the London Institution and the Geological Society of London. Invented the mercury gasometer, president of the Royal Institution 1816.

Samuel Phelps 1804–78
Shakespearean actor and for twenty years manager of Sadlers Wells theatre.

George J. Pinwell 1842–75
Watercolour painter and successful book illustrator.

Sir Thomas Platt 1790–1862
Solicitor and Baron of the Exchequer.

Louis Prevost 1796–1858
French born keeper of prints at the British Museum. An exceptional linguist, he learned forty languages and catalogued the Museum's collection of Chinese books.

Alfred Prosser –1923
North London sports goods manufacturer.

Bernard Quaritch 1819–1899
German born antiquarian bookseller.

Peter Robinson 1804–74
Founder of the Oxford Street department store.

Carl Rosa 1843–89
German born musician, founded the Carl Rosa opera company in 1875.

Sir William Ross 1794–1860
Miniature painter, he painted over 2,200 works, including portraits of the Royal Family.

Rossetti family:
Gabriele 1783–1854
Italian poet and political refugee, professor of Italian at Kings College, London.

His son William Michael 1829–1919
Poet and editor of the Pre-Raphaelite magazine *The Germ*.

His daughter Christina 1830–94
Poet and theological writer.

His daughter-in-law Elizabeth Siddal 1829–1862
Wife of Dante Gabriel, was buried here with a manuscript of some of his poems which he retrieved from her coffin in 1869. He is buried at Birchington, Kent.

JAMES RISIEN RUSSELL 1863–1939
Chairman of the National Society for Lunacy Law Reform, advocated insanity as a ground for divorce.

WILLIAM SALT 1805–63
Banker and historian of Staffordshire.

FREDERICK SAYER –1868
Soldier and magistrate of Gibraltar, author of a *History of Gibraltar*, 1862.

THOMAS SAYERS 1826–65
Last of the bare-fisted prizefighters. Fought a world championship bout of forty-two rounds against the American John Heenan which ended in a draw by intervention.

JAMES SELBY 1844–88
Whip of the 'Old Times' coach, set a speed record of seven hours fifty minutes for the journey from London to Brighton and back. The procession of coaches and mourners at his funeral exceeded a mile in length.

GEORGE SOWERBY 1788–1854
Conchologist and dealer in shells.

CHARLES GREEN SPENCER 1837–90
Balloonist, head of C.G. Spencer & Sons, aeronauts.

ALFRED STEVENS 1818–75
Artist and sculptor, designed the Wellington Memorial in St Paul's Cathedral.

CHARLES STEWART 1840–1907
Comparative anatomist, a founder of the Anatomical Society, president of the Linnean Society 1890–1894.

COL. STODARE (ALFRED INGLIS) 1832–66
Magician and illusionist, performed for the Royal Family.

SIR HENRY STORKS 1811–74
Served in the Crimean war, High Commissioner of the Ionian Islands 1859 and subsequently Governor of Malta and Jamaica.

ANNA SWANWICK 1813–99
Writer and advocate of higher education for women, president of Bedford College and a founder of Girton College, Cambridge and Somerville Hall, Oxford.

CHARLES TURNER 1838–1913
Controller-General of the Inland Revenue 1876–1900.

ANDREW URE 1778-1857
Chemist, one of the first in Britain to adopt the modern notation for the elements. Experimented on resuscitation methods by electrical shock.

JAMES VETCH 1815-69
Engineer. He designed fortifications during the Peninsular War, a scheme for a Suez canal and a drainage system for Windsor Castle. Conservator of harbours for the Admiralty 1853-63.

ADM. GEORGE WALDEGRAVE, LORD RADSTOCK 1786-1857
Served in the Peninsular war, concluded a treaty with Ali Pasha in 1810. His library on naval history was left to the Royal United Service Institution.

ARTHUR WALEY 1889-1966
Poet, assistant keeper at the British Museum, translator of Chinese and Japanese literature.

GEORGE WALLIS 1811-91
Deputy commissioner for the 1851 Great Exhibition, keeper of the South Kensington Museum.

FREDERICK WARNE 1825-1901
Publisher specialising in illustrated children's books.

STELLA DOROTHEA WEBB 1902-89
Novelist who wrote under the pseudonym Stella Gibbons, best known for *Cold Comfort Farm*.

THOMAS WEBSTER 1773-1844
Gave up an architectural career to become a geologist, the mineral Websterite is named after him.

CHARLES WESLEY 1793-1859
Chaplain to the royal household from 1837, officiated at the confirmation, coronation, marriage and first churching of Queen Victoria.

SIR GEORGE WILLIAMS 1821-1905
Founder in 1844 of the Y.M.C.A. (Memorial only).

GEORGE WOMBWELL 1788-50
Founded Wombwell's Menageries with two boa constrictors, later the largest travelling menagerie in England.

MRS HENRY WOOD 1814-87
Novelist best known for *East Lynne* (1861). Her tomb is modelled on that of Scipio Africanus in Rome.

STANISLAUS WORCELL 1799-1857
Polish aristocrat, who gave up his position to join Polish revolutionaries in exile. Buried with other Poles at White Eagle Hill, so called after the eagle on his grave.

MATTHEW COTES WYATT 1777–1862
Sculptor and painter, a royal favourite, he decorated thirty-three of the ceilings at Windsor Castle and sculpted several figures of royalty including the statue of George III in Cockspur Street.

ALEXANDER WYLIE 1815–87
Missionary and Chinese scholar, translated many Chinese works into English.

BENJAMIN WYON 1802–58
Chief engraver of seals and medals at the Royal Mint.

HILLINGDON AND UXBRIDGE CEMETERY
HILLINGDON HILL, HILLINGDON, MIDDX.

Founded   1855 (Uxbridge) and 1867 (Hillingdon)
Owner: London Borough of Hillingdon
Acreage: 45

Situated on a dual carriageway, the triple gabled entrance to Hillingdon Cemetery is through a Gothic arch with generous living accommodation above and at either side. The drive curves up to the two small chapels again in the Gothic style all designed by Benjamin Ferrey.[1] They were built by the firm of Fassridge of Uxbridge using Kentish rag and Bath stone at a cost of £1,800 and are set at right angles to each other. Both are equipped with the unusual feature of two sets of adjacent double doors. The Anglican chapel is distinguished by its bell cote and three lancet windows in the apse, the Dissenters' chapel now serves as a tool store.

The cemetery is L-shaped, a reminder that originally it was two separate grounds with a dividing wall, part of which survives. The four acre Uxbridge cemetery had its own chapels and a lodge on Kingston Lane, designed by Charles Shoppe, but all are now demolished and the lodge replaced in the 1970s.[2]

Maintenance is minimal and apart from new signage the cemetery has an air of neglect; the arch and the replacement lodge on Kingston Lane are unoccupied and the trees need attention. These include some fine monkey puzzles north of the main path. Particularly unattractive are the iron frames at the entrances which prevent vehicles of a certain height from entering the cemetery.

Hillingdon: The entrance on Hillingdon Hill by Benjamin Ferrey (1855).

A handful of interesting memorials include the mid-nineteenth century Hollingworth sarcophagu. Immediately in front of the chapels is an attractive winged angel holding a palm carved into a headstone commemorating Maud Youngs (1943).

HILLVIEW CEMETERY
Wickham Street, Welling, Kent

Founded: 1985
Owner: London Borough of Bexley
Acreage: 12

The cemetery is on a flat site containing both lawn and a variety of traditional memorials. The emphasis of the latter is on imported white and grey marble headstones relieved by photographic portraits of the deceased and gilt lettering. Near the car park is a circular section for cremated remains surrounded by a beech hedge. There is no chapel and the only building is an office and lavatories. This is not a cemetery worth a detour.

HITHER GREEN CEMETERY AND LEWISHAM CREMATORIUM
Verdant Lane, SE6

Founded: 1873
Owner: London Borough of Lewisham
Acreage: 65

A comparison of the old and new at Hither Green portrays as well as anywhere the richness of the nineteenth century cemetery and the vacuity of its twentieth century counterpart. A visitor to the old cemetery is under no illusions about the place he is in as soon as he passes the extravagantly decorated iron entrance gates. Until the 1960s, when it was demolished, a Gothic style lodge contributed to the *mise en scène*. From there meandering paths lead to either of the two Gothic chapels with complex plans and intricate Decorated style tracery. Little belfries with highly imaginative gargoyles and octagonal spires rise above the evergreen trees. Not unnaturally, the cemetery's architect Francis Thorne also chose to be buried here in 1885. The builder was William Webster and the plans for landscaping were drawn up by a pupil of William Paxton, Edward Milner. While one of the chapels remains in use the other is now derelict and in a poor state of repair. Nearby is the cemetery's only mausoleum in which John Taylor was interred in 1903. It is a thirteenth-century style Gothic structure, rendered, painted and bristling with pinnacles.

In this part of the cemetery tombstones of varied design fill the ground in satisfying disarray which create the atmosphere of a country churchyard. Here would feel at home men such as Horatio Nelson John 'who lost his life while suppressing Dacoity in the Bassein District Burmah 1886' or Major Houdron 'Inspector of Hill Roads in the Himalayas' (died 1887), or William Macorquodale 'Captain of the West African Frontier Force' (died 1902). Symbolism appreciated by Victorians is also here, for example the rope and anchor motif around the grave of naval architect Bernard Waymouth (1890) and the charming bronze panel entitled 'Sleep' on the grave to Joseph Hill (1895).

Beyond the boundary of this Victorian ideal, now marked only by a ridge of tree stumps, sprawl acres of the new cemetery, the crematorium and the garden of rest. A first impression is of rigidly planned

Hither Green: The chapel by Francis Thorne (1873)

paths and gravestones and the unvarying low profile of the thousands of stone memorials. Any imaginative landscaping has been discouraged. Trees are limited to small ornamental flowering varieties, tomb design is reduced to the minimal slab. At the rear of the crematorium all memorials are restricted to the lawn grave. One significant, but neglected, memorial commemorates six teachers and thirty-eight children killed by a bomb which devastated their school in 1943. Among the several stereotypical angel images, many have been decapitated, the uniformed figure of William Priestman (10th Forest Hill Group Boy Scouts) 'taken suddenly for higher service, April 1929 aged 17½ years' is surprisingly still unscathed. The only building in this part of the cemetery could be confused with a small bus shelter – the place, in short, is unbelievably drab.

Two rows of mature poplars segregate the cemetery from the crematorium which was added during 1956 in a travesty of taste.[1] Responsible for the scheme was the borough architect, H.H. Forward. The approach is via a little bridge, necessary to negotiate the artificial lake created in the clipped urban garden. Heralded by the wilting remnants of floral tributes, still wrapped in sweating cellophane, the crematorium chapel is reached, dominated by a silver angel. It is built of red brick and roofed with copper, now coloured green. Inside, all is varnished wood and gold chrome. A red carpet leads up the nave to a bier constructed in fake black and white veined marble. The waiting room is furnished with black plastic chairs and rubber plants, more like a saloon bar than a crematorium, perhaps intentionally, to avoid any contemplation of death. The cremation dilemma, caught by a lack of ecclesiastical precedent in crematorium design and the failure to come to terms with death is nowhere more forcibly apparent than in this model of artless deceit.

PATRICK FOLEY 1836–1914
Founder of the Pearl Assurance Company in 1864 and M.P. for Connemara 1885–95.

HUGUENOT BURIAL GROUND
EAST HILL, SW18

Founded: 1687
Owner: London Borough of Wandsworth
Acreage: ¼ acre

A large pedimented memorial on the north side of this obscure little cemetery explains its origins. After the Revocation of the Edict of Nantes in 1685, French Huguenot families took refuge in Wandsworth where 'they established important industries and added to the credit and prosperity of the town. . . ' Carved below, but now rather indistinct, are some thirty names.

The ground was twice enlarged and finally closed to burials in 1854 but reopened as a public garden. In fact the triangular site is entirely enclosed by railings (restored in 2003) in addition to three busy roads making it well nigh inaccessible. Anyone managing to negotiate these hazards will discover a traditional eighteenth century burial ground filled with headstones and chest tombs in the classical tradition. Many are now in poor condition. The cemetery is also known as Mount Nod.

ISLEWORTH CEMETERY
PARK ROAD, ISLEWORTH

Founded: 1879
Owner: London Borough of Hounslow
Acreage: 2 ½

This small ground is dominated by twin chapels and their shared octagonal spire. Although characteristically Gothic in style they are unusual for being built largely in polychrome brick. The architect was Augustus Rovendino and it is regrettable that such imposing cemetery buildings together with the old mortuary should now be disused and allowed to fall into disrepair. Happily a small lodge built with the same Ruskinian brickwork remains in use.

The chapels aside, the cemetery is remarkable for its oddities. The two tallest monuments both commemorate disasters. One of these is a fine polished granite classical structure erected for the Pears family, including Thomas Pears, lost on the *Titanic* 15 April 1912. The other, a red granite obelisk, was paid for in 1885 by public subscription in memory of Alice Ayres, killed in a fire. The inscription dramatically records:

> Amidst the sudden terrors of the conflagration with true courage and clear judgement she heroically rescued the children committed to her charge. To save them three times she braved the flames, at last, leaping from the burning house, she sustained injuries from the effects of which she died.

Elsewhere the names on three tombstones have a fortuitous relevance: 'Ghost', 'Deadman' and 'Skull'.

ALBERT BALDWIN 1858–1936
The 'noted numismatist', he founded in 1872 the coin dealing firm bearing his name.

GEORGE MANVILLE FENN 1831–1909
Author, editor and dramatist.

SIR THOMAS WILLIAMS 1853–1941
Director of the L.M.S. and several other railway and canal companies.

JEWISH CEMETERY
ALDERNEY ROAD, E1

Founded: 1697
Owner: The United Synagogue
Acreage: 1 ¼

Like all Jewish cemeteries in Whitechapel this one is hard to find hidden behind its brick wall. A notice 'Beware Guard Dog' does not encourage casual visitors, but inside all is peaceful. The cemetery was bought for the Ashkenazim community in London by a wealthy merchant, Benjamin Levy, on a 999-year lease and enlarged in 1733. Most tombstones, inscribed in Hebrew, have decayed to anonymity; originally many were richly carved chest tombs but these have collapsed leaving only their capping on the ground. The few survivors display a lively variety of eighteenth-century tomb designs incorporating motifs like the skull and crossbones, shovel and pick, curtains and palms. The inscription on a granite slab near the gate explains, 'Within this cemetery lie the mortal remains of the founders, lay readers and rabbis of the Ashkenazim community of this country . . .'

RABBI SAMUEL FALK 1708–82
The 'Ba'al Shem' of London. English Cabalist and mystic.

PHILAS FRANKS 1722–65
A great beauty, painted by both Gainsborough and Reynolds.

AARON HART 1670–1756
Polish born, the first chief rabbi of the Ashkenazim in Britain, 1709–56.

MOSES HART 1676–1757
Merchant, the Great Synagogue was built at his expense (1721), he also bequeathed money to the London Hospital.

BENJAMIN LEVY –1705
Merchant, he bought a 999-year lease of this cemetery ground for £190 in 1696.

DAVID LEVY 1740–99
Published a Hebrew grammar in three volumes and several other books on Jewish ritual.

DAVID SCHIFF –1791
Chief rabbi 1765–91.

JEWISH CEMETERY
BRADY STREET, E1

Founded   1761
Owner: The United Synagogue
Acreage: Approx. 4

The old Jewish cemeteries are small secretive places, a few acres hidden by high walls and locked doors, often cheek by jowl with new buildings and identified from outside only by the trees that overhang walls topped with broken glass. Brady Street is an oasis in a wilderness of East End urban desolation comprised of waste land and forbidding council house blocks. Originally it was a brickfield adjacent to Ducking Pond Lane but was leased to the New Synagogue in 1761 for an annual rent of twelve guineas. Like the other Jewish cemeteries in Whitechapel it is now closed to burials (since 1858) but is still crowded with tombstones.

It is Jewish law that coffins should be separated by a distance of six hands' breadths and only one body buried in each grave at least 6ft from the surface. At Brady Street, which was soon filled, this rule was overcome by heaping new earth over a portion where Jews, who belonged to no particular congregation, had been buried. This area was called the Strangers Ground and is still noticeably hilly with pairs of headstones placed back to back.

ABRAHAM GOLDSMID 1753–1808
Financier who, with his brother Benjamin, had a near monopoly of influence on the Stock Exchange; also a generous philanthropist. Both committed suicide.

SOLOMON HERSCHELL 1761–1842
Chief rabbi of the Ashkenazim in England.

HYMAN HURWITZ 1770–1844
Polish-born Jewish professor of Hebrew at London University, 1828. A friend of Coleridge.

MOSES JACOB –1781
A founder of the New Synagogue.

MIRIAM LEVEY 1801–56
Welfare worker who opened the first soup kitchen for the poor in Whitechapel.

NATHAN MOSES 1692–1799
Died aged 107 and 6 months.

NATHAN MEYER ROTHSCHILD 1777–1836
Founded the London branch of the family's bank in 1805, helped fund the government during the Napoleonic wars. His remains were brought from Germany, where he died.

NATHANIEL, 3RD LORD ROTHSCHILD 1910–90
Zoologist, government advisor, banker and oil executive, he also had a distinguished career in military intelligence.

JEWISH CEMETERY, EAST HAM
SANDFORD ROAD, E6

Founded: 1919
Owner: The United Synagogue
Acreage: 25

A strange charmless place crammed with black lettered, tall, white marble headstones and, sporadically, traditional classical monuments such as draped urns or columns. Since Able Seaman Jacob Emanuel was the first to be buried here in January 1919 there is little space left. The prayer hall, linked to the cohanim and mortuary by cloisters is a scruffy white-washed building, architecturally more suited to a Mediterranean seaside resort than a cemetery.

ISIDORE BERLINER 1869–1925
Founder and president of the London Jewish Hospital.

TED 'KID' LEWIS 1896–1970
Real name Solomon Mendeloff, world champion welterweight boxer 1915, 'one of the all time greats'.

MARCUS LIPTON 1900–78
Labour M.P. for Lambeth 1945–78.

JEWISH CEMETERY
FULHAM ROAD, SW3

Founded: 1815
Owner: The Western Synagogue
Acreage: Approx. 1

The impression given by this tiny cemetery is more typical of Prague than London and is totally unexpected in the Fulham Road. It is walled in save for a locked rusty iron gate but a plaque on the wall discloses its existence. The site was originally well known for its mulberry trees associated with the silk industry, but was bought by the Western Synagogue to create the first Jewish burial ground west of the City.

The small prayer hall and office building erected near the entrance has long since been demolished. The ground, however, is still densely covered by some 300 headstones shaded by ash trees and a large plane. The general condition of the cemetery appears good and it seems a pity, albeit understandably so, that no better use has been made of it following its closure to burials in 1886, except for the use of reserved graves.

SOLOMON HART 1806–81
Artist, the first Jewish Royal Academician, professor of painting at the Academy 1854–63.

ZADOK JESSEL 1792–1864
Wealthy merchant and father of Sir George Jessel, Master of the Rolls.

Jacob Waley 1818–73
Professor of political economy at London University, first president of the Anglo-Jewish Association 1870.

Simon Waley 1827–75
Stockbroker, pianist and composer.

JEWISH CEMETERY
Hoop Lane, NW11

Founded: 1895
Owner: West London Synagogue
Acreage: 16½

This cemetery stands opposite Golders Green crematorium. Twin red brick and terracotta tiled halls for conducting the burial service are sited just inside the gates and beyond them the distinctive prostrate slabs of the Sephardim Jews fill the east side, and the upright monuments of the West London Synagogue the west. Apart from the old closed Sephardi cemeteries off the Mile End Road and a section at Edgwarebury, this is the only Sephardi cemetery left in London. The stones are almost invariably laid flat, occasionally with slightly curved tops and often tilted so the inscription is more easily read. Most are now white marble slabs. The origin of the design is said to emanate from the time when Sephardi cemeteries were built in poor swampy ground and the flat stone proved more stable than others. Theoretically the bodies beneath are orientated with the feet towards the east.

The Sephardi simplicity contrasts markedly with the sometimes very grand monuments in the west ground, such as the huge classical ensemble for Henry Bishoffscheim (1908) or the shrouded sarcophagus for Emanuel Belilios (1905). As usual in Jewish cemeteries, planting is minimal and strong doses of weed killer have left arid patches.

WEST SIDE

Emanuel Belilios 1837–1905
A Hong Kong businessman, educational philanthropist and member of the colony's Legislative Council 1882–1900.

Sir Bernard Cohen 1886–1965
Lost both his legs during the Great War and served on many committees thereafter concerned for the disabled.

Sir Frederick Cowen 1852 1935
Composer and conductor of the Hallé Orchestra.

Julia Goodman 1812–1906
Portrait painter.

Sir Basil Henriques 1890–1961
Spent a lifetime working in the boys' clubs of East London.

Leslie, Lord Hore-Belisha 1893–1957
Liberal M.P. for Devonport 1923–45, as Minister of Transport he introduced the 'Belisha' beacon.

Gerald Isaacs, 2ND Marquess of Reading 1889–1960
Barrister, took an active role in foreign of Reading affairs, particularly during the Suez Crisis in 1956.

Sir Albert Levy 1864–1937
Benefactor of the Royal Free and Eastman Dental hospitals.

Hans Liebeschuetz 1893–1978
German historian, an authority on German Jewish historiography.

Sir Philip Magnus 1842–1933
Mathematician, took an active interest in education and science.

Baron Sterling Nahum 1906–56
Photographer well known for his photographs of the royal family, he was official photographer at the Queen's Coronation.

Lawrence Phillips 1842–1922
Artist and inventor of patent sketching boxes, calculating machines and the rocking bar keyless watch.

Napoleon Sadek 1905–70
Lawyer, writer and journalist.

Sir Harry Samuel 1853–1934
Banker and M.P. at various times for St Pancras, Limehouse and Norwood.

Sir Edward Sassoon 1853–1934
Banker with business interests in the East.

Sir John Simon 1853–1934
The first M.P. for Dewsbury 1868–88 and the second Jew to practise as a barrister, mainly in Jamaica.

Sir Frederick Stern 1884–1967
Banker and horticulturalist, he specialised in growing lilies and daffodils; chairman of the John Innes Horticultural Institute, 1947–61.

EAST SIDE (SEPHARDI)

Arthur Blok 1882–1974
Principal examiner H.M. Patents Office, first director of the Israel Institute of Technology.

Philip Guedalla 1899–1944
Barrister, civil servant and historian. Author of many books on modern European history.

Stanley Setty 1902–49
Car dealer murdered by Donald Hume, his dismembered torso was discovered in the Essex marshes having been dropped into the sea by Hume from an aeroplane.

JEWISH (WEST LONDON REFORM) CEMETERY
Kingsbury Road, N1

Founded: 1843
Owner West London Synagogue
Acreage; Approx. ½

One of the unknown corners of London which still maintains a quiet dignity despite the depredations of a wartime landmine that fell across the road, vandals and the invasion of nature. The cemetery is no longer in use but was once the burial ground of many prominent Jewish families among the founders of the Reform movement, both Sephardi and Ashkenazi. Tomb design varies considerably and includes the Lawson sarcophagus of 1879, a splendid pink granite affair with bronze embellishments standing on four mighty bronze paws.

Interesting statistics can be gleaned from the burial register for the early years. Between 1843, the date of the first burial, and 1853, forty-two burials are recorded, seven were still births and the average age of the remaining deceased was only thirty-three.

Sir Isaac Goldsmid 1778–1858
Financier and bullion broker, a founder of University College, London and patron of University College Hospital. He was the first Jew to be made a baronet in 1841.

Sir Julian Goldsmid 1838–1934
M.P. for St Pancras 1885–96, Vice Chancellor London University and an art collector.

Lionel Lawson 1824–79
Made a fortune from manufacturing printing ink, a large shareholder in the *Daily Telegraph*.

Joseph Levy 1812–88
Founder of the *Daily Telegraph* 1855 which was sold for only 1*d*, the first London newspaper at that price. The Levy family changed their name to Lawson.

DAVID MARKS 1811–1909
Minister of the West London Synagogue, professor of Hebrew at London University for fifty-six years.

DAVID MOCATTA 1803–82
Architect who designed railway stations and synagogues, a founder of the West London Synagogue. He was 'endowed with superior mental gifts'.

CAMILLO ROTH –1888
Stockbroker. First professing Jew to be cremated, his ashes are interred in the grave.

JEWISH CEMETERY
LAURISTON ROAD, E9

Founded: 1788
Owner: The United Synagogue
Acreage: 2 ¼

One of the many Jewish cemeteries that are dotted about East London, this one originally belonged to the Hambro Synagogue. Unlike the others, Lauriston Road is not entirely enclosed by high walls and inside it is grassed rather than cindered. The nineteenth-century lodge is by H.H. Collins. The most distinctive feature is a central row of granite sarcophagi supported on granite paws, the last resting places of the rich philanthropist Magnus family. Many of the other headstones are now becoming illegible. By order of the Council, the cemetery was closed to burials in 1886, and had virtually ceased to operate by 1870 being then full, save for reserved space.

ISAAC VALENTINE 1822–98
Founder of the Jewish Orphan Asylum.

MORRIS VAN PRAAGH 1809–71
A president of the Hambro Synagogue.

JEWISH NEW SEPHARDI CEMETERY
MILE END ROAD, E1

Founded: 1733
Owner: Spanish and Portuguese Jews' Congregation
Acreage: Approx. 1

By 1724 the old Sephardi cemetery was almost full and a new ground (the 'Novo') about 200 yards to the east was acquired, known as 'The Cherry Tree' on account of the orchard that grew there. In 1732 this was cut down to make way for a mortuary building (demolished in 1922) and the ground was walled round ready for burials. For over 100 years almost all Anglo Sephardim were buried here. They included such prominent members as Diego Pereira, adviser to Maria Theresa of Austria, who created him Baron Aguiler, one of the first Jews in modern history to be ennobled;

Sampson Gideon, influential financier in eighteenth century England; Solomon da Costa Atias, whose Hebrew library is now in the British Museum; the moneylender Don Pacifico, whose British citizenship almost provoked a war in 1850 and the boxer Daniel Mendoza. The graves of these men and some 7,000 others filled the new ground so that an adjacent plot was needed in 1849, which served for another fifty years, when the Golders Green cemetery was bought.

Since then the 'Novo' has undergone drastic changes. In 1940 eighty graves were destroyed by bombs and a commemorative monument now marks the place of the original reinternment. Then in 1974, despite unprecedented demonstrations by many rabbis, the original Cherry Tree plot was sold to the neighbouring Queen Mary College for redevelopment, and all remains interred prior to 1873, moved to a one acre site in Brentwood. Only some 2,000 nineteenth- and twentieth-century graves now remain, marked by battered horizontal slabs. Inscriptions still reveal the names of distinguished Jewish families, among them Sassoon, Lindo and Montefiore.

Henry Hart 1818–91
Merchant in South America, he established the first synagogue in Argentina.

Jacob Montefiore 1801–95
The 'last survivor of the commissioners appointed in 1834 by William IV for the colonisation of South Australia'.

JEWISH OLD SEPHARDI CEMETERY
Mile End Road, E1

Founded 1657
Owner: *Spanish and Portuguese Jews' Congregation*
Acreage: *1½*

Somehow, while all around has been devastated for redevelopment, this small dusty ground manages to survive, combining its role as a cemetery with that of garden for the temporary residents of the old hospital, now a students' hostel, on its southern flank. For over 300 years the land has been a cemetery and as such is the oldest surviving Jewish cemetery in the country.

The Sephardim, refugees of the Spanish inquisitions, had lived a sequestered life in London until the Commonwealth, when they successfully petitioned Oliver Cromwell for permission to establish a synagogue and a cemetery. As a result the Mile End Road site was acquired, known as the Old or 'Velho' cemetery, and first used for the interment of Mrs Isaac de Brito in 1657 with assistance from the Churchwardens of St Katherine Cree who tolled their bell and lent a pall for a fee of 2s 4d. In 1684 the brick wall was first built and a carved stone slab set into the present wall records the event. The cemetery was soon much in demand, the registers report a number of plague victims in the 1660s and an appalling record of infant mortality. There are over 600 entries prefixed 'el angelito' to indicate a child's interment. Not surprisingly, by 1737 the cemetery was full and a new ground was acquired further east in the Mile End Road.

Today, the characteristic flat marble tomb slabs of the Sephardim merchants lie flush to the ground. A few have been rebuilt in recent years, but for the most part only faint Spanish or Hebrew inscriptions or the odd skull and crossbones symbol have outlived the rigours of East End transformation.

Antonio Carvajal −1659
A merchant from Amsterdam and largely responsible for establishing the new Jewish community in England. The cemetery ground was leased to him in 1657.

Simon de Caceres −1704
Merchant, he advised Cromwell on the defence of Jamaica and on plans for the conquest of Chile.

Don Isaac Lindo 1636−1712
One of the first Jewish brokers in the City and an ancestor of Disraeli.

Don Fernando Mendes −1724
Physician to John IV of Portugal, accompanied Catherine of Braganza to England and attended Charles II in his last illness.

David Nieto 1654−1728
Hebrew scholar and rabbi at the Bevis Marks synagogue. His epitaph reads: 'Sublime theologian, profound sage, distinguished physician, famous astronomer, sweet poet, elegant preacher, subtle logician, ingenious physician, fluent rhetorician, pleasant author, expert in languages, learned in history.'

JEWISH CEMETERY
Montagu Road, N18

Founded: 1884
Owner: Federation Burial Society and the Western Synagogue
Acreage: Approx. 20

A busy cemetery with a steady stream of visiting relatives. There must be more marble and polished granite per square yard here than anywhere else in London. The style is nearly always the same, tall headstones, sometimes with an embellishment of classical derivation, in row after row with scarcely a distracting feature, not even a blade of grass, between them. There are two brick mausolea, one commemorating a Russian rabbi who died in 1910 on a fundraising visit to London. Like most Jewish cemeteries it is secured behind high walls.

In stark contrast to the marble finery is the little brick prayer hall, totally unfurnished save the religious texts in Hebrew.

Samuel Montagu, 1ˢᵗ Lord Swaythling 1832−1911
Banker, founder of the firm Samuel Montagu dealing in the foreign exchange market, Liberal M.P. for Whitechapel 1885–1900. Supported conversion to the metric system as president of the Decimal Association; philanthropist.

JEWISH CEMETERY
Plashet Park, High Street, East Ham, E6

Founded: 1896
Owner: The United Synagogue
Acreage: 14

A small rectangular cemetery laid out in characteristic Jewish style. The tombstones are closely packed in straight rows with only one spinal path, a few stunted trees and no flowers or shrubs. The *Ohel* (prayer hall) still exists to the rear of the courtyard behind the main gates, although the Victorian lodge has been sold off and much altered. The Plashet is now a forlorn place, deserted by mourners, very different from the scene witnessed by T.W. Wilkinson in 1906:

Plashet: Consecrating a memorial, from *Living London* (1906)

> From the little synagogue [Ohel] comes the sound of a wild sobbing incantation. We enter. Immediately the central figure arrests the eye. It is that of the minister, who stands by a coffin in the middle of the hall, chanting the psalm in Hebrew, his voice rising and falling in minor cadences that vibrate the heartstrings like the most inspired music of sorrow... Presently the mourners – all males – break out into a kind of response. Then there is a sudden move. The coffin is placed on a bier, carried through the doorway, and, after a short halt just outside, conveyed straight to the rude grave which has been prepared for it alone. Never do the Jews place two bodies in one grave. The pall is withdrawn from the coffin – that plain, unpolished, undecorated shell of deal in which the Jew, whether a Rothschild or a pauper, usually returns to Mother Earth. A moment later and there is an intermittent rattle as each of the party, the minister included, seizes a shovel and casts some gravel into the gulf. And now all is over.[1]

LIBERAL JEWISH CEMETERY
Pound Lane, NW10

Founded: 1914
Owner: The Liberal Jewish Synagogue (St John's Wood)
Acreage: 4

The Liberal Jewish Cemetery is one of a trio of burial grounds in Willesden; adjacent is that of the United Synagogue and the Willesden Cemetery in Franklyn Road. Accessed from a private road next to the fire station, and having passed the caretakers' house, the drive sweeps round to the prayer hall (*Ohel*). It was designed by Ernest Joseph, Lord Bearsted's architect who worked mainly for the Shell Oil Company, for which he designed the Shell-Mex Building on the Embankment. In contrast, the prayer hall resembles a brick pavilion in the Queen Anne revival style with a hipped roof, a pediment over the door and arched windows. The foundation stone was laid in January 1925.[1] A stone at the rear records the construction of an extension: 'This building erected in 1963 to celebrate the Liberal Jewish Synagogue's Golden Jubilee and to commemorate the life and works of Lily Montagu is dedicated to the worship of God and advancement of a living Judaism.' Directly in front of the prayer hall is a war memorial cenotaph crowned by a stone lamp.

The cemetery is well maintained and is comparatively well planted for a Jewish burial ground. Hedges enclose a number of family plots while some areas are grassed and a cluster of trees can be found in the centre of the cemetery; a row of poplars stand isolated near the caretakers' house.

The most interesting memorials are near the prayer hall. Of prominence is the mourning bronze figure commemorating the sculptor Benno Elkan and his wife. A further work by Elkan appears on the rear of the Holocaust memorial in the centre of the cemetery. Erected in 1957 a bronze tondo depicts a partly kneeling male figure, head bowed and holding an upturned torch. Nearby is a large grey granite chest tomb detailed in Egyptian revival style commemorating the Baron family. The most unusual memorial dated 1936, comprises four stone tortoises which support a curved sided pedestal confined between two discs, the upper inscribed with the name Conchita Rubenstein who 'Died with her daughter'.

Older memorials include draped urns, obelisks and a few sarcophagi in a variety of materials, but the remaining examples are more conventional. Unusually for a Jewish cemetery, a columbarium can be found against a wall near the prayer hall. Further evidence of the Reform movement's acceptance of cremation is signified by the rows of dedicated rose trees marking the burial of ashes.

BENNO ELKAN 1877–1960
Sculptor.

JEWISH CEMETERY
ROWAN ROAD, SW16

Founded: 1915
Owner: West End Chesed V'Emeth Burial Society.
Acreage: 5½

This cemetery is typical of Jewish cemetery design.[1] The recently renovated prayer hall, or *Ohel* (meaning 'tent'), stands near the entrance, from which a path cuts directly down the centre of the ground surrounded by a forest of tall white marble headstones which fill every available space. There are no trees, virtually no flowers and little variation in the design of the marble slabs. Conformity even extends to the inscriptions which, with slight variations, follow the formula: 'deeply mourned by a devoted wife (husband), son, daughter-in-law, grandchildren, brother, sisters, brother-in-law, sisters-in-law, nephews, nieces, relatives and friends'. Only the deceased's name appears, it being the custom that the names of the living are not mentioned.

Most of those buried here are of Eastern European origin who settled in the Soho area of London working as tailors, cabinet makers, shopkeepers and so on. The cemetery is now closed, superseded by a new one at Cheshunt.

JEWISH CEMETERY, WEST HAM
BUCKINGHAM ROAD, E15

Founded: 1857
Owner: The United Synagogue
Acreage: 10½

Duplication of land use at Brady Street was only a temporary solution to the New Synagogue's burial problem and in 1857 the congregation joined with the Great Synagogue to buy five acres from the banker, Samuel Gurney, adjoining the new cemetery of West Ham. Today the contrast between the two could not be more marked. Whereas the latter enjoys an expansive garden setting, the Jewish cemetery is conspicuous for its burnt grass, grey cinder paths and decaying monuments. The central avenue of pollarded trees have now been removed and it is well worth walking to the end of this path where stands one of London's architectural curiosities, the magnificent mausoleum built in 1866 for Evelina de Rothschild. She died in childbirth aged twenty-seven and her heartbroken husband, Ferdinand, employed the distinguished architect Sir Matthew Digby Wyatt (he was currently at work on the India office in Whitehall and had just been awarded the R.I.B.A. gold medal) to design a suitable memorial for her.

Ferdinand de Rothschild was a collector with an extravagant taste for Renaissance art and this is reflected in the peripteral domed rotunda he had built. Everywhere the name Eva or the initials E.R. have been entwined in the building's decoration. On his own death in 1898 he too was buried here, beside his wife.

The cemetery's prayer hall, which was little more than a corrugated iron shack, has been demolished. It was built on an extension of land in 1874 and replaced by an earlier building. Other monuments too are insignificant. The older ones tend to be of York stone but white marble is now preferred. What they lack in size however is often compensated for by the standard of rhetorical epitaphs. A typical example of the genre reads:

> Passenger! At this sad shrine drop a tear;
> O'er innocence and beauty that slumber here.
> Alas! A consuming fire has laid low
> These flowers than which sweeter ne'er did show,
> Yet this sacred spot conceals but their earthly clod,
> Their spirits now bloom in the Paradise of God.

Lines which commemorate three children who died in 1897.
Another headstone, now fading with age is, ironically, inscribed:

> Though cold in death alas! Our rainy tears will keep his memory green for years and years.

At the north end of the cemetery several of the paths were excavated in 1960 for reinterring remains moved from the Old Jewish Cemetery in Hoxton Street. This was a tiny quarter-acre ground used between 1707 and 1878 by the Hambro Synagogue of Fenchurch Street.

Ferdinand de Rothschild 1839–98
Built Waddesdon Manor, Buckinghamshire 1874–89 to resemble a French chateau, furnished with French eighteenth-century furniture. M.P. for Aylesbury 1885–98. He endowed the Evelina Hospital for Children in Southwark Bridge Road in memory of his wife Evelina 1839–66.

Sir Benjamin Phillips 1810–89
Fancy goods warehouse owner, the first Jew elected as a common councilman in London, Lord Mayor of London 1865–66.

David Salomons 1797–1873
A founder of the London and Westminster Bank, he was active encouraging legislation permitting Jews to hold municipal offices; appointed the first Jewish magistrate in Kent in 1838, first Jewish Lord Mayor of London 1855–56, Liberal M.P. for Greenwich 1859–73.

James Samuel 1797–1866
Founder of the firm J. Samuel and Son, monumental masons which has carved many of the better monuments in London's Jewish cemeteries.

JEWISH CEMETERY, WILLESDEN
Glebe Road, NW10

Founded: 1873
Owner: The United Synagogue
Acreage: 23

The cemetery is tucked behind the Rolls Royce coachworks of Ward Mulliner and is, appropriately, the Rolls Royce among London's Jewish cemeteries. Here are buried members of some of the most important Jewish families in Britain, including numerous Rothschilds.

The cemetery was designed by Nathan Joseph, a Jewish architect who specialised in artisan dwellings and synagogues. His Willesden buildings, each designed for a specific purpose in the ritual of Jewish burial practice, were described by *The Builder* in 1873 as follows:

> A central one, intended for the reception of the coffin, with the mourners, during the recital of the preliminary prayers, being in fact, what in other communions is designated a chapel, but which, perhaps, we may call an oratory. It has broad windows. On the left side of this structure is a building for the cohanim, who are not permitted to enter in close proximity to a grave. This is a single room. Opposite it is a third building, consisting internally of two portions, a 'tahara' room, or room for the performance of the rites of ablution of the dead, and a lavatory, with necessary retiring rooms.[1]

The choice of the English Gothic style for these buildings in traditional Kentish ragstone seems curious and they stand incongruously amid a vast sea of marble and granite. Moreover, the size and close proximity of the 30,000 monuments, the well maintained plants and paths suggest something more akin to Père Lachaise than a London cemetery.

Willesden: The Rosenberg tombs (1904-35)

New tombs are now confined to an area near the main gate. The first of the old tend to be near the main axial path with all the Rothschilds to the west and south of it, several in little balustraded and railed enclosures. At Willesden the monumental mason has had a field day, usually working with combinations of pink and grey coloured granites, or, in the case of the Joel family plot, incorporating marble as well, cordoned off by elaborate ironwork (which has been stolen). The Rosenbergs from Newcastle preferred quantity; a quartet of exactly matching tall grey granite shrines are an imposing sight. Walter Samuel's family from Liverpool chose white marble on a grand scale, and built an enclosure with enormous Corinthian columns. Amid this polished finery Sir Israel Gollancz's rough hewn granite monolith, carved with a quotation from Beowulf, is a refreshing surprise.

Hermann Adler 1838-1911
German born chief rabbi of the United Hebrew Congregations of the British Commonwealth 1891-1911.

Nathan Adler 1803-90
German-born chief rabbi of the United Hebrew Congregation of the British Commonwealth 1844-90.

Barney Isaacs Barnato 1852-97
Hatton garden diamond merchant with interests in South Africa including a 1/10 stake in de Beers; committed suicide by jumping overboard from a ship in the mid-Atlantic.

Marcus, Lord Bearsted 1853-1927
Developed the Near East oil industry, shipping oil through Suez for the first time. Lord Mayor of London 1902-3.

Gerald Bright 1904–74
Known as Geraldo, a popular 'big band' leader in variety and cabaret.

Sir Israel Brodie 1895–1979
Chief rabbi in the United Kingdom, co-founder of the Zionist Federation of Australia.

Sir Charles Clore 1904–79
Businessman, property developer, financier, with particular interests in shoe manufacture and shipping; a director of the Ritz Hotel.

Sir John Cohen 1898–1979
The founder of Tesco Stores.

Sir Anthony de Rothschild 1811–76
Banker, first president of the United Synagogue 1870.

Charlotte, Baroness de Rothschild, 1819–1884
A philanthropist who maintained a soup kitchen in East London, patroness of young musicians.

Meyer de Rothschild 1818–74
Banker, builder of Mentmore and racehorse owner, he won the Derby in 1871.

Joseph, Lord Duveen of Millbank, 1869–1939
Art dealer and benefactor of many British art galleries and the British Museum.

Sir Joseph Duveen 1843–1908
Dutch born art dealer, he financed the Turner galleries at the Tate Gallery and gave many paintings to the nation.

Sir Israel Gollancz 1863–1930
Professor of English literature at London University and prolific author on many aspects of the subject.

Joseph Hertz –1946
Czech born chief rabbi 1913–46.

Solomon Joel 1865–1931
Director of several South African diamond mining companies and a motor-racing enthusiast.

Sir Eric Miller 1927–77
Chairman of the Peachey Property Corporation, knighted in Sir Harold Wilson's controversial resignation honours list, took his own life soon afterwards on the Jewish day of Atonement.

Louis Montagu, 2nd Lord Swaythling 1869–1927
Together with his son Stuart Montagu, 3rd Lord Swaythling (1898–1990), both bankers and farmers.

Hannah, Countess of Rosebery 1851–90
Born a Rothschild, she inherited Mentmore in 1874. A philanthropist, she died of typhoid.

Alfred Rothschild 1842–1918
Banker, a director of the Bank of England and an art collector.

Lionel, Lord Rothschild 1868–1937
Zoologist, established his own natural history museum at Tring, the contents of which were left to the British Museum.

Lionel Rothschild 1808–79
Manager of the family's banking interests in England, M.P. for the City of London 1859–74. Race horse owner, he won the Derby in 1879.

Nathan, Lord Rothschild 1840–1915
Owned 10,000 acres and a pack of staghounds in Buckinghamshire. M.P. for Aylesbury 1865–85.

The Hon. Nathaniel Rothschild 1877–1927
Banker and entomologist.

Herbert Samuel, 1st Viscount Samuel 1870–1963
A leader of the Liberal party, M.P. for Cleveland 1902–19 and Darwen 1929–35. He was appointed Home Secretary in 1916 and 1931 and was High Commissioner in Palestine 1919–25.

Simeon Singer 1846–1906
Author of the *Singer's Siddur*, the Authorised Daily Prayer Book of the United Synagogue.

Edward Solomon 1855–1890
Pianist and composer of comic operas.

Sir Isidore Spielman 1854–1925
Served on the board of numerous art galleries and museums, an enthusiastic promoter of British art.

Sir Meyer Spielman 1856–1936
Banker and member of many committees on education, he wrote *Romance of Child Reclamation*.

Marc Tager –1988
One of the 270 passengers and crew killed in an aeroplane crash at Lockerbie as a result of a terrorist bomb explosion.

KENSAL GREEN CEMETERY AND WEST LONDON CREMATORIUM
Harrow Road, W10

Founded: 1833
Owner: The General Cemetery Company
Acreage: 72

Many people would regard Kensal Green as the most distinguished of London's cemeteries. Not only is it older than the others with an early history synonymous with the early history of the whole English cemetery movement, but it also retains its original range of buildings and boasts an unequalled array of mausolea, three of which commemorate royalty.[1]

Its story begins with George Carden, the barrister who began campaigning for burial reform in the 1820s and who was largely responsible for establishing the General Cemetery Company in 1830. He succeeded in persuading a number of architects, aristocrats and business men to join the board including a banker, Sir John Dean Paul, who, in 1831, purchased fifty-four acres of land for the company at Kensal Green for the price of £9,500. (The fact that the ground was heavy London clay seems to have been ignored by the enthusiastic company promoters). Only a few months later London was experiencing its first cholera epidemic and Parliament needed little persuasion to pass a Bill 'for establishing a General Cemetery for the interment of the Dead in the Neighbourhood of the Metropolis'[2] in July 1832. The Act provided a model copied by other private cemetery companies set up in the following twenty years. (An important clause provided for the compensation of parish clergy who might otherwise have benefited from burial fees, at a rate of between 1s 6d and 5s depending on the type of burial).

The company had earlier taken steps to commission a designer of cemetery buildings, but without success. Several members of the board had artistic pretensions including the architects John Griffith and Thomas Willson, the artist A.C. Pugin and the sculptor Robert Sievier. Not surprisingly the issue became highly contentious. Architects who had been considered, and rejected by the end of 1831, were Benjamin Wyatt, who refused the job, Charles Fowler, Francis Goodwin and Thomas Willson. In November 1831 it was decided a competition might solve the problem for designing a chapel costing no more than £10,000 and a gateway for £3,000. From forty-six entries, Henry Kendall was declared the winner with his Gothic designs, but almost immediately these attracted criticism from a number of directors. A review of the drawings in The Gentleman's Magazine perhaps sums up the opposition's opinion. Kendall's Gothic was:

> A rather florid style of architecture ... the slender proportions as well as the number of Mr Kendall's spires and pinnacles seem to us to be at variance with the sepulchral character of the edifice ...[3]

The crux of the problem was one that dogged English architects of the period – whether to build in the Gothic or the classical style. In this case the classicists finally won the day and Carden, a Gothic advocate, was voted off the Board. Thus it was that the classical chapels, gateway and lodges were designed by John Griffith and finally completed in 1837, over four years after the cemetery's dedication and the first interment of Margaret Gregory on 31 January 1833.

The chapels are austere Greek revival in style, the Anglicans having the Doric order, the Nonconformists, Ionic, and both with flanking colonnades and brick vaulted catacombs beneath with space, apparently, for 4,000 bodies. The Anglican chapel had the additional novelty of a hydraulic catafalque which lowers coffins directly from the chapel to the catacombs where they were stacked, some covered in velvet, and secured behind iron grilles, stone panels or glass windows. (The catafalque was restored in 1997.)

The main gateway resembles a triumphal arch with an attic story over the centre.[4] It gave access to the grounds landscaped by Griffith with the assistance of A.C. Pugin and the ideas of at least one previous unsuccessful planner, a Mr Liddell who had been a pupil of John Nash. Certainly the influence of Nash's formal design for Regent's Park is noticeable at Kensal Green which also has a central path circle divided into quadrants. The plan ensured careful demarcation between the forty-seven acres of consecrated ground for the established church and only seven allocated to others, in the approved fashion.

> The left hand road, as will be anticipated, leads to the abodes of the Turks, Jews, Infidels, Heretics and 'unbaptised folk' and the right hand after passing among the beautiful and consecrated graves of the faithful, leads to the Episcopal chapel. This chapel is a beautifully executed work, in the same style as the entrance buildings and is fitted up in excellent taste.[5]

Wrote a contemporary observer.

Kensal Green was an immediate success attracting the cream of the West End trade. By 1842 Laman Blanchard was:

> startled by the number of monuments. It is scarcely ten years since the sheep were driven from their pasture, and already has there been about 6000 interments...[6]

The number of enormous mausolea was certainly something to marvel at. For maximum satisfaction some occupants, like James Morison, built them during their lifetime. *The Builder* was stuffy in its comments; while conceding 'some show excellent work and a lavish expenditure' it referred to the tombs generally as 'dreary inanities' and Andrew Ducrow's Egyptian mausoleum in particular as 'ponderous coxcombery'.[7] But after the Duke of Sussex chose Kensal Green as his final resting place in 1843 the cemetery's popularity was assured. The Centre Avenue and the area round the chapels has the highest concentration of large mausolea, representing most architectural styles. There are towering Gothic confections (John Gibson 1892 and the Molyneux family 1864, Egyptian caprices (Ducrow 1842); classical caryatids (Sir William Casement 1844); and temples (John St John Long 1834); Renaissance effigies (William Mulready 1863); huge obelisks (Sir Richard Mayne 1868); and many others less easily defined.

A number of distinguished architects designed tombs in Kensal Green; for example, George Basevi (Hankey family 1838); Edward Blore (Gen. Foster Walker 1866); William Burges (Capt. Charles Ricketts 1867); C.R. Cockerell (Lady Pulteney 1849); John Gibson (Molyneux family 1864); Owen Jones (Chappell family 1849); and J.B. Papworth (Galloway family 1838). A host of sculptors are represented including several by Robert Sievier, a director of the company, and Prince Albert's own artistic advisor, Professor Grüner, who designed Princess Sophia's charming sarcophagus in 1848. The memorial to Marigold Frances Churchill was by Eric Gill, but this has been stolen.

By the beginning of the new century the cemetery directors were obliged to issue a notice to the public because 'many persons labour under the impression that the vacant space in this cemetery is becoming exhausted' and they made clear this was not the case. In fact an additional plot of land west of the old cemetery had been acquired which at the time was 'practically untouched.'[8]

However, even this part is now filling up and the company, which has outlived all its rivals, has been forced to sell plots on the verge of the old paths for new burials. This is unfortunate as it spoils the original spacious layout. Decay and vandalism have also played their part in altering the appearance of the cemetery and some *ad hoc* attempts to prevent destruction such as the brutal bricking up of mausolea doors are very unsatisfactory. Nevertheless, a more optimistic picture for Kensal Green was signalled in 1984, when part of the cemetery was designated a conservation area. Six years later the Friends of Kensal Green cemetery was launched. Increased awareness of the qualities of the cemetery and active help from The Friends have done much to save one of London's most important nineteenth-century architectural monuments. They have instigated the restoration of the Dissenters' chapel together with its catacomb, the reinstatement of the curved colonnades and conservation work on a number of memorials. The Friends produce literature, organise regular lectures and tours and arrange an annual open day.

Burials continue in the cemetery and near the western entrance are a number of new mausolea and memorials, some of them undoubtedly expensively produced but of dubious merit. A black granite seat decorated in the style of a market stall complete with coloured fruits and hanging light bulbs must be unique. There is a further collection of thirteen new brick mausolea in the burial area near the crematorium which, from a distance, look like a row of beach huts.

A large island area to the west of the old cemetery has recently been acquired by the Christian Orthodox Church and was consecrated in 2005. Beyond is the West London Crematorium opened by Lord Horder in 1939. The architect of the building, G. Berkeley Willis, must be credited for attempting to maintain the classical idiom of the original chapels, albeit in a rather ponderous fashion, using for the most part unattractive cream coloured bricks. Above the entrance is the inscription *Mors Janua Vitae* (death the gateway to life). The fumes from the cremators are cunningly carried up flues in the angles of the wall so that the chimneys are practically invisible. The west chapel was left unfinished and unused until 1996 when the paved courtyard between the chapels was enclosed at each end by large glazed panels and entrance doors.

At the rear of the chapels are the usual loggias and garden of memory, planned by Edward White, although the water features have now been replaced by flower beds. A former president of the Institute of Landscape Architects, White specialised in crematoria gardens with Stoke Poges Memorial Gardens his most prominent work.

A more extensive list of those buried at Kensal Green can be found in *Paths of Glory* published by The Friends of Kensal Green cemetery (1997).

Kensal Green: The 'towering gothic confection' tomb of John Gibson (1894)

Kensal Green: Sir William Casement's Mausoleum (1844)

Col. Frederick Aikman 1828–88
Won the V.C. during the Indian Mutiny when he led his 100 men in routing 700 rebels.

Harrison Ainsworth 1805–82
Journalist, playwright and author of some forty novels. He lived for a while at Kensal manor, near the cemetery.

James Albery 1838–89
Dramatist and playwright.

Thomas Alllom 1804–77
Architect and artist.

Henry Angelo 1780–1852
'Superintendent of sword exercise to the army and navy', he ran a well known fencing school in St James's Street.

Charles Apperley 1778–1843
Alias 'Nimrod' the sports writer.

Henry Ashbee 1834–1900
City merchant in the silk trade, bibliophile and author. He owned the finest collection of books on Cervantes outside Spain.

Sir William Atherton 1806–64
M.P. for Durham 1852–64, solicitor general 1859, attorney general 1861.

Augustus Frederick, Duke of Sussex, 1773–1843
Sixth son of George III. He chose to be buried at Kensal Green following the confusion he witnessed at William IV's funeral in Windsor. His wife Cecilia is also buried here.

John Auldjo 1805–86
Mountaineer and geographer, he made the fourteenth ascent of Mont Blanc in 1827 and afterwards wrote of his experiences.

Charles Babbage 1791–1871
Distinguished mathematician. His calculating machines were forerunners of modern computers.

Michael Balfe 1808–70
Irish musician, he composed for the theatre. There is a memorial to him in Westminster Abbey.

William Banting 1826–1901
A royal undertaker. The family firm conducted minor royal funerals throughout the nineteenth century and until 1932.

Rev. Richard Barham 1788–1845
Author of the *Ingoldsby Legends* (reinterred from St Mary Magdalen, Fish Street 1891).

Thomas Barnes 1785–1841
Editor of *The Times* 1817–41; 'the most powerful man in the country', said Lord Lyndhurst.

'James' Barry 1795–1865
The first woman doctor, she concealed her sex while serving as an army surgeon. She was inspector-general of hospitals 1858–59 and only discovered to be a woman when laid out after death.

Gaetano Bartolozzi 1757–1821
Italian engraver and father of Madame Vestris (see below), his passion for music and fencing caused him to neglect his trade and he died in poverty.

Hezekiah Bateman 1812–75
American actor and theatre manager who gave Irving his first chance in *The Bells*.

Sir William Beatty –1842
Naval surgeon, he attended Nelson at his death at Trafalgar in 1805 and afterwards kept the fatal ball mounted in gold.

William Behnes 1791–1864
Sculptor, at one time very successful and appointed sculptor in ordinary to the Queen, he died 'in the gutter with threepence in his pocket'.

Sir Julius Benedict 1804–85
German born conductor of opera in London and the Norwich music festival 1845–78.

William Cavendish Bentinck-Scott, 5th Duke of Portland, 1800–79
Spent £4 million at his seat Welbeck, Notts., in his enthusiasm for privacy, gardening and horse-racing. Projects included one and a half miles of tunnels, a 1,000ft long glass peach house, a glass covered gallop and riding school.

GEORGE BIRKBECK 1776–1841
Doctor and founder of the London Mechanics' Institute which became Birkbeck College.

JAMES BISHOP 1783–1854
London organ builder, his firm in Kensal Green is still in existence.

REV. JOHN BLAKE 1839–1906
Clergyman, scientist and geologist, he was president of the Geological Association 1891–92 and wrote numerous works on the subject.

EMILE BLONDIN 1824–97
Tightrope walker who achieved fame by crossing a tributary at Niagara Falls. He died at Niagara House, Ealing.

BRIG.GEN.GUY BOISRAGON 1864–1931
Won the V.C. in India in 1891. (Headstone replaced 2006).

SIR SAMUEL BONHAM 1803–63
Colonial governor, his last post was governor and commander in chief, Hong Kong.

RICHARD BONINGTON 1802–28
Landscape painter trained in France and a friend of Delacroix. His remains were exhumed from Pentonville churchyard in 1837.

JOHN BRAHAM 1774–1856
Tenor opera singer.

WILLIAM BRODERIP 1789–1859
Judge, conchologist and a founder of the Zoological Society, his shell collection was left to the British Museum.

CHARLES BROOKS 1816–74
Novelist, editor of *Punch* 1870–74 and author of comic verse.

ISAMBARD BRUNEL 1806–59
Engineer, his achievements include the designs for the 'Great Eastern', the Clifton Suspension Bridge and the Great Western Railway.

SIR MARC BRUNEL 1769–1849
Born in France and father of Isambard. An engineer, he designed the Thames tunnel at Rotherhithe in 1825 which was opened by Queen Victoria in 1843.

PETER BURROWES 1753–1841
Lawyer and Irish M.P. renowned for his opposition to Union and as supporter of Catholic rights.

GAZETTEER

DECIMUS BURTON 1800–81
Architect, his stuccoed classical buildings include the Athenaeum and estates in Bloomsbury and Tunbridge Wells.

ANNE, LADY BYRON 1792–1860
Wife of Lord Byron, for a year.

SIR AUGUSTUS CALCOTT 1779–1844
Landscape and seascape artist. Also his wife, Maria, 1785–1842, author of children's books, traveller and historian.

JOHN CARADOC. 2ND LORD HOWDEN, 1799–1873
A.D.C. to Wellington in Paris and subsequently ambassador to Brazil and Spain.

GEORGE CARDEN 1798–1874
Barrister and cemetery reformer. Founder of The General Cemetery Company.

GEN.SIR WILLIAM CASEMENT 1780–1844
Member of the Council of India, his tomb was sculpted by F.M. Lander, a local monumental mason, using artificial stone.

SIR ERNEST CASSEL 1852–1921
German born financier, philanthropist and friend of Edward VII.

JOHN CASSELL 1817–65
Self educated publisher, *Cassell's Illustrated Family Paper* was his most successful venture. A strict teetotaller.

MARIGOLD CHURCHILL 1918–1921
Infant daughter of Sir Winston and Lady Churchill.

SIR CASPAR CLARKE 1846–1911
Director of the Victoria and Albert Museum for nine years and the Metropolitan Museum for a further five, 'were he blindfolded he would know spurious objects from their odour'.

DR JOHN CLIFFORD 1836–1923
Baptist minister and president of the World Federation of Brotherhoods, 1919–20.

JAMES COBBETT 1806–42
Cricketer who excelled as a slow round arm bowler.

ADM.SIR GEORGE COCKBURN 1772–1853
Served under Nelson and conveyed Napoleon to St Helena where he remained as governor of the island for a year, later a Tory M.P.

Wilkie Collins 1824–89
Novelist, writer of 'sensation' novels, the best known being *The Woman in White* (1860) and *The Moonstone* (1868).

Robert Collum 1806–1900
President of the Royal College of Surgeons, for many years served in India.

Sir Michael Costa 1808–84
Neapolitan born musician, he was conductor Covent Garden 1846–60 and was the first in England to conduct with a baton instead of a violin bow in 1832.

Sir Cresswell Cresswell 1793–1863
M.P. for Liverpool 1837–42 and a judge in the Court of Probate and Divorce. He adjudicated upon 1,000 cases in only one of which was his judgement reversed.

Allan Cunningham 1784–1842
Scottish writer and art historian, he wrote *Lives of the most eminent British Painters Sculptors and Architects* in six volumes.

Thomas Daniell 1749–1840
Landscape artist who specialised in oriental subjects, having travelled in India sketching 1788–93.

James Dark 1795–1871
Cricketer, umpire and proprietor of Lords cricket ground 1836–64.

George Darley 1795–1846
Irish lyric poet and mathematician.

John de Courcy, Lord Kingsale 1827–65
Premier baron of Ireland. He astonished onlookers in 1859 by reviving the old de Courcy privilege of remaining covered in the presence of the Sovereign.

Thomas de la Rue 1793–1866
Printer. Founded family firm in 1821.

Lowes Cato Dickinson 1819–1908
Portrait painter of royalty. Co-founder of the Christian Socialist Movement and the Working Men's College. His monument is by Eric Gill.

Gen.Sir Collingwood Dickson 1817–1904
An artillery officer, he won the V.C. in the Crimea in 1854.

Charles Dilke 1789–1864
Literary critic, antiquary and editor of *The Athenaeum*. The ashes of his son, Sir Charles Dilke (1843–1911) are buried in this family vault. A left wing M.P. for Chelsea, his career was curtailed by a sensational divorce case in 1886.

GEN. SIR MOORE DISNEY 1766–1846
Distinguished himself as commander of the reserve force that covered Sir John Moore's retreat at Corunna.

MAJ. GEN. MATTHEW DIXON 1821–1905
Won the V.C. at the siege of Sebastopol in 1854.

SIR WILLIAM DON 1825–62
Actor and racehorse owner, he sold his horse Newtondon for £85,000.

ANDREW DUCROW 1793–1842
'The Colossus of equestrians' and circus owner. His mausoleum by Danson cost £3,000 to build and was decorated by John Cusworth. Inscribed on it are the words 'this tomb erected by genius for the reception of its own remains'.

JOSEPH DURHAM 1814–1877
Sculptor with a speciality in fountain design.

Kensal Green: Baroque angels over Mary Gibson's Corinthian temple monument (1870)

GEORGE DYER 1755–1841
Bibliophile and historian of Cambridge University.

SIR CHARLES EASTLAKE 1793–1865
President of the Royal Academy, director of the National Gallery 1855–65 and author of many books on art. He was buried first in Florence and reinterred here in 1866.

JOHN PASSMORE EDWARDS 1823–1911
Newspaper proprietor and philanthropist who established schools, libraries and hospitals.

SARAH FAIRBROTHER 1816–90
nown as Mrs Fitzgeorge, she was married to George, Duke of Cambridge (see below).

HUGH FALCONER 1808–65
Superintendent of the Botanical Gardens, Calcutta, he helped to establish the Assam tea industry.

ROBERT FELLOWES 1770–1847
Theologist and philanthropist, he helped to endow University College, London.

ALLEYN FITZHERBERT, LORD ST. HELENS, 1753–1839
Diplomat, as ambassador to Russia he was a friend of Catherine the Great. Subsequently Lord of the Bedchamber to George III and a trustee of the British Museum. His valuable art collection was destroyed by fire.

RICHARD FLEXMORE 1824–60
Dancer and clown, well known for his imitations of leading contemporary dancers.

JOHN FORSTER 1812–76
Drama critic, biographer and executor of Charles Dickens.

SIR FRANCIS FREELING 1764–1836
Secretary to the Post Office, he reformed the use of mail coaches. Also a book collector.

DR HENRY GAUNTLETT 1805–76
Organist and composer, wrote the tune for 'Once in Royal David's City'.

GEORGE, DUKE OF CAMBRIDGE 1819–1904
Grandson of George III. Commander in Chief of British Army 1856–95, served in the Crimea. Funeral attended by Edward VII, the Prince of Wales and foreign royalty.

JOHN GIBSON 1817–92
Architect, he designed several banks and the Middlesex Guildhall.

GEN. SIR WALTER GILBERT 1785–1853
Member of the Council of India, sportsman and racing enthusiast.

ISABELLA GLYN 1823–89
Shakespearian actress, imprisoned for two years in 1874 for declining to release documents related to her divorce.

SIR JOHN GOSS 1800–80
Organist at St Paul's Cathedral for thirty-five years, he composed the anthem played at Wellington's funeral.

GEN. HUGH GOUGH 1833–1909
Won the V.C. during the Indian Mutiny. His brother also won the medal, one of four cases where brothers have achieved this distinction.

THOMAS GRATTAN 1792–1864
Author of *Highways and Byways* and some fifteen other works. British consul in Massachusetts 1839–46.

GEORGE GREENOUGH 1778–1855
Geologist and president of the Royal Geographical Society 1839–40 and the Geological Society 1811–18 and 1833–35.

BARNARD GREGORY 1796–1852
Actor and editor of *The Satirist*, imprisoned twice for libel, his vilification of the Duke of Brunswick caused the latter to lead a riot at Covent Garden where he was playing 'Hamlet'.

GEORGE GROSSMITH 1847–1912
Entertainer, singer of light opera and co-author with his brother Weedon of *The Diary of a Nobody* (1894).

ADM. SIR EDWARD HAMILTON 1772–1851
In 1799 'cut out' a Spanish frigate from Puerto Cabello, 'a feat unsurpassed in naval annals', subsequently commander of the royal yacht *Mary*.

THOMAS HANCOCK 1786–1865
Founded the India rubber trade in England, collaborated with Macintosh in manufacturing waterproof garments.

PHILIP HARDWICK 1822–92
Architect, specialising in banks and commercial buildings in London.

JOHN HARLEY 1786–1858
Comedian, singer and collector of walking sticks.

SIR GEORGE HEAD 1782–1855
Served in the Peninsular war, deputy knight marshal at William IV's and Queen Victoria's coronations and a writer of travel books.

EDWARD HINGSTON c.1823–76
London theatre manager and Mark Twain's literary editor.

JOHN HOBHOUSE, LORD BROUGHTON DE GYFFORD, 1786–1869
Politician, friend of Byron and a founder member of the Royal Geographical Society.

MARY HOGARTH 1819–37
Dickens' sister-in-law and reputedly his mistress.

THOMAS HOGG 1792–1862
Barrister, friend and biographer of Shelley. His widow Jane was formerly married to Edward Williams who drowned with Shelley.

WILLIAM HOLLAND 1779–1856
Upholsterer, cabinet maker and funeral furnisher.

JAMES HOLWORTHY 1781–1841
Watercolour artist and a founder member of the Royal Society of Watercolourists.

THOMAS HOOD 1799–1845
Poet and humourist. *The Builder* judged his monument by Noble as 'the best thing' in Kensal Green, but the bronze decorations have since been stolen.

William Horsley 1774–1858
Organist and composer, he wrote the music for 'There is a green hill far away'. Also his daughter Sophia to whom Mendelssohn dedicated his fourth book of *Songs Without Words*.

Joseph Hume 1777–1855
Indian army surgeon and subsequently a radical politician, for thirty years he was leader of the radicals in Parliament.

James Leigh Hunt 1784–1859
Journalist and author, friend of Keats, Byron and Shelley, he was present at the latter's cremation in Italy.

Frederick Huth 1777–1864
Prussian merchant in the City, he died worth over £½ million. His mausoleum is the largest in the cemetery with a capacity for over forty coffins.

Anna Jameson 1794–1860
Irish born authoress and art historian.

Charles Kemble 1775–1854
Actor, together with his actress daughter, Fanny 1809–1893.

Henry Kendall 1776–1875
A prolific and versatile architect. He won first prize for his designs for Kensal Green in 1831 but they were later rejected.

Sir William Knighton 1776–1836
Confidant and keeper of the privy purse to George IV and physician to the Prince of Wales.

Sarah Lane 1822–99
Made a fortune as actress manager of the Britannia theatre pantomimes.

Sir George Larpent 1786–1855
Authority on Turkish affairs and the East India Company, M.P. for Nottingham 1841–42.

William Leake 1777–1860
Historian of classical Greece, left his collection of antiquities to the Fitzwilliam Museum.

John Leech 1817–64
Illustrator, chief artist for *Punch* 1842–64.

Charles Leslie 1794–1859
Author and artist, he wrote biographies of Constable and Reynolds.

Wyndham Lewis 1779–1846
Tory politician, his widow married Disraeli.

ROBERT LINDLEY 1775–1855
Violoncellist and composer. Appointed professor at the Royal Academy of Music 1822.

JOHN LISTON 1776–1864
Highest paid comic actor of his day.

MAJ.GEN.SIR OWEN LLOYD 1854–1941
Won the V.C. in Burma in 1893. A big game hunter, he killed 150 head of game in 1897.

JOSEPH LOCKE 1805–60
Civil engineer who designed railways in England and on the continent.

CHARLOTTE LOCKHART 1799–1837
Sir Walter Scott's daughter and wife of John Lockhart, his biographer.

JOHN ST JOHN LONG 1798–1834
Purveyor of quack medications. 'Stranger as you respect the receptacle for the dead (as one of many that will rest here) read the name of John St John Long without comment.' Sculpture by Sievier depicts a statue of Hygeia within an Ionic peristyle.

JOHN LOUDON 1783–1843
Writer on architecture and furniture, gardening and authority on cemetery landscaping.

SAMUEL LOVER 1797–1868
Songwriter and miniature painter.

SIR WILLIAM LUMLEY 1769–1850
Served under Wellington, governor of Bermuda 1819–25, during which time he illegally assumed episcopal powers and was fined £1,000. Groom of the bedchamber to Queen Victoria.

SIR ANDREW LUSK 1810–1909
Banker and businessman, Liberal M.P. for Finsbury 1865–85, Lord Mayor of London 1873–4.

SIR WILLIAM MCCORMACK 1836–1901
President of the Royal College of Surgeons and surgeon to Edward VII.

SIR JAMES MCGRIGOR 1771–1858
Chief of medical staff in the Peninsular war, physician extraordinary to Queen Victoria.

CHARLES MACKAY 1814–89
Scottish poet, songwriter and journalist, New York correspondent for *The Times* during the American civil war.

DANIEL MACLISE 1806–70
Irish born historical painter. He painted several large murals in the Palace of Westminster.

Kensal Green: Renaissance effigy on the Mulready tomb (1863)

Sir Peregrine Maitland 1777–1854
Commanded the 1st and 3rd battalions of Grenadier Guards at Waterloo, lieutenant governor Upper Canada 1818–34, and governor of the Cape of Good Hope 1843–46.

John Malcolmson 1835–1902
Won the V.C. in Persia in 1857. Gentleman at Arms 1870–1902.

Joseph Manton 1766–1835
Gunmaker and inventor, he took out several patents for improving his guns, none of which were ever known to burst, despite that he was bankrupted in 1826.

Adm. Sir Thomas Martin 1773–1854
Admiral of the Fleet 1849–54, M.P. for Plymouth 1818–32.

Sir William Maule 1788–1858
A Baron of the Court of Exchequer, Justice of the Court of Common Pleas and a member of the financial committee of the Privy Council.

Henry Mayhew 1812–87
Founder of *Punch* and writer on the state of London's poor.

Sir Richard Mayne 1796–1868
First joint Chief Commissioner of the Metropolitan Police 1850–68.

Freddie Mercury 1946–91
Rock star. Cremated here, the whereabouts of his ashes are unknown.

Sir William Molesworth 1810–55
M.P. for Southwark 1845–55 and Colonial Secretary 1855. An authority on Thomas Hobbes.

Lord Robert Montague 1825–1902
Conservative M.P. for Huntingdon 1869–74 and Westmeath 1874–80, held office as Minister of Education; on his retirement from politics he devoted himself to religious controversy.

NICHOLAS MORI 1796–1839
Violinist, his motto was 'memento Mori'.

JAMES MORISON 1770–1840
'The Hygeist', he invented the vegetable universal medicine known as Morison's Pills. His mausoleum was built in his lifetime by William Milligan.

JOHN MORRIS 1810–86
Professor of geology at London University 1844–78, an authority on coal mining and fossils.

JOHN MOTLEY 1814–77
American ambassador to Britain 1869–70, author of *The Rise of the Dutch Republic*.

SURG.-GEN.SIR JAMES MOUAT 1815–99
Won the V.C. the day after the battle of Balaclava in 1854.

WILLIAM MULREADY 1786–1863
Irish born artist specialising in sentimental genre subjects. Tomb by Godfrey Sykes.

REV. GEORGE MURRAY 1784–1843
Bishop of Rochester 1827–60, he confirmed the Crown Prince at Hanover in 1838.

JOHN MURRAY
Publisher, he founded the *Quarterly Review* in 1809, published Byron's works and travel books. A newspaper enterprise with the twenty-year-old Disraeli lost him £26,000.

RT. REV. THOMAS MUSGRAVE 1788–1860
Archbishop of York 1847–60 and Arabic scholar.

JOHN NICHOLS 1779–1863
Printer, proprietor of *The Gentleman's Magazine* 1833–56, published most of the important county histories produced during the first half of the nineteenth century.

ADM.JAMES NOBLE 1774–1851
Served as Nelson's flag lieutenant at the battle of St Vincent.

SIR PATRICK O'BRIEN 1823–95
Irish M.P. and traveller.

FEARGUS O'CONNOR 1794–1855
Chartist leader. 'While philanthropy is a virtue and patriotism not a crime will the name of O'Connor be admired and this monument Respected.'

ADM.SIR ROBERT OTWAY 1770–1846
Joined the navy at the age of twelve, enjoyed an active career, during six years in the West Indies he is said to have destroyed 200 enemy ships.

Sir Robert Owen and Reformers Memorials 1771–1858
Twin granite obelisks commemorate Owen, the philanthropist and pioneer socialist and eighty-two other reformers. Many, including Owen, are buried elsewhere.

Walter Peart –1898
Railway engine driver, he was in the cab of the Windsor express when the boiler exploded. He sacrificed his life while attempting to save others.

John Philip 1817–67
Artist, strongly influenced by Spanish painters. Admired by Queen Victoria who commissioned 'The Marriage of the Princess Royal with the Crown Prince of Germany' in 1858.

William Pickering 1796–1854
Publisher and pioneer in the use of cloth bound editions.

Jeanette Pickersgill –1885
First person to be cremated at Woking Crematorium on 26 March 1885. Her ashes are in the catacomb.

James Pope-Hennessy 1916–74
Literary editor of *The Spectator* and biographer, died after being attacked at his home in London.

Rev. Baden Powell 1796–1860
Professor of geometry and father of the founder of the Boy Scout Movement.

Winthrop Praed 1802–39
Founder of *The Etonian*, Tory M.P., and humorous poet. Sculpture by Raymond Smith.

Adelaide Proctor 1825–64
Poet and hymnwriter.

Sir Terence Rattigan 1911–77
Playwright.

Thomas Mayne Reid 1818–83
Novelist and correspondent for *The New York Times*.

James Rendel 1799–1856
Harbour and bridge building engineer, he constructed harbours at Portland and Holyhead.

Sir John Rennie 1794–1874
Engineer architect. He completed his father's work on London Bridge and was responsible for several major works in the royal dockyards.

Kensal Green: Charles Ricketts' tomb by William Burges (1867)

GEORGE REPTON 1786–1858
Architect. He assisted his father Humphrey and John Nash before establishing a reputation as a designer of country houses in the West Country.

JOSEPH RICHARDSON 1790–1855
A Cumberland mason, he discovered that by striking pieces of mica schist or whinstone, melodious sounds were produced. He arranged several in an instrument called 'The Rock Harmonicon' which his sons played to admiring audiences.

CAPT. CHARLES RICKETTS 1788–1867
Joined the navy aged seven and served under Nelson, married an heiress and retired aged twenty-seven. High Sheriff of Buckinghamshire. He was father of Charles Ricketts, the artist, by his mistress. Tomb by William Burges.

RICHARD ROBERTS 1789–1864
Railway engineer and inventor of machine tools.

REV. ARTHUR ROBINS 1834–89
'The Soldiers' Bishop'. Chaplain to Queen Victoria and the Household Brigade.

FREDERICK ROSEN 1805–37
Oriental scholar, professor of oriental languages at London University.

ADM. SIR JOHN ROSS 1777–1856
Arctic explorer and subsequently British Consul in Stockholm.

ADM. HENRY ROUS 1795–1877
Naval officer, discovered the Richmond and Clarence rivers in Australia. On retirement he became a successful racehorse owner and manager at Newmarket.

Edmund Routledge 1843–99
Publisher of magazines for boys and author of books on sports.

Henry Russell 1812–1900
Musician, a pupil of Rossini, author of 760 songs sold for a total of approximately £400.

Joseph Sabine 1770–1837
Trained as a barrister, he became a notable horticulturalist and one of the first fellows of the Linnean Society. An authority on British birds.

Joseph Samuda 1813–85
Engineer, a founder member of the Institution of Naval Architects, he designed *Thunderer*, the first armour cased ship in the navy. M.P. for Tavistock 1865–68 and Tower Hamlets 1868–80.

Anne Scott 1803–33
Daughter of Sir Walter Scott.

Edward Scriven 1775–1841
Engraver and founder of the Artist's Fund. Tomb by C.H. Smith.

Edward Seaton 1815–80
Surgeon, founder and president of the Epidemiological Society. Under his guidance compulsory vaccination was introduced in 1853 against smallpox.

John Shaw 1803–70
Architect, he designed several schools and was surveyor of Eton College.

Charles Shaw-Lefevre, Viscount Eversley, 1794–1888
Speaker of the House of Commons 1839–57, governor of the Isle of Wight.

Henry Sherry 1850–1933
London funeral director. Founder and first president of the British Undertakers' Association.

Sir Carl William Siemens 1823–83
German born electrical engineer. With his brothers set up the Siemens factory and constructed overland and submarine telegraphs.

Robert Sievier 1794–1865
Sculptor and promoter of the General Cemetery Company in 1830. Several monuments in Kensal Green are by him.

Kensal Green: The Sevier family monument (1865)

Kensal Green: The Cooke family monument (1866) by Thomas Milnes photographed in 1980

Sir George Smart 1776–1867
Composer and conductor, he conducted the music at the funeral of George IV and the coronations of William IV and Victoria.

Robert Smirke 1753–1845
Painter and illustrator.

Rev. James Smirnove 1756–1840
For sixty years chaplain at the Russian Embassy.

Sir John Mark Smith 1790–1874
General who was Commandant of the Royal Marines, M.P. for Chatham

Rev. Sydney Smith 1771–1845
Canon of St Paul's, wit and promoter of Catholic emancipation.

William H. Smith 1792–1865
Stationer who inherited a bookselling business founded by his mother which he expanded to become the largest in the country. His son and successor, another William, 1808–76, is also buried here.

George Smythe, Viscount Strangeford, 1818–57
Tory M.P. with the Young England group, promoted the welfare of the working classes taking an interest in allotments. He fought the last duel in England in 1852.

Princess Sophia 1777–1848
Daughter of George III and victim of an unfortunate love affair. Her epitaph reads 'Come unto me all ye that labour and I will give you rest.' Sarcophagus carved by Signor Bardi.

Elizabeth Soyer 1813–42
Prodigy painter known as 'the English Murillo', she died in labour. Her husband was the Reform Club chef Alexis Soyer, a dietician and author of the popular *Charitable Cookery or the Poor Man's Regenerator*, and also buried here.

Allan Steel 1858–1914
Barrister and cricketer, he played for England between 1880 and 1888. President of the M.C.C. 1902.

BENJAMIN STEVENS 1833–1902
American antiquary and bookseller, he came to England in 1860 as agent for numerous American libraries.

RT. REV. CHARLES STEWART 1775–1837
Missionary to Canada and Bishop of Quebec 1826–37.

WILLIAM STRANG 1859–1921
Painter, etcher and illustrator.

JOHN STUART 1815–66
Explorer, he reached the centre of Australia in 1860 and was the first to cross the continent in 1861. He was awarded 1,000 square miles in South Australia and a £2,000 prize for the achievement.

SIR JOHN TENNIEL 1820–1914
Political cartoonist in *Punch* and illustrator of *Alice in Wonderland*.

WILLIAM MAKEPEACE THACKERAY 1811–63
Novelist and contributor to *Punch*. Dickens attended his funeral which was 'very plain and commonplace'.

CHARLES THOMSON, LORD RITCHIE, 1838–1906
Chancellor of the Exchequer 1902–3.

THERESA TIETJENS 1831–77
Hungarian mezzo-soprano.

SIR NICHOLAS TINDAL 1776–1846
Tory M.P. and Chief Justice of Common Pleas 1829–46.

ADM. SIR RICHARD TRACY 1837–1907
Assisted in the foundation of the modern Japanese and Chinese navies. President of the Royal Naval College, Greenwich 1897–1900.

MAJ. GEN. WILLIAM TREVOR 1831–1907
Engineer and marksman. He won the V.C. in India in 1865.

ANTHONY TROLLOPE 1815–82
Novelist and post office official, he introduced the pillar box into this country.

Kensal Green: The Dissenters' Chapel, restored in 1997.

Edward Troughton 1753–1835
Optician and inventor of navigational instruments.

Rev. Thomas Turton 1780–1864
Mathematician, musician and Bishop of Ely 1845–64.

David Unwins c.1780–1837
Physician who made his reputation with a treatise on mental illness, an early convert to homeopathy.

Richard Valpy 1754–1836
For fifty years master of Reading School, his mausoleum was erected by his eleven surviving children.

Mme. Lucia Vestris 1797–1836
Actress and opera singer, she assisted her husband Charles Mathews in managing Covent Garden.

Thomas Wakley 1795–1862
Medical and social reformer, founder and first editor of *The Lancet* in 1823.

Robert Wallace 1831–99
Presbyterian minister, lawyer and M.P. for Edinburgh 1886–99.

William Wallace 1814–70
Composer of operas, including 'Maritana'.

James Ward 1769–1859
Painter and engraver, particularly of animal subjects. Sculpture by J.H. Foley.

Col. Marcus Waters 1794–1868
Served in the Royal Engineers, 'the last surviving officer of his corps who was engaged in the battles of Quatre Bras, Waterloo'.

Sir Frederick Watson 1773–1852
Master of the Household to George IV, William IV and Queen Victoria.

Friedrich Welwitsch 1806–72
Austrian born botanist employed by the Portuguese government to explore the flora of its African colonies. He discovered *Welwitschia mirabilis* which can live for over 1,500 years.

William Whiteley 1831–1907
Founder of Whiteleys in Queensway. Shot dead by a blackmailer in his shop.

Horace Wilson 1786–1860
Doctor who practised in India, professor of Sanskrit at Oxford. He published many works on oriental subjects.

MAJ. WALTER WINGFIELD 1833–1912
Inventor of 'Sphairistike' in 1874, later developed into lawn tennis.

FREDERICK WINSOR 1763–1830
Originator of public gas lighting in London and Paris, where he is buried. Pall Mall was the first street he illuminated, in 1808. (Memorial only).

JAMES WYLD 1812–87
Geographer and map maker known for his maps of the gold mining areas of California and famous for his illuminated Great Globe exhibited in Leicester Square. M.P. for Bodmin for many years.

KENSINGTON HANWELL CEMETERY
UXBRIDGE ROAD, W7

Founded: 1855
Owner: Royal Borough of Kensington and Chelsea
Acreage: 19

A Gothic arch straddles the entrance to this cemetery which helpfully bears the date 1855 and the name of the architect, Thomas Allom. Allom was surveyor to the Ladbroke estate in Kensington but also had a special interest in sepulchral architecture. He had trained with Benjamin Baud and came second to him in the competition for the Brompton Cemetery design in 1838. He built the charming Gothic funerary chapel for the third Earl of Caernarvon at Highclere, and in 1865 a more fanciful Gothic mausoleum for George Dodd at West Norwood cemetery.

The Kensington cemetery does not compare with such extravagances; nevertheless, all the hallmarks of a mid-Victorian cemetery are evident. Originally it had two chapels but the Dissenters' chapel has gone and the survivor suffered from partial demolition of its east end in 1972. All that remains is an arched colonnade attached to the rear of the existing building. The Anglican chapel is a little fourteenth-century style building originally with 'an extremely plain and dull interior'.[1] In the 1890s stained glass, a mosaic dado, marble columns, a painted roof and new piers were added to brighten it up. It is now unused. The cemetery grounds were generously planted with coniferous trees, willows and suitably funereal holly and yew, which line the entrance drive, now in a state of advanced maturity. As a result when walking round the meandering paths one barely sees the neighbouring houses and the main line railway to the north. Despite the modest number of burials recorded each year the cemetery is very well maintained and more recently Victorian-style street lights have been installed.

Kensington Hanwell: memorial to Edgar Smith, conchologist (1916)

The cemetery's catchment area was the comfortable middle class parish of St Mary Abbots in Kensington which had been built up with stuccoed terraces between 1830 and 1850. The residents chose equally respectable but seldom showy tombs. There are one or two exceptions, particularly the dotty monument southwest of the chapel erected for Mr Wheeler, a Notting Hill builder. It incorporates most nineteenth-century tomb materials in an unprecedented design. A tall marble cross and statue is the focal point, and in front of it is a mosaic and lead inlaid pavement surrounded by granite posts and iron railing. Less flamboyant are the shell memorial to Edgar Smith, a conchologist, and a most unusual half circular classical cistern on the Rubens grave.

By the 1870s interments at Hanwell were averaging 800 per annum and an additional three and a half acres adjacent to the west side were bought as a matter of urgency. At the same time the Burial Board decided to forbid the burial of those who lived outside the parish. In 1880 ambitious plans were made to tunnel under the railway line to a new thirteen acre plot but they proved abortive. It was decided in 1924 that accommodation at Hanwell was 'drawing near to exhaustion'[2] and it became necessary to start a new cemetery which opened eventually at Gunnersbury.

Kensington Hanwell: The entrance arch by Thomas Allom (1855).

Sir Arthur Benn 1858–1937
Politician and president of the Council of Federation of Chambers of Commerce of the British Empire 1931–34.

Edward Blanchard 1820–89
Playwright, drama critic, writer of London guidebooks and founder of the *Astrologer*.

Brig.Gen. John Carroll 1870–1927
Cavalry officer who commanded a Russian force at Morjegorskaia, 1919.

Sir Henry Cartwright 1823–99
Colonial administrator, Sheriff of Londonderry 1884.

Marta Cunningham –1937
American concert singer and founder of the 'Not Forgotten' Association 1920.

Austin Dobson 1840–1921
Journalist, poet and authority on eighteenth-century English literature.

Surg. Gen. Alfred Eteson 1833–1910
Served in the Indian medical service during the Indian mutiny.

FRANK FELLER 1848–1908
Victorian military artist of swiss origin.

SIR RICHARD HAWES 1893–1964
Doctor specialising in tropical diseases; consulting physician to the Colonial Office 1941–61.

SIR JAMES INGLIS 1851–1911
President of the Institute of Civil Engineers and general manager of the G.W.R.

GEN.SIR EDWIN JOHNSON 1825–93
Served for many years in India, a member of the Council of India, Director General of Military Education 1884–86.

THOMAS KEMP 1836–1905
Recorder of Norwich.

SIR ROBERT MCCALL 1847–1934
Judge in Northern Ireland.

ADM.SIR FRANCIS MCCLINTOCK 1819–1907
Arctic explorer, 'he discovered the fate of Sir John Franklin' in 1859.

SIR JAMES PEILE 1833–1906
Member of the Council of India.

JOHN BYAM SHAW 1872–1919
Pre-Raphaelite artist and founder of the Byam Shaw Art School in 1911.

EDGAR SMITH 1847–1916
Conchologist at the British Museum, the shell on his tombstone is a large tridacna.

GEORGE THOMAS 1850–1923
Australian born landscape artist.

LT.GEN.SIR HENRY WEARE 1825–98
Veteran of the Maori wars.

HENRY WILLIS 1810–84
Landscape painter in the style of Constable.

KINGSTON CEMETERY AND CREMATORIUM

BONNER HILL ROAD, KINGSTON, SURREY

Founded: 1855
Owner: Royal Borough of Kingston upon Thames
Acreage: 27½

Visually Kingston starts well but tails off badly. The main path from the gates leads to the two chapels which occupy the highest point in the cemetery. Their style is much pinnacled Decorated with a common vaulted *porte cochère* supporting a hexagonal belfry and spire. The architects were Messrs Aickin and Capes.[1] One chapel is now a 'Hall of Memory', the other houses the Book of Remembrance, a more fitting use than the customary tool shed alternative.

East of the chapels the road sweeps down between the best of the tombs, circumnavigates the war memorial and continues its axial way to the doors of the crematorium whose foundation stone was laid on the 19 December 1950. It was designed by the Borough's surveyor, G.L. Paling, with the chief assistant architect, C.A. Trim, and was opened in 1952 by Lord Horder. The style is in pedestrian brick 'stripped classical', but the interior is a ghastly shock. The conventional dreary fittings are bathed in a death-like pallor cast by hideous yellow stained glass, surely an unintentional mistake? Of the twenty-five crematoria in the London areas it is only one of two where the catafalque containing the coffin descends to the basement crematory. A viewing gallery permits inspection of the cremation process. More recently a modern *porte cochère* has been added in front of the chapel doors.

Kingston : The bronze figure by Richard Goulden on the Burton grave (1908)

Adjacent to the crematorium building are the usual brick cloisters, which accommodate bronze tablets and beyond, an unkempt pergola, rose beds, a pond and a weed-infested rockery. A lumpish plinth dates this ill-assorted complex at 1958.[2] Mr Chapman, in writing his guidebook of Kingston in 1877 was spared these adjuncts when he noted:

> The improvements effected during the last few years in the design and construction of memorials of the dead are clearly perceptible in this cemetery. Nearly the whole of those erected are the work of the resident artists, and the various emblems depicted on the stone display much merit and skilful execution.[3]

Since that was written two unusual additions have appeared, the massive stone pile commemorating Arthur Ranyard in 1894 topped by a female figure, well out of reach of potential vandals, and the Diana Burton bronze angel of 1908. This was designed by sculptor Richard Goulden and cast by her father, a metal founder in Thames Ditton, who also cast the Queen Alexandra memorial fountain outside Marlborough House. Further along the same path is a sculpted bronze relief commemorating Ernest Von Bransthausen (1900). Elsewhere a baldacchino on barley sugar columns shelters a pair of angelic figures on the Macrae Memorial (1901).

The southern and more recent section of the cemetery is reached by terracotta steps over a ha ha. Several Kingston worthies are buried here, including three mayors, but nothing else is of interest.

SIR WILLIAM BOVILL 1814–73
Lord Chief Justice of Common Pleas, he was the judge who tried the ejectment case of Tichborne v. Lushington over ten months 1871–72.

SIR CHARLES BURGE 1846–1921
Mayor of Kingston 1912–19.

SIR COLVIN COLVIN SMITH 1829–1913
Surgeon General of the Indian Medical Service, honorary surgeon to Queen Victoria and Edward VII.

JEFFREY DEAR –1938
Wireless operator for Imperial Airways, killed in the Wallington aircrash.

THOMAS HANSARD 1813–91
Proprietor and editor of Hansard's parliamentary debates 1833–88.

SIR WILLIAM HARDMAN 1828–90
Recorder of Kingston-on-Thames, editor of *The Morning Post* 1872–90.

DR JOSEPH MOLONEY 1857–1896
Explorer of the African Congo.

ARTHUR RANYARD 1845–94
Secretary of the Royal Astronomical Association and editor of 'Knowledge' 1888–94.

JOHN SIM 1810–75
High Sheriff of Surrey.

ALFRED, LORD WEBB-JOHNSON OF STOKE ON TRENT 1880–1958
Surgeon, during the 1920s played a major role in organising the rebuilding of the Middlesex Hospital, the longest serving president of the Royal College of Surgeons 1941–49, president of the Royal Society of Medicine 1950–52.

WILLIAM YOUNG –1901
Governor of the Gold Coast.

LAMBETH CEMETERY AND CREMATORIUM
BLACKSHAW ROAD, SW17

Founded: 1854
Owner: London Borough of Lambeth
Acreage: 41

Lambeth is not in the same class as the Borough's great cemetery at Norwood. The flat site and proximity of the suburban railway line are partly responsible but so too has been the devastating policy of flattening or breaking up old tombstones. Acres of ground are now grassy wastes and new walls have been built from smashed stones.

The early history of the cemetery is conveniently recorded on plaques set above the doors to the two chapels. In 1853 thirty acres of land were 'purchased of Samuel Martin of Garratt Lane as a burial ground for the parish of St Mary Lambeth'. The architects of the simple brick Gothic buildings were Frederick Wehnert and John Ashdown, the total cost of land and buildings: £21,500. One of the chapels is now derelict.[1]

By 1874 nearly 50,000 interments had taken place and an additional eleven acres were purchased by a worried Burial Board whose members discovered that since 1853 the value of land had increased by 65 per cent due to the rapid expansion of the suburbs.[2] The purchase is recorded on a panel on one of the brick pillars supporting the railings along Blackshaw Road. The Board's action was none too soon for by 1889 only Brompton and the City of London cemeteries exceeded in number Lambeth's 109,010 burials. Discussing the problem, *The Builder* rightly said, 'The time is fast approaching for earnest reconsideration of our mode of sepulture'.[3]

Eighty-four years later the crematorium was built. The scheme, devised by Sir Guy Dawber, Fox and Richardson, consists of an insipid brick complex which the designer has attempted to articulate with a few unconvincing stabs at Wrenaissance detail.[4] This is particularly discernible

Lambeth: A perspective view of the cemetery from *The Builder* (1854)

from the cenotaph type design behind the catafalque. Above the entrance to one of the side doors is carved a robed figure rather in the style of Eric Gill. A second chapel which formed part of the original plan was never built. Separate from the crematorium chapel is the Chapel of Meditation housing the Book of Remembrance. The complex is a sorry contrast to the confident Victorian architecture of the chapels but, unfortunately, not untypical of its genre. Beyond is the usual area for scattering ashes and the obligatory rose bushes. It is particularly unfortunate that large blue warehouses now overlook the grounds.

The pressure on land at Lambeth meant it was never planned with picturesque qualities in mind. *The Builder* wrote:

> The architects have divided the whole of the ground into parallelograms, as better adapted to an economical appropriation of the ground for interment; the plots being calculated for a regular number of graves when the rest of the ground is full.[5]

Like Lambeth's neighbour, Streatham Cemetery in Garratt Lane, the best memorials are those in the circular section just inside the main gate, but having escaped the onslaught of clearance, they are now completely overshadowed by a row of disproportionately large fir trees. Unusual for its date and material is the big black slate and marble baldacchino built for the Smith family in 1932. A marble balustrade marks out the grave of the south London funeral directing family of Ashton, and behind this there is a splendid art deco pink granite urn on the Wood grave. A riderless horse stands on top of Thomas Allen's plinth and elsewhere a lion rests couchant on the Calvin grave (1897). The Lambeth connection with Doulton is represented by the miniature memorial marking Harriett Shannon's grave (1912) and also some terracotta common grave markers. The nautical epitaph to John Cairns is a neat metaphor, 'Tho his body is under hatches, his soul has gone aloft'. Near the boundary with the railway is a low level wall of remembrance commemorating the war dead.

THOMAS ALLEN 1861-98
Equestrian.

ROBERT BOWERS 1822-1908
Social reformer and historian of Southwark.

CHARLES CHAPLIN -1901
Music hall ballad singer and father of the actor comedian. An alcoholic, he is buried in a pauper's grave.

GEORGE GALVIN (DAN LENO) 1860-1904
Music hall star and pantomime performer, known as 'The King's Jester'. Began his career in 1864 as 'Little George the Infant Wonder', he appeared on stage almost daily for thirty-six years. Died after a mental breakdown in 1903.

SAMUEL GOVETT (SAM POLUSKI) 1866-1922
Comedian.

LAVENDER HILL CEMETERY
LAVENDER HILL, ENFIELD, MIDDX.

Founded: 1870
Owner: London Borough of Enfield
Acreage: 28 (and 12 acre Strayfield Road extension)

The site was opened by the Enfield Burial Board which furnished it with all the requisites of the Victorian cemetery: a sandstone lodge next to the entrance gate and two gothic chapels on either side of the entrance; they are good examples of fourteenth century Gothic architecture and were designed by Thomas J. Hill.[1] The Nonconformist chapel retains its broach spire, but is now derelict.

This is a well-maintained cemetery on an undulating site. The planting is now mature and sombre coniferous trees surround the entrance. A fence marks the Strayfield Road extension which was opened in 1997.

The island sites in the road system contain the best memorials; the Celtic cross to Benjamin Godfrey M.D. is an example. Others near the Anglican chapel include the memorial to Philip Twells, a former MP for the City of London (1880), Heinrich Faulenbach's grave marked by a bronze plaque on a substantial granite vault, and the large chest tomb for the Enfield branch of the Bosanquet family. The memorials in the extension, where lawn memorials dominate, are of little interest.

MANOR PARK CEMETERY AND CREMATORIUM
SEBERT ROAD, E7

Founded: 1874
Owner: Manor Park Cemetery Company
Acreage: 50

Manor Park is one of the few private cemeteries that continues to be run by its founding company. Access is both from Sebert Road and from Whitta Road where the name of the cemetery is proclaimed in large metal letters.

On the right of the main gates is the lodge which serves as the office. The chapel, designed by a J. Winter, was originally built in 1877 but, with the exception of the spire, it was demolished by a bomb in 1944. It has been rebuilt using brick in no nonsense stripped Gothic style with a crematorium added to the east end in 1955.[1] There are attractive stained glass windows in the chapel.

An unusual number of memorials featuring angels border the main drive to the chapel and among others include that commemorating William Ecclestone 'Jolly Jumbo' (1915) and a reclining figure on the Edwards grave (1931). Most have fortunately escaped the vandals. There is one modest mausoleum, a gothic tabernacle supported on pink granite columns containing the Serle family. Near the entrance is a headstone with the sculpted relief of ten-year-old John Clinton, below which reads, 'The little hero who died trying to save a companion from drowning.'

Beyond the chapel is the Garden of Remembrance with an abundance of rose bushes and at its centre a copper-domed shelter. Nearby is the recent addition of walled enclosure containing an open air columbarium. The 1919 Ordnance Survey map indicates that a small Nonconformist chapel stood on this site, although it was of the 'tin tabernacle' variety and has long disappeared.

Maintenance in certain areas is minimal so that when combined with the avenues of mature horse-chestnut trees a welcome rural atmosphere is achieved in this quiet backwater of east London.

John Travers Cornwall 1900–16
VC – the second youngest holder of the decoration; he was awarded it posthumously for his gallantry at the battle of Jutland.

Pte. Sidney Godley 1889–1957
The first private soldier to win a V.C. during the Great War on 23 August 1914.

Col. Albert Martin –1936
M.P. for Romford 1918–23.

Mary Orchard 1830–1906
She served Princess Alice's children for forty years. Her monument was 'erected in grateful memory by Victoria, Princess Louis of Battenberg, Elizabeth, Grand Duchess Sergius of Russia, Ernest Louis, Grand Duke of Hesse, Alix, Empress of Russia'.

MERTON AND SUTTON JOINT CEMETERY
Garth Road, Morden, Surrey

Founded: 1947
Owner: Merton and Sutton Joint Cemetery Board
Acreage: 57½ (only 22 in use)

This is the largest of the few post-war cemeteries founded in the Greater London area, in which functionalism dominates. Originally accommodating traditional memorials, the lawn concept was soon adopted. Straight lines are the overwhelming feature – in the stripped classical style of the chapel, in the grid iron pattern of tarmac paths and in the gleaming rows of monuments placed back to back. Surprisingly the architect involved, Albert Thomas, who completed the building in 1955, was in part responsible for the art deco Institut Français, built in Kensington eight years earlier. Only the entrance is impressive, with gate piers supporting Portland stone urns. Beyond them is a large brick lodge and opposite, a waiting room. Rising to the chapel, the main drive is lined with beech trees and firs softening this rigidly deployed landscape. Behind the chapel is the Admadiyya Muslim Burial Ground.

MITCHAM CEMETERY
Church Road, Mitcham, Surrey

Founded: 1883
Owner: London Borough of Merton
Acreage: 7

The cemetery's limits are difficult to define, being no more than an extension to the churchyard surrounding Mitcham's parish church. That dates from the thirteenth century and its churchyard was enlarged in 1855. The cemetery was founded in 1883 and enlarged in 1908. What remains of a sundial contains this information on the base.

Whereas the churchyard is appropriately bosky with yews and chestnuts predominating, the cemetery for the most part is flat and bare of trees. At one time it had a chapel, on the north side, but all trace of this has gone, as have the railings. The boundary hedge is patchy and with this lack of protection vandalism has been a major problem – many memorials have been badly damaged and the place is now a rather desolate island surrounded by busy roads.

One monument is of some interest – a tall Gothic cross designed for his family by Henry Downing, an architect specialising in the design of Gothic churches in the early twentieth century. Unique in a London cemetery is an iron graveboard, although this example has rusted badly. Near the north gates there is a little group of monuments erected in the 1930s, among them the subtly incised slab above Ida Beutell's grave (1932), which is an unusually successful attempt by the artist to abandon tradition for a contemporary design. Local folklore claims that an unmarked rusty iron cross near the north wall marks the grave of a gypsy queen, reputedly buried in a concrete tomb accompanied by all her gold jewellery.

One early nineteenth-century tomb in the churchyard records a remarkable and tragic tale. It commemorates Mary, Sarah and Eliza Atwood,

> who were poisoned by eating funguous (*sic*) vegetables mistaken for champignons on the 11th day of October 1808 and died at the ages of 14, 7 and 5 years within a few hours of each other in excrutiating circumstances. The Father, Mother and now, alas, an only child, partakers of the same meal, have survived with debilitated constitutions and to lament so dreadful a calumny. This monument is erected to perpetuate the fatal event as an awful caution to others, let it be too a solemn warning that in our most grateful enjoyments even in our necessary food may lurk deadly poison . . .

Henry Downing 1865–1947
Church architect, he designed St Barnabas, Mitcham; author of several books on mediaeval monumental brasses.

Col. C.A. Edwards 1864–97
Commandant of the British Central African armed forces and the youngest officer of his rank then serving in the army. He died of fever at Zomba aged thirty-three.

Gen. Sir James Lindsay 1815–74
Served in Canada, Inspector General of reserve forces 1868–70.

Cecil Stringer 1900–41
Killed on board the battleship H.M.S. *Hood*, when it was sunk by the *Bismarck*; there were only three survivors among the Hood's crew of 1,419.

MITCHAM CEMETERY
London Road, Mitcham, Surrey

Founded: 1928
Owner: London Borough of Merton
Acreage: 18

Situated opposite Figges Marsh and opened by the Mitcham Urban District Council, first impressions of this cemetery are not promising. Although the lodge is impressively large and the boundary with the main road marked by a tightly packed row of tall fir trees, the site is flat, planting minimal and the layout symmetrical with a simplified Gothic chapel set squarely in the middle. This was designed by Chart & Sons, architects of Reading. Many of the older memorials are near the main entrance including an attractive trio of graves each with angels which, surprisingly, have managed to remain unscathed. Beyond the chapel a hedge encloses a number of war graves. Further sections at the back of the cemetery are gradually filling up.

Nevertheless, in this austere setting and among the acres of banal lawn type monuments dedicated to 'Sis' or 'Pop', are remnants of Mitcham's history. A few of the larger tombs have been erected by 'travellers'' families: the Greys, Dixies and Hunts, who regularly attended Mitcham fair. A well known local totter glorying in the name of Albert Sparrowhawk is also here. Two unusual monuments bear attributes of the deceased's trade, one a diver's helmet, the other an anvil and hammer. More recently a large bronze figure of the Blessed Virgin Mary holding Christ's body has been installed on a grave near the chapel.

MORTLAKE OLD CEMETERY
South Worple Way, SW14

Founded: 1854
Owner: London Borough of Richmond upon Thames
Acreage: 6

A small squarish plot divided by a diagonal path between gates at each end. (The unconsecrated acres to the west were added in 1877). Like several other London cemeteries it is located next to a hospital. At the Avenue Gardens entrance a rather tame Edwardian style lodge stands inside the main gate with its highly decorative iron gate pillars now painted bright green. A small Gothic chapel with a bell cote which stood at the centre of the ground was demolished in 1969, a loss partly compensated for by some very large horse-chestnut trees.[1]

The cemetery is now a quiet backwater but at the end of the last century religious fanaticism caused a near-riot when Patrick Hurley, an Irish Catholic murdered in a local pub, was buried in the Protestant ground. The police were called to disperse the angry crowd.

There are no very significant memorials, but a handful of larger ones stand against the north wall, including the obelisk commemorating Admiral Ommaney.

ARTHUR CECIL BLUNT 1844–96
Actor, 'more remarkable for neatness than robustness or strength'.

ROSANNA CASTLE 1802–1906
Lived to the age of 104.

SIR EDWIN CHADWICK 1800–90
Served on the Poor Law Commission and Board of Health. In 1843 produced an influential report on the 'Practice of Interment In Towns'.

LT.GEN.SIR WILLIAM DENISON 1804–71
Engineer and colonial administrator. Governor of New South Wales 1854–61 and Madras 1861–6.

CHARLES DICKENS 1837–96
Eldest son of the author and editor of his Works.

FRANCIS GODFREY 1811–68
Waterman to Queen Victoria.

GEORGINA HOGARTH 1827–1917
Sister-in-law, friend and housekeeper to Charles Dickens. She edited his letters for publication.

SIR ADOPHUS LIDDELL 1818–85
Lawyer and permanent Under Secretary of State for the Home Department 1867–85.

ADM.SIR ERASMUS OMMANEY 1814–1904
Served on the Arctic Expeditions of 1838 and 1850 when the first winter quarters of Franklin's ships were discovered.

THOMAS GERMAN REED 1817–88
Together with his wife Priscilla (1818–95), devised the 'German Reed Entertainment' in 1855 'to provide dramatic amusement for that class of society which was reluctant to visit the theatres'.

REV.HENRY VENN 1796–1873
Prebendary of St Paul's and for over thirty years honorary secretary of the Church Missionary Society.

SIR HENRY WILLOCK 1790–1858
Diplomat, he served in Persia 1822–30, chairman of the East India Company 1844–47.

MORTLAKE ROMAN CATHOLIC CEMETERY
North Worple Way, SW14

Founded: 1852
Owner: Southwark Roman Catholic Diocesan Corporation
Acreage: Approx. 3

Mortlake cemetery is so obscurely sited it is not even marked on the A-Z map of London. Nevertheless it repays discovery, sandwiched higgledy-piggledy between the church of St Mary Magdalene and a Catholic primary school, which has adopted a corner for its playground. Maintenance of the cemetery has recently improved but it is still a rough and ready place.

The most famous attraction is the rendered stone mausoleum built like an Arab tent for Sir Richard Burton and his wife Isabel. Burton died in Trieste in 1890 but his embalmed body was shipped to England by his wife who cajoled contributions of £688 from his friends for the construction of the 'tent', apparently designed by herself. After vandals had attacked it in 1951 the tent was restored and its Carrara marble doors bricked up. A panel on the door contains lines by Justin Huntley McCarthy, 'Farewell, dear friend, death hero! The great life is ended, the great perils, the great joys; And he to whom adventures were as toys.' An iron ladder gives access to a glass panel in the roof to permit a view of the interior with its two dusty coffins festooned with an assortment of lanterns, bells and other religious paraphernalia installed by Lady Burton who liked to conduct séances here before a little altar.

The cosmopolitan element at Mortlake does not end with the Burton tomb. There are a number of other old European families represented, like the D'Erlangers, the Esterhazys and a large Gothic mausoleum built for Guillaume Henry, Comte de Vezlo who died aged seven in 1901. (Unfortunately, this is now in a poor state of repair with the roof of the apse covered by plastic sheeting and the windows smashed.) Three distinctive coffin shaped tombs commemorate the Stokes family, probably designed by the architect Leonard Stokes who is also buried here.

Sir Albert Beckett 1840–1904
Assistant Accountant General of the Army.

Edward Bellasis 1800–73
Parliamentary lawyer and Lancaster Herald. He was a Catholic convert.

John Bentley 1839–1902
Architect who specialised in designing churches for the Catholic Church, including Westminster Cathedral.

Mortlake R.C.: Sir Richard Burton's stone 'tent' (1890).

WALTER BLOUNT 1807–94
Genealogist and Clarenceux King at Arms 1882–94.

KATHERINE BRADLEY 1848–1914
Together with her niece Edith Cooper 1862–1913, also buried here, wrote thirty volumes of poetry and plays under the pseudonym Michael Field.

CONSTANCE BURD 1860–1939
Foundress of the Sisters of Consolation.

SIR RICHARD BURTON 1821–90
Explorer and orientalist, he travelled to Mecca in 1853, explored Central Africa and translated the 'Arabian Nights'. Also his wife Isabel 1831–96.

HENRY CLUTTON 1819–91
Architect, he made his reputation by winning the Lille Cathedral competition with William Burges (q.v.).

HENRY DE COLYAR 1846–1925
Gold Staff officer at the coronations of Edward VII and George V. A judge and author of several legal textbooks.

CHRISTOPHER ENNIS –1904
Yeoman of the King's Bodyguard.

JOHN JONES 1839–1929
Chief Commissioner, Dublin Metropolitan Police.

DONALD MACGREGOR 1839–1911
Liberal M.P. for Inverness.

SIR JAMES MARSHALL 1829–89
A one-armed Catholic convert, formerly an Anglican clergyman, who became a lawyer and in 1880, Chief Justice of the Gold Coast where he re-established the Catholic church.

JOHN MORRIS 1812–80
Domestic chaplain to Coventry Patmore and author of theological works.

MARY PROBYN 1855–1909
Poet.

LEONARD STOKES 1858–1925
An inventive architect who designed many Catholic churches and Telephone Company buildings. He won the RIBA Gold Medal in 1919.

WILLIAM TOWRY-LAW 1809–86
Soldier, chancellor of the Diocese of Bath and Wells from 1839 until 1851, when he joined the Catholic Church.

RICHARD VAN ZELLER 1844–92
Portuguese consul in London.

NEW BRENTFORD CEMETERY
SUTTON LANE, HOUNSLOW, MIDDX.

Founded: 1902
Owner: London Borough of Hounslow
Acres: 8

Adjacent to a busy underground line, this small rectangular shaped cemetery is symmetrically divided into ten sections. The original railings remain although the lodge has been replaced with a bland 1950s house. The drive leads to the chapel designed by the architects Thomas H. Nowell Parr and A.E. Kates. Nowell Parr was surveyor to Brentford District Council and in private practice a specialist in the design of pubs including The Beehive in Brentford. The chapel was erected in 1909 and built of honey coloured bricks with a squat tower banded by pink bricks. Both the chapel and the nearby Cross of Sacrifice are sheltered by the mature pines and cedars.

Two memorials on the right of the main drive are worth noting; the 1925 McKenzie grave with crossed branches in white marble, and the bronze sundial on the red granite Newnham grave of 1911. Beyond the chapel most of the memorials are headstones only. Additional burial space is likely to be found by reclaiming the neighbouring allotments now that the cemetery is nearly full.

NORTH SHEEN CEMETERY
LOWER RICHMOND ROAD, SW14

Founded: 1909
Owner: London Borough of Hammersmith and Fulham
Acreage: 26

Bulbous stone piers along the perimeter wall indicate the cinema *moderne* style of the 1920s. They are the best feature of this cemetery which succumbs to mediocrity as soon as one passes the gate. The lodge is no different from any other ribbon development house and the layout beyond a dreary grid plan.

The cemetery opened for burials in September 1909 and a temporary chapel was provided before the Borough of Fulham surveyor and engineer, Arthur Holden, designed the little brick Gothic chapel which was officially opened on 5 November 1931. Its only surprise is the colourful modern stained glass depicting New Testament scenes installed in 1953 to replace windows damaged in the war; the artist was Antoine Acket.[1]

The monuments play safe, nothing vulgar or very large, and granite has given way to polished marble. The only exceptions are two gaunt mausolea standing near the entrance (Broughton,

1919 and Thornton) and, on the west side, a stone sheepdog patiently guards his master's grave. The cemetery has a large Roman Catholic section and many Poles have chosen to be buried here. At the north end, low-maintenance lawn cemetery principles have been adopted.

MORGAN PHILLIPS 1902–63
General Secretary of the Labour Party 1944–62.

ALEXANDRA PILSUDSKA 1867–1963
Widow of the Polish soldier and statesmen Joseph Pilsudski 1867–1935.

NUNHEAD CEMETERY
LINDEN GROVE, SE15

Founded: 1840
Owner: London Borough of Southwark
Acreage: 52

Nunhead: The chapel by Thomas Little (1840) Photographed in 1980.

Nunhead ranks among the best of London's large nineteenth century cemeteries, but its history has always been troubled and its condition is now critical.[1] It began life in 1840 as the cemetery of All Saints. Like its sister cemetery at Highgate, Nunhead was owned by the London Cemetery Company, and like Highgate, it was built on a fine hill top site near the old Nun's Head Tavern, once the 'favourite resort of smoke dried London artisans'.[2]

The Company also had a first rate surveyor, James Bunstone Bunning, to lay out its cemetery. Subsequently he was appointed architect to the City of London but probably more than any other important Victorian architect, Bunning's buildings have been fated to suffer untimely destruction. Among them were the huge Caledonian Market, the bizarre Holloway Prison and above all, the incomparable Coal Exchange. Until recently it seemed that his neo-classical gate lodges

Nunhead: The chapel after restoration

at Nunhead would suffer likewise. Two were included in the scheme, but after both suffered severe dilapidation one was restored in the 1980s, and is now occupied, while the east lodge is currently awaiting renovation. Together with the imposing entrance gates, hung on stone piers embellished with iron inverted torches, (symbolising life extinguished,) they compose a marvellously solemn approach to the main drive that proceeds uphill to the Anglican chapel.

This was designed by Thomas Little who won the commission in competition. (He was also the architect at Paddington Old Cemetery). It is planned as an octagon, with a short nave and transepts, entered from a palatial *porte cochère*. Beneath it was a crypt. The architectural style is 'Decorated Gothic' as was the now demolished Nonconformist chapel, sited to the south west of the main entrance, a simple rectangular building with an ante chapel. As an additional attraction, the company excavated catacombs east of the gates. The larger consisted of a chamber, entered by a staircase, which was brick barrel vaulted and contained 144 cells. The other was a strange brick catacomb shaft, approximately 8ft across and 17ft deep. Circulating around all these buildings were meandering paths and luxurious planting. With the gradual addition of some fine tombs, the balance of nature and architecture that Loudon advocated was brilliantly achieved.

For twenty-five years Nunhead prospered, recording over 200 burials per year. Then in 1865, when the first superintendent died, it was discovered he had defrauded the company of many thousands of pounds. Additional problems were the threat of take-over by the local burial board, economic recession and lower rates of mortality, following sanitary improvements. With difficulty the cemetery survived and in the next fifty years greenhouses and a new south entrance were built. There was also talk of building a crematorium in 1911 but this came to nothing.

Between the wars, mounting wages and maintenance bills caused concern and removal of the iron railings for scrap during the Second World War led to Nunhead suffering the increased effects of wanton vandalism. In 1960 efforts were made to revive the cemetery's fortunes. Nunhead was bought by a property company that planned to build on part of the land. Local reaction was hostile and the scheme rejected. By the end of the decade the situation was acknowledged as hopeless as the cemetery was losing £5,000 each year even though one third of it was still unused. Its owner, United Cemeteries, ceased business in February 1969.

In July 1969 an eager *The Times* reporter advised his readers to visit Nunhead as soon as they could because 'its like may never be seen in London again'.[3] He was right. However, by then the Nonconformist chapel had been demolished and the remaining buildings were in a shocking state. The Anglican chapel was burnt out by vandals, the lodges were in ruins and the vaults and catacombs plundered for their lead and jewellery. Two exceptional monuments had been damaged, a bronze figure by Sir Giles Gilbert Scott had been stolen from the grave of nine Boy Scouts, drowned in a boating accident on the Thames in 1912,[4] and the Romanesque style Doulton terracotta mausoleum of the Stearnes family had been invaded. Wild stories of black magic rituals appeared in newspapers and a white robed ghost had been reported hovering among the graves. Only the trees and undergrowth flourished, but in an unchecked rampage.[5] By 1975 the Borough of Southwark decided enough was enough and succeeded, with the aid of an Act of Parliament, in buying the cemetery for £1.

A firm of surveyors was employed and as a result of their findings, Southwark set about dividing the cemetery into three parts. Twenty-two acres were destined to remain as a cemetery, with burial space for another fifty years, twenty-one acres would be a nature reserve and nine acres tamed to become Waverley Park, all at a cost of over £½ million. The scheme did not materialise and since then the cemetery's fortunes have been mixed.[6]

In 1981 the Friends of Nunhead Cemetery was founded. They and the Borough successfully applied to the Heritage Lottery Fund in 1999 for £1¼ million to carry out urgent work. As a result one of Bunning's lodges has been restored, the chapel has been stabilised (but without a roof) and repairs have been carried out on the boundary railings and fifty monuments, including the Stearnes mausoleum and Allan monument. The cemetery is now listed as a Grade II* historic landscape.

Sir Frederick Abel 1827–1902
Military chemist and authority on explosives. He invented cordite with James Dewar in 1889 and wrote *The Modern History of Gunpowder*.

Robert Abel 1857–1936
England test cricketer, in 1899 he made 357 runs in an innings, a record until 1938.

William Ackland 1820–95
Medical galvanist and optician, wrote *Hints on spectacles: when to wear and how to select them*.

Henry Adams 1799–1887
Principal clerk with Lloyd's Register of Shipping which he served for seventy-four years.

Robert Armstrong 1788–1867
Gaelic lexicographer, scientist and schoolmaster. He was author of the first Gaelic dictionary to be published, in 1825.

Rev. Charles Banks 1806–86
Baptist minister, printer and publisher. He published the *Kentish Times* among other newspapers, founded the Baptist journal *The Earthen Vessel* and wrote a life of Calvin.

Lavinia Bartlett 1806–75
Baptist preacher with a huge following at the Metropolitan Tabernacle.

Frederick Beckwith 1821–98
Assumed the title of world swimming champion although 'really only a passable swimmer'. Coached many swimmers including Captain Webb for his cross channel swim.

William Beckwith 1857–92
Champion swimmer, son of Frederick (q.v.) at the age of five performed as 'Baby Beckwith, the Wonder of the World'. In 1881 he beat Captain Webb in a six day race.

William Bennett 1820–95
Poet and journalist. He assisted Gladstone in his campaign to become Liberal M.P. for Greenwich in 1868.

Francis Bristow –1911
Died in her 105th year.

Above: Nunhead: The restored terracotta Stearnes Mausoleum (*c.* 1900).

Right: Nunhead: Detail on the Stearnes mausoleum

SAMUEL BROOME 1805–70
Gardener to the Inner Temple for forty years. His annual chrysanthemum show was a well-known London spectacle.

HORACE BROWN 1848–1925
Chemist, brewer and viticulturist, he became governor of Imperial College, London.

WILLIAM BROWNING 1797–1874
Historian, and uncle to Robert Browning the poet. He wrote several books including histories of the Huguenots and Henry V.

SIR ERNEST BUDGE 1857–1934
Keeper of Egyptian antiquities at the British Museum and archaeologist. He conducted excavations in Mesopotamia and Egypt.

JOHN CALLOW 1822–78
Artist brother of William Callow.

HENRY CAPEL 1795–1887
Wine merchant and historian of the Coopers' Company.

CHARLES CARPENTER 1858–1938
Civil engineer. President of the Institution of Gas Engineers 1895 and pioneer in chemical warfare during The Great War.

Nunhead: James Bunning's entrance gates

Thomas Carter c.1818–67
Clerk in the Adjutant-General's office and military historian, wrote *Curiosities of War and Military Studies* (1860).

William Chadwick 1797–1852
Builder and railway engineer. He built the chapels at Kensal Green cemetery, worked on the Great Western Railway and was involved in the development of the Ladbroke estate.

Col. Joseph Chester 1821–82
American born writer and genealogist. Published *The Register of Westminster Abbey* in 1876.

Charles Cheyne 1838–77
Schoolmaster and astronomical theorist.

Charles Clarke 1849–1908
Chemist, active in Southwark local government, he became Liberal M.P. for Peckham in 1906.

Cuthbert Collingwood 1826–1908
Physician, naturalist and writer on the Swedenborgian church.

William Collyer 1782–1854
Congregational minister, founder of Peckham's Hanover chapel, patronised by the Dukes of Kent and Sussex.

Peter Cunningham 1789–1864
Surgeon superintendent of convict ships to Australia. Later wrote of his experiences and of a visit to the Falkland Islands.

William 'Mutton' Davies 1795–1867
A tailor who always ordered mutton when out to dinner. A local character, he was at times a boxer, wrestler and acrobat.

Sir Polydor de Keyser 1832–98
First Catholic Lord Mayor of London since the Reformation, 1887–88, owner of the Royal Hotel, the largest in London.

William Distant 1845–1922
Naturalist. He was director of the Anthropological Institute, secretary of the Entomological Society and editor of the *Zoologist*.

Bryan Donkin 1768–1855
Engineer, inventor and astronomer. His inventions included a paper-making machine, the composition roller and a method for preserving meat in airtight cans. He built an observatory in his garden.

Sir Horatio Donkin 1845–1927
Grandson of the above, he was an eminent doctor and director of convict prisons.

Rev. George Drew 1818–80
Clergyman and ecclesiastical scholar. His son Julius founded the Home and Colonial Stores and built Castle Drogo.

Augustus Durandeau 1848–93
Writer of popular music hall songs including 'If you want to know the time ask a policeman.' Buried in a pauper's grave.

Benjamin Edgington 1794–1869
In 1835 established the company that became the largest tent and marquee manufacturing business in the country.

George Elkington 1824–97
Architect with a practice in south-east London. Two of his most important works, the town halls of Lewisham and Bermondsey have been demolished.

Barnard Farey 1827–88
Engineer and inventor. He designed the gas valve with rack and pinion and invented a double cylinder rag boiler for paper making.

Henry Field 1803–88
A lineal descendant of Oliver Cromwell, appointed the Queen's assay-master in 1851. He introduced precision to the minting of coinage.

James Figgins 1811–84
Son of Vincent Figgins (q.v.). Typefounder and prominent in City government, Tory M.P. for Shrewsbury 1868–74.

Vincent Figgins 1776–1844
Eminent City of London type founder. His tomb was designed by W.P. Griffith, the architect.

Sir Charles Fox 1810–74
Engineer. He worked on the London and Birmingham railway with Robert Stephenson before starting his own business. He built many bridges but achieved lasting fame by erecting the Crystal Palace in nine months.

LT. COL. FRANCIS FULLER 1791–1853
Served in the Peninsular Campaign, at Waterloo, the capture of Paris and subsequently in India.

CHARLES GANDON 1837–1902
Gas engineer. Developed gas works in Turkey, India and Brazil before becoming
President of the Society of Gas Engineers and the Gas Institute.

HAROLD GLANVILLE 1854–1930
Accountant and Liberal M.P. for Bermondsey 1910–22.

F.M. SIR WILLIAM GOMM 1784–1875
Joined the army aged ten and served in the Peninsular Campaign and at Waterloo. Governor of
Mauritius 1842–9, commander-in-chief in India 1851–55 and constable of the Tower 1872–5.

FREDERICK GORRINGE 1831–1909
London draper and founder of Gorringe's department store in Victoria.

WILLIAM GOVER 1822–94
Actuary, founder and managing director of the British Equitable Assurance Company. Took
an active part in City affairs.

CDR. JOHN HARROLD 1876–1948
Registrar General of Shipping and Seamen from 1921–38 and honorary commander R.N.R.

WILLIAM HENSHAW 1791–1877
Composer and organist of Durham Cathedral 1813–62.

FRANCIS HILL 1801–60
Journalist and editor of the *Daily News*.

JENNY HILL 1850–96
Entertainer from the age of ten. As a cockney music hall star she was famous for
songs such as 'The boy I love is up in the gallery'.

TOM HOOD 1835–74
Son of Thomas Hood (q.v.), poet, novelist, journalist and illustrator.

REV. THOMAS HORNE 1780–1862
Biblical scholar. At the British Museum he catalogued the Harleian manuscripts and edited
Simeon's twenty-one volume commentary on the Bible.

GEORGE HOWELL 1833–1910
Left school aged eight and eventually became a bricklayer and trade union leader. Lib/Lab M.P.
for N.E. Bethnal Green 1885–92.

JAMES HOWELL 1787–1866
Architect and surveyor to the City of Westminster, president of the Surveyors Club 1832–49.

WILLIAM JENKINS −1778
A seven-foot-tall clerk exhumed from the former churchyard of St Christopher-le-Stocks in 1934. The remains of several other priests and clerks from that church were moved to Nunhead in 1860 when it was built over by an extension to the Bank of England.

JOSEPH LEICESTER 1825−1903
Glass maker and trade union leader, Lib/Lab M.P. for South West Ham 1885−86.

SIR GEORGE LIVESEY 1834−1908
Chairman of South Metropolitan Gas Company and local philanthropist, built Camberwell's first free library.

WILLIAM LUCEY −1893
Shipowner.

WILLIAM MCCORMICK 1801−78
Builder and M.P. for Londonderry 1860−65.

HUGH MACLAUCHLAN 1852−99
Journalist, editor successively of the *Hampshire Telegraph*, *Portsmouth Evening News* and *London Star*.

GEORGE MANSELL 1805−70
Together with his son George (1841−97), they were prominent South London newspaper publishers.

PETER MARSH 1828−1909
Took part in the charge of the Light Brigade.

THE MARTYRS' MEMORIAL 1851
An obelisk built with funds collected by Joseph Hume M.P. to commemorate five Scottish nationalists transported to Australia in 1793 for advocating parliamentary reform. A similar monument was built in 1846 at Calton Hill Cemetery, Edinburgh.

WILLIAM MORRIS 1808−74
Engineer, worked on building Hammersmith bridge and Southend Pier, engineer to the Kent Water Works for thirty-eight years.

ANTHONY NEWMAN c.1774−1858
Printer, publisher and bookseller. Owned the Minerva Press 1820−48.

EDWARD NEWMAN 1801−76
Naturalist. Founder and editor of *The Entomologist*, *The Zoologist*, *The Phytologist* and from 1858 editor of *The Field*. Author of books on ferns, insects, birds, moths and butterflies.

ADM. MATTHEW NOLLOTH 1810−82
Naval officer, surveyed the coast of West Africa. Port Nolloth in South Africa is named after him.

Cicely Nott 1832–1900
Actress and singer. Married Samuel Adams, a proprietor of several London music halls.

George Oke 1821–74
Legal writer, his *The Magisterial Synopsis* (1849) was published in fourteen editions.

Francis Ravenscroft 1828–1902
Banker son of Humphrey Ravenscroft (q.v.). Founded the Birkbeck Bank in 1815 and was the driving force behind the creation of Birkbeck College of which he was governor 1849–1902.

Humphrey Ravenscroft 1784–1851
Wigmaker, he introduced wigs made of white horsehair which obviated the wearing of hair powder.

Rev. Thomas Ravenshaw 1829–82
Antiquary and botanist. Author of *Flowering Plants of Devon* (1860) and *Ancient Epitaphs from A.D.1250 to 1800* (1878).

Frederick Rogers 1846–1915
Bookbinder, trade unionist and first chairman of the Labour Representation Committee. As a scholar of English literature he promoted working class education.

Charles Rolls 1799–1885
Engraver and artist. Engraved plates for Finden's *Royal Gallery of British Art* (1840).

Rev. Joshua Russell 1796–1870
Solicitor, poet and, after 1835, Baptist minister. In 1850 he visited Ceylon and India and published an account of his travels.

Henry Schiller 1807–71
Artist, composer, photographer and writer, he also invented a way of laying undersea cables. Buried with his wife, Annie, who wrote *German National Cookery for English Kitchens* (1873).

Lord Justice Sir Charles Selwyn 1813–69
Barrister, elected Tory M.P. for Cambridge 1859, appointed Solicitor General in 1807 and Lord Justice of Appeal in 1868.

Dr. David Smart 1848–1913
Surgeon and astronomer. He built a reflecting telescope in his Bermondsey garden. Joint author of *The Perturbations of Halley's Comet in the Past*.

Alfred Smith 1828–91
Composer and chorister. Professor of music at the Royal Academy of Music and Guildhall School of Music.

Harriet Tebbutt 1815–93
Nurse, she served in the Crimea as superintendent of the Scutari hospital under Florence Nightingale.

George Thornbury 1828–76
Journalist and writer of over twenty books including *The Life of J.M.W. Turner* (1862) and two volumes of *Old and New London*. Died of overwork in Camberwell Lunatic Asylum.

Sir John Thwaites 1815–70
Appointed chairman of the Metropolitan Board of Works in 1855 and directed the first stage in building London's drainage system.

Thomas Tilling 1825–93
Pioneered horse drawn bus routes in South London, he became London's largest omnibus proprietor.

Joseph Tomlinson 1823–94
Engineer and sometimes driver of the Royal train. Designed the locomotive works at Neasden and the network of telephone wires over London for the Northern Telephone Company. President of the Institute of Mechanical Engineers 1890–92.

Alfred Vance 1839–88
Music hall comedian known as 'The Great Vance'. He toured the country with Vance's Concert Company. Over 1,000 admirers attended his funeral. His monument has now gone.

John Vernham 1854–1921
Organist from the age of thirteen, professor of music at King's College.

Dr Charles Verral 1780–1843
Devised the 'Prone System' for the treatment of spinal deformity.

John Waller 1813–1905
Artist and antiquary. Designed a stained glass window commemorating Chaucer in Westminster Abbey and with his brother wrote *A Series of Monumental Brasses* (1841–46).

Joseph Wallis 1825–83
London piano manufacturer and maker of prize winning flutes.

James Ward 1800–84
Barefist boxer, champion of England 1825–32. On retirement became a publican and artist.

John Warriner 1860–1938
Organist. Professor of pianoforte at Trinity College, London, president of the London Society of Organists and author of several books on music.

Rev. James Wells 1803–72
An illiterate farm labourer who became a self-taught Baptist minister and popular preacher in Walworth. Published a volume on the Book of Revelation.

Edward Weston 1822-74
Publican and founder in 1857 of Weston's Music Hall, later renamed the Holborn Empire.

Thomas Wing 1802-89
Left £70,000 in his will for the benefit of blind persons.

Capt. John Woodriff 1791-1868
Between 1802-05 served on a convict ship to Australia, circumnavigated the globe and took part in the battle of Trafalgar. Later saw action in South America and commanded a slave ship to South Africa.

John Yeats 1814-1902
Fellow of the Royal Geographical Society, founder of a school for boys in Peckham and author of books on commerce.

PADDINGTON CEMETERY, MILL HILL
Milespit Hill, NW7

Founded: 1936
Owner: The City of Westminster
Acreage: 26

An immaculately maintained cemetery with tombstone names that reflect the cosmopolitan nature of west London. East Europeans are especially well represented. The chapel, with more than a hint of Dudok, is by the architect Eric E. Lofting. Not unlike the chapel at Chiswick, the demolished Anglican chapel at Gunnersbury and the smaller Kingston Crematorium, it is a substantial and dignified brick building although the interior is plain and disappointing. Had not others opened in the immediate north London vicinity, such as at Hendon and St Marylebone, it could easily have been converted into a crematorium.

The architectural link with Holland is appropriate as the cemetery contains a plot reserved for the Netherlands Field of Honour opened in 1965 in the presence of the Duke of Gloucester and H.H. Prince Bernhard. It contains the graves of 270 Dutch citizens killed during the war, the remains of many transferred from graves all over the country. A bronze figure of a dying man by van Kralingen stands at the head of this small but impressive plot.

Air Vice Marshal Owen Boyd 1889-1944
Balloon commanding officer 1938, escaped from a P.O.W. camp in 1944.

Princess Diana de Faucigny-Lucinge et Coligny, 1922-73
Of the French aristocratic family established in the thirteenth century.

Billy Fury (Ronald Wycherley) 1941-83
Pop singer, 'greasiest, sexiest, most angst ridden Brit rocker of them all'. He died of a heart attack.

Sir John Laing 1879-1978
President of John Laing and Son, contractors; president of the London Bible College.

JULIAN MACLAREN-ROSS 1912–64
Novelist, Literary dandy and hard-drinking chronicler of Fitzrovia.

MICHAEL O'LEARY 1890–1961
Won the V.C. in 1915 and served as a Major in World War II.

PADDINGTON CEMETERY
WILLESDEN LANE, NW2

Founded: 1855
Owner: London Borough of Brent (since 1986)
Acreage: 24

Paddington was one of the earliest public cemeteries to be built following the 1852 Metropolitan Interment Act, aimed to relieve hard-pressed urban churchyards. The architect and planner was Thomas Little, already experienced in cemetery work having designed Nunhead's chapel.[1] The entrance gates, off axis to the north east, are within close proximity of those other Victorian institutions in Willesden Lane, the flamboyant Prince of Wales pub, the church schools and, above all, the former premises of John Cramb, the monumental mason at no. 138 which was built by F.C. Dare in 1883–4. Like his premises at Hampstead it is essentially a three story Victorian house but decked out with a mongrel array of classical and Egyptian revival detail.

Within the cemetery, the full range of white painted lodges and two chapels with a *porte cochère* each plus a central belfry remain. These stand within a regular scheme of paths (equipped with iron foot scrapers) in the shape of a horse shoe.[2] *The Builder* commented that grouping the chapels and their ancillary buildings in this way obviated 'the unsatisfactory and diminutive appearance which small detached chapels in large open spaces always present'.[3] The architectural style is

Paddington: The chapels by Thomas Little (1855)

correct thirteenth-century Gothic. Unique in any London cemetery is the recent addition of a picnic area complete with metal tables.

In 1894 the Cremation Society of England discussed the building of a crematorium at Willesden following a scheme by the architect of Woking Crematorium, Edward F.C. Clarke.[4] The Society and the Burial Board could not agree on terms and their objective was eventually realised with the opening of Golders Green in 1902.

Despite some clearance, the cemetery contains a surprising number of interesting monuments, not least John Cramb's own (1902) in polychrome, carved and polished granite. On entering, attention is immediately caught by the florid bronze embellishments on the Coetze memorial (1877). In the centre of the granite cross is a depiction of the Ascension encircled by an art nouveau flourish of angels and drapery. Railings at the base support mourning figures at each corner in the same fluid style. The monument opposite sports a fine bust of Jabez Burns (1876).

On the north boundary path beyond the immaculately maintained war grave, is a winged angel kneeling above the memorial to Lady Lidiard (1924) and next to it two mausolea. One is a plain Gothic cell but still retaining its original wooden door, but the other is a lavish exercise in the fourteenth-century Gothic style including a sculpture of the Ascension in the tympanum, fearsome oversized gargoyles and a three sided apse with shattered fragments of stained glass in the lancet windows. It is a tragedy that such an extraordinary building has suffered from neglect and vandalism. Elsewhere, the doorways into the Strude and Calland mausolea have been crudely protected by corrugated iron sheeting.

Two substantial Celtic crosses mark the burial areas for religious orders one of them bearing a striking bronze figure of Christ. A number of chest memorials can also be found; one to F.C. Anstey and a more substantial but anonymous example overloaded with heraldry shelters under a yew tree.

There are some early examples of porcelain photographs of the deceased, such as Daisy Clark (1927) and several graves retain their original iron railings. Of note is the bronze lettering on the Mannooch grave (1883), the carving of a rifle, axe and army cap on the headstone commemorating Frederick Stock, sapper Royal Engineers who was 'Called to higher service' in 1918, and the figure of Ivy Margaret 'who entered heaven after a few hours illness' in 1931 aged eight years, dressed in the fashion of the time.

Burials continue in the cemetery towards the south where a raised section of ground provides space for more. Maintenance here is at a lower level as this has been designated a 'nature area'.

Edward Barry 1830–80
Architect, he succeeded to his father's practice in 1860. Designed the Royal Opera House and Charing Cross Station Hotel.

Edward Beesley 1831–1915
Professor of history at University College, London. President of the London Positivist Society 1878–1900.

Thomas Bowlby 1818–60
The Times war correspondent; shipwrecked in the Malabar, he was tortured to death by Tartars and buried in the Russian cemetery, Peking. (Memorial only).

Jabez Burns 1805–76
'Preacher, author, philanthropist and temperance reformer.' He delivered thirty-five annual temperance sermons between 1839–75.

Sir James Cockle 1809–95
The first Chief Justice of Queensland, Australia, and a mathematician.

William Fyfe 1835–82
Scottish artist who painted portraits, historical and genre subjects.

Alfred Gilbert 1828–1902
Composer and organist.

Danny Maher 1881–1916
'The Famous Jockey'. American born, he became champion jockey of the U.S.A. aged seventeen, won the Epsom Derby in 1902, 1905 and 1906 and was champion jockey in Britain 1908 and 1912.

Edward Moore, 6th Earl Mount Cashel, 1829–1915
Irish peer, the last of his line.

Arthur Orton 1834–98
The claimant in the famous Tichborne trial. The personation case lasted 103 days, the criminal case another 188, Orton was convicted of perjury in 1874 and sentenced to seven years' imprisonment. (An unmarked grave).

William Purkiss 1827–99
Publican and theatre manager, he opened the Central Hall, High Holborn, in 1889.

Thomas Robertson 1858–95
Veterinary surgeon, actor and theatre manager.

Edward Spencer 1833–78
Founder of the *Western Morning News* in 1860, which he edited until his death by drowning.

PAINES LANE CEMETERY
Paines Lane, Pinner, Middx.

Founded: 1860
Owner: London Borough of Harrow
Acreage: 2½ acres

Paines Lane Cemetery looks very like a country churchyard largely on account of its proximity to Pinner's medieval parish church.[1] Entering through the gates the drive rises between a pair of cedars beyond which once stood the chapel. It was a lofty brick Gothic building, very plain, with a cavernous porch facing the drive, until it was demolished in 1982. The architect was

T. Lavender of Watford. There is no lodge and railings are replaced by hedges.

Near the site of the chapel is a Celtic cross set on a curious stone platform on which one would expect an inscription, but there is none. To the west are a number of brick vaults many with their iron railings still in place. One contains Horatia, the daughter of Admiral Nelson.

Elsewhere there are the usual marble crosses, some adorned with birds, and a few intact angels and distinctive art deco memorials. The two wives of Sir Ambrose Heal, founder of the Tottenham Court Road furnishing store, are commemorated, respectively, by an Arts and Crafts bronze cross (1901) and an unusual floral cross raised over a classical plinth (1938). Another Celtic cross with especially intricate carving commemorates the Scotsman James Gairdner (1912).

Although the grass is regularly cut, maintenance appears to be at a low level and some memorials are completely swamped by brambles. The cemetery is now only used when an existing grave is reopened and the safety of memorials is clearly a concern. Many are staked to prevent them toppling over, treatment that is preferable to the drastic practice of laying them flat on the grave.

Sir Francis Milman, 4th Baronet 1842–1922
Soldier, his great grandfather had been physician to George III.

Horatia Nelson Ward 1801–81
Daughter of Lord Nelson and Emma Hamilton, married to the Rev. Philip Ward. She died in Pinner.

PINNER CEMETERY
Pinner Road, Pinner, Middx.

Founded: 1933
Owner: London Borough of Harrow
Acreage: 22½

This is the flagship of the Borough's cemeteries. A bronze plaque attached to the lodge announces that it was consecrated and dedicated on 13 May 1933, under the direction of the committee chairman, A. Hannibal and the architect S.W. Richardson.

The cemetery forecourt and heavy iron gates act a sort of architectural centrepiece tucked into a road of white painted and green roofed blocks of flats. Lodge and chapel are modestly gothicized and the lavatories discreetly hidden behind the laurels between the two. Planting around the plots first used for burials is copious but over the hilltop is a desperate wasteland with barely a tree. To the right of the main drive a curious phenomenon has been created, the children's graveyard, a border of flat marble slabs some 100 yds long mostly filled with green glass chippings. Near them, but a long way from home, are the graves of Czech soldiers killed during the last war.

One monument stands out among the sober rows and alone justifies a visit to the cemetery. It is a life-size red granite armchair, 1954 model, erected over the grave of Susan Dunford, who it is written, 'left her chair vacant' in that year. It is a delight worthy of any nineteenth century cemetery.

SIR DAVID ROSEWAY 1890–1969
Under Secretary of State War Office 1945–55.

MAJ.GEN.GEOFFREY WHITE 1870–1959
Commandant Royal Military Academy, Woolwich.

PLAISTOW CEMETERY
BURNT ASH ROAD, BROMLEY, KENT

Founded: 1892
Owner: London Borough of Bromley
Acreage: 4

Entry to the cemetery is via a corridor of land, as so often occurs where sufficient ground for cemetery use was only available isolated from the road. In this case the architect, W.R. Mallett, made the best of it by designing a bulky Gothic lodge under which the drive passes. In the cemetery proper he placed a compact Early English style chapel topped by a flèche.

Like many of the small outer London cemeteries, Plaistow is well kept and used primarily by local people, with a limited capacity for new burials. There are few celebrities and tombs are conservatively designed with the cross symbol predominant. A touching epitaph on the tomb of Alice Johnstone, who died in 1920, illustrates the point:

> This humble stone is erected as a token of affection, remembrance and gratefulness by all who knew her at the Silver Grill, Bishopsgate, employer, employees and customers.

In such places the residents tend not to die but follow the example of one Bromley gentleman who in 1938 'passed into the keeping of the great Architect of the Universe'.

JOSEPH JOHNSON 1839–1906
Curator of the Royal Botanic Gardens, Belfast (monument only).

JAMES LAIDLAW 1836–1921
Pioneer missionary of the English Presbyterian church in Formosa.

ROGER YELVERTON 1845–1912
Chief Justice of the Bahamas and 'Chairman of the League of Criminal Appeal by whose agitation a Court of Criminal Appeal has been secured' (in 1907).

PLUMSTEAD CEMETERY
WICKHAM LANE, SE2

Founded: 1890
Owner: London Borough of Greenwich
Acreage: 30½

The advantage of a hillside position is once again demonstrated at Plumstead which was built on parkland first laid out in the seventeenth century. Entrance is through an arched gateway; on one side is the cemetery office, with the original enamel 'Superintendent's Office' sign on the door, and on the other side is a rebuilt lodge sensitively incorporating original stone. The main path then ascends to the chapels which enjoy a site rarely equalled by London's parish churches. The architectural style is also unusual, taking its cue from the French 'Flamboyant' rather than any English source. These unusual elements are pursued further by the introduction of a great deal of brightly coloured glass similar in style to Victorian pub windows. Another feature is the semi-circular mortuary chapel forming part of the *porte cochère*. The architects were Church, Quick and Whinchop, also responsible for Woolwich Cemetery.

The ground around the chapels undulates and at one point is actually carved out of the hillside to create a cliff. One solitary mausoleum can be found here; to Robert Webb, the year 1915 is carved above the door. There are few other interesting monuments. A number refer to those killed at work in the notorious Woolwich Arsenal. In particular, a pink granite obelisk north of the chapels was 'Erected to the memory of the men who lost their lives in the Guncotton and Lyddite explosions', two separate incidents when eleven men died in 1903.

REV. I.P. DICKERSON −1900
Born at Wytheville, USA, 'ex-slave and jubilee singer'.

ALBERT GORMAN 1883−1959
Mayor of Woolwich 1940−41, a chairman of the Metropolitan Water Board.

COL.SIR EDWIN HUGHES 1832−1904
Solicitor, company director, M.P. for Woolwich 1885−1902, first mayor of Woolwich 1900−01.

ALFRED SMITH 1861−1932
Awarded the V.C. during the Sudan Campaign in 1885.

PUTNEY LOWER COMMON CEMETERY
MILL HILL ROAD, SW13

Founded: 1855
Owner: London Borough of Wandsworth
Acreage: 3

A cemetery in miniature situated in an unusually rural setting of land bought from Lord Spencer on the edge of Barnes Common. Unlike nearby Barnes Common Cemetery, Putney is still handsomely railed in (including a bishop's mitre design above a letter 'P' on the finial) and has a full Gothic complement of two entrance gates, a lodge (unoccupied) two chapels and a belfry (boarded-up) built for £2,314 to the design of the cemetery specialists Messrs Barnett and Birch. A plaque records that they were built by the local builders W. and R. Aviss (their family tomb is in the cemetery).

The epitaph on Hannah O'Ryan's tombstone of 1868 is classic Victorian pathos, part of which runs as follows:

This tomb carved by affection's memory, wet with affection's tears, is erected by her afflicted daughter as a mournful tribute of tender affection to her dearly beloved and best of mothers.

Sir Alfred Dryden 1821–1912
Descendant of the poet John Dryden, barrister and land-owner at Canons Ashby, Northamptonshire.

PUTNEY VALE CEMETERY AND CREMATORIUM
Kingston Road, SW15

Founded: 1891
Owner: London Borough of Wandsworth
Acreage: 45

On one side of the A3 is Richmond Park, hidden behind Gothic railings on the other is the hard marmoreal glitter of Putney Vale, built on fields that had been farmland since mediaeval times. It was, and probably still is, one of the most popular cemeteries south of the river, having superseded the once fashionable West Norwood and Nunhead.

Land was first bought in 1887 with additional acres acquired in 1909 and 1912, so that the cemetery now extends up to the edge of Wimbledon Common. Along the parallel boundary to the road a Garden of Remembrance was opened in 1937. Its genteel neo-Georgian style of brick enclosures, rose garden and fountain court, attempts to disguise the sepulchral function. A contemporary brochure described the scene in a masterpiece of euphemistic prose:

> The grace of Nature and the architectural skill of man have combined to make a thing of beauty in a quiet spot among God's green acres near the western boundary of the great Borough of Wandsworth. . . Bright flowers, green lawns and stately trees painted by the Master Artist, give back the smile that we knew and soft waters echo the voice that we remember.[1]

Coyly engraved on plaques set in the walls are such elegies as:

Putney Vale: The entrance (1900). The chapel was converted to a crematorium in 1938, badly burned by fire in 1946 and reopened in 1956

> The kiss of the sun for pardon
> The song of the birds for mirth
> We are nearer God's heart in a garden
> Than anywhere else on earth.

A sentiment rudely destroyed by the roar and fumes of traffic not 20 yards away.

At the end of the now closed drive from the A3 is a Gothic chapel with a stumpy spire, built in 1890 to the designs of David Brown.[2] A second chapel was converted into a crematorium to a scheme prepared by the borough engineer, Ernest J. Elford, and opened in May 1938 by Lord Horder. It was badly burned in a fire in December 1946 but due to war time exigencies rebuilding was delayed until 1956 when the other chapel was also converted for cremation services. One of the chapels has delightful coloured abstract designed stained glass. A new chimney was added to the rear of the building in the late 1990s. Clement Attlee, the Labour prime minister, was cremated here in 1967 and Clementine Churchill, widow of Sir Winston in 1977, but neither is commemorated by a monument. On the approach to the crematorium a free standing catacomb range was constructed in 2003. A new single-storey office was opened in the 1980s when the vehicle entrance from the busy A3 was closed. Access to the cemetery is now from Stag Lane.

The real glory of Putney Vale lies beyond the buildings. Here are the massed ranks of monuments erected around the turn of the century in every imaginable size and shape before expense and byelaws put an end to such extravaganza. They range from the sublime, such as the towering Egyptian style mausoleum containing the remains of Alexander Gordon (1910), to the ridiculous, exemplified by the flower strewing angels in the blue and orange tiled loggia on Caroline Lyons' tomb (1924). Nearby is a reclining female figure on the Marsh grave (1920) and the very striking carved figure on the Vickery grave (1922). Granite, marble, limestone and bronze jostle in frenzied commemoration of wealthy residents from Wimbledon, Putney and Streatham.

The older tombs were built in a broad sweep following the line of the south eastern perimeter railings. At the top end is the unique Ismay tomb of 1937 carved with three masted schooners sailing in a choppy sea. Halfway is the Sainsbury mausoleum, a finely proportioned Bathstone temple. It is a tragedy that the proximity of these tombs to the Common footpaths has resulted in attacks by vandals. Few of the angel figures have escaped unscathed.

Towards the centre of the cemetery there is nothing comparable, it is being overwhelmed by the stark black and white marble slabs of the modern mason's art. Some are distinguished by beautifully cut lettering but the trend is towards the banal monotony of the lawn cemetery.

MAJ. GEN. ERNEST ALEXANDER 1870–1934
Artillery office who won the V.C. in 1914. Medal was sold for £80,000 in 1999.

COL. SIR JOHN ALKINS 1875–1963
Physician and a deputy director of Medical Services in Great Britain.

SIR FREDERICK ALLEN 1864–1934
Managing Director of the P. & O. Shipping Line.

SIR WILLIAM BATTEN 1865–1938
A judge in the Indian Civil Service.

SIR WILLIAM BENNETT 1852–1931
Physician and H.M. Inspector of Anatomy.

ADM. LORD CHARLES BERESFORD 1846–1919
Friend of the Prince of Wales, arch-opponent of naval modernisation.

TERENCE BLACKWOOD, 2ND MARQUESS OF DUFFERIN AND AVA, 1866–1918
Secretary in the Diplomatic Service.

LIEUT. WILLIAM BOULTER 1892–1955
Won the V.C. in 1916.

SIR THOMAS VANSITTART BOWATER 1862–1938
Lord Mayor of London 1913–14 and M.P. for the City of London 1924–38.

SIR HARRY BOYD 1876–1940
Civil servant and Registrar of Baronetage.

SIR FRANCIS BRAKE 1889–1960
Engineer.

HARRY BRODIE 1875–1956
Colonial merchant, M.P. for Reigate 1906–10.

ROBERT BURNHAM, LORD RENWICK 1904–73
Stockbroker and a chairman of the Institute of Directors.

SIR ANDREW CAIRD 1870–1956
Managing director of the 'Daily Mail' 1922–26.

HOWARD CARTER 1874–1939
Draughtsman, archaeologist and Egyptologist, in 1922 he discovered the tomb of King Tutankhamun.

BYRON CARY, 12TH VISCOUNT FALKLAND, 1845–1922
Art collector, representative peer for Scotland.

PETER CHEYNEY 1896–1951
Actor, soldier and author of detective novels.

HENRY CLASPER 1858–1931
Queen Victoria's waterman.

SIR HUGH CLIFFORD 1866–1941
Between 1912 and 1929 was successively governor of the Gold Coast, Nigeria, Ceylon, and the Straits Settlements. Author of a Malay/English dictionary.

Sir Charles Clipperton 1864–1927
Inspector General of Consulates.

Ivy Compton Burnett 1892–1969
Novelist.

Sir Anderson Critchett 1845–1925
Surgeon oculist to Edward VII and George V.

Anthony Devas 1911–58
Artist, he was a member of the New English Art Club.

Sir Henry Dickens 1849–1933
Last surviving son of Charles Dickens, Common Serjeant of the City of London 1917–32.

Laurie Doherty 1876–1919
He and his brother Reggie (see below) were the first English tennis stars. Wimbledon singles champion 1902–06 and doubles champion 1897–1901, 1903–05. US singles champion 1903 and doubles champion 1902–03.

Reggie Doherty 1874–1910
Wimbledon singles champion 1897–1900 and doubles champion 1903–05.

Sir John Ellerman 1862–1933
Shipowner and art collector, reputedly the richest man in England at his death.

Sir Hugh Ellis-Rees 1900–74
Financial advisor to the government, chairman O.E.E.C. 1952–60.

Sir Jacob Epstein 1880–1959
Sculptor, he executed the statuary on Oscar Wilde's tomb in Père Lachaise (1909), one of his earliest works.

Douglas Eric, 2nd Lord Hacking of Chorley, 1910–71
Solicitor and company director.

Sir Stephen Finney 1852–1924
English rugger international 1872–3. Railway engineer in India.

Sir Pierson Frank 1930–46
Chief engineer and county surveyor L.C.C.

Reginald Fraser –1966
Scientist and inventor.

William Fraser, 1st Lord Strathalmond, 1888–1970
Chairman of B.P. 1941–56 and a director of the National Provincial Bank.

WILLIAM FRASER, 2ND LORD STRATHALMOND, 1916–76
Chairman of B.P. 1962–76.

SIR PERCY GREENAWAY 1881–1956
Lord Mayor of London 1932–33.

COL. HARRY GREENWOOD, D.S.O. AND BAR, 1881–1948
Won the V.C. in 1918, also recipient of the O.B.E. and M.C.

SIR DOUGLAS HALL 1866–1923
M.P. for the Isle of Wight and instigator of the water ambulance during the Great War.

SIR EDWARD HAWKE 1895–1964
Recorder of London 1959–64.

SIR JOHN HAWKE 1869–1941
Judge of the Kings Bench Division 1928–41.

LT. COL. REGINALD HAYWARD 1881–1970
Won the V.C. in 1918. Games manager at the Hurlingham Club 1952–67.

SIR FREDERICK HOBDAY 1869–1939
Honorary vet to George V and George VI, dean of the Royal Veterinary College.

SIR EDWARD HULTON 1859–1925
Newspaper proprietor, he owned the *Daily Sketch*, *Evening Standard* and numerous other papers. In 1923 he sold his interests to Allied Newspapers for an estimated £6 million.

BRUCE ISMAY 1862–1937
Shipowner, chairman of the White Star Line and a director of the L.M.S.

SIR CHARLES JACKSON 1848–1923
Authority and writer on English goldsmiths.

SIR HENRY JACKSON 1876–1937
M.P. for Wandsworth 1924–29 and 1931–37.

SIR WILLIAM JOHNS 1873–1937
Director of naval construction 1930–36.

SIR CHARLES JOHNSTON 1848–1933
Lord Mayor of London 1914–15.

SIR JOHN JORDAN 1852–1925
H.B.M. Envoy Extraordinary and Minister Plenipotentiary at Peking 1906–20.

ALEXANDER KERENSKY 1881–1970
Prime minister of the provisional government in Russia during the months before the Bolsheviks seized power in 1917.

ADM. SIR HERBERT KING-HALL 1862–1936
Director of Naval Intelligence, formerly Commander-in-Chief Cape of Good Hope 1912–15 during which time he sank the German cruiser *Konigsberg*.

SIR CLEMENT KINLOCH-COOKE 1854–1944
Lawyer, politician, journalist and founder editor of the *Empire Review* 1901–41.

SIR JOHN LAVERY 1856–1941
Society artist, president of the Royal Society of Portrait Painters 1932–41.

SIR CHARLES LEWIS 1825–93
Solicitor, politician and author of legal textbooks.

SIR FRANK LOCKWOOD 1847–97
Solicitor General 1894–5 and *Punch* cartoonist.

ROBERT LORAINE 1876–1935
Aeronaut, the first man to fly in a storm, the first to fly the Irish channel and the first to use a wireless from the air in 1910.

JOSEPH LOSEY 1909–84
Film director. Cremated here.

LORD MACDONNELL OF SWINFORD 1844–1925
Colonial administrator in India, member of the Council of India 1902.

SIR PATRICK MACDOUGALL 1819–94
Military historian, wrote *The Campaigns of Hannibal*.

SIR JOHN MACFADYEAN 1866–1929
Principal of the Royal Veterinary College.

SIR WILLIAM MADGE 1845–1927
Founder of *The People* magazine.

SGT. MARTIN –1981
Head linksman at the Royal Opera House Covent Garden for thirty two years.

SIR ALEXANDER MATHESON 1861–1929
Australian politician and member of the senate of Australia 1901–06.

SIR CHARLES MATHEWS 1850–1920
Director of Public Prosecutions 1908–20.

Left: Putney Vale: The Ismay Memorial (1937). **Right:** Putney Vale: Reclining figure on the Marsh grave (1920)

AIR CHIEF MARSHAL SIR WILLIAM MITCHELL, 1888–1944
Gentleman Usher of the Black Rod 1941–44.

FERGUS, LORD MORTON OF HENRYTON, 1887–1973
Lord of Appeal 1944–59.

SIR DERMOD MURPHY 1914–1975
Governor of St Helena 1968–71.

SIR WILLIAM NOBLE 1861–1943
Engineer in Chief of the G.P.O. in London, a director of G.E.C.

SIR HENRY OAKLEY 1823–1915
Director of the Great Northern Railway.

SIR CHARLES OWENS 1845–1933
General manager of the L.S.W.R. 1908–11 and director of the Southern Railway 1923–30.

GEN. SIR ARTHUR PAGET 1851–1928
Commanding officer British forces in Ireland 1911–17. (Memorial only – buried at Cannes).

SIR GEORGE PATON 1859–1934
Managing Director of Bryant and May.

CAPT. GEORGE TATHAM PATON 1895–1917
V.C. posthumously awarded while serving in France. (Monument only, his remains were buried in Metz-en-Couture, France).

SIR ROY PLOMLEY 1914–1985
Radio presenter, devised the 'Desert Island Discs' programme.

SIR SAMUEL POWER 1863–1932
Gentleman Usher of the Black Rod of St. Patrick.

SIR DAVID PRAIN 1857–1944
Botanist, director of Kew Gardens 1905–22.

SIR PATRICK QUINN 1855–1936
Detective Superintendent in the Special Branch with special responsibility for protecting foreign sovereigns on visits to the U.K.

SIR EDWARD REED 1830–1906
Naval architect and chief constructor in the Royal Navy 1863–71. He assisted in improving the design of ironclads. Liberal M.P. for Cardiff for twenty years.

SIR GEORGE REID 1845–1918
Helped to frame the constitution of the Commonwealth of Australia. Premier of New South Wales 1894–99. First High Commissioner of Australia in London 1910–16.

SIR HARRY RENWICK 1861–1932
Electrical engineer, he masterminded the installation of London's first super power station at Barking in 1925.

SGT. ALFRED RICHARDS 1879–1953
Won the V.C. at Gallipoli in 1915 when he lost a leg. He was one of six V.C.s awarded to the Lancashire Fuseliers on the same day.

SIR RONALD ROSS 1857–1932
Doctor and pioneer in the treatment of malaria.

WILLIAM ROUTLEDGE 1859–1939
Explorer and anthropologist. He sailed a schooner built by himself and his wife to survey the south east Pacific 1913–16.

SIR EDWIN SAUNDERS 1814–1901
Dentist to Queen Victoria and Edward VII.

SIR OWEN SEAMAN 1861–1938
Author and editor of *Punch* 1906–32.

SIR PHILIP SMYLY 1896–1953
Chief Justice of the Gold Coast 1911–29.

Henry Saxon Snell 1830–1904
Architect who specialised in designing hospitals.

Sir Dudley Stewart-Smith 1857–1919
Judge and Vice Chancellor of the County Palatine of Lancaster.

Sir Thomas Storey 1851–1933
Chairman of Lloyd's Register of Shipping.

Vesta Tilly 1864–1952
Born Matilda Powles, the greatest of music hall male impersonators, she was the original Burlington Bertie. Her career spanned fifty years.

Sir Tudor Walters 1868–1933
Liberal M.P. for Sheffield 1906–22 and Falmouth 1929–31, Paymaster General 1919–22 and 1931. First president of the Educational Association.

Sir Charles Watson 1844–1916
Colonial administrator and author of *Fifty Years Work in the Holy Land*.

John Wheatley 1892–1955
Watercolour artist and engraver.

Sir Richard Winstedt 1878–1966
Colonial administrator in Malaya and authority on the country's history and language. President of the Royal Asiatic Society for sixteen years.

QUEEN'S ROAD CEMETERY
Queen's Road, Croydon, Surrey

Founded: 1861
Owner: London Borough of Croydon
Acreage: 26

After 145 years and over 37,000 burials, the cemetery is an oasis of green in an area of dense housing. The land was purchased in 1860 for £5,079; including the buildings, walls, railings and laying out of the grounds at a total cost of £16,000. Archbishop Sumner consecrated part of the cemetery on 18 July 1861 and the Bishop of Southwark, Dr Grant, blessed the Roman Catholic section on 28 August the same year. In the first year sixty-three burials took place but Croydon is now only used for the reopening of existing graves.

Surrounded by roads on three sides, the original railings – painted in the borough's corporate colour of bright blue – remain on Queen's Road. Inside the entrance is a ragstone lodge, and tucked away in the corner is a large air raid shelter. Mature cedars line the main drive to the prominently situated chapels. These were built in the Decorated style with plenty of variety in the tracery patterns. The architect was C.E. Robins whose designs were selected in competition with eleven others.[1] Oddly enough, instead of providing a *porte cochère* common to both, he designed two, but perversely added a broach spire to only one. The Anglican chapel has a semi-octagonal apse at the east end. Both chapels are now unused, boarded up and in a sorry state, although one serves as a tool store.

A narrow flat site does not offer much scope for landscaping but variety has been achieved with tree planting. The cemetery used to extend just east of the twin chapels and it is within this original ground that monuments of interest can be found. Regrettably, many have been cleared, but those remaining around the chapel are worth noting. None are very big but they include a rare cast iron Gothic-style tomb of 1865. Isabella Saward was 105 years old when she was buried beneath it in 1950. Almost as rare as iron is the use of slate in London cemeteries. The four headstones of the Couch family demonstrate its imperishable qualities. There is a splendid angel carved into a headstone on the grave of bellfounder, Cyril Johnston, and Joseph Philpot is commemorated by a fine chest tomb with original railings.

A welcome feature at Croydon is the recent addition of large interpretation boards giving the history of the cemetery.

JOSHUA ALLDER 1838–1904
Founded Allder's department store, Croydon in 1862.

JOHN ANDERSON 1827–1907
Author, artist and historian.

FRANCIS BARRAUD 1824–1900
Stained glass artist in the Covent Garden firm of Lavers, Barraud and Westlake.

SIR REUBEN BARROW 1838–1917
Liberal M.P. for Bermondsey.

EDMUND DUFF 1869–1928, VERA SYDNEY 1889–1929, VIOLET SYDNEY –1929
Husband, sister and mother of Mrs Grace Duff and all victims of arsenic poisoning. The newspapers reported 'unseemly scenes' when crowds flocked to witness the three exhumations, but despite three inquests, no one was ever charged with the sensational crime known as the Croydon Poisoning Mystery.

ADM. SIR STEPHEN LUSHINGTON 1803–77
Crimean war veteran and governor of Greenwich Hospital.

JOSEPH PHILPOTT 1802–1869
Theologian and writer of religious tracts.

COL. W.H. SNELL 1822–1910
Served in the army for seventy-one years.

FREDERICK WALTERS 1849–1931
Architect. He designed numerous churches including Buckfast Abbey.

RICHMOND CEMETERY
Grove Road, Richmond, Surrey

Founded: 1853
Owner: London Borough of Richmond upon Thames
Acreage: Approx. 15

Richmond is an unusually rural cemetery which in spring simulates a country churchyard beneath a disguise of primroses, daffodils and forsythia – even rabbits are not uncommon. A Victorian flavour is added by the presence of yews, cypresses, two suitably lugubrious Gothic chapels and a thatched shelter. The Nonconformist chapel was sold in 1982 and following the repositioning of the gates now stands outside the boundary of the cemetery. Distinguished by heavy plate tracery and sculpted decoration, rare for a cemetery chapel, it has been restored and a small house added to one side. The name of the architect is unknown. The ragstone Anglican chapel is more conventional Early English ragstone, designed by Sir Arthur Blomfield and built about 1870. After declining into a tool store it was restored by the Richmond Borough Environment Trust and listed in 1990. A feature of the chapel is the triptych reredos decorated with brightly coloured mosaic depicting censing angels on a gold ground. It once rejoiced in a west window filled with stained glass but all that remains is a panel at such a height that even the vandals have been defeated.

Richmond: detail on a grave (1902)

The cemetery's origins are vague. It appears that one and a half acres of land were provided for burial purposes by George III. Steps were taken to acquire it for municipal use in 1853 but the burial board was not formed until 1868. In 1873 the cemetery was enlarged and the Vicar 'created considerable excitement . . . by erecting a wall to divide the consecrated from the unconsecrated ground', a tactic which was roundly condemned and 'one fine morning it was found levelled to the ground' – to the Vicar's annoyance. He offered a £20 reward for the apprehension of this 'evil and maliciously disposed person',[1] apparently without result. Two further enlargements occurred in 1898 and 1902, north of a footpath which divides the ground.

The monuments meanwhile decay gently into the undergrowth although some clearance has taken place around the Anglican chapel. William Harvey's granite tombchest has subsided but the incised palette in pink granite remains discernible. The floral carving on the Prendergast family's crosses, a virtuoso work, seems especially appropriate in these surroundings. About the turn of the century the contemporary taste for the Renaissance inspired a few brick monuments in the style. In the cemetery's northern half are two large memorials. A granite cenotaph designed by Sir Edwin Lutyens, with a foundation stone laid by General Smuts in 1915, marks the graves of South African soldiers killed during the Great War. The lion was sculpted by Cecil Thomas. Nearby is a curious classical structure built in the 1950s commemorating those servicemen who have died in Richmond's Star and Garter home.

Among the epitaphs there is a cricketing classic beneath the name of Tom Richardson, a Surrey and England player:

> He bowled his best but was himself bowled by the best on July 2nd 1912.

More allusive is that of Alfred Ellis, who died in 1888:

> Eleven years summoning officer at Richmond.
> Blessed are the Peacemakers.

And enigmatic, the undated:

> Annie's Grave. Aged 21
> It matters little who the maiden was
> We called her Annie, and she was beloved
> By all who knew her – Reader if you knew
> This good and truthful girl then will you
> Breathe a pious benediction on her soul
> And sanctify her memory with a tear.
> Erected by her master
> As a tribute to fidelity and attachment.

Sir Charles Burt 1832–1913
Solicitor and active member in Richmond's local government.

Sir Arthur Church 1834–1915
Chemist, he discovered churchite, a native cerium phosphate, and other new minerals. President of the Mineralogical Society, he also published works on English porcelain, of which he was a collector.

Sir Frederick Cook 1844–1920
City businessman and Conservative M.P. for Kennington 1895–1906.

Maj.Gen. Godfrey Dyer 1889–1977
Indian army officer and chairman of the British Association for Cemeteries in South Asia.

Richmond: The tomb of William Harvey, engraver (1866)

SGT. FREDERICK EDWARDS 1894–1964
He won the V.C. in 1916.

WALTER FITCH 1817–1892
Botanical artist. During his lifetime he published nearly 10,000 drawings including contributions to the *Botanical Magazine* and *Gardener's Chronicle*.

CHARLES GARVICE 1851–1920
Novelist, dramatist and journalist. President of the Farmers and Landowners Association, chairman of the Author's Club 1908–20.

LORD CLAUD HAMILTON 1843–1925
A.D.C. to Queen Victoria in 1887, a Lord of the Treasury and a Tory M.P. for Londonderry, Kings Lynn, Liverpool and South Kensington. Chairman of the Great Eastern Railway 1893–1922.

SGT. HARRY HAMPTON 1870–1922
Won a V.C. during the Boer War. Committed suicide on the railway track in Richmond.

GEORGE HARNEY 1817–97
'The Last of the Chartist Leaders, After Life's Fitful Fever he sleeps well.'

WILLIAM HARVEY 1796–1866
Engraver, served his apprenticeship under Thomas Bewick. His wood engraving of Haydon's 'Assassination of Dentatus' in 1821 was the largest block ever cut in Britain.

ARTHUR HUGHES 1832–1915
Pre-Raphelite painter and book illustrator.

JULIUS JEFFREY 1801–77
Surgeon, he served in India, pioneered the use of limes in forming citric acid and invented a respirator for treating pulmonary attacks (1835).

WILLIAM MACMILLAN 1887–1977
Sculptor, his best known works are the statues of George VI overlooking the Mall and Alcock and Brown at Heathrow Airport.

SIR RALPH MILLBOURNE 1862–1942
Stockbroker and president of the Ex-Servicemen's Welfare Society.

Richmond: Passion flowers and Lilies.

Sir William Olpherts 1822–1902
Served in the Royal Artillery, won a V.C. in 1857 during the relief of the Residency at the siege of Lucknow in the Indian Mutiny. Known as 'Hell-fire Jack'.

George Osborn 1808–91
Wesleyan preacher, president of the Wesleyan Methodist Conference 1863–81; he published several works on the Wesleys.

Sir Andrzej Panufnik 1914–91
Polish born composer and conductor.

John Pigott –1923
War correspondent.

Felix Pissarro 1874–97
Painter, third son of Camille Pissarro the French Impressionist.

Gen.Sir Harry Prendergast 1834–1913
Won a V.C. during the Indian Mutiny when he was severely wounded. Ccommanded an expedition that annexed an area of Upper Burma for which he was thanked by the Queen.

James Ramsbottom 1891–1925
Pioneering horticulturalist who is credited with saving the British daffodil industry from extinction.

Thomas Richardson 1870–1912
England fast bowler, in one season he took 290 wickets, a record that stood for thirty-three years.

Maj.Gen.Sir Dudley Ridout 1866–1941
Member of the executive and legislative council of the Straits Settlements 1915–21.

Robert Allen Rolfe 1855–1921
First curator of the orchid herbarium at Kew and founder of *The Orchid Review*.

Leslie Stuart 1862–1928
Composer, he wrote the 'Lily of Laguna'.

Mgr. Montague Summers 1880–1948
Demonologist, writer of ghost stories and historian of early English drama.

Sir James Szlumper 1834–1914
Twice mayor of Richmond, a civil engineer, he was concerned with the construction of London's underground railways.

Thomas Taylor 1879–1932
Curator of the Royal Botanical Gardens at Kew.

Sir Max Waechter 1837–1924
German born, he published a pamphlet on the federation of the States of Europe which he submitted to all the European governments and sovereigns. Presented Petersham Ait and Petersham Lodge to Richmond, founded and supported several convalescent homes; High Sheriff of Surrey.

RIPPLESIDE CEMETERY
Ripple Road, Barking, Essex

Founded: 1886
Owner: London Borough of Barking and Dagenham
Acerage: 31

Rippleside Cemetery was established to provide burial space for the parish of St Margaret's, Barking. In November 1884 the Burial Board purchased 12 acres of land and employed a local architect, Charles James Dawson, to design the lodge chapel and railings.[1] The chapel is an ambitious exercise in the perpendicular Gothic style, notable for its entrance tower and stair turret, using Kentish rag with Portland stone dressings. This and the east gable are decorated with flint flush work, an East Anglian specialty. Dawson said that the style was '. . . characteristic of the historical part of Barking' and it certainly bears a resemblance to both St Margaret's Parish Church and the local Curfew Tower.

Spreading cedars line the entrance drive to the chapel around which are the best memorials like the marble triptych to Margaret Gow (1929), and an impressive angel, resembling a winged victory, dominating the early twentieth-century Kerry family grave. On the approach to the chapel is a standing uniformed figure above the Rowley grave with a bronze medallion portrait of the deceased beneath. Although the date is illegible the Portland stone statue has survived both vandalism and the weather. Less fortunate is the Ager monument on which stands a sadly mutilated sculpture relief of a horse. Six victims of an explosion at Hewett's works in Barking were buried in the cemetery on 12 January 1899.[2]

Charles James Dawson 1850–1933
Local architect who designed the magistrates court, fire station and swimming baths in Barking and planned Barking Park.

Samuel Hewett –1904
Commemorated by a large anchor, an appropriate symbol for a member of a family which owned Barking fishing fleet, at one time the largest in the world.

Joseph Leftley 1844–87
Local road haulier whose firm was reputed to be the oldest in the country founded in 1800.

RODING LANE NORTH CEMETERY
Roding Lane North, South Woodford, Essex

Founded: 1940
Owner: London Borough of Redbridge
Acreage: ½

Fenced in among the football pitches this cemetery must be one of the smallest in London. Having been allocated for graves of those in the Borough who lost their lives through enemy action, the twenty-three small gravestones that for years were forgotten and forlorn have been joined by more recent memorials following the Council's decision to reopen the cemetery. Planting is minimal and there are no memorials of significance.

ROYAL HOSPITAL CHELSEA BURIAL GROUND
Royal Hospital Road, SW3

Founded: 1692
Owner: The Royal Hospital
Acreage: 1

Whereas Sir Christopher Wren was singularly unsuccessful in segregating the post fire City churches from their traditional graveyards, he achieved his aim at Chelsea where there was more room to manoeuvre on the new Hospital site. The narrow little ground lies east of the Hospital and, until its closure in 1854, accommodated some 10,000 bodies. In-pensioners were not normally given a headstone and the ground was used over and over again. There is now just a scattering of table tombs, headstones and slabs, several handsomely carved in the eighteenth century.

The earliest interment was of Simon Cox in 1692, a soldier who had served under four monarchs. Similar versatility and longevity are recurring features of the old soldiers who followed him. There are records of two aged 112, one 111 another 107. William Hiseland, one of the centenarians, even married 'when above one hundred years old'. Equally unusual are Christiana Davis (died 1739) and Hannah Snell (died 1792), two women who joined the army as soldiers, both buried in unmarked graves.

In 1854 the Hospital acquired a new plot in Brompton Cemetery which was used until 1893 when Brookwood Cemetery provided the Hospital's present burial ground, although since 2004 the burial of ashes has been allowed here.

Gen. Sir Walter Braithwaite 1865–1945
Served with distinction during the Boer and Great Wars, aide de camp to George V, governor of the Hospital 1931–38. (Memorial only.)

Charles Burney 1726–1814
Musician and astronomer, wrote *The History of Music* in four volumes 1776–89, appointed organist to the Hospital 1783. He was father of Fanny Burney, the novelist.

William Cheselden 1688–1752
Surgeon, he perfected the 'lateral operation for the stone' which he could perform in under one minute. Wrote the beautifully illustrated *Osteographia*, attended Sir Isaac Newton on his deathbed, appointed surgeon to the Hospital 1737.

Col. Thomas Chudleigh 1664–1739
Lieutenant governor of the Hospital and father of the beautiful and notorious Elizabeth, the bigamous wife of the 3rd Earl of Bristol and 2nd Duke of Kingston.

James Cock 1737–1810
Master cook of the Hospital and for many years director and honorary secretary of the Chelsea Savings Bank.

William Daniel 1664–1739
Master cook of the Hospital and cook to the Duke of Marlborough in all his campaigns. 'He was to the King Loyal to his Wives tender to his Relations kind.'

Christiana Davis 1667–1739
Irish born, she joined the army to search for her husband, was imprisoned by the French, served at Blenheim and Ramillies when she was wounded and her sex discovered. In 1712 she was presented to Queen Anne and given a pension. Three volleys were fired at her burial.

Gen. Sir David Dundas 1735–1820
Military tactician, wrote *The Principles of Military Movements* (1788) and regulations on Army discipline. Governor of the Hospital 1803–20.

Isaac Garnier 1630–1711
A Huguenot, he escaped to England in 1685 and served the Hospital as an apothecary, establishing his own physic garden and laboratory in the grounds.

William Hiseland 1620–1732
Served in the army for eighty years, he was present at the battle of Edgehill and all Marlborough's campaigns. Became a pensioner in 1713.

Thomas Keate 1745–1821
Surgeon general to the army 1793, surgeon to George IV and the Hospital. The first to tie the subclavian artery for aneurism.

Gen. Sir Neville Lyttleton 1845–1931
Served at the battle of Omdurman, Commander in Chief South Africa 1902–4 and Ireland 1908–12. Governor of the Hospital 1912–31. (Memorial only.)

Sir Thomas Ogle 1618–1702
An impoverished royalist, Charles II made him first governor of the Hospital in 1685.

Gen. Sir Edward Paget 1775–1849
Served in the Peninsular Campaign and lost his right arm at Oporto. Governor of Ceylon 1821–23, retired following criticism of his conduct during the Burma Campaign 1825.

Sir Thomas Renton 1665–1740
Physician extraordinary to George I.

Hannah Snell 1723–92
Served in both the Army and Navy in the search for her missing husband, on one occasion being punished with 500 lashes. Published her adventures in 1750 and appeared on the stage. Died insane.

Samuel Wyatt 1737–1807
A successful architect, he specialised in the design of neo-classical country houses and experimented with cast iron construction. Appointed clerk of the works at the Hospital in 1792.

ROYAL HOSPITAL GREENWICH CEMETERY
Chevening Road, SE10

Founded: 1857
Owner: London Borough of Greenwich
Acreage: 6

Following the foundation of the Royal Naval Hospital at Greenwich in 1694, pensioners who died could be 'safely anchored' in either of two cemeteries, one near the Dreadnought Seamen's Hospital, the other near Maze Hill. By 1857 these were both filled and the present Pleasaunce site was bought. According to a plaque now set into the wall, the remains of some 3000 former pensioners were moved here from the old ground. In 1926 the Pleasaunce was sold to the Borough, although the Admiralty reserved the right to conduct further burials. Part of the ground is now a children's park and the cemetery appears rather forlorn, shorn of its railings and dotted with holly bushes, but kept tidy. More recently a large bench has appeared with the appropriate inscription from Psalm 107, 'They that go down to the sea in ships – that do business in great waters.'

There are no buildings or large tombstones and the graves are in four clusters. Many of the inscriptions are now illegible but the naval association is immediately obvious due to the number of anchors embellishing the memorials. Naval etiquette prevailed to the last, so that ratings are buried in the west plot, officers in the east.

Lieut. James Berry 1843–1930
Curator of the Royal Naval Museum for seventeen years.

Charles Burney 1826–87
Superintendent of the Royal Hospital School 1870–87.

Capt. Edmund Cooper-Key 1862–1933
Superintendent of the Royal Hospital School, his wife Florence, buried with him, died in 1974 aged 101.

John Donaldson 1818-81
Doctor and Inspector General of the Royal Navy.

Sir George Hill 1855-1928
Record keeper in the Probate Registry, Somerset House, and president of the Rugby Football Union.

John Holman 1824-83
Deputy Inspector of Hospitals and Fleets to the Royal Navy.

Sir John Liddell 1794-1868
Director of the medical department, Royal Navy, 1854-64.

Adm. Henry May 1853-1904
Captain of the Royal Naval College, Greenwich.

Thomas Mott 1841-1913
Crimean war veteran and seamanship instructor to George V.

Capt. Henry Parker 1789-1873
A midshipman at the battle of Trafalgar 1805.

Anthony Sampayo 1818-62
French ambassador to England.

James Shepherd 1835-1907
Crimean war veteran and for eighteen years Queen Victoria's boatswain's mate on the Royal Yacht *Victoria and Albert*.

Capt. Mark Sweny 1783-1865
Served at the battle of Trafalgar 1805.

ST MARYLEBONE CEMETERY AND CREMATORIUM
East End Road, N3

Founded: 1854
Owner: The City of Westminster (Cemetery) & The London Cremation Company (Crematorium)
Acreage: 33

The site, described in 1854 as 'a retired and rural spot',[1] was farmland before the cemetery was built by architects Barnett and Birch, winners of a competition. Considering a limit imposed of £15,000 for the entire project, they succeeded in devising a cemetery of remarkably generous proportions.

From the road it is immediately recognisable by its black spiky railings, two fine cedar trees and substantial gates with entrance arch. A large Gothic lodge (with the gates and railings it cost £3,000) and a Decorated Gothic chapel (£1,400) stand at either end of the broad entrance drive. The recently cleaned ragstone chapel has an elaborately buttressed belfry and a cunningly planned

St Marylebone: The consecration service from The Illustrated London News *(1855)*

exit (now blocked) behind the altar to allow coffins to pass straight through to the cemetery ground. A smaller dissenters' chapel (only £700) was built in a less conspicuous position and is not now used.[2]

This manicured cemetery has always catered for the affluent middle classes of Marylebone, Highgate and Hampstead, a high proportion in professional and military occupations, and this is reflected in the number of large monuments flanking the yew tree avenues. Commendable planning has ensured that the best of these occupy strategic positions at the main junctions, with impressive results. Their variety of design and materials is enormous, but notable by any standards are several large early twentieth century monuments incorporating bronze sculptures. That commemorating an Australian, Thomas Skarratt Hall (died 1903) and his family, is a massive grey and pink granite sarcophagus on an island site, modelled, it seems, on Napoleon's tomb in Paris, with a bronze angel at each corner. (These were stolen in 1989.) East of the chapel, the engineer Sir Peter Russell's granite monument supports a bronze bust of the deceased and a life size young engineer being steered heavenwards by a gesturing angel. It is the work of Sir Edgar MacKennal, who subsequently designed the stately effigies of Edward VII and Queen Alexandra on their tomb in St George's Chapel, Windsor. An even more theatrical composition is the bronze of a dying youth propped up on the Renaissance style tomb of Thomas Tate (1909). The sculptor was F. Lynn Jenkins well known for his large scale decorative works of the period. Immediately opposite there is a more modest and appealing work of 1914, a draped mourner, above Harry Ripley's tomb, by Sir William Reid-Dick, a sculptor whose most distinguished sepulchral work was the great lion above the Menin Gate Memorial at Ypres. It is similar to an unidentified bronze in Hendon Cemetery.

There is one outstanding mausoleum built for Algernon Borthwick, Lord Glenesk the proprietor of *The Morning Post*. It houses the remains of his wife and son, who had both predeceased him, and eventually himself on his death in 1908. The mausoleum was designed as a mortuary chapel in the Decorated style by Sir Arthur Blomfield. The exterior west gable bears a relief of the Resurrection, and inside, beneath a vaulted roof, are three alabaster sarcophagi which rest before a marble reredos lit by stained glass windows. Most of the glass is intact but it is perilously vulnerable and the growth of unchecked vegetation on the roof is not an encouraging sight.

In 1937 a gate and small lodges were added to the west of the cemetery to provide a separate approach for the new crematorium. This is a large Italianate style brick building by Sir Edwin Cooper, one of the last British architects to design in the classical grand manner. His main London works are Marylebone Town Hall and the Port of London Authority building at Tower Hill. The crematorium is not in the same class but its dignified vaulted interior and standard of craftsmanship in brick, stone, marble and oak is at a high level rarely equalled by postwar crematoria.[3] Beyond the chapel is a cloistered courtyard with central fountain and around it, the well kept Gardens of Remembrance with the usual rose bushes and memorials.

Whereas the great nineteenth-century cemeteries like City of London, Kensal Green, Highgate, Norwood and Brompton and the crematorium at Golders Green are fairly well documented, those more representative of the early twentieth century are less well known. St Marylebone Cemetery, despite its early foundation date, must qualify as another worthy of study.

Sir George Barham 1836–1913
Founder chairman of the Express Dairy Company, High Sheriff of Middlesex 1908–09 and Mayor of Hampstead 1905–06.

Henry Bates 1825–92
He explored the Amazon basin 1848–59 during which time he discovered 550 new species of butterfly and returned to England with a collection of 14,700 species. Assistant secretary to the Royal Geographical Society 1864–92, resident of the Entomological Society 1869–78. He wrote several books about his Amazonian travels.

Alfred Bentley 1878–1923
Artist and engraver.

Sir Henry Bishop 1786–1855
Composer, he wrote numerous musical dramas for the Covent Garden, Kings and Drury Lane theatres. Knighted in 1842, the first musician ever to receive that honour, professor of music at Oxford 1848–55.

Keith Blakelock 1945–85
A police constable murdered during race riots in Tottenham.

Algernon Borthwick, Lord Glenesk 1830–1908
Editor and proprietor of the *Morning Post*, friend of Napoleon III and Conservative M.P. for South Kensington 1885–95. His family mortuary chapel was designed by Sir Arthur Blomfield.

Sir James Boyton 1855–1926
Unionist M.P. for East Marylebone 1910–18, president of the Auctioneers and Estate Agents Institute 1905–06.

Sir Austen Chamberlain 1863–1937
Unionist M.P. for East Worcestershire 1892–1914 and Birmingham West from 1914, Chancellor of the Exchequer 1903–06 and 1919–21, member of the War Cabinet, leader of the House of Commons 1921–22 and Foreign Secretary 1924–29.

Austin Claflin 1865–1928
The American manager and director of the Underwood Typewriter Company.

Sir Cyril Cobb 1918–38.
Barrister and Unionist M.P. for West Fulham

Sir Edwin Cooper 1873–1942
Yorkshire architect specialising in large public buildings in the grand classical manner.

Sir Nicolas de Villiers 1902–58
Deputy secretary Ministry of Works 1945–51.

Sir Edmund Gosse 1849–1928
Librarian to the House of Lords 1904–14 and man of letters. He specialised in Scandinavian literature and introduced Ibsen to the English theatre.

Alfred Harmsworth, Lord Northcliffe, 1865–1922
Newspaper proprietor of the *Evening News, Daily Mail* and *The Times.* The cortège route of seven miles from Westminster Abbey was 'through a practically unbroken avenue of spectators' and an aeroplane overhead dipped in salute at the internment.

Cecil, 1st Lord Harmsworth 1869–1948
Liberal M.P. for Droitwich 1906–10 and South Bedfordshire 1911–22; a British member of the Council of the League of Nations 1922. Brother of Lords Northcliffe and Rothermere.

Sir Robert Harmsworth 1870–1937
Liberal M.P. for Caithness 1900–22.

Sir George Hayter 1792–1871
Portrait and miniature painter, 'principal painter in ordinary to H.M. Queen Victoria'.

Quintin Hogg 1845–1903
Businessman, sportsman and founder president of the Regent Street Polytechnic in 1882.

Edward Hollingdale –1956
'Private Chamberlain of Cape and Sword of H.H. Pope Pius XII.'

Dame Fanny Houston 1857–1936
One of the first five Dame Commanders of the British Empire, supporter of woman's suffrage, founder of the Rest Home for Tired Nurses during the Great War. She gave £100,000 towards the Schneider Trophy flying contest.

Thomas Huxley 1825–95
Surgeon and zoologist, he supported Darwin's theory of the origin of the species, secretary of the Royal Society 1871.

Sir Harold Kenyon 1875–1959
Funeral director. Six times Mayor of Paddington and three times Mayor of Kensington.

Daniel Luckenbill 1881–1927
'Assyrologist at the University of Chicago' where he was professor.

Brig.Gen.Sir Arthur Maxwell 1875–1935
Director of several merchant shipping lines and president of the Institute of Bankers 1931–32.

Sir Alfred Mays-Smith 1861–1931
Company director, president of the Society of Motor Manufacturers and Traders.

Jimmy Nervo 1897–1975
Came from a circus family, began his career in music hall with Fred Karno, a member of the Crazy Gang, formed in 1922.

Sir Louis Newton 1867–1945
Lord Mayor of London 1924, High Sheriff of Kent 1940, a prominent freemason.

St Marylebone: Tomb of Thomas Tate by F. Lynn Jenkins (1909)

St Marylebone: Tomb of Harry Ripley by Sir William Reid-Dick (1914)

St Marylebone: The memorial to Thomas Skarratt Hall (1903) showing the bronze angels which were stolen in 1989

VASLAV NIJINSKY 1888–1950
Ballet dancer. His body was exhumed and reburied in Montmartre in 1953.

SIR JAMES PAGET 1814–99
Surgeon to Queen Victoria and the Prince of Wales, president of the College of Surgeons 1875, vice chancellor of London University 1884–95.

SIR WILLIAM PETERSEN 1856–1921
Scottish born classical scholar, principal of McGill University 1895–1919.

SIR JOHN QUAIN 1816–76
Judge of the Court of Queen's Bench, author of a book on common law procedure, presented his law library to University College, London.

St Marylebone: The interior of the Glenesk mausoleum by Sir Arthur Blomfield (1908) (Courtesy of English Heritage)

RICHARD QUAIN 1800–1887
Professor of surgery at London University, surgeon to Queen Victoria, wrote *Elements of Anatomy* 1848.

SIR JOHN RIGBY 1834–1903
Solicitor-General 1892–94, Attorney General 1894, a Lord Justice of Appeal 1894–1901.

SIR PETER RUSSELL 1816–1905
Australian engineer, he founded the school of engineering at Sydney University.

SIR THOMAS SMITH 1833–1909
Surgeon to Edward VII, vice president of the Royal College of Surgeons.

LEOPOLD STOKOWSKI 1882–1977
Conductor of the Cincinnati, Philadelphia, N.B.C. and New York Philharmonic Orchestras and well known for his transcriptions of music by J.S. Bach.

MATILDE VERNE 1865–1936
Pianist and music teacher, among her pupils was H.M. the Queen Mother.

JAMES WEIR 1892–1971
M.P. for Ross and Cromarty 1892–1911.

SIR EDWARD WHITE 1847–1914
A chairman of the L.C.C.

SIR ARTHUR WORLEY 1871–1937
President of the Chartered Insurance Institute and the Insurance Institute of London. Member of the Royal Commission on National Health Insurance.

ALBERT YORKE, 6TH EARL OF HARDWICKE, 1867–1904
Stockbroker and Under Secretary of State for India.

CHARLES YORKE, 5TH EARL OF HARDWICKE, 1836–1897
Soldier and sportsman, M.P. for Cambridgeshire 1865–73, comptroller of the Queen's household, kept racehorses, bankrupted 1881.

ST MARY'S ROMAN CATHOLIC CEMETERY
HARROW ROAD, NW10

Founded: 1858
Owner: St Mary's Catholic Cemetery Company
Acreage: 29

A bleak place adjacent to Kensal Green Cemetery and sandwiched between the Great Western railway, the Underground and the Grand Union canal. Despite this, the fine collection of mausolea and many exceptional memorials make it a cemetery well worth visiting.

A tour of St Mary's begins with a Gothic lodge followed by a drive up to the chapels, the cemetery office and beneath them a catacomb with provision for 500 coffins. The designer of these buildings was the Roman Catholic architect Samuel Nicholl who could be relied upon, said Eastlake, for 'honest and substantial work'.[1] Masses are still regularly celebrated here for the souls of the deceased and the buildings are well maintained. Richly coloured glass which was installed in 1978 includes images of SS Michael and George. Near the entrance is a relief portrait of Francis Babington Tussaud (by R. Vanlinden), grandson of Madame Tussaud complete with scroll of music manuscript and quill pen. His parents repose in the catacombs beneath.

Like its neighbour at All Souls', St Mary's has an hydraulically operated catafalque which descends to the subterranean level, although the carpeted chapel hides all evidence of an aperture in the floor. Beyond the office is a surface level catacomb dominated at one end by a coloured relief of the Resurrection.

St Mary's first burial in a common grave, took place in 1858. In the next eight years 12,500 burials were recorded, many of them Irish immigrants escaping the potato famine. These common graves are now being reused and a large section to the south of the cemetery, now devoid of any planting, has been banked up with earth over which rows of lawn graves have appeared. A further area is also being reclaimed. The level of vandalism is regrettable; many figures appear to have been decapitated and several of the mausolea are in a poor condition. Although most have not been invaded there is a tendency to have the entrance unsuitably blocked with brick and concrete blocks. The Frosi mausoleum is one example. Another, now devoid of its door and windows, is reduced to serving as a wood store.

The foreign element among those buried here are predominately Italian and Irish but against the east wall of the cemetery is

St Mary's R.C.: Bronze relief of the Holy Family on the Connolly grave (1933)

a large memorial commemorating the Belgian soldiers who died in Britain from injuries received in the Great War. Another well represented group are numerous priests and nuns, such as the Sisters of the Little Company of Mary. As the large signs outside the chapel state, surplus revenue from burial fees is used to assist invalid priests.

Of St Mary's twenty-four mausolea, that to the Conde de Bayona y Marquis de Misa is the most decorative. It is a little gothic chapel demonstrating the Spanish custom for surface decoration. Lurid stained glass windows depict scenes of the Crucifixion and Resurrection above an altar table and sculpture of the Pieta. There are also two mausolea with a strong Byzantine flavour. One commemorates the Whigham family (1928) and the other the Campbell's by C.H.B. Quennell (1904) which is constructed in courses of thin red bricks and Portland stone beneath a pendentive dome.[2] Its interior is faced with Devonshire marble and the dome speckled in gold mosaic above a narrow blue line. Stained glass, by Paul Woodroffe, includes a Resurrection scene and on either side a lamb and pelican. A cross on the dome, by silversmith Omar Ramsden, has now disappeared and more ominously the copper sheathed door has been damaged. Nearby is the mausoleum to the Gatti family resembling a little Gothic chapel beneath a traceried copper roof. Inside, carved on the arcaded walls, are the names of Sir John Gatti and his descendants. The largest mausoleum in the cemetery is the French flamboyant-style chapel built for the Emmet family (1915). Two recent marble mausolea, erected by Italian families (the Giordano's at the entrance in particular), demonstrate that this method of commemorating the dead is still not extinct, although they exhibit none of their predecessors architectural fantasy.

Beside the chapel is a memorial to the Brazilian Luisa Fowke, attended by the sculpted figures of her husband and son (1890). In the centre of the cemetery a ponderous stone sarcophagus bears the name and portrait of a Frenchman Auguste Cagniere who died in 1874, and another commemorates the Irish, Mary Anastasia Power (1880) with kneeling angels in support at the four corners.

Two bronzes are particularly dramatic. One near the Belgium war memorial is a relief panel of the Holy Family, with Joseph holding a carpenter's saw. It makes a sombre group on the Connolly grave (1933). In the north west corner of the cemetery there is a small but striking low relief image by Josef Braunsteiner on the Meixner grave (1936) depicting Mary supporting Christ's head,

Augusta Mary, Princess Edward de Ligne, –1872
The de Ligne family is one of the oldest in Belgium with a history that can be traced to the eleventh century.

Sir John Barbirolli 1899–1970
Conductor of the Hallé and New York Philharmonic orchestras.

Prince Louis Bonaparte 1813–91
Nephew of Napoleon I and a philologist who lived in London. At his death, 'his coffin was so designed that having been placed in the sarcophagus, its sides and lid could be removed, and the Prince revealed in court dress lying on a mattress of violet satin fringed with gold. His chest was aglitter with orders.'

Sir Timothy Coghlan 1857–1926
Australian statistician, a member of various Royal commissions concerned with statistical reports on Australasia.

St Mary's RC: The Emmet Mausoleum

St Mary's RC: The Campbell family's Byzantine mausoleum by C.H.B. Quennell (1904)

Maj. Thomas Crean 1875–1923
Doctor, and Irish international rugger player, he won a V.C. during the Boer War.

Sir John Day 1826–1908
High Court judge and collector of pictures of the Barbizon school.

Hugh Delargy 1908–76
Labour M.P. for Thurrock and party whip 1950–52.

Baron Frederic d'Erlanger 1868–1943
Businessman and musician, he composed several operas, symphonies, choral works and ballets.

Richard Doyle 1824–83
Caricaturist, he designed the original title page for *Punch*.

William Eassie 1832–88
Engineer and first honorary secretary of the Cremation Society of England.

Sir John Gatti 1872–1929
Theatre proprietor, chairman of the L.C.C. 1927–28 and Mayor of Westminster 1911–12.

Christine Granville 1915–52
Polish born, she was the Countess Krystyna Skarbek. During the war she worked in the French resistance and won the G.M. Murdered by a former lover.

Gilbert Harding 1907–60
Television personality well known for his appearances on 'What's my Line?'

Dick Henderson 1891–1958
Music hall comedian, he sang ballads and jokes while soberly dressed in a suit and a small bowler hat.

Josef Jakobs 1898–1944
German spy during the Second World War, the last person to be executed at the Tower of London.

Al Mancini 1903–68
Welterweight boxer.

James Mann 1838–99
Chamberlain to Pope Leo XIII.

Cardinal Henry Manning 1808–92
Cardinal archbishop of Westminster. Took an active interest in working class education, housing and the temperance movement. His remains were removed to Westminster Cathedral in 1907.

Phil May 1864–1903
Punch cartoonist.

Pius Melia 1800–83
Professor of belles lettres, Jesuits' College, Rome. Came to England in 1848 and ministered to the Italian community in London.

Sir James Melville 1885–1931
Labour M.P. for Gateshead 1909–31 and Solicitor General 1929–30.

Alice Meynell 1847–1922
Poet and journalist, she cared for Francis Thompson (see below) during his addiction to opium.

Sir George Mivart 1827–1900
Zoologist, author of several works on the origin of the species. As a consequence Cardinal Vaughan instructed priests not to administer the sacrament to him.

Sir John Mooney 1874–1934
M.P. for Dublin 1900–06 and a member of many parliamentary select committees.

Maj.Gen.Sir Luke O'Connor 1832–1915
Won the V.C. at the battle of the Alma, one of six awarded in the battle when soldiers were first given the medal.

Thomas O'Connor 1848–1929
Irish patriot, journalist, founder and editor of the *Star* and *Sun* newspapers.

Charles Palmer 1819–1900
Dominican friar, he wrote several books on the history of the Order.

Sir Anthony Panizzi 1797–1879
Italian-born principal librarian of the British Museum and instrumental in having the reading room built.

Sir Henry Parker 1825–94
Solicitor and a president of the Law Society.

Carlo Pellegrini 1839–89
Italian-born caricaturist who signed his work 'Ape'.

Mary Seacole 1805–81
Born in Jamaica, served as a military nurse in the Crimea and Jamaica.

Sir Charles Skerrett 1863–1929
Chief Justice of New Zealand.

Clarkson Stanfield 1793–1867
Began his career as a scenery painter, latterly a successful marine artist.

Francis Thompson 1859–1907
Mystical poet who suffered from addiction to opium, biographer of St Ignatius Loyola. The inscription on his tomb was carved by Eric Gill.

Francis Tussaud 1829–58
Grandson of Mme Tussaud, also his parents Joseph (died 1865) and Elizabeth Tussaud (died 1863).

Thomas Wingham 1846–1903
Composer, professor of music at the Royal College and choirmaster at the Brompton Oratory.

Cardinal Nicholas Wiseman 1802–65
First cardinal archbishop of Westminster, biblical scholar, writer and preacher, his remains were transferred to Westminster Cathedral, together with a monument designed by E.W. Pugin, in 1907.

ST PANCRAS AND ISLINGTON CEMETERY AND ISLINGTON CREMATORIUM

HIGH ROAD, N2

Founded: 1854
Owner: The London Boroughs of Camden and Islington
Acreage: 185

No sooner was the 1852 Metropolitan Interment Act made law than the St Pancras Burial Board bought eighty-eight acres of Horse Shoe Farm on Finchley Common and there established the first publicly owned cemetery in London. The loamy soil was the main attraction of the site because there were still fears that cemeteries might harbour noxious waste and, 'a period of fourteen years would be sufficient to effect the decay of a corpse in such soil'.[1] A further ninety-four acres were added in 1877 to form an immense rambling cemetery divided between the

St Pancras and Islington: Percival Spencer – Aeronaut (1905). The balloon has been removed

St Pancras & Islington: The lodge (1900). It was demolished in 1970

GAZETTEER 311

two Boroughs, the largest in London. The authorities were well pleased,

At present no other cemetery can compare with, much less surpass in size and loveliness this beautiful park-like ground, with its splendid trees of ever varying tints.[2]

– wrote a Burial Department registrar. The cemetery was consecrated by the Bishop of London on 25 July 1854. By 1900, over 365,000 burials had taken place and one hundred years later the figure is around one million. Today, although the limes, cedars, monkey puzzles and cypress trees are still there, the sheer size of the cemetery appears to have defeated its owners. Only those areas in regular use are maintained, leaving large tracts totally overgrown by brambles and dark conifers.

The original lodge was demolished in 1970 and replaced by a functional box which looks very mean compared with the old pinnacled Gothic railings at the entrance. The two original chapels were by Barnett and Birch, a Decorated Gothic Anglican chapel with a 100ft spire survives; the Dissenters' chapel, which was demolished after the Sexond World War, had a six-sided lantern apparently 'similar to some mortuary chapels in Belgium and the south of France'.[3] In 1896 a Roman Catholic chapel was added to the designs of Seagrave, Bravett and Taylor (which is now derelict) and Islington's own Anglican chapel, a pleasant brick and stone dressed Arts and Crafts building by architects Forsyth and Maule, winners of a competition.[4] Its quality is conspicuous compared to the crematorium added in 1937 by Albert Freeman, an architect who specialised in crematoria. His design closely follows a blueprint Freeman had described at length to the Society of Architects in 1906 but any practical advantages it may have are negated by the feeble red brick and Portland stone building with a glass dome.[5] It is now totally enclosed by trees and a tightly packed Garden of Remembrance.

Bordering the main drives near the cemetery entrance there are the usual scattering of Victorian mausolea but the glory of the cemetery is the Mond mausoleum and crypt, near the centre. It is

St Pancras & Islington: Memorial commemorating Harry Gardner

St Pancras & Islington: The grave of William French (1896).

an enormous grey granite and stone Ionic temple superbly sited on a tree-lined slope. With the Ralli mortuary chapel at Norwood it must rate as the finest classical building in any of the London cemeteries. The architect was Darcy Braddell, later a vice-president of the R.I.BA. .Other monuments worth seeing are more curious than artistic. There is Percival Spencer's balloon ascending from a plinth (although this has been removed) and the parachute descending on Captain Alfred Smith's grave which also commemorates Harry Gardner, the famous Lyceum clown. At the base of another monument squats a large dog commemorating William French, 'who lost his life on July 13th 1896 while saving a dog from drowning in Highgate ponds'. The monument, raised by public subscription 'was contributed to by all classes of lovers of dumb animals'. On another insignificant headstone six centenarians are remembered, including Sarah Lamb aged 106. Eighteenth century Islingtonians are also here, their remains moved from St Mary's parish church following road widening in 1865 and again in 1883, which encroached on the churchyard in Upper Street. They fill two large plots, one so overgrown by holly bushes that even the memorial stone is hard to see.

In the Roman Catholic section is a large bronze by Francesco Nagni of Rome on the Manzi grave (1962). It depicts two angels emerging from a stone sarcophagus carrying the supine body of the deceased wearing a shirt neatly buttoned. Nagni was a major Italian sculptor whose most important work was the figure of Pope Pius XI above his tomb in St Peter's Rome. Sadly, the figure of pearly king Henry Croft (1930) was smashed by vandals in 1994, although a photo plaque on the grave depicts the original memorial.

On the pathside of an overgrown section is the resplendent life-size kilted figure of Alexander Lamond (1926) and next to the Roman Catholic chapel is a mausoleum adorned with gold mosaic containing Letizia Melesi. Killed by a motor cab on Holborn Viaduct in January 1914 the scene is depicted on panels beside the iron grille entrance. Nearby the victim of another accident is commemorated in the relief portrait of John Baptista Demanio who died in Lisbon in 1913.

PTE. VALENTINE BAMBRICK 1837–64
Won the V.C. during the Indian Mutiny. His medal was forfeited for misconduct in 1863, he committed suicide.

CORA CRIPPEN 1875–1910
Professionally known as Belle Elmore, the failed actress wife of Dr Crippen. She was murdered by him on 1 February 1910, a crime for which he was subsequently hanged.

HENRY CROFT 1862–1930
Municipal road sweeper and the original pearly king. 400 pearlies attended his funeral which was filmed by Pathé News.

St Pancras & Islington: The Mond mausoleum by Darcy Braddell (1909)

Sir William Crump 1851–1923
City solicitor active in helping to acquire recreational facilities for north Londoners including Alexandra Palace in 1875. First Mayor of Islington.

Henry D'Alcorn 1827–1905
Composer, who wrote the 'Ta-ra-ra-boom-de-ay' melody.

George Fortescue 1847–1912
Departed this life 'at the British Museum as Keeper of the Printed Book Department'.

Sir Eugene Goossens 1893–1962
Violinist and conductor.

John Hickey –1896
A survivor from the charge of the Light Brigade. His monument was 'erected by a few admirers', including J.K. Jerome. Two other Brigade members were less fortunate and are buried here in a common grave.

Ken 'Snakeships' Johnson –1941
West Indian dance band leader. Killed by a bomb with the rest of his band at the Café de Paris.

Ford Madox-Brown 1821–93
Pre-Raphaelite artist and associate of William Morris. Together with his wife Emma whom he married when she was aged fifteen.

Frank Manzi 1913–62
Chairman of the Amusement Trades Association.

Ludwig Mond 1839–1909
Millionaire German industrialist and chemical technologist, his Lancashire factory was the largest alkali producer in the world. He donated large sums to charity and bequeathed his collection of early Italian paintings to the National Gallery.

Alfred Mond, Lord Melchett 1868–1930
Director of I.C.I., Liberal M.P. for Swansea 1910–23 and Camarthen 1924–28.

Robert Morrell 1823–1912
Founder of the Sunday League. In 1896 he secured the opening of national museums on Sundays.

Sir Horace Regnart 1841–1912
President of Maples in Tottenham Court Road.

Mary Shepherd –1989
Resident in playwriter Alan Bennett's front garden about whom the play *Lady in the Van* was written.

George Spencer –1916
'The Boy' from a famous ballooning family and a gymnastic equipment manufacturers. He introduced the Velocipede to England in 1868.

Percival Spencer 1864–1913
Balloonist, cyclist and gymnast, and nephew of George Spencer (see above).

ST PATRICK'S ROMAN CATHOLIC CEMETERY
Langthorne Road, E11

Founded: 1868
Owner: St Mary's Catholic Cemetery Company
Acreage: 43

A scruffy closely packed cemetery sited on the edge of the Central Line. Few trees and the lack of coherent landscaping contribute to its desolate appearance. It was opened to cope with the nineteenth century population explosion in Hackney which increased from 38,000 in 1861 to 125,000 in 1871. The tombstone names indicate the Roman Catholic status of the cemetery, most are Irish, Italian and Polish. 168,000 burials have been recorded and to cater for the continuing demand the land is being reclaimed by adding a six feet deep layer of earth over old graves.

Near the entrance is a brutalist gothic concrete mausoleum resembling a black Bedouin tent with coloured glass added to the windows and a forbidding steel grating in the doorway. It commemorates Lucia Ferrari 'Mamma adorabile' (1965) behind it is a more conventional classical mausoleum commemorating the Mills family (1972). Its decorative iron gates and colourful stained glass windows have somehow escaped the vandals as have a host of neighbouring statues depicting Christ, the Virgin Mary, various saints and angels.

The cemetery has a Gothic chapel, office and lodge designed by S.J. Nicholl, the same architect who designed St Mary's, Kensal Green, the sister cemetery, and numerous Roman Catholic churches in London.

Mary Kelly 1864–88
The last of Jack the Ripper's prostitute victims, she was disembowelled at a house in Miller's Court, Spitalfields. (An unmarked grave).

St Patrick's RC: The Ferrari mausoleum (1965)

STREATHAM CEMETERY
GARRATT LANE, SW17

Founded: 1892
Owner: London Borough of Lambeth
Acreage: 36

Originally opened by the Streatham Borough Burial Board, the cemetery has few subtleties except for an attractive pair of chapels designed by William Newton-Dunn. These are the usual ragstone Gothic, but very unusual in having vestigial transepts and spacious arcaded *portes cochères* set at right angles to the main building.[1] A circular east window made up from foiled tracery employs angels as label stops. These days plastic protects the windows of one chapel, which is infrequently used, and the other is derelict. Either side of the vehicle entrance are a pair of pedestrian gateways bearing the words 'Streatham' and 'Cemetery'. Inside is a substantial lodge with a helpful panel naming the members of the Streatham Burial Board, the clerk, architect and contractor. There is a more modest lodge at the north end of the boundary wall and the cemetery retains the unusual feature of an air raid shelter.

There are a few memorials of above average interest, particularly around the circular section between the two chapels. They include the pile of black granite blocks on the Krall grave (1903), a style known in the trade as 'a garden job'; Henry Budden's little blue terracotta temple (1907) with the inscription 'called, justified; glorified'; Edward Stimson's chest tomb, and the angel with trumpet on Beryl Hall's grave. Many memorials have been declared unsafe and have been crudely supported by two wooden stakes.

Beyond the Cross of Sacrifice, the remainder of the cemetery is rather dismal. Some attempt was made in its early years to plant firs which have now darkly matured, but recent planting has been meagre. In the late 1970s the decision to flatten or remove some of the older headstones has resulted in sections simply being grassed with the occasional memorial protruding. In 2007 an area occupied by greenhouses was cleared and made available for burials by sinking concrete chambers into the ground.

Streatham: 'A Garden Job' on the Krall grave (1903)

Sir Wyke Bayliss 1835–1905
Painter, president of the Royal Society of British Artists.

Thomas Lewis 1833–1915
Organ builder in Stockwell.

Charles Wilson –1990
One of the great train robbers who in 1963 stole £2.6 million from the Glasgow/Euston Express. He was murdered at his Spanish home.

STREATHAM PARK CEMETERY AND SOUTH LONDON CREMATORIUM
Rowan Road, SW16

Founded: 1909
Owner: The Crematorium Company
Acreage: 70

In 1994 this cemetery was dismissed as a 'sad and graceless' place on account of its woeful presentation. Since then its fortunes have taken a turn for the better as the buildings and grounds have benefited from substantial investment.

The origins of the cemetery can be traced back to 1890 when the New London Cemetery and Crematorium Limited) issued its prospectus, '... proposing to establish a new cemetery on a

Streatham: The blue terracotta temple commemorating Henry Budden (1907)

Streatham Park: 'He lived as he died a cyclist' – Maurice Selback (1935)

plot of 52 acres of land near Mitcham, Surrey' but nothing further developed until 1907.[1] The Great Southern Cemetery, Crematorium and Land Company then resurrected the idea of a south London equivalent to the Great Northern Cemetery. The five directors, including three undertakers required a capital of £40,000, and after surveying the financial results of two privately owned cemeteries – Manor Park and Woodgrange Park – they believed dividends of at least 10 per cent could be paid annually to investors. The flotation was successful, the land acquired and the first burial took place on the 14 January 1909.

The cemetery proved popular and apparently catered for about 20 per cent of all burials in south London. By the end of the first year (1909) 2,000 burials had taken place while by October 1917 just under 30,000 burials had been recorded rising to 43,000 in 1921. An Anglican chapel, whose chief merit was its rich floral patterned stained glass, and a little brick Roman Catholic chapel, were built to the designs of John Bannen of Bannen and Rowe, in East London. The Anglican chapel was capable of accommodating one hundred persons and had room for eight funerals to take place simultaneously. It has now been converted into the cemetery office following demolition of the lodge in 1973, the site of which was developed for housing. The Catholic chapel too has been demolished.

As its name suggested, the Company always intended to build a crematorium and in 1913 foundations were laid, but the intervention of the war delayed the project which got no further until 1936, when The South London Crematorium was built to new designs by Bannan with the help of an engineer, Mr Joseph. The thirty-first in the UK and the fifth crematorium in London, it cost £11,000 and is built of Berkshire mottled brick with stone facing. Its style was the faintly pompous stripped classical that 1930s architects used indiscriminately for shops, banks or hotels, as well as crematoria. At one stage the tower which disguises the chimney was illuminated. Prior to radical alterations in the late 1990s it was a large complex comprising three chapels for cremation services in addition to a Chapel of Remembrance, erected in 1958 by members of the Variety Artistes' Benevolent Fund, an organisation closely linked with the cemetery. The north chapel was remodelled after a fire in July 1980.

The large chapel, crematory and the columbarium, situated on the upper level, are all that remains of the original scheme. The old columbarium is about as attractive as a post office sorting room. Stacked at one end of this chilling place are pathetic rows of plastic flowers, photographs and lurid mementoes of the deceased, besides their ashes. Nevertheless, this part of the building still retains many original art deco features such as window grilles, door handles and woodwork. A new columbarium is housed in one of the former chapels while the site of the third chapel

Streatham Park: South London Crematorium which opened in 1936.

is occupied by an outside catacomb range that has been popular with Italian families. In the cemetery there is also a new gated area heralded as 'The Glade Memorial Garden' containing low level mausolea.

Immediately beyond the buildings, the garden of remembrance complete with pergola comprises the usual assortment of commemorative artefacts associated with cremation; wall tablets, memorial vases, stepping stones, bird baths, sundials, garden features or a choice of rose bushes. The gardens were laid out by Major L. Milner White of Milner, White who were responsible for the design of many UK crematoria gardens of remembrance. These are typical of their genre and reflect the trend for scattering of ashes at crematoria followed by garden memorials. More contemporary forms of remembrance are found near the catacomb range including a fountain and a large granite open book for recording the names of deceased children.

Either side of the main drive beyond the former chapel are clusters of modest memorials; most do not deserve a second glance. Exceptions are the attractive trio of angels on the main drive, a sleeping lion on the Groves memorial, and the memorial to Maurice Selback, a cyclist killed in 1935 which incorporates a portrait of the deceased, his bicycle, a wheel symbol and the inscription, 'he died as he lived a cyclist'. Another large stone bears the name of 200 variety artistes buried here between 1921 and 1944. Reflecting the east European communities of south London and Balham in particular, there are many Poles buried in the cemetery. Significant clearance of memorials and trees in the 1970s has left large areas of the cemetery without any planting, although these areas have now been grassed.

Ownership of the cemetery passed from the Great Southern Group to Service Corporation International in 1998; the Crematorium Company is a subsidiary of the present proprietor, Dignity Funerals.

Lizzie Collins 1870–1938
With her two sisters, Marie and Lottie, originated the famous 'ta-ra-ra-boom-de-ay!' song and dance number of the naughty nineties.

Tom Costello 1863–1943
Comedian and vocalist with a long variety career.

Arthur Cross –1965
Awarded the V.C. in 1918 on overcoming seven heavily armed German soldiers equipped with only a revolver. His family also buried here were killed in the Blitz.

Gus Elen 1863–1940
A coster comedian who sang cockney songs, one of his most popular being, 'It's a great big shame'.

Henry Fanshawe, Lord Badeley 1874–1951
Clerk of the Parliaments 1934–49.

Frederick Field –1923
Undertaker and a founder director of the cemetery.

Richard Fitzgerald 1906–59
Professor of law, University College, London, an authority on English constitutional law.

Will Hay 1888–1949
Comedian famous as the bogus schoolmaster of the 4th Form at St Michael's. A keen astronomer and vice president of the Variety Artistes' Federation 1945.

Sir Thomas Hughes 1856–1938
A judge and chairman of the General Council of the Bar 1920–31.

Walter Hunt 1857–1946
Sailor, authority on the aborigines, chimney sweep, lecturer and cyclist, he cycled 120 miles on his seventieth birthday.

Charlie Kunz 1896–1968
Jazz pianist.

Tom Learmore 1866–1939
Character comedian in the 1890s, his most famous song was 'Percy from Pimlico'.

Nellie Navette 1865–1936
Solo dancer and popular principal boy.

Dorothy Richardson 1873–1957
Pioneer of the 'stream of consciousness' modernist novel. She was an intimate friend of H.G. Wells.

Dorothy Squires 1915–98
Singer, Her worldwide popularity brought her a fortune of £2.5 million in the 1970s. By the time of her death she was penniless following numerous taxation lawsuits.

ST THOMAS'S ROMAN CATHOLIC CEMETERY
Rylston Road, SW6

Founded: 1849
Owner: Westminster Roman Catholic Archdiocesan Trustee
Acreage: Approx. ½

Although A.W.N. Pugin's Rylston Road Church is well known, the architectural attractions of the cemetery beyond it are less familiar even though they include the graves of several distinguished Catholic architects and a tomb designed by Philip Webb.

The ground, once cultivated as part of the Fulham Fields market gardens, was bought by St Thomas's benefactress Elizabeth Bowden as part of the church complex to provide an alternative to the Catholic burial plot at Brompton. It is now a neglected melancholic little place but once received commendation from the *Illustrated London News*.

> The church with its spacious cemetery, schools and rectory, seen amid the semi-rustic labourers' cottages of Fulham Fields, form a highly picturesque group of buildings, creditable to the munificence of the foundress.[1]

The first interment in 1849 was of a ten-year-old named, ironically, William Littleboy. The inscription reads:

> Of your charity pray for the repose of the soul of
> William Littleboy,
> Who died August 10th 1849, in his 11th year,
> being the 1st interment in this Cemetery,
> Also
> Jacob Littleboy, brother of the above,
> accidentally drowned August 23rd 1851. In his
> 11th year
> R.I.P.

Burials were frequent thereafter and by 1857 the cemetery was partially closed. Now it is no longer used save when family vaults are re-opened. One large canopied monument, built in 1881 for Thomas Loughnan, an official in India, is notable. Pevsner compared it to a monastic well and alleges it was imported from Boulogne.[2] There is also a charming copper domed mausoleum of Mathilde Harwarth who died in 1942.

JOHN BALL 1818–89
The first president of the Alpine Club, he crossed the Alps forty-eight times and wrote *The Alpine Guide* in three volumes (1863–68). M.P. for Co. Carlow 1852–57.

ELIZABETH BOWDEN –1896
Wife of J.W. Bowden the ecclesiastical writer, she employed Pugin to build St Thomas's in memory of her husband.

SGT. EDWARD DWYER –1916
Won the V.C. in 1915 at Hill 60 in Belgium. On returning to London he was employed as an army recruiter before being killed in action, (memorial only).

SIR JOHN ENNIS 1842–84
M.P. for Athlone 1868–74 and 1880–84.

HERBERT GRIBBLE 1847–94
Architect of the Brompton Oratory, 1878.

JOSEPH HANSOM 1803–82
Inventor of the hansom cab, founder editor of *The Builder* 1842 and architect of numerous Catholic churches and Birmingham town hall.

JOSEPH STANISLAUS HANSOM 1845–1931
Son of the above, architect and first secretary of the Catholic Records Society.

Sir Thomas Henry 1807–76
Chief magistrate of London 1864–76. He assisted in drafting legislation on extradition, licensing and gambling.

Adm. Sir Henry Kane 1843–1917
Director of Naval Ordnance 1894–97.

Lord Alexander Gordon Lennox 1825–92
Fourth son of the Duke of Richmond. After a military career became M.P. for New Shoreham 1849–59.

Sir Donald MacFarlane 1830–1904
M.P. for Co. Carlow 1880–85 and Argyllshire 1885–92.

Titto Mattei 1841–1914
Musician. An infant prodigy, he gave his first concert aged five. He composed numerous popular songs and several operas and was at one time pianist to the King of Italy.

Dennis O'Connor 1840–83
M.P. for Co. Sligo 1868–83.

Francis O'Gorman –1923
A private Chamberlain to the Pope.

William Palgrave 1826–88
Jesuit priest and missionary in Syria and Arabia. Subsequently he was laicised and served in the Foreign Office. He died while acting as Government Minister in Uruguay.

Charles Parker 1799–1881
Architect, surveyor of the Duke of Bedford's London estates, author of *Villa Rustica* 1832.

Sir James Power 1884–1914
Landowner and chairman of Sir John Power & Sons, the Dublin distillers.

Joseph Scoles 1798–1863
Architect of several Catholic churches including the Immaculate Conception, Farm Street, London.

Helen, Countess Tasker –1888
Philanthropist who assisted in many Catholic causes; Pius IX bestowed on her the title of Countess in 1870.

Joseph Tasker –1848
Linguist and traveller; he died in Persia and his body was brought back to St Thomas's.

Warrington Taylor 1838–70
Business manager to William Morris's firm. He died of consumption and his tombstone was designed by Philip Webb.

William, Lord Tyrrell of Avon, 1866–1947
Civil servant in the Foreign Office where he became a permanent under secretary. British ambassador to France 1928–34, president of the British Board of Film Censors 1935–47.

SURBITON CEMETERY
Lower Marsh Lane, Surbiton, Surrey

Founded: 1918
Owner: Royal Borough of Kingston upon Thames
Acreage: 11

Located down a cul-de-sac and packed in between a sewage works, a busy railway line and industrial units, Surbiton nevertheless enjoys a surprisingly peaceful atmosphere and is well kept. Beech and cherry trees line the drive which leads to the chapel designed by John Bannen. It is a simple brick building with buttressed walls and a Gothic belfry above the tiled roof. The same architect was responsible for Streatham Park Cemetery and South London Crematorium and he may well have designed the chapels at Tottenham Park and Eastbrookend which bear a close similarity to Surbiton.

There are few memorials of note and most appear to have come direct from the monumental masons catalogue of the interwar years. Angels have been a popular choice including four diminutive examples at each corner of the Hussey grave (1931) and its covering of green glass chippings.

SUTTON CEMETERY
Alcorn Close, Sutton, Surrey

Founded: 1889
Owner: London Borough of Sutton
Acreage: 19 1/2

Two giant pylons straddle the cemetery and high tension cables whir westwards towards the neighbouring business park which has replaced the sewage works. In such circumstances there has been little chance for Sutton to develop any picturesque qualities but it makes up for this lack by a high standard of maintenance. Near the entrance with its original gates and gate piers, grass is clipped to resemble a bowling green. The drive is flanked by the Borough's new mortuary (the old one is now a store) and the little flint Gothic chapel by E.W. Crickmay, surveyor to the local Board, is immaculately kept. No weeds hide the monuments which include a bronze harp embedded in a granite rock, erected in 1929 for Anna Sabatini, and a large Renaissance-style headstone commemorating five munitions workers killed during the First World War at Brocks munitions factory nearby. Other memorials of note are the anchor and heraldic cat carved on the Sutherland grave, and the late nineteenth century memorial to the Miller family in which a hand clutching a scroll is protected beneath a gothic tabernacle.

George, Lord Ebbisham of Cobham, 1868–1953
Lord Mayor of London 1926–7, M.P. for Epsom 1918–28, treasurer of Dr Barnardo's Homes.

Sutton: The chapel (1900).

Sir Edward Holland 1865–1939
High Sheriff of Surrey 1931, he 'served on numerous committees'.

Joseph Rank 1854–1943
Chairman of the Yorkshire-based milling company and father of J. Arthur Rank.

Robert Smith –1970
Local historian.

TEDDINGTON CEMETERY
Shacklegate Lane, Teddington, Middx.

Founded: 1879
Owner: London Borough of Richmond upon Thames
Acreage: 9

If one had to choose a typical Victorian cemetery, Teddington would be as good a choice as any. It has all the ingredients, including the ubiquitous railway line on one side and opposite the gates once stood the office of the local funeral director and mason in very respectable premises dated 1881 and the words 'Statuary and mason' carved on a stone escutcheon. Sadly, this building was demolished in 2005. Inside the cemetery gates is the lodge, a gabled bargeboarded villa and rising above the dark conifers beyond, the two crocketed spires belonging to the chapels. The pair were designed by T. Goodchild in fashionable Decorated style connected by a barn-like entrance arch. They are built of attractive honey coloured Bargate ragstone with Bathstone dressings. A contemporary description in *The Builder* is very precise:

> The chapels are each 30 feet by 20 feet internal dimensions, lined with white bricks and relief stamped tiles by Minton. Seats are arranged stall-wise and are, with the open roofs, all of deal stained and varnished. The reading desks are of pitch pine by Hammer, from the architect's design.[1]

Around the chapels the paths circulate among green algae stained tombstones. A number of retired soldiers are buried here, the battle honours of long forgotten imperial wars sometimes added to their epitaphs. Several accidental drownings in the nearby Thames are also recorded and Reginald Witt, 'killed by a ball while playing hockey in Bushey Park Oct.21st 1893'.

Hidden among bushes to the west is the old mortuary, in an incongruously Gothic style. A section of adjacent allotments has recently been absorbed for burials and the remainder will be acquired when needed.

RICHARD D. BLACKMORE 1825–1900
Author of *Lorna Doone*, (1869), he sold the produce from his Teddington garden at his own Covent Garden stall.

EDWARD CHAPMAN 1821–1904
Professor of mineralogy at University College, London and Toronto.

SIR GEORGE HASTINGS 1853–1943
Physician and president of the Coaching Club, he married Alice (died 1931) daughter of the artist W.P. Frith, whose other two children Mary and Walter are also buried here.

COL. ALEXANDER MACDONALD 1839–89
'The last chief of the old historic family of Glencoe... (died) after thirty-six years great suffering caused by 21 wounds received in the Crimea at the battles of Alma and Inkerman.'

SIR THOMAS NELSON 1826–85
Solicitor to the City of London 1862–85, he conducted litigation that secured the freedom of Epping Forest.

WILLIAM OSBORNE 1814–1891
Headmaster of Rossall School 1849–69.

JOHN WAGLAND –1892
State coachman to Queen Victoria 1857–73. The Queen ordered his tombstone to be erected in the cemetery.

SIR ALFRED WOODGATE 1860–1943
Civil servant and Mayor of Kingston 1832–34.

Teddington: 'Typically Victorian'

TOTTENHAM CEMETERY
Prospect Place, N17

Founded: 1856
Owner: London Borough of Haringey
Acreage: 56

Pevsner described this area of Tottenham as a 'deliciously rural oasis'.[1] Over half a century later it remains so, partly on account of the mediaeval parish church and graveyard, partly the Elizabethan Bruce Castle and its grounds, partly the Georgian vicarage and especially because of this spacious nineteenth-century cemetery.

Its early history compares with many that were founded soon after the 1852 Metropolitan Interments Act. Land was bought by the local burial board in small parcels from several vendors and an advertisement was placed in *The Times* for architects to submit plans for the two chapels, 'the whole cost not to exceed £1000'.[2] Within three weeks several had been submitted and number thirty-four, signed 'Labor et Spes' selected. This was George Pritchett, who had already designed identical chapels for Saffron Walden's cemetery in Essex. These were inspected by members of the board who pronounced them satisfactory and within a year all was ready. Mr Pritchett had designed two Gothic chapels with stained glass, the ground had been drained and landscaped, £57 1s 6d worth of shrubs and evergreens planted and the Bishop of London had performed the ceremony of consecration.[3]

The cemetery filled rapidly and was extended beyond a bisecting footpath to the north-west in 1883 linked by an underground pathway. Part of the newer ground contains an extensive Gardens of Remembrance with a lake much favoured by Canadian geese, and a rockery.

There is little that is remarkable about either the tombs or their occupants except one, designed by William Butterfield for himself and his family. It is a mediaeval-style coffin tomb with a sculpted cross on its top. Butterfield had a close association with Tottenham, his sister lived there and he restored All Hallows Church for the vicar who lies in the next grave.

WILLIAM BUTTERFIELD 1814–1900
Architect of High Victorian churches. All Saints, Margaret Street is his most celebrated work.

TOTTENHAM PARK CEMETERY
Montagu Road, N18

Founded: 1912
Owner: Badgehurst Ltd.
Acreage: Approx. 6

Compared with the neatly packed rows of the Western Synagogue's tombs across the party wall, this cemetery is a shambles. Opened in 1912 by some of the directors of the Great Southern Cemetery, Crematorium and Land Company, who had established both Streatham Park and Ilford Park (now Eastbrookend) cemeteries, land was purchased at £135 per acre.[1] The chapel (now in a state of collapse), lodge and office were completed by mid 1913.[2] The architect was John Bannen who had designed the chapels at Streatham Park Cemetery and Surbiton. (He was also probably responsible for the buildings at Eastbrookend).

Tottenham: The chapels by George Pritchett (1856) before enlargement of the cemetery.

Today, although signs proudly declare the name of the cemetery, the small brick office inside is derelict and a notice on an adjacent wall claims that the only maintenance is carried out by Friends of the Cemetery.

The dismal state of Tottenham Park would be little better than its sister cemetery at Woodgrange had it not been saved by the Muslims. On the south side of the only path, an eruption of bright flowers, some plastic, some real, decorate Muslim graves, many grave stones displaying the red crescent emblem. The atmosphere is positively Asiatic on a sunny day, when brightly clothed mourners burn joss sticks over the graves, filling the air with pungent scents. It is unique in London.

Tottenham: The tunnel under the footpath dividing the cemetery.

TOWER HAMLETS CEMETERY
SOUTHERN GROVE, E3

Founded: 1841
Owner: The London Borough of Tower Hamlets
Acreage: 33

As the docks in east London developed during the early nineteenth century, so the population increased, only to be decimated by the cholera epidemics of the 1830s and 40s. Tower Hamlets Cemetery, incorporated by Act of Parliament in 1841, was one of seven large privately owned cemeteries that formed a cordon around central London intended to cope with the capital's burial problem.

The attraction of the new cemeteries as viable commercial propositions encouraged businessmen to invest in them, Tower Hamlets being no exception. Included on the board of the City of London and Tower Hamlets Cemetery Company, as it was called, were John Hammack, the chairman, a surveyor and local timber merchant and John Pirie, a ship owner who was Lord Mayor of London in 1841, and knighted the following year. The Company's capital, which was limited by the Act to £20,000 divided into £10 shares, soon earned a handsome interest. Within months of its incorporation, the cemetery was consecrated by the Bishop of London and the first burial conducted, all on the same day, 4 September 1841. Business was less brisk for the remainder of the year but in 1845 over 500 burials were recorded and over 1,000 in 1850. By 1889 approximately 250,000 bodies had been interred, the vast majority in common graves costing 25s each. By the time Mrs Holmes inspected the cemetery in 1896 it was already getting out of hand. She witnessed:

> ... a regular ocean of tombstones many of which are lying about apparently uncared for and unclaimed; in fact most of the graves, except those at the edges of the walks look utterly neglected ...[1]

Fifty years later Pevsner described Tower Hamlets as 'astonishingly overcrowded and overgrown'.[2]

By this time the company was impoverished and following lengthy discussions the Greater London Council (GLC) bought the cemetery in 1966, after which burials were discontinued. The buildings which had suffered bomb damage were by then derelict and all demolished in 1972. The chapels had been designed in 1848 by the architectural partnership of Thomas Wyatt and David Brandon, fresh from their

Tower Hamlets: The Anglican chapel by Thomas Wyatt and David Brandon

Tower Hamlets: The Nonconformist chapel. From *The Illustrated London News* (1849)

triumph with the parish church of Wilton, Wiltshire, one of the most admired buildings of the period. The *Illustrated London News* commented that the Anglican chapel,

> in consecrated ground is in the early decorated period, with a belfry at one angle in which are some nicely ornamented windows; and at the sides are attached cloisters for the reception of mural tablets, so constructed as to afford an effectual screen from the weather. The octagonal Dissenters' Chapel is in the Byzantine style ... Beneath both chapels are dry and extensive catacombs ...[3]

The other buildings were a little Egyptian style mortuary and the lodge, now replaced by a mean brick house.

Having demolished the chapels the GLC planned to turn the cemetery into a public park but there was considerable opposition to this idea not least because the proposals included removal of many of the trees and tombstones. Part of the southern section of the cemetery was nevertheless cleared of memorials.

Vandalism went unchecked and it became a dumping ground for rubbish. No other London cemetery had been allowed to grow wild for so long. In describing it in an article in *East London Papers* 1969–70, Denis Keeling likened it to:

> A map of the USA and Mexico, the 'Mexican territory' being largely unused. To the north of the latter lies a sparsely used area which is thick with tall grass and weeds. The rest alternates between heavily wooded areas filled with graves, and pleasant grassy clearings.[4]

Today, it remains one of the eeriest cemeteries in London and away from the perimeter the undergrowth remains like a jungle. However, there is evidence to show that the cemetery is beginning a new lease of life. Clearance of trees and the dense vegetation has taken place in areas surrounding the perimeter; a large section has been enclosed by railings to create a wildlife area, there is new signage and markers for a nature trail. In 1993 the single story Soanes Centre designed by Robson Kelly Architects was built at the entrance. It provides environmental and ecological courses and also acts as a base for the Friends of Tower Hamlets Cemetery Park, as the cemetery is now known. This makes sense as it is a haven for wildlife; 100 species of birds have been recorded as well as foxes and other small mammals.

Most of those buried here are east Londoners, often in paupers' graves (in the 1850s they accounted for some 80 per cent of burials) and good monuments are few. The best commemorates Joseph Westwood (died 1883) in the size and style of a mediaeval market cross, except that the finials are metal, with a Gothic canopy and spire sheltering a female figure. It stands near the centre of the cemetery at an intersection of the main paths, but most of the other larger memorials are in the north west corner. Designs derive mainly from classical sources, the draped urn is a particular favourite. One such urn crowns the sarcophagus of the Llewellyn family on which an inscription reads:

Sacred to the memory of Ellen, daughter of Llewellyn and Ellen Llewellyn, who died 6th Feb. 1854 aged 14 months. Also Emily, sister of the above, who died 29th March 1858, aged 3 years and 9 months. Beatrice Ada, who died 26th July 1860, aged 15 months. Horace, who died 20th Dec. 1864, aged 3 months and 3 weeks. Cuthbert Llewellyn, who died 29th Jan. 1865, aged 5 months.

In this tragic and modest way Tower Hamlets provides much that is interesting to the local or social historian.

Where occupations are mentioned on tombstones it transpires that many were sailors, often drowned at sea. Some, like Captain Lusby of Hull, ended their days more dramatically; he was accidentally shot aboard his ship in London in 1874. Another, Peter Slader, aged only fourteen, fell from the masthead of a ship in the West India Dock before drowning in 1848. Henry and James Mead, watermen, were run down by the Woolwich steampacket *Plover* in 1863. William Fisher was one of the unfortunate 550 day trippers drowned in 1878 when their paddle steamer, the *Princess Alice* collided with the collier *Bywell Castle* and sank at Galleon's Reach.[5] Another illfated voyager was Emma Simpkins:

She died at sea
of dysentry
On her passage to India 1854.

Death was never very distant from the Victorians, as Augustine Tuson discovered when he was 'struck by death with an instantaneous blow without a premonitionary symptom on the 5th of October 1848'. The inscription continues, 'Reader be warned by this event that ye be found in a waiting posture'.

Closely related to the occupation of 'mariner' are a number of ancillary trades whose practitioners are buried here. One can find engineers, mastmakers, ropemakers, shipping surveyors, excisemen and telegraph operators. There is also a sprinkling of foreign names, especially Germans who had settled in the east end following eighteenth century religious persecution in the Palatinate. One of the most spectacular funerals Tower Hamlets witnessed was of a French exile, M. Rougée, in 1857. The *Illustrated London News* reported:

The funeral started from the residence of the deceased in Charlotte Street, Blackfriars Road. As soon as the coffin was placed in the hearse, and the widow and the immediate friends in the mourning coach, the foreign exiles, to the number of about 2,000 formed in procession, and followed, carrying flags bearing various Republican devices, encircled with crape fringed with silver . . . Large as the procession was at the starting, it increased in magnitude as it proceeded, until by the time it arrived at the canal bridge in the Mile End Road it could not have numbered less than 10,000. When the coffin was lowered into the grave, M. Pyat pronounced a funeral oration over the grave. M. Tilandier, M. Louis Blanc, M. Dillart and Mr Nash addressed the assemblage. At the conclusion of the orations cries of 'Vive la République démocratique et sociale' resounded through the multitude.[6]

Even this funeral was dwarfed by the extraordinary rites that attended Alfred Linnell's burial on 18 December 1887. Linnell had been killed by a police charge at a socialist rally in Trafalgar Square and his funeral was organised by W.T. Stead and Annie Besant's Law and Liberty League. The procession, which started from a Soho undertaker's shop, took three quarters of an hour to pass any one spot. It was headed by a band playing the Dead March from 'Saul' and fifty stewards carrying wands guarded the coffin. The crowd grew larger as the cortège travelled east. By the time the cemetery had been reached it was dusk and raining. An unsympathetic *Times* reporter wrote:

> A cry was raised of 'hats off' and many of those nearest the hearse showed this sign of respect to the dead, but the crowd, which sprawled over the tombs, and graves and monuments, made no sign of being animated by any feeling of respect. In the darkness which was illuminated for a few seconds now and then fitfully by matches being struck, evidently by smokers, the Burial Service of the Church of England was read, but it was heard by few outside the immediate crowd around the grave for the others were talking more or less loudly.[7]

Two speeches followed, one by William Morris, but:

> The speakers were rendered almost inaudible by the retreating feet of many who were not inclined to stop in the drenching rain and in a few minutes the cemetery was deserted by all but a few who chanted a 'death song' composed by William Morris.[8]

The vitality of the east end funeral survived to the end. One of the last interments at Tower Hamlets was described by Barbara Jones in her book *Design for Death*:

> On October 22nd 1965 the cemetery could show a beautiful piano four feet long made of white chrysanthemums outlined with pink ones. The keyboard was scarlet carnations and the pedals and sharps were silver paper. In silver on a purple ribbon 'Good Night Pop', On a card 'In loving memory of Dear Dad'. On a sheet of paper:
>
> > 'Around a Piano we have
> > Gathered through the years
> > A legacy of happiness and
> > Laughter that shines
> > Through our tears'[9]

Scenes like these are now history but the cemetery itself remains and the dilemma raised by its future is the same that affects many other wild and picturesque nineteenth century cemeteries all over the country. With luck a happy balance of gentle decay and discreet maintenance can be achieved.

For a more extensive list of those buried in the cemetery see *Every Stone Tells a Story: A short History and History Trail of Tower Hamlets Cemetery Park* by Rosemary Taylor (1996).

Charlie Brown –1932
'Uncrowned king of Limehouse', licensee of the Railway Tavern, West India Dock Road and antique collector. His funeral attracted over 10,000 mourners.

Capt. John Buckley 1813–76
Won the V.C. in the Indian Mutiny. His two wives and eight children either died of fever or were murdered in India.

Will Crooks 1852–1921
Trade unionist, member of the L.C.C. and Labour member for Poplar and Woolwich 1903–21.

Thomas Mullins 1839–99
A survivor of the 17th Lancers who rode in the charge of the Light Brigade at Balaclava.

Harry Ordel 1858–1914
National organiser of the Dockers' Union 1894–1914, member of the 1889 Dock Strike Committee, founder member of the I.L.P.

Joseph Westwood –1883
Iron shipbuilder and wrought iron manufacturer. His company's football team became West Ham United.

TRENT PARK CEMETERY
COCKFOSTERS ROAD, COCKFOSTERS, HERTS

Founded: 1960
Owner: London Borough of Islington
Acres: 6

The cemetery is located next to Cockfosters Underground station some distance from the Islington borough boundary, but a visit cannot be recommended. Trent Park ranks among the least interesting of all London cemeteries.

The single brick chapel in the now unfashionable style characteristic of its period was designed by Sir John Brown and A.E. Henson. It incorporates a waiting room with a Book of Remembrance and lavatories. Light and airy with stained glass and blue fabric furnishings it is reminiscent of a church hall or scout hut. It is surprising it was built at all considering the increased number of cremations in the 1960s.

Outside the chapel the ground is flat with minimal planting except evergreens, and a central avenue between the graves. As a new breed of cemetery, the lawn concept triumphs with bronze plaques at ground level and concrete troughs with vases placed strategically at the side of the roadway. Most of the section behind the chapel is already full. An average of ninety burials a year take place in the southern area but why anyone should wish to be commemorated in this desolate place is a mystery.

TWICKENHAM CEMETERY
Hospital Bridge Road, Twickenham, Middx.

Founded: 1868
Owner: London Borough of Richmond upon Thames
Acreage: 20

The cemetery occupies a flat rectangle of land once surrounded by orchards and fields. It avoids dullness thanks to the Victorians' practice of lavish tree planting and the triple spires of the two Decorated style chapels with their uniting *porte cochère* near the centre of the original eight-acres ground. They were designed by Charles Jones, the Ealing borough surveyor, and built at a cost of £3,000 including the stained glass and stone altars.[1]

The monuments are not spectacular with one exception, a charming bronze ensemble of fishing tackle commemorating Francis Francis, the author, with an epitaph, 'And angle on, and beg to have a quiet passage to a welcome grave.' There are also three memorials to members of the variety artistes' profession who ended their days at 'The Briars'.

Allotments at the far end of the cemetery are being converted into burial space with provision for around 1,000 graves.

Francis Francis 1822–86
Angler and novelist, he was angling editor of *The Field* for twenty-five years. There is a memorial to him in Winchester Cathedral.

Edward Stanley Gibbons 1840–1913
Stamp dealer, his firm was founded in Plymouth in 1865 and moved to London in 1874.

James Lewis 1856–1924
Composer, author of numerous music text books and principal of the Victoria College of Music, London.

Robert Martin 1821–1906
'For 42 years professor of clarinet at Kneller Hall.'

Twickenham: Francis Francis' tomb (1886). Regrettably the fishing rod is now missing.

Rt. Hon. Jonathan Peel 1799–1879
M.P. for Huntingdon 1831–68, Secretary of State for war 1858–59 and race horse owner. His horses won first and second places in the 1844 Derby.

Dr. Ernst Roth. 1896–1971
Czech born music publisher with Boosey and Hawkes, friend and adviser of Stravinsky.

Col. Robert Thompson 1833–90
Commandant of Kneller Hall 1880–1888.

Maj. Frederick Walter 1904–31
Commandant of the corps of commissionaires

Maj. Gen. Sir Willoughby G. Watkin 1859–1925
Chief of General Staff in Canada.

Fred Williams –1916
Music hall actor well known for his pantomime dame roles.

WALTHAMSTOW CEMETERY
Queen's Road, E17

Founded: 1872
Owner: London Borough of Waltham Forest
Acreage: 11

The land was bought for £5,000 by the Walthamstow Burial Board which then invited six architects to submit 'plans and specifications for the erection of two chapels with entrance lodge and fence and gates on the south front of the burial ground,' the cost not to exceed £2,250. An unusual adjunct to the lodge was 'a Room about 20 by 14 feet for Inquest Room'. Other buildings required were, 'a Coach House and Tool House with Dead House'.[1] R.C. Sutton from Nottingham was finally appointed architect and all his buildings survive, with the

Walthamstow: The chapels (1872). Unusually, they are positioned at right angles

Coroner's Court still using the Inquest Room. The well-kept Gothic chapels, joined by a *porte cochère* surmounted by a belfry, are typical cemetery architecture except in their planning, being joined at right angles.

Apart from Sutton's buildings, Walthamstow is disappointing. Only the wretchedly mean Hooke mausoleum (1913) breaks the monotonous acres of indistinguishable small tombstones. Near the green painted railings along Queens Road is an anchor cast onto a rock above the Taylor monument and there is a rare example of a small cast iron memorial adorned with a draped urn. Although a few trees line the entrance, the site is devoid of grass or vegetation on account of the extravagant use of weedkiller. Perhaps Jack Williams (died 1917) described on his headstone as, 'Pioneer, comrade, socialist' might have approved. Epitaphs such as there are tend towards the sentimental, like the lament on the death of a one year old:

> A sweet little flower nipped in the bud
> No sin or sorrow knew
> Just came to win a parent's love
> And then to heaven withdrew.

WANDSWORTH CEMETERY
MAGDALEN ROAD, SW18

Founded: 1878
Owner: London Borough of Wandsworth
Acreage: 34

A large wedge-shaped cemetery that slopes a full one-third of a mile between the length of Magdalen Road and a busy railway line to the north west. When opened by the Wandsworth Burial Board the cemetery was only 12 acres in extent, now the northern part of the existing cemetery with access from Magdalen Road. Inside the gates was the lodge and a short drive lead to two small Gothic style chapels centrally placed and end to end, adding to the formality of the overall design. Only the non-conformist chapel is now in use, but the cemetery is maintained to a high standard. Two tablets at the entrance to the disused Anglican chapel record the original opening and enlargement of the cemetery in 1898–9, the Burial Board members and the builder. The Board's minutes were destroyed in World War Two but an account of the cemetery's opening names the architect of the chapels as the local surveyor, H.W. Young. The listed entrance gates built of brick and stone with gabled pinnacles complements the lodge constructed at the time of the extension.

The cemetery's most interesting features can be found at the thick end of the wedge where a gridiron pattern of paths meet in a series of *ronds-points* around which the older and better monuments have been erected with some sense of artifice. These tend to have solid plinths topped by urns, obelisks or crosses, certainly nothing frivolous as befitted local dignitaries like Sir Edward Evans, (died 1928), who listed his recreations in *Who's Who* as 'motoring and work'. Towards the back of the cemetery a miniature domed temple built of ceramics commemorates the Carr family (1911), not dissimilar to one in the nearby Streatham Cemetery. Others worth a second glance are the towering granite structure above Emma Cock's grave (1886), the Gothic twin arched gable commemorating Jurgan and Emily Pfeiffer (1889) with detail reminiscent of Rosslyn chapel and the more traditional praying figure of the Lake memorial (1938) and the weeping willows on the Harding headstone (1880).

Wandsworth houses no fewer than eight separate war memorials and, curiously, the remains of two air raid shelters. Lance-Corporal Davey's individual monument of 1917 is especially touching. Modelled propped against a cross are his Lee Enfield rifle and fallen hat. And one wonders if the premature death of General George Washington, a Brixton nine-year-old who died in 1895, cut short his parents' vision of a brilliant military career.

In the late 1980s a large section of the ground running parallel with the railway which had already been used for burials was banked up with earth. Now sheltered by well developed poplars, it no longer looks new and its popularity has meant that this supply of additional space has nearly been exhausted.

SIR JAMES CARMICHAEL 1858–1934
Builder and Director General of Housing in England and Wales 1918–20.

GUNNER JAMES COLLIS 1860–1918
Won the V.C. during the retreat to Kandahar in the second Afghan War. It was for a time forfeited after he had been convicted of bigamy. Headstone restored in 1998.

SIR EDWIN EVANS 1855–1928
Local businessman and director of several building societies.

SIR EDWARD FITHIAN 1845–1936
Lawyer and secretary of the Association of Chambers of Commerce.

SIR HENRY HOLLOWAY 1857–1923
President of the Institute of Builders.

MAJ. THOMAS HOLMES 1808–93
'The Nestor of British Cyclism.' Sportsman, actor and tricyclist record holder.

BERTRAM MATZ 1865–1925
Publisher and authority on Dickens.

JAMES NOBLE 1865–1925
Journalist, wrote for *The Spectator* and editor of the *Liverpool Argus*.

Wandsworth: The entrance from Magdalen Road following enlargement of the cemetery in 1898–9. The chapels are on either side of the drive

Sir James O'Grady 1886–1934
Trade unionist and secretary of the National Federation of General Workers.

William Parker 1823–90
Surgeon, president of the Microscopical Society 1871–3, he made a minute study of the skull.

John Wimperis 1829–1904
Architect, he designed many of the terracotta buildings in Mayfair.

WEST HAM CEMETERY
Cemetery Road, E7

Founded: 1857
Owner: London Borough of Newham
Acreage: 20

With the passing of the Burial Acts in the 1850s a West Ham Burial Board was set up directed to secure an appropriate plot of cemetery land. This was achieved only after it was reported:

> Many meetings of the Board and of Committees have taken place, that there has been much correspondence attendant upon the obtaining of 'Tenders of Land' that twelve advertisements have been inserted in the London and County papers that ten Auctioneers and Land Agents have been written to as well as several Landowners...[1]

Finally twelve acres were bought from Samuel Gurney (this area was enlarged in 1871) and it is very apparent that little regard was paid to the landscaping potential during these negotiations, good drainage and cost being considered more important.

Thus West Ham is remarkable more for its lack of distinctive features than anything else. A substantial barge boarded lodge precedes a

West Ham: Memorial to Sub-Officer Henry Vickers and Fireman Frederick Sell, who died in the Silvertown explosion in 1917

straightforward grid plan of paths and a typical ragstone Decorated Gothic Anglican chapel designed by T.E. Knightley, an architect responsible for several east end churches (the Nonconformist chapel has been demolished). There are no prominent monuments but cemetery poets have been busy. For example William Chapman, who died in 1872, is remembered thus:

> No more confined to grovelling scenes of night
> No more a tenant pent in mortal clay
> Now should we rather hail thy glorious flight
> And trace thy journey to the realms of day.

Albert Wardale was drowned in the *Egypt* which sank in 1922 with the loss of ninety-six lives and £1,054,000 worth of gold and silver. His epitaph is as follows:

> Rocks and storms I fear no more
> When on that eternal shore
> Drop the anchor and furl the sail
> I am safe within the vale.

The victims of two other terrible disasters are also commemorated here:

GEORGE AND CATHERINE BARRETT −1878
Two of the 550 victims drowned in the Thames when the pleasure boat *Princess Alice* sank following a collision.[2]

FREDERICK SELL AND HENRY VICKERS −1917
Two of the firemen killed at the great Silvertown munitions factory explosion in 1917 which killed sixty-nine people and injured 390 others. A procession a quarter of a mile long followed their hearses.[3]

WESTMINSTER CEMETERY
UXBRIDGE ROAD, W7

Founded: 1854
Owner: The City of Westminster
Acreage: 23

The Metropolitan Interment Act 1850 was made law none too soon for the St George's Hanover Square burial board. Already there had been complaints about the nauseating smells emanating from the burial ground in the Bayswater Road and some unpleasant consequences caused by an exploding coffin in the vaults of St Mark's, North Audley Street. The Board was therefore lucky to find a plot of land near the Uxbridge Road still undeveloped by speculative house builders and sufficiently well drained that coffins and 'the Bodies deposited would be compounded with dust in about 20 or 30 years'.[1] So said Robert Jerrard, the board's architect who designed the cemetery and its buildings for £14,741.17.11d.[2] It was extended by 11 acres in 1883.

Jerrard's lodge is a very substantial house, the largest lodge in London, which carries a high relief sculpture of St George above the main door. The gate piers are tall and Gothic, the reverse of one records the names of the Burial Board members.[3] A row of stately cedars (part of the 1850s £1,000 planting programme) leads to the chapels. There is, as one would expect from a wealthy borough, a sense of opulence about the cemetery which is still very well maintained. Only the chapels are disappointing; although large, their lumpy Gothic style does not fulfil the promise of the approach. The stained glass windows in the Anglican chapel depicting some thirty biblical symbols were installed in 1945. Opposite the entrance to this chapel, under the *porte cochère*, are double door to the mortuary. Unusually, the complex also possesses two-story office accommodation.

The cemetery was consecrated by the Bishop of London on 6 July 1854 with appropriate ceremony, followed by a cold collation and half a pint of sherry per guest. Burials began in the same month, but surprisingly few have been commemorated by remarkable monuments. Several mausolea line the path from the gates but they are strangely box-like, with the exception of the pink granite Keller mausoleum in the Egyptian style. Remarkably, a mausoleum, the size of a small house, has recently been built by the Arma family. It is designed as a traditional classical temple, albeit in brick, faced with paired pilasters and an entablature at the entrance.

Elsewhere stone angels in every imaginable posture are the favourite unimaginative motif, frequently adorning tombs of the innumerable retired colonial gentry, soldiers, planters and missionaries who are buried here. South-east of the chapels is the grave of one of these tough empire builders, Himalaya Robinson, who died in 1902. 'The daughter of a soldier she was as an infant borne on the strength of Wellington's Peninsular Army'. A civilian memorial to 200 who died in World War Two was unveiled in 1950. Built into the cemetery's west wall is a small catacomb range. Over 100,000 burials have taken place in this cemetery.

SIR JOHN AKERMAN 1825–1905
Mayor of Pietermaritzburg and colonial delegate for Natal in London.

AL BOWLEY 1890–1941
Singer and bandleader. Killed in an air raid and buried in a communal grave.

RT. HON. HENRY FITZROY 1807–59
Tory M.P. for Lewes 1837–59.

FREDDIE FRINTON 1916–68
TV comedian with a cult following in Germany and Scandinavia

WILLIAM HILL 1817–95
Violin maker of the London firm W.E. Hill and Sons, founded in 1762.

SIR JOHN HUNT 1859–1945
The first town clerk of the City of Westminster 1900–28.

REV. WELLBORE MCCARTHY 1840–1925
The first Bishop of Grantham.

RICHARD NEWTON 1854–1926
Palaeontologist on the staff of the British Museum.

COL. SIR DAVID SEMPLE 1856–1937
Director of medical research studies in India and Egypt.

COL. SIR JOHN YOUNG 1843–1932
A much decorated soldier awarded medals in nine of the ten campaigns in which he took part, twice specially mentioned in despatches to Queen Victoria.

WEST NORWOOD (SOUTH METROPOLITAN) CEMETERY AND CREMATORIUM
NORWOOD HIGH STREET, SE27

Founded: 1836
Owner: London Borough of Lambeth
Acreage: 40

Despite years of poor maintenance, war time bombing, demolitions, and a programme of 'lawn conversion' from the late 1960s, vestiges of this once magnificent cemetery still survive. Unlike the shamelessly convenient flat cemeteries of today, the Victorians preferred something infinitely more romantic, best realised on an elevated site, and Norwood is second only to Highgate in achieving this picturesque ideal.

The land was bought from Lord Thurlow's trustees and the cemetery built by the South Metropolitan Cemetery Company for £75,000. It lies opposite the imposing Greek revival church of St Luke's (1822), but in complete contrast the chosen style for the cemetery was Gothic, including the railings. This massive iron enceinte, bolstered by an equally hefty wall intended to ensure safety from grave robbers and vandals, was designed by Sir William Tite, the architect also responsible for the chapels and original gate lodge. Inscribed above the entrance arch is 'South Metropolitan Cemetery AD MDCCCXXXVI' and a shield with the arms of the dioceses of Winchester and Canterbury. Above the pedestrian gate are the words 'Deus Deo' and '1887' on the inner side. Tite later became President of the RIBA and a specialist railway station architect, although his best known works are probably the Royal Exchange (1841) and the huge Brookwood Cemetery in Surrey (1854). An early print of the cemetery at Norwood illustrates a wonderfully spacious design, with clumps of deciduous trees and concentrations of tombs, rather like a park by Capability Brown. It is interesting that J.C. Loudon was critical of this planting, preferring a more even spread of pines, yews, junipers, box and weeping willows. But both he and Tite would be appalled at the cemetery's present state.

The two chapels have been demolished above ground. They stood on the summit of the hill, built of stock brick with stone dressings in the Perpendicular style. The Church of England chapel was the larger, with its front extended on either side by arcaded cloisters providing space for memorial tablets. Its lofty rectangular shape and flanking turrets resembled King's College Chapel, Cambridge. Beneath it, catacombs were excavated with room for 2,000 or more coffins. George Collison in 1840 described how

> In the centre of the chapel stands a kind of high oblong table, covered with black drapery; its purpose is to conceal the very ingenious machinery which at a given secret signal conveys the coffin placed on its top, slowly down into the vaults below, without the slightest noise to indicate the nature of the agency which is the hydraulic pump.[1]

In what was the first conversion of cemetery buildings in London, a crematorium was added to the Nonconformist chapel and opened in 1915.[2] Tragically both chapels were damaged in 1944 and demolished instead of being repaired, the Nonconformist chapel in 1955 and the Anglican in 1960. In their places stand a walled rose garden of remembrance and a new crematorium, the latter designed by Alwyn Underdown in 1956. It is a squat ill-proportioned architectural disaster in pink brick with some terrible ironwork decoration.[3] Incorporating the chimney from the original crematorium, the facility comprises two chapels, the obligatory Book of Remembrance, and a columbarium. Grilles at the base of the walls, the only remaining evidence of the chapels, secure the old catacombs where Tite himself is buried.[4] In 1936 his Gothic lodge was also demolished, a replacement being in turn bombed and replaced in 1950 by the present building.

West Norwood: Completed before his death in 1939, the mausoleum commemorates Edmund Distin Maddick.

Apart from the walls, railings and entrance arch, only one other fragment thought to be Tite's work survives: a monument for the banker J.W. Gilbart. Tite had collaborated in the design of The London and Westminster Bank for Gilbart and in 1866 designed his tomb whose spire and pinnacles would fit comfortably on a parish church. Carved in a spandrel is a squirrel gathering nuts, a reference to Gilbart's banking interests.

After passing through the entrance one of the most striking mausolea in any London cemetery is encountered. It commemorates the physician Edmund Distin Maddick who built it before his death in 1939. The rectangular Portland stone vault, which stands on a stepped base, is fitted with a grand doorway and windows bearing a coat of arms and carved architraves in a manner reminiscent of a town hall rather than a tomb. Above is a concave roof pierced by tall glazed crosses on each side which supports the figure of Christ and a child some 40 feet above ground.[5]

The boundary road then leads to the most outstanding group of

West Norwood: The Anglican Chapel, demolished 1960.

memorials in the Greek burial ground, a plot to the north east of the cemetery reserved in 1842 for the Brotherhood of the Greek Community in London.[6] In 1872 Stephen Ralli, a merchant, built a chapel on an adjoining plot of land in memory of his young son, Augustus, who had died of rheumatic fever at Eton. It has been suggested that the architect was John Oldrid Scott who at the time was working with his father, Sir Gilbert Scott. The building is a superb essay in Greek revival architecture, a rarely used style at that time. On either side of the Doric porticos are flanking burial chambers, whilst the cella itself is richly coffered.

The same family commissioned the mighty mausoleum nearby for John Ralli in 1863. The architect was George Edmund Street, best known for his many churches and the London Law Courts. The Ralli mausoleum, despite its relatively small scale, displays Street's talent for using massive forms with calm assurance and his interest in polychromy displayed by the use of different stones. Yet another Ralli, Eustratio, was immured in 1875 in a domed Renaissance style mausoleum nearby. The architect was Edward Barry, who in 1858 had designed Alexander Beren's monument on the brow of the hill. Barry succeeded to his father's practice in 1860 and with it the burden of completing the Houses of Parliament. In comparison the Berens monument is small and little known but it has been described as 'one of the finest High Victorian monuments in the country'.[7] Standing on a granite plinth it resembles a mediaeval sarcophagus – a nineteenth century equivalent of Edward the Confessor's shrine in Westminster Abbey. The materials used are rich and varied, creating a highly intricate Gothic design which cost £1,500 to build.[8] Another exotic prototype was chosen by Thomas Allom in 1865 as the model for George Dodd's mausoleum. This pink and white marble confection resembles a north Italian Gothic church. Regrettably, it is in a shocking state and needs conservation before it deteriorates any further.

Among the Gothic and the marble are some less conventional tombs. The hard wearing properties of Victorian terracotta are demonstrated by the well preserved mausolea built for Sir Henry Doulton in 1897 and Sir Henry Tate in 1890 and in the highly decorative obelisk to James Brown (1884). There is even less chance of weathering affecting John Britton's millstone grit monolith of 1857 designed by George Godwin. Nothing so colossally plain in funerary architecture had been seen since Edward I was interred in his box-like Purbeck marble tomb chest in 1307.[9]

A complete list of notable Norwood monuments would be too long to include here. Many can be found in the Greek

West Norwood: Contrasts. Rear is Sir William Tite's monument for the banker J.W. Gilbart (1866). In the foreground is a millstone grit momlith by George Godwin for John Britton (1857)

cemetery and on the higher ground and also near the entrance. Worth mentioning are the delicately lobed canopy of the Schilizzi tomb, the bronze bust embedded in Benjamin Colls's granite plinth, a relief carving designed by William Burges on his own and his mother's tomb and the tapered sarcophagus with surrounding ironwork built for Dr Gideon Mantell by A.H. Wilds, the Brighton architect. There is also the iron tracery of Anne Farrow's 1854 tomb (restored in 1999), and the ship *sans* iron masts on the memorial to Captain John Wimble (1851) with stone reliefs of ships on three panels.

One curiosity in the south east corner of the cemetery is a little plot purchased for parishioners of Wren's city church, St Mary at Hill. Another is the number of German nationals buried here, on account of the German church that once existed near Forest Hill.

Historically and architecturally, Norwood compares favourably with those old favourites, the monuments in St Paul's Cathedral or even Westminster Abbey, but unlike them, it has been left to Lambeth's planning department to look after it. When the Borough acquired Norwood by compulsory purchase in 1966 from an undercapitalised company, ambitious schemes were formulated, in conjunction with the Victorian Society, for preserving the most important monuments and landscaping the ground to provide an 'attractive open air history book'.[10] Admittedly the task was a formidable one. As early as 1905 Algernon Ashton was writing letters to the press complaining that:

> This beautifully situated God's Acre has for some time past been in a surprisingly shocking condition, many of the headstones being quite crooked, others lying broken on the ground, whilst the grass is allowed to grow wild.[11]

In 1971 emphasis was placed on the 'urgent need of repair' of the best monuments and clearance carried out with 'careful detailing of edgings, retaining walls, paths, etc.'[12] Instead, the Council indiscriminately flattened over 10,000 monuments, with little effort made to record them, in an attempt to create an easily maintained parkland. In response the Friends of West Norwood Cemetery were founded in 1989 to halt the destruction of memorials and in 1994 the

West Norwood: Memorial to John Wimble (1851) on Ship Path

West Norwood: Detail on the Brown memorial (1884)

Council's policy was judged to be illegal by the Southwark Diocesan Consistory Court. By then, however, a number of important monuments had disappeared, including one by J.L. Pearson erected in 1855 (all we know of this is an entry in a list of Pearson's work).

Happily, it is not all bad news. The Council have undertaken scrub clearance along the Ship Path, including opening up a route by the side of the listed Grissell monument leading up to the site of the former Anglican chapel. Other grass paths have been opened up by mowing. Individual listed monuments repaired with funds from various sources include those of Sir Henry Tate (1899), Sir Henry Doulton (1897), and Baron Julius de Reuter (1899) to name just 3 of over 100 monuments which have been reinstated with support from the Friends.

Finally, the Ecology and Landscape Survey required under the Court judgment has at last been commissioned. This should provide the basis for medium/long term development of the cemetery as well as providing a secure footing to allow for fund raising from bodies such as the Heritage Lottery Commission. In the meantime The Friends plan to continue their work on smaller projects especially the reinstatement of memorials.

Sir William A'Beckett 1806–69
First Chief Justice of Victoria, Australia, 1851–63. Author and journalist, he wrote *A Universal Biography* in five volumes.

Charles Alcock 1842–1907
Journalist, writer and sportsman. He played cricket for the Gentlemen of Essex and football for the Wanderers and England. He played in the first football international against Scotland. As secretary of the F.A. 1870–96 he promoted the F.A. challenge cup. He also organised the first England v. Australia test match in England. Tomb recently restored.

Sir James Alderson 1794–1882
Physician extraordinary to Queen Victoria, president of the Royal College of Physicians 1867–82.

Arthur Anderson 1792–1868
Founder member and chairman of the P. & O. Shipping Line, Liberal M.P. for Orkney 1847–52.

John Appold 1800-65
Inventor. His two most important inventions were the centrifugal pump and refinements in laying underwater cables. His house was renowned for its domestic gadgets.

Florence Armitage -1915
An inscription on the memorial to her father, John Burke, records her death on 7 May 1915 as a result of the *Lusitania* being torpedoed off Ireland.

Sir Richard Baggalley 1816-88
Lord Justice of Appeal 1876-85, responsible for steering the 1875 Judicature Act through Parliament.

Sir Joseph Barnby 1838-96
Composer, music master at Eton College and conductor of the Royal Choral Society for twenty-four years.

Edward Barratt 1844-91
Plumber, publican and cricketer. He played for England v Australia in 1878 taking ten wickets in their first innings. Memorial demolished.

Sir Frederick Barthorpe 1857-1942
Banker and president of the Chartered Institute of Secretaries.

James Bassett (Charles Bertram) 1854-1907
The foremost conjurer of his time. His audiences included Queen Victoria, the Prince of Wales (22 times), the Czar and the German emperor.

Mary Bayly 1816-99
Founder of the Mothers' Meetings, authoress of *Workmen and their Difficulties*, etc.

Thomas Willert Beale 1828-94
Musical impresario and promoter of Berlioz. He wrote songs, piano pieces, plays and an operetta as well as his autobiography.

Henry Beaufoy 1786-1851
Educational philanthropist, he built and endowed the Lambeth Ragged Schools.

Col. William Beck 1804-73
Colonel in the service of H.M. Fath Ali, Shah of Persia.

Isabella Beeton 1836-65
Authoress of *Mrs Beeton's Book of Household Management* first published in 1861; died in childbirth.

Samuel Beeton 1831-77
Husband of the above; a bookseller and publisher, he published the first English edition of *Uncle Tom's Cabin*.

JOHN BELCHER 1841–1913
Architect, his mature work is representative of some of London's best Edwardian Baroque buildings. Memorial restored.

WILLIAM BENNETT 1811–71
Landscape artist. Memorial destroyed.

ALEXANDER BERENS –1858
Linen draper in the 'fancy trade'.

SIR HENRY BESSEMER 1813–98
Engineer and pioneer in the manufacture of steel. He patented 114 inventions between 1838 and 1894, including a means to produce bronze powder and gold paint.

ELHANEN BICKNELL 1788–1861
Made a fortune in whaling, a connoisseur and collector of nineteenth century British painting.

MARTIN BLADEN, LORD HAWKE 1860–1938
Yorkshire county cricket captain 1883–1910, he also played for England and was manager of numerous England tours abroad. Ashes only.

SAMUEL BLANCHARD 1804–45
Author and journalist, he wrote an article on Kensal Green Cemetery in *Ainsworth's* magazine in 1842. Committed suicide. Memorial destroyed.

HENRY BOHN 1796–1884
Successful bookseller, publisher, linguist and bibliographer, also well known for his hobbies as rose grower and art collector. Memorial destroyed.

ROBERT BOWLEY 1813–69
Musician and general manager of Crystal Palace. He committed suicide in the River Thames. Memorial destroyed.

CHARLES BRAVO 1846–76
The poisoned victim of one of the most celebrated unpunished Victorian crimes. The inquest jury examined the corpse through a glass panel in the coffin: 'the face had acquired the dark hue of a mummy and the teeth were almost entirely black'. Monument restored.

JOHN BRISTOWE 1827–95
Physician and lecturer at St Thomas's hospital. His books included a standard work on medicine for students.

THOMAS BRISTOWE 1833–92
Stockbroker and M.P. for Norwood 1885–92, 'died suddenly in the refreshment room at Brockwell Park'.

John Britton 1771–1857
Antiquary, author and publisher of numerous illustrated architectural and topographical books.

Lionel Brough 1836–1909
Comedian and journalist, he instituted the practice of selling newspapers on the street. Memorial destroyed.

Robert Brown 1842–95
Geographer. He travelled widely and varied geographical with botanical research. Published many popular geography books. His name is commemorated on Vancouver Island and elsewhere.

Samuel Brown 1810–75
Actuary and statistician. A keen promoter of decimal coinage and president of the Institute of Actuaries 1867–69.

Richard Brunton 1841–1901
Civil engineer, he planned the construction in Japan of lighthouses and lightships essential for trade with the West, and founded Japan's first school of civil engineering. His memorial was replaced in 1991 by the Japanese.

Edward Bumpus 1832–96
London bookseller.

William Burges 1827–81
High Victorian architect with a penchant for mediaeval inspired decoration, his principal works are Cork Cathedral and the remodelling of Cardiff Castle; his parents Alfred and Elizabeth Burges are also buried in the tomb designed by their son.

James Busby 1800–71
British Resident in New Zealand, he introduced the vine into Australia and New Zealand 1832–3.

Maria Cassavetti (Zambaco) 1843–1914
Friend and model to Rossetti and Burne-Jones, she was also a painter and medallist.

George Cattermole 1800–68
Watercolour painter and book illustrator, chiefly of historical subjects. Dickens attended his funeral.

Sir Joseph Causton 1815–71
Stationer and printer.

Paul Cinquevalli 1859–1918
Polish born juggler and clown.

William Clarke 1798–1856
Autocratic one-eyed Nottingham county cricketer 1816–45 who in 1840 established the Trent Bridge cricket ground. In 1846 he founded and captained the touring All England XI.

William Clowes 1779–1847
Founder of the printing firm that bears his name. He was the first to use steam machinery in printing. Also his son, William Junior, 1807–83.

Benjamin Colls 1815–78
Founder of the London building firm Colls & Sons, father of William (q.v.).

William Colls –1893
Building contractor, his funeral was attended by 400 employees and twenty carriages.

Sir Francis Cook 1817–1901
Warehouse owner and art collector, he died a millionaire.

Thompson Cooper 1837–1904
With his father compiled the first two volumes of *Athenae Cantabrigienses* and wrote 1,422 entries for the first edition of the D.N.B.

Dr James Cornwell 1812–1902
Schoolmaster and author of school textbooks that became models of their kind. His *School Geography* (1847) went through ninety editions.

David Cox 1809–85
'The younger'; watercolour painter.

Frederick Crace 1779–1859
Architectural decorator of Brighton Pavilion, Windsor Castle and Carlton House. His famous collection of maps and drawings was left to the British Museum. Memorial destroyed.

John D Crace 1838–1919
Architectural decorator. See John G. Crace (q.v.).

John G Crace 1808–89
Son of Frederick Crace (q.v.) who with his son John D. Crace were the foremost interior decorators of the nineteenth century. The Houses of Parliament, Windsor Castle and the Crystal Palace were decorated by them.

Col. Joseph Crowe 1826–76
First South African holder of V.C., won during the Indian Mutiny. His remains have since been removed to South Africa. Monument destroyed.

Thomas Cubitt 1788–1855
Building contractor responsible for housing developments in Islington, Bloomsbury, Belgravia and Clapham. He worked for the Queen at Osborne House and Buckingham Palace. His will is the longest ever made. The tombstone is a ten ton slab of granite.

Sir William Cubitt 1785-1861
Engineer involved in the construction of numerous canal, port and railway enterprises; he invented the treadmill in 1818 and, as president of the Institution of Civil Engineers, supervised the construction of the Crystal Palace in 1851. Memorial destroyed and reinstated.

George Davidge 1794-1842
Actor manager at the Royal Coburg, City and Surrey theatres, renowned for his miserliness.

William, Lord de Blaquiere 1778-1851
Great Alnager of Ireland, he committed suicide while suffering from smallpox.

Alphonse de Normandy 1809-64
Chemist, he patented a method for distilling sea water for drinking. Memorial destroyed and reinstated.

Baron Paul de Reuter 1816-99
German-born founder of the famous press agency in 1851.

George Dodd -1854
A gentleman of the Privy Chamber and M.P. for Maidstone 1841–53.

George Dolland 1774-1852
Optician, astronomer and optical instrument maker.

Sir Henry Doulton 1820-97
Potter of Lambeth, he developed the manufacture of Doultonware; also his father, John Doulton, who founded the firm in 1828.

William Dowton 1763-1851
Actor manager. Memorial destroyed.

Henry Dunn 1801-78
Author on theological subjects and scripture teacher.

William Edgar 1791-1869
Of Swan and Edgar, established by him in Piccadilly in 1834.

Thomas Edwards 1879-1933
Ventriloquist, he performed at all the leading London theatres and elsewhere.

Col. John Enoch 1785-1855
Served in the Peninsular Campaign and at Waterloo.

James Epps -1907
Introduced cocoa as a popular drink in Britain.

James Esdaile 1808–59
Surgeon and mesmerist. Memorial destroyed.

Dr Charles Fagge 1838–83
Distinguished physician at Guy's Hospital.

Robert Fairlie 1831–85
Railway engineer, he patented the double-bogie engine in 1864.

James Field 1845–1902
Restorer of Southwark Cathedral, 'to whose untiring energy the restoration of Southwark Cathedral was largely due'. Monument demolished.

Joshua Field 1786–1863
Engineer, with Joseph Maudslay (see below) he designed the engines of the 'Great Western'; founder member and president of the Institute of Civil Engineers 1848–50.

Alfred Forrester 1804–72
Illustrator known as 'Crowquill' and author of burlesques and children's books.

Sir Thomas Gabriel 1811–73
Timber merchant and Lord Mayor of London 1866–67.

Henry Gallup–1885
An American who made a fortune by the sale of Fragrant Floriline and Mexican Hair Restorer.

John Gassiot 1797–1877
Amateur scientist, experimented in the use of electricity. His firm, Martinez Gassiot still imports vintage port.

James Gilbart 1794–1863
Banker and writer of many books on banking practice.

Joseph Glass 1791–1867
Inventor of the first successful chimney sweeping machine. Memorial destroyed.

James Greathead 1844–96
South African born engineer who adapted Sir Marc Brunel's (q.v.) tunnelling shield for use in the construction of London's underground railways.

Thomas Grieve 1799–1882
Together with his son, two of the famous Grieve family of theatrical scene painters. Memorial destroyed.

John Grover 1836–92
Railway and waterworks engineer and antiquarian, he wrote *Old Clapham*.

William Brodie Gurney 1777–1855
Shorthand writer who between 1803 and 1844 recorded many of the most important state trials and proceedings of Parliament. A founder and later president of the Sunday School Union.

Frederick Gye 1810–78
Opera impresario and manager of Covent Garden, Drury Lane and the Lyceum theatres. Rebuilt Covent Garden after a fire in 1856. Killed accidentally at a shooting party.

George Hackenschmidt 1877–1968
Estonian born world champion wrestler and weightlifter, he also wrote many books on physical fitness and wrestling. Cremated here.

William Haines 1778–1848
Engraver and painter specialising in miniatures.

Walter Hann 1838–1922
Artist and scenery painter, his work included the scenery for the first production of *Peter Pan*. Memorial destroyed.

Sir James Hannen 1821–94
A Lord of Appeal, he presided over the Parnell Enquiry 1888–1889.

Henry Harrod 1817–71
Lawyer, antiquary and author of *Gleanings Among the Castles and Convents of Norfolk* (1857).

Walter Hedgcock 1864–1932
Composer, organist and musical director and conductor at Crystal Palace.

John Herapath 1790–1868
Mathematician and journalist. Manager of *Herapath's Railway Journal* in which he advocated the atmospheric railway.

Lewis Hertslet 1787–1870
Librarian at the Foreign Office.

William Higgs 1824–83
Of Higgs and Hill, building contractors, founded in 1874.

John Hilton 1804–78
Surgeon extraordinary to Queen Victoria and a president of the Royal College of Surgeons.

Alfred Hunter 1828–1911
Organ builder, his finest work is the organ at St James's, Spanish Place. His firm was absorbed by Willis.

SIR WILLIAM HUNTER 1781–1856
Lord Mayor of London 1851–52.

DOUGLAS JERROLD 1803–57
Author, journalist and newspaper proprietor. He edited *Lloyds News*. Memorial destroyed but reinstated.

LAWSTON JOHNSTON 1839–1900
Invented the manufacture of Bovril 1875, sold his company for £2m in 1896 and died on his yacht in Cannes.

SIR HORACE JONES 1819–87
Architect-surveyor to the City of London, he designed several markets and assisted in the design of Tower Bridge.

CAPT. JAMES JONES –1878
Surveyor and H.M.'s representative in the Persian Gulf 1853–58.

WILLIAM KEARNS 1794–1856
Irish born composer, violinist and singing teacher. Memorial destroyed.

SAMUEL KERSHAW 1836–1914
Librarian at Lambeth Palace for forty years and historian of Surrey.

SIR JOHN KEY 1794–1858
Lord Mayor of London 1830–31.

THOMAS KING 1835–88
Prize fighter, a champion of England 1862, and bookmaker.

JAMES KNOWLES 1806–84
London architect, he laid out Leicester Square in 1874.

KATHERINE LANNER (MRS GERALDINI) 1829–1908
Austrian born ballet dancer who performed all over Europe and in New York. Having retired to London she produced numerous ballets and pantomimes.

ALEXANDER LEE 1802–51
Composer and manager of Drury Lane and Strand Theatres. Memorial destroyed.

JAMES LEE –1880
Editor of *Bells Weekly Messenger* and the *Farmers' Journal*.

THOMAS LETTS 1803–72
Manufacturer of calendars, interest tables and especially diaries, he issued twenty-eight varieties in 1839.

Richard Limpus 1824–75
Composer and founder of the College of Organists. Monument destroyed

Hannibal McArthur 1788–1861
Queensland pioneer and M.P. in New South Wales. Memorial destroyed.

Gilbert H. MacDermott 1845–1901
Singer, famous for the song, 'We don't want to fight, but by jingo if we do', hence the word 'jingoism'

John MacGregor 1797–1856
At an early age emigrated to Canada and became a member of the House of Assembly. Returning to Scotland he became M.P. for Glasgow (1847) and wrote extensively on commercial and historical subjects. Defrauded the Royal British Bank of which he was a director and died a fugitive abroad.

Edmund Maddick –1939
Surgeon. He also built the Scala Theatre, Charlotte Street, and was director of cinematography during the First World War.

Robert Mallett 1810–81
Irish born civil engineer. Joined the family iron foundry which built bridges, railway stations and the Fastnet lighthouse. Author of numerous scientific papers.

William Maltby 1763–1854
Librarian of the London Institution 1809–54.

Sir Augustus Manns 1823–1907
Director of music at the Crystal Palace for fifty years.

Gideon Mantell 1790–1852
Geologist, archaeologist and discoverer of the iguanodon. The tomb was badly damaged in 1987 but restored in 1992 with the help of grants from English Heritage and the Geologists' Association.

Edward Mappin 1827–75
One of the original partners in the cutlery firm which bears his name.

William Marsden 1796–1867
Founder of the Royal Free and Marsden Hospitals.

Joseph Maudslay 1801–67
Engineer in partnership with Joshua Field (q.v.); pioneer of marine engine technology.

Sir Hiram Maxim 1840–1916
Inventor of the Maxim gun, he also conducted experiments in powered flight.

Moses Merryweather 1791–1872
Steam fire-engine manufacturer.

Thomas Miller 1807–74
Began life as a basketmaker, became an author and historian of London. Memorial demolished.

William Miller 1817–70
Professor of chemistry at King's College, London, 1845–70. He published work on wide ranging subjects: astronomy, deep sea soundings, meteorology and chemistry. Memorial demolished.

Robert Moffat 1795–1883
Missionary to South Africa, his daughter married David Livingstone.

William Mortlock 1832–81
Cricketer, known as 'Old Stonewall' he played longstop for Surrey and was a member of the first England touring team in Australia 1861. Memorial base only.

Dr Charles Murchison 1830–75
Physician, president of the Pathological Society 1877–79. He published 311 scientific works.

Alexander Murray –1888
Scottish born author of numerous guides and history books.

George Myers 1803–75
Builder, he executed all Pugin's major buildings besides many important public and military contracts. Memorial demolished.

Lt.Col.Sir William Napier 1785–1860
Served under the Duke of Wellington and author of the *History of the Peninsular Campaign*.

Edward Neale 1805–46
Prize fighter.

Henry Noad 1815–77
Professor of chemistry at St George's Hospital 1847–77. He specialised in the study of electricity and its properties. Memorial demolished.

John Oakley 1813–87
Prize winning emery paper and knife polish manufacturer.

Edith O'Gorman 1842–1929
'The escaped nun'. She was a member of an American convent 1862–68 following which she denounced the Catholic Church in her books and lectures.

George Oliver (George Conquest) 1837–1901
Acrobat and pantomime performer, he developed the 'flying ballet' in which actors 'flew' about the stage suspended from wires. Subsequently as a theatre manager he wrote and produced his own pantomimes and melodramas.

David Osbaldiston 1794–1851
Shakespearian actor and controversial manager of Sadlers Wells and the Royal Victoria Theatre (the Old Vic). Memorial demolished.

Princess Eugenie Palaeologu –1934
'Descendant of the Grecian Emperors of Byzantium', she claimed descent from Constantine the Great.

Alexander Parkes 1813–90
Inventor, he took out forty-six patents, most of them connected with the deposition of metals by electricity, also the method of using zinc for desilverisation of lead and the discovery of celluloid. Memorial demolished.

Charles Pearson 1793–1862
Solicitor and promoter of the Metropolitan underground railway.

John Pepper 1821–98
Chemist, teacher, author, illusionist and inventor of 'Pepper's Ghost' (1862) which he exhibited worldwide.

Rev. William Phelps 1776–1856
A Somerset vicar for forty years. Author of the *History and Antiquities of Somerset* which he did not live to complete.

Philip Phillips 1802–1864
Theatrical scene painter and artist. Memorial demolished.

Sir John Pirie 1781–1851
Shipowner and Lord Mayor of London 1841–42. Memorial demolished.

Christopher Pond 1826–81
Wine merchant and builder of the Criterion theatre and restaurant. He helped finance the first England cricket team to tour Australia in 1861.

Edward Poole 1830–67
Arabic and Biblical scholar, editor of three volumes of *The Thousand and One Nights*.

Sophia Poole 1804–91
Lived in Egypt 1842–49 and wrote extensively on the country, especially her book *Englishwoman in Egypt* (1844–46).

COL. JOHN PORTE 1884–1919
Revolutionised the design of the British flying boat during the Great War.

SAMUEL PROUT 1783–1852
Watercolour painter specialising in architectural subjects.

REV. WILLIAM PUNSHON 1824–81
Methodist minister, he spent many years in Canada, president of the Wesleyan Conference 1874.

MARIO RAGGI 1821–1907
Italian born sculptor, his work includes the statue of Disraeli in Parliament Square.

SOPHIA RAINCOCK –1890
Artist. Her sister, Harriet, was the first person to be buried in Norwood in 1837. Memorial destroyed.

AUGUSTUS RALLI –1872
Eldest son of a Greek merchant, who, with his four brothers originated from the Island of Scios. The five traded as Ralli Bros. Three other brothers: John, Eustratio and Pandia are also buried here.

ELEANOR RATHBONE 1872–1946
M.P. who campaigned for the introduction of the Family Allowance.

ANGUS REACH 1821–56
Journalist on the *Illustrated London News* and *Punch*; author of *The Natural History of Bores*, *The Natural History of Humbugs*, etc. Monument destroyed.

DAVID ROBERTS 1796–1864
Artist, specialising in Near East topographical subjects.

THOMAS ROBSON 1822–64
Comedian, 'the greatest comic actor of his day'. Memorial destroyed.

WILLIAM ROUPELL 1831–1909
Illegitimate son of a lead ash smelter whose estate he acquired through forgery. M.P. for Lambeth 1857 until 1862 when he was convicted of his crimes. Memorial destroyed.

JOHN SAUNDERS 1867–1919
Violinist with the John Saunders Quartet and leader of the Royal Philharmonic Society and the Russian Ballet orchestra.

MARY SCRIVEN –1936
Died aged 104, the oldest person buried in the cemetery.

DR EDWARD SEYMOUR 1796–1866
Physician and medical writer. Specialised in treating mental diseases for which he freely prescribed opium.

Sir George Shenton 1842–1907
Australian banker, businessman and goldmine owner. Eleven times mayor of Perth and president of the Legislative Council of Western Australia 1892–96.

William Simms 1793–1860
Mathematical instrument maker especially of equipment used in observatories. Monument destroyed but new stone on site of grave.

William Simpson 1828–97
Librarian at St. Pauls for sixteen years, he wrote a history of the cathedral.

Sir Lumley Skeffington 1771–1850
Fop and playwright, confidant of the Prince Regent and inventor of the colour Skeffington brown. Caricatured by Gillray and dubbed 'an admirable specimen of the florid Gothic'. Memorial destroyed.

John Smith –1892
Originator of the words 'Not Negotiable' for crossed cheques.

Sir Lumley Smith 1834–1918
Judge in the Central Criminal Court 1901–13.

Richard Smith 1786–1855
Actor, specialising in 'infernal parts'. His collection of theatrical memorabilia was presented to the British Museum. Memorial destroyed.

Thomas Sopwith 1803–79
Mining engineer and pioneer in the recording of geological features in mines. Kept a diary for fifty-eight years, contained in 170 volumes.

Tom Spring 1795–1851
Prize fighter, a champion of England in 1821, he lost an eye while boxing in 1818.

Rev. Charles Spurgeon 1834–92
Preacher and founder of the Metropolitan Tabernacle in 1861. His funeral attracted a greater number of mourners than any other in the cemetery's history.

Edward Stephens –1861
An early settler in South Australia and a member of the Colonial Legislative Council.

Mill Stephenson –1937
Antiquary, best known for *A List of Monumental Brasses in the British Isles* (1926). Cremated, no memorial.

John Stevens –1861
Railway engineer, inventor and patentee of the semaphore signalling system.

JAMES STIFF 1808–97
Potter and founder in 1862 of the stoneware and terracotta manufactory named after him.

THOMAS STOUGHTON 1848–1917
Founder, with Matthew Hodder, of the publishing company bearing their names in 1868.

THOMAS STRANGE 1808–84
A judge in India for thirty-one years and a biblical scholar.

SIR THOMAS TALFOURD 1795–1854
Judge and playwright of historical tragedies.

SIR HENRY TATE 1919–99
Sugar merchant, philanthropist and founder of the Tate Gallery (terracotta mausoleum designed by E. George and Peto).

DAVID THOMAS 1813–94
Hymn writer and congregational minister, he helped found the University of Wales at Aberystwyth in 1872.

DR THEOPHILUS THOMPSON 1807–60
Physician. He specialised in the treatment of consumption and introduced the use of cod liver oil into England.

HENRY THORNTON 1800–81
Banker and partner in William Deacon & Co.

RICHARD THORNTON 1776–1865
Lloyds underwriter and philanthropist, sometimes known as the 'Duke of Dantzic'.

GEORGE TINWORTH 1843–1913
One of the most gifted artists at Doulton's pottery, he executed numerous religious works. Memorial demolished.

SIR FRANCIS TRUSCOTT 1824–95
Lord Mayor of London 1879–80, he erected the griffin in place of Temple Bar.

JAMES TURLE 1802–82
Organist and choirmaster at Westminster Abbey from 1831 until his death, during which time he composed a great deal of church music. His son Henry Turle (1835–83), editor of *Notes and Queries* is buried in the same vault.

SHARON TURNER 1768–1847
Lawyer and historian of the Anglo-Saxons.

NATHANIAL WARD 1806-93
Doctor and botanist, he invented 'Wardian Cases' for the transport of living plants. Memorial demolished.

JOHN WATTS 1786-1858
Partner of John Doulton in the Lambeth pottery firm that bore their name.

WALTER WATTS-DUNTON 1832-1914
Poet, novelist and friend of Swinburne.

HARRIET WAYLETT 1800-51
Actress, known as Kate Kearney. Memorial demolished.

RICHARD WEBSTER, LORD ALVERSTONE, 1842-1915
Lord Chief Justice of England 1900-13. While at the bar he earned more money than any other barrister had done before. M.P. for the Isle of White 1885-1900

THOMAS WEBSTER 1810-75
Lawyer, he wrote a standard work on patent law in 1844. As a member of the Society of Arts he was active in promoting the Great Exhibition of 1851.

JAMES WESTMACOTT 1823-1900
One of the famous Westmacott family of sculptors.

SIR JOSEPH WHITAKER 1820-95
Publisher and founder of *Whitaker's Almanac* in 1868. Memorial demolished.

SIR ARNOLD WHITE 1830-93
Solicitor to Queen Victoria.

WILLIAM WILLIAMS 1820-92
Traveller, lecturer and scientific writer. His interests were various and the subjects of his books included walking, cooking, chemistry, explosives and phrenology.

JOHN WITHERS 1823-1911
A survivor from the charge of the Light Brigade.

WILLIAM WOODINGTON 1806-93
Sculptor and painter, he designed the bronze relief of the Battle of the Nile on Nelson's column. Memorial demolished.

SIR ALBERT WOODS 1816-1904
Garter King of Arms 1869-1904.

CHARLES WOOLLEY 1846-1922
Accountant, collector of pottery and historian of Lambeth. Memorial demolished.

WILLIAM WRIGHT 1837–99
Editor of the British and Foreign Bible Society publications, historian of the Hittites.

WILLIAM WYON 1795–1851
Engraver and medallist at the Royal Mint. He designed the profile of Queen Victoria for the Penny Black.

JOHN YARROW 1818–98
Poet, orator and painter.

WILLESDEN CEMETERY
FRANKLYN ROAD, NW10

Founded: 1891
Owner: London Borough of Brent
Acreage: 26

A flat square-shaped ground, what it lacks in notable tombs is compensated for by some fine chestnut trees and, originally, a pair of unique 'Pont Street Dutch' brick chapels. They were the competition winning designs of Charles H. Worley and a source of deliberation by the Burial Board, which 'found that the labours of the hanging committee of the Royal Academy were as nothing to theirs in exhibiting the designs in the vestry hall'.[1] After 'stormy, tempestuous, passionate' debate the decision was made and at a solemn stone laying ceremony the newspapers of the day and the names of the Willesden Burial Board were placed in bottles beneath the foundation stones of each chapel. A customary marquee lunch followed and a number of less solemn toasts. F.A. Wood, a local worthy and historian, standing in for the absent vicar, was uncertain how to propose a toast, 'success to the cemetery', he said, amid laughter, 'would look as though he wished the cemetery to be filled as soon as possible'.[2] £20,000 was spent on the cemetery including the cost of land and it is deplorable that now, after so much care had been taken with their foundation, the chapels were closed in 1982 and demolished four years later. A tarmac turning point has replaced them. Not only that but at the entrance the Borough has continued to spoil Worley's original design by adding a pair of incongruous urns on the piers and building a new lodge instead of adapting the chapels.

Over 80,000 burials have taken place at Willesden and in an attempt to create room for further burials, graves now fill one of the main paths which resemble a marble traffic jam. As an alternative solution, towards the back of the cemetery earth has been piled up to provide space for yet more.

Only a few monuments are worth discovering. There is a large granite globe above the Allen grave (1919), and a carved child angel holding a lace edged funeral pall commemorating four year old Leopold William (1896), while the mawkish figure of Georgina 'Georgie' Robinson in her wedding dress records that she was killed in a car accident while returned from her honeymoon in France in 1965. Near her is a crouching winged angel holding a scroll in the grave of Margaret Royance (1945) and beyond that a headstone on the Golds grave (1947) revealing three musical quotations, including one on the reverse. Sadly the bust of Leah Nathan (1913) which sheltered under a canopy is missing. Another memorial that catches the imagination is a heap of granite rocks and the enigmatic inscription, 'Ernest Schwarz of the Kalahari', who died in Senegal in 1928. *The Times* described him as being '. . . remembered chiefly for his persistent advocacy of a scheme for the irrigation of the Kalahari desert, or, more accurately, a considerable portion of that vast area.'[3] Behind it is a curious memorial to Lolita Strauss (1958) bearing a small bronze aeroplane and relief sculpture.

WIMBLEDON CEMETERY
Gap Road, SW19

Founded: 1877
Owner: London Borough of Merton
Acreage: 28

The cemetery must be placed firmly in the second division. Two Gothic chapels, each with a small broach spire, were by Sir Banister Fletcher and the ground 'laid out' for £6,000, but it is not a very distinguished complex and rather spoiled by a glass roofed mortuary placed squarely in the middle.[1] This and the Roman Catholic Chapel are now disused. The best memorial is the Cooke mausoleum, dated 1885, which stands vulnerably abandoned near the western boundary. It is a mongrel Italianate structure with a stepped pyramid roof built using quantities of pink and grey granite and originally stained glass, but its prominence has attracted vandals and it is now in a sorry state.

The prime grave plots near the main path have been cornered by local dignitaries, mayors and councillors of the Borough. A stone commemorating Belgian refugees who died in Wimbledon during the Great War stands in the south east Roman Catholic corner, among a strong Irish contingent. Here, a large statue of the martyr, St Barbara and her emblem, a tower (she is the patron saint of gunners and miners), is a prominent feature on the Fakler grave (1928).

The original twenty acres of the cemetery were enlarged by a further eight near the railway, isolating the original brick gate piers which now stand adrift.

Frederick Barnard 1846–96
Artist, cartoonist for *Punch* and *The Illustrated London News*, he also illustrated works by Dickens and Thackeray.

Sir Thomas Molony 1865–1949
The last Lord Chief Justice of Ireland 1918–24.

Sir Westby Perceval 1854–1928
Agent General for New Zealand 1891–96 and Tasmania 1896–98.

Sir Colin Scott-Moncrieff 1836–1916
Colonial administrator, he took part in suppressing the Indian mutiny.

Wimbledon: The Cooke Mausoleum (1885). It has been vandalised since this photograph was taken in 1980.

WOODGRANGE PARK CEMETERY
Romford Road, E7

Founded: 1888
Owner: Badgehurst Ltd
Acreage: 28

Woodgrange Park has seen better days. The cemetery was dedicated during a short ceremony on 12 February 1888 immediately prior to the first interment: a child from Bromley. In declaring the cemetery open, the chairman of Woodgrange Park Cemetery Company, Henry Laurence Hammack, said that '. . . those who entrusted their dead to the Company for interment, might rest assured that the remains of their friends would receive most careful and reverential guardianship.' Shamefully, that promise has not been fulfilled as today the cemetery is in a shocking state. Where memorials have not been cleared there is thick undergrowth and rubbish. The only trees are those that line the short avenue leading from the gates to the area once occupied by the brick Gothic style chapel designed by W. Gillbee Scott.[1] Inside, a memorial plaque recorded the efforts of Mr Hammack, an alderman of the ward of Bishopsgate who died in 1894. By the 1990s the chapel was totally derelict having been stripped of all furnishings, covered in thick ivy and the roof in a state of collapse. Demolition took place in October 2006 following a fire. More recently a new two-storey office has appeared at the entrance to the cemetery.

There are few exceptional tombs save some polished granite examples that line the drive. A squat temple on a plinth protects the relief portrait of William Matthews (1915) and a marble vase sheltered beneath stone slabs on columns commemorates the Murphy family. Clearance of memorials has made way for new Muslim graves and a padlocked enclosure is reserved for The Muslim Patel Burial Trust. In an unmarked grave are the bodies of five Iranian terrorists, shot during the Iranian Embassy siege of 1980. In another section is the memorial to Miss M. McLean who died in 1904. It was erected by officers and sailors of the Imperial Japanese navy and the

Woodgrange Park: Artists' impression of the chapel by W. Gilbee Scott from *The Architect* (1889)

Woodgrange Park: The Chapel in 2005: It was demolished a year later.

inscription is of Japanese characters. There is also a fine terracotta memorial now displaced from the Gamble grave (1904).

A large area near the railway has been cleared of graves and their contents to make way for a new housing estate. In 1990 a proposal to build a crematorium was explored but this came to nothing.

Frederick Charrington 1850–1936
'The Great Temperance Advocate', despite being a member of the well known family of brewers.

Walter Cornish –1919
Murdered with his wife and two daughters at Forest Gate, victims of Henry Perry a former soldier.

Charles Mare 1814–98
Ship and bridge builder. He pioneered the use of iron in the construction of H.M.S *Warrior* (1861) and built the Britannia bridge at Conway and the Albert bridge at Saltash.

WOOD GREEN CEMETERY
WOLVES LANE, N22

Founded: 1995
Owner: London Borough of Haringey
Acreage: 8

Opened on land that was formerly a nursery and recreation ground, Wood Green is an unusual attempt to create a modern cemetery in an urban setting. It is described as being popular with borough residents – particularly the Cypriot and Turkish community – possibly on account of pebbles used in place of grass interspersed with palms and cordylines as well as more traditional rose beds. Add to that the zany bamboo shelters with their hanging baskets and the cemetery takes on a Mediterranean air.

The Muslim burial ground shelters behind a line of dense fir trees on Wolves Lane with graves facing east and marked out by wooden surrounds. More conventional are the rows of lawn memorials in black granite and white marble beyond the car park. Much thought has been given to the overall landscaping of the site which is well maintained and generously planted. As a result the borough has created both a tranquil and innovative setting for this busy cemetery.

WOOLWICH CEMETERIES
KING'S HIGHWAY AND CAMDALE ROAD, SE18

Founded: 1856
Owner: London Borough of Greenwich.
Acreage: 32 ½

The cemetery is divided into two sections. The old part of twelve acres, fronting Kings Highway, is an excellent example of how Victorian cemeteries can be adapted successfully into something like a country park while preserving their main features. It has the advantage of a hillside position, formerly part of Plumstead Common, surrounded by a large number of large flourishing trees – cedars, Scots pine and copper beech. The south London architectural practice of Church, Quick and Whinchop, who also designed Plumstead Cemetery and several local public buildings, were responsible for the Early English style chapel with its sizeable tower. It sits on the brow of the hill providing the main architectural accent in the landscape now that a small dissenters chapel and a lodge have been demolished. Around it a number of tombstones have been pruned but the best are retained. These include a white marble Celtic cross of massive proportions which commemorates the *Princess Alice* disaster in 1878 and is inscribed on the plinth as follows:

The Saloon Steamer 'Princess Alice' returning from a pleasure excursion was wrecked off Tripcock Point by collision with the steamer collier 'Bywell Castle' on the night of September 3rd 1878. It was computed that 700 men women and children were on board, of these about 550 drowned and 120 were buried near this place. To the memory of those who perished this cross was erected by a National Sixpenny Subscription to which more than 23,000 persons contributed.[1]

Woolwich: The lodge and the chapel on the right have been demolished

Compared with this unprecedented tragedy the inscription on another, rather smaller Celtic cross nearby, is of little consequence, but the import of its message sums up much that is peculiar to the Victorian age:

> To the memory of Temple Leighton Phipson-Wybrants late Captain
> 75th Regiment (Gordon Highlanders) who died on his 34th birthday
> November 29th 1880 while in command of an expedition exploring the
> Sabi River, Eastern Africa. His body through his mother's devotion
> October 7th 1881 now rests here.[2]

The later section of the cemetery which was brought into use in 1885 can be reached through the gates past the chapel. It is comparatively uninteresting save for a small relief sculpture of Sister Gladys Richards-Lockwood M.M. (1955) depicted in spectacles and nurse's uniform and the angel standing next to a suited figure on the Ellis grave (1932).

Brompton: Notice to visitors

Notes

AUTHORS' NOTE TO THE FOURTH EDITION
1. Curl, J.S. *Death and Architecture* (Stroud, 2002)
2. For full contact details of all the cemeteries and crematoria see Wolfson, P. *Greater London Cemeteries and Crematoria* (6th edition revised by Cliff Webb) (London: 1999)

INTRODUCTION
1. Sims.G.R. (Ed.), *Living London,* (London, 1906), pp. 81–87
2. Stone, Mrs, *God's Acre of Historical Notes Relating to Churchyards,* (London, 1858), p.115

HISTORY
1. For more detailed accounts of the development of the nineteenth century cemeteries see Curl, J.S. *Death and Architecture,* (Stroud, 2002); Elliot, B. 'The Landscape of the English Cemetery' *Landscape Design,* No 184 (October, 1989), pp. 13–14; Rugg, J. 'The Origins and Progress of Cemetery Establishment in Britain' in the *Changing Face of Death: Historical Accounts of Death and Disposal* Jupp, P.C. and Howarth, G. (Eds.) (Basingstoke, 1997); Arnold, C. *Necropolis: London and its Dead,* (London, 2006)
2. *The Builder,* Vol. 1, 8 April 1843, p.104
3. Dickens, C. *The Uncommercial Traveller,* (London, 1860), p. 233
4. Dickens, C. *Bleak House,* (London, 1852–3), p. 207
5. *Household Words,* Dec 14 1840, quoted by Mrs Basil Holmes, *The London Burial Grounds,* (London, 1896), p. 217
6. Dickens, C. *The Uncommercial Traveller,* (London, 1860), p. 91
7. Walker, G. *Gatherings from Graveyards . . . ,*(London, 1839), p. 202
8. Victoria Park was one of the few cemeteries to open and close in London during the nineteenth century. Comprising 11 acres, the cemetery was privately owned and managed until being laid out in 1894 by the Metropolitan Public Gardens

Association. Nothing remains of the cemetery except the entrance arch on Usk Road E2, and the enclosed parkland is now called Meath Gardens. See Holmes, B. op.cit; Tegg, W. *The Last Act Being the Funeral Rites of Nations and Individuals.* (London, 1876), and *The Builder*, Vol. 8, 1 September 1860, p. 558; Vol. 29, 21 October 1871, p. 822; Vol, 31. 15 March 1873, p. 201

9 Holmes, Mrs Basil, op. cit. p.192 ff
10 Walker, George, op. cit. p.154
11 See Jupp. P.C. 'Enon Chapel: No Way for the Dead' in the *Changing Face of Death: Historical Accounts of Death and Disposal* Jupp, P.C. and Howarth, G. (Eds) (Basingstoke, 1997)
12 From 'Mr Van-Brugg's Proposals about Building ye new Churches' Bodleian Ms. Eng. Hist. B.2. ff. 47, published in Laurence Whistler, *The Imagination of Vanburgh and his Fellow Artists*, (London, 1954), Appendix 2, p.251
13 The history of the development of British cemeteries is described by Brooks, C. *Mortal Remains...* (Exeter, 1989)
14 See Nierop-Reading, B. 'The Rosary Cemetery' *Landscape Design*, No 184 (October, 1989), pp. 48–50
15 Chadwick, E. *A. Supplementary Report to Her Majesty's Secretary of State for the Home Department form the Poor Law Commissioners on the Results of a Special Inquiry into the Practice of interment in Towns*, (London, 1843). p.199
16 See *The Builder*, Vol. 8, 2 March 1850, p. 204 and Vol. 14, 25 October 1856, p. 587
17 *The Builder*, Vol. 8, 5 January 1850, p.10
18 Parsons, B. *Committed to the Cleansing Flame: The Development of Cremation in Nineteenth Century England*, (Reading, 2005)
19 'Golders Green Crematorium, brief History,' typescript provided by the Company, n.d.
20 *Special Report: Memorial Safety in Local Authority Cemeteries*, Local Government Ombudsman, (2006)
21 Located in Birchen Grove, Kingsbury near the Brent Reservoir, the cemetery was purchased in 1929 by the Borough of Willesden. The site was purchased and partly enclosed by railings and massive gate piers; a single chapel, lodge and shelter were also constructed. The scheme was abandoned when Willesden merged with Wembley Borough to form Brent Council in 1965 and it was decided that sufficient burial space existed at Carpenders' Park Cemetery which Wembley had opened in 1954. The site now accommodates a nature reserve, garden centre and buildings although the chapel, lodge and shelter still remain.
22 *Planning for Burial Space in London*, London Planning Advisory Committee, (1997)
23 Davies, D. & Shaw, A. *Reusing Old Graves*, (Kent, 1995)
24 *The Builder*, Vol. 1, 11 March 1843, p.53

PLANNING

1 Letter to *The Morning Post*, (undated but sold as part of lot 137 at Sotheby's, Bond Street, 12 June 1980)

2 From an unidentified newspaper cutting (sold at Sotheby's as above)
3 Willson, Thomas, *The Pyramid, A General Metropolitan Cemetery to be erected in the vicinity of Primrose Hill,* (London, 1842), p.1. ff
4 *The Builder,* Vol. 3, 12 April 1845, p.177
5 *The Builder,* Vol. 8, 2 March 1850, p.104
6 Loudon, John, op. cit, Preface
7 Loudon, John, op. cit, p.14
8 Loudon, John, op. cit, p.38
9 Loudon, John, op. cit, p.44
10 Loudon, John, op. cit, p.44
11 Chadwick, Sir Edwin, op. cit, (Ch. 11 ref. 10) p. 144
12 See Rugg, J. 'Lawn Cemeteries: the emergence of a new landscape of death' *Urban History* Vol. 33, No. 2 (2006) pp.213–233
13 *The Times,* 7 December, 1936.

MONUMENTS AND BUILDINGS

1 Hakewill, Arthur, *Modern Tombs, or gleanings from the Public Cemeteries of London* (London, 1851), p. 4 ff.
2 *The Builder,* Vol. 37, 1879, p 250
3 Pugin, A.W.N., *An Apology for the Revival of Christian Architecture in England,* (London, 1843), p 37
4 British Institute of Industrial Art, *The Art of Graveyard Monuments,* (London, 1925), p.17
5 Jones, B. *Design for Death,* (London, 1967), p.229
6 At the back of Croft, H.J. *Guide to Kensal Green Cemetery,* (London, 1881)
7 *The Builder,* Vol. 40, 11 June 1881, p741
8 Quoted in the *Survey of London. Northern Kensington',* Vol. 37, London, 1973, p.337
9 Loudon, John, *On the laying out, planting and managing of Cemeteries and on the improvement of Churchyards* (London, 1843). (ch. 111 ref .6), p.153

EPITAPHS

1 *The Builder,* Vol. 40, 11 June 1881, p.741
2 *Ainsworth's Magazine,* Vol. 2, 1842, p.180
3 Graham, H. *More Ruthless Rhymes for Heartless Homes,* (London, 1930), p.42

FLORA AND FAUNA

1 Loudon, J. *The Gardener's Magazine,* 1843, p.105
2 Wright, T. *History and Antiquities of London,* (London, 1837), p. 397
3 Quoted by Loudon, J. *On the laying out, planting and managing of Cemeteries* (1843) (ch. III, ref. 6), p. 46
4 Clark, B. *Handbook for Visitors to Kensal Green Cemetery,* (London, 1843), p. 8 ff
5 Collison, G. *Cemetery Interment,* (London, 1840), p. 112
6 *The Builder,* Vol. 21, 24 October 1863, p. 755

7 *Abney Park Cemetery Company*, Hendon Park Cemetery, (London, 1903), p. 8 ff
8 ibid
9 Sims, G.R. (Ed.), op. cit. (ch. I, ref. 1), p. 82 ff
10 Holmes, Mrs B. *The London Burial Grounds. Notes on their History from the earliest times to the Present Day* (London, 1896), p.303
11 The 'Friends of Highgate Cemetery Newsletter' (1978)
12 Howard, J. and R. *A Self-Guided Walk Around the Trees of Brompton Cemetery*, (London, 2003)
13 London wildweb
14 Loudon, op.cit,. p. 21

ABNEY PARK
1 Abney Park Cemetery Company, op.cit, (ch.VI, ref.8), p.6
2 Loudon, John, op.cit, (ch.III, ref.6), p.22
3 In 1872 the 18th century Fleetwood House was demolished and its grounds added to the cemetery.
4 Barker, Rev. T. *Abney Park Cemetery: A Complete Descriptive Guide . . .* etc., 1869, p.21 ff
5 Barker, Rev. T. op.cit., p.32
6 They were listed in 1975 along with many memorials.
7 In an advertisement in Barker, Rev. T. op.cit
8 Holmes, Mrs Basil, op.cit, (ch.II, ref.4), p.256
9 Holmes, Mrs Basil, op.cit, p.136.
10 Barker, Rev. Thomas, op.cit., p.20.

BANDON HILL
1 See *The Sutton and Epsom Advertiser and Surrey County Reporter*, 13 January, 1900

BARNES COMMON
1 For a photo of the lodge, entrance gates and chapel see Brown, M. (Ed.) *Barnes and Old Mortlake Past with East Sheen*, (London, 1997)
2 See Parsons, B. *Committed to the Cleansing Flame: The Development of Cremation in Nineteenth Century England*, (Reading, 2005)

BATTERSEA NEW
1 See *The Builder*, Vol. 51, 7 April 1893

BATTERSEA ST. MARY'S
1 The Parsee burial custom is probably the most extraordinary of all. The body, clad in white, is carried by Parsee Zoroastrian bearers to a Tower of Silence. These Towers have no roof or windows, only a small iron door. The body is placed inside and left exposed to the sun and the vultures. This ritual is determined by the Zoroastrian belief that fire, earth and water are sacred elements that should not be contaminated by the dead. In England there is no Tower and the rules have been

relaxed to permit earth burial or cremation, preferably in a furnace fuelled by gas or electricity.

Brompton
1 Collison, George, op.cit, (ch.VI,ref.5),p.180
2 *The Builder*, Vol. 30, 7 September 1872, p.710

Brookwood
1 See Clarke, J.M. *London's Necropolis: A Guide to Brookwood Cemetery*, (Stroud, 2004) for a comprehensive history of the cemetery
2 Clarke, J.M. *The Brookwood Necropolis Railway*, Fourth Edition, (Usk, 2006)

Bunhill Fields
1 From Maitland's *History of London*, 1756 quoted by Mrs Basil Holmes, op.cit.(ch. ii,ref.4),p.134 See also Light, A.W. *Bunhill Fields* (London, 1915) two volumes. *The Official Guide to Bunhill Fields*, (London, 1991)

Camberwell
1 Blanch, W. *Ye Parish of Camberwell . . . etc.*, (London, 1875), p.131
2 The cemetery was used extensively in the film *Entertaining Mr Sloane*, (1969)
3 Letter to the *South London Press*, 11 June, 1890
4 Blanch, W. op. cit. p.130
5 Letter to the *South London Press*, 30 April, 1892
6 Woollacott, R. *Camberwell Old Cemetery: London's Forgotten Valhalla*, (London, 2000)

Camberwell New
1 See *The Builder*, 12 April, 1929 for an illustration of the chapels
2 Pevsner, Sir Nikolaus, *The Buildings of England, London 2 South*, 1983, p.618.
3 See *The Architects' Journal*, 6 April, 1939. See also *The Municipal Journal and Public Works Engineer*, 31 March 1939. The crematorium entrance buildings and cemetery chapels were listed in 1998.

Charlton
1 *Illustrated London News*, 10 January 1857, p.13

Chingford Mount
1 Report on the opening of the cemetery May 1884, in the Waltham Forest Central Reference Library
2 Brown, W. *St Pancras, Open Spaces and Disused Burial Grounds*, (London, 1902), p.67

Chiswick New
1 Parsons, B. 'Mortlake and the Art Deco Influence' *Journal of the Institute of Burial and Cremation Administration*, Vol. 71 No. 3 (2003), pp.20–23

City of London

1. Vaes, G. *Les Cimetières de Londres*, (Brussels, 1978), p.33. For a history of the cemetery see Lambert, D. *The Cemetery in a Garden: 150 Years of the City of London Cemetery and Crematorium*, (London, 2006)
2. Haywood, W. *Report to the Honourable Commissioners of Sewers of the City of London*, (London, 1849), p.7.ff
3. Haywood, W. *Report*... etc. 1852, p.144
4. Minutes of the City Cemetery Board, September 1854, p.24
5. *The Builder*, Vol. 13 1855, p.578
6. *The Builder*, Vol. 14 1856, p.102
7. Haywood, W. *Report*... etc. 1858, p.26.
8. See *The Building News*, 2 August 1901, p.137 and 16 August 1901, p.207 and *The Undertakers' Journal*, 15 November 1904, pp.230–231 and Jones, P.H. and Noble, G. E, (Eds.) *Cremation in Great Britain*, Second Edition (London, 1931), p. 24. The entrance, lodges, cottages, cemetery chapels and old crematorium have all been listed.
9. Holmes, Mrs Basil, op.cit, (ch.II,ref.4),p.191

Crystal Palace

1. See *The Builder*, Vol. 32, 7 November 1874, pp.923–24

Eastbrookend

1. See *The Undertakers' Journal*, September 1914, pp.259–60 for photos of the construction work, chapel and lodge. See also September 1917, p.247

East London

1. See *Pharos*, Vol. 20 No. 1, (1954) p.15
2. For an account of this tragedy see Neal, W. *With Disastrous Consequences: London Disasters 1830–1917* (London, 1992) pp.1–28. Other victims were buried at Woolwich, West Ham and Tower Hamlets
3. Sims, G.R. (Ed.),op.cit. (ch.I,ref.1), p.86

East Sheen

1. A full history of the cemetery can be found on the Council's website. The cemetery records are also available for searching online.

Edmonton

1. See *The Building News*, 4 March 1887, and 17 May 1889

Enfield

1. See Jones, P.H. *Cremation in Great Britain*, Third Edition, (London, 1945) pp.66–67 See also *The Times*, 20 October, 1938

Golders Green Crematorium

1. See Grainger, H. 'Golders Green Crematorium and the architectural expression of cremation' *Mortality,* Vol. 5 No. 1 (2000), pp. 53–73; Jupp, P.C. and Grainger, H.J. (Eds.) *Golders Green Crematorium 1902–2000: A London centenary in context* (London, 2002); For descriptions of the buildings and photographs see Freeman, A.C. *Crematoria in Great Britain,* (London, 1906); Jones, P.H. and Noble, G.E. (Eds.) *Cremation in Great Britain* Second Edition (London, 1931) pp.20–22, and Johns, C. 'Golders Green Crematorium: A history and tour of Great Britain's most famous crematorium,' *Pharos International,* Vol. 59 No 3 (1993), pp. 134–9
2. *Building News,* Vol. 83 1902,p.789

Great Northern

1. Parsons, B. *Committed to the Cleansing Flame: The Development of Cremation in Nineteenth Century England,* (Reading: 2005) pp. 45–47
2. *The Builder,* Vol.19 1861,p.809. See Dawes, M.C. The End of the Line: The Story of the Railway Service to the Great Northern London Cemetery (Barnet, 2003)
3. *The Builder,* Vol. 20, 11 January, 1862, p.25
4. *The Builder,* Vol. 19, 23 November, 1861, p.809
5. *The Builder,* Vol. 20, 11 January, 1862, p.25

Greenlawn

1. *The Times,* 7 December, 1936

Gunnersbury

1. See *The Architects' Journal,* 4 July 1928. See also *The Builder,* Vol 152, January 22 1937. A defeated competitor was the country house architect, Sir Edward Guy Dawber.

Hammersmith New

1. See *The Builder,* 17 September, 1926
2. Hines, C. and Cheetham, K. *Art Deco London,* (London, 2003) p.56, and Parsons, B. 'Mortlake and the Art Deco Influence' *Journal of the Institute of Cemetery and Crematorium Management* Vol. 71 No. 3 (2003), pp. 20–23,and Jones, P.H. *Cremation in Great Britain,* Third Edition, (London, 1945), p.72 and p.118

Hampstead

1. See *The Architect,* Vol. 14, 9 October 1875, p.200 for illustrations see *The Builder,* Vol. 2, 25 November 1874, p.1147. The chapels were listed in 1974. The Bianchi and a number of other memorials are also listed.
2. See *The Architect,* Vol. 14, 7 August 1875, p.76
3. See *The Architect,* Vol. 67, 6 June, 1902

Hendon

1. See *The Builders' Journal and Architectural Record*, 11 November, 1896, p.219
2. Abney Park Cemetery Company, op.cit, (ch.VI, ref.8), p.8 ff.
3. *The Undertakers' Journal* 15 July, 1903 p.161
4. *The Undertakers' Journal* 15 March, 1922, p. 84
5. Ibid.

Highgate

1. See www.highgate-cemetery.org for details of opening times and access
2. 6 and 7 William IV c.136, local and personal. For a further history of the cemetery see *Highgate Cemetery: Victorian Valhalla* Photographs by John Gay and Introduction by Felix Barker (London, 1984) and Curl, J.S. *Death and Architecture*, (Stroud, 2002), pp.224–239
3. Minutes of the London Cemetery Company, 9 January, 1837
4. Justyne, W. *Guide to Highgate Cemetery*, (London 1865), p.1
5. Justyne, W. op.cit, p.38.
6. Lloyd, J. *The History, Topography and Antiquities of Highgate . . . etc.*, (Highgate 1888), p.494
7. Justyne, W. op.cit, p.16
8. Girouard, M. *Country Life*, 5 Aug 1971, p.334
9. Justyne, W. op.cit, p.33
10. *The Builder*, Vol.17, 1859, p.861.
11. Lloyd, J. op.cit, p.495
12. See Brooks. C. *Burying Tom Sayers: Heroism, Class and the Victorian Cemetery*. (London, 1989)

Hillingdon and Uxbridge

1. See *The Builder*, Vol. 25, 20 April, 1867, p.1149. The entrance arch was listed in 1974.
2. See *The Builder*, Vol. 55, 10 November, 1855, pp.546–47

Hither Green

1. See *Pharos*, Vol. 22 No. 2 1956 p.5, and *Funeral Service Journal*, 15 June, 1956 p.275

Jewish Cemetery Plashet Park

1. Sims, G.R. (Ed.), op.cit, (ch.1, ref.1), p.86

Liberal Jewish Cemetery Pound Lane

For further details of this cemetery and other Jewish cemeteries in the London area see Kadish, S. *Jewish Heritage in England: An Architectural Guide*, (London, 2006) (ch. 4)

Jewish Rowan Road
1 See *The Undertakers' Journal*, September, 1915 p.320

Jewish Cemetery Willesden
1 *The Builder*, Vol.31, 1873, p.822

Kensal Green
1 See Curl, J.S. (Ed.) *Kensal Green Cemetery. The Origin and Development of the General Cemetery of All Souls, Kensal Green, London, 1824–2001* (Chichester, 2001) for a comprehensive history of the cemetery.
2 2 and 3 William IV C.110, local and personal
3 *The Gentleman's Magazine*, Vol.102, 1832, pt.ii, p.246.
4 The entrance arch is not dissimilar to that at Brompton Cemetery
5 Collison, G. *Cemetery Interment*, (London, 1840) (ch.VI, ref.5), p.157
6 *Ainsworth's Magazine*, Vol.2, 1842, p.179
7 *The Builder*, Vol.12, 1854, p.460
8 Notice issued by the General Cemetery Company 1910

Kensington Hanwell
1 Report on Hanwell Chapel, Kensington, 1889. Kensington Central Library Ms.2295
2 Minutes of Kensington Council, 15 April, 1924

Kingston
1 The cemetery chapels were listed in 1983
2 The extension to the Garden of Remembrance was designed by Sidney C. Wilson and dedicated on 15 June 1958 by the Bishop of Kingston.
3 Chapman, W., *Handbook of Kingston*, (Kingston, 1877), p.89

Lambeth
1 *The Builder*, Vol. 12, 29 April 1854, p.222
2 *The Builder*, Vol. 32, 11 July 1874, p.582
3 *The Builder*, Vol.32. 28 March 1874, p.261
4 See *Pharos*, Vol. 25 No. 4 pp.18–19. The wood work in the chapel was carried out by the firm of George Hammer who also fitted out the following crematoria – Charing, Enfield, Finchley, Golders Green, Hither Green, Mortlake, Oxford, Torquay, Porchester, North East Surrey (Battersea New), Leeds and St Marylebone.
5 *The Builder*, Vol.12, 1854, p.222

Lavender Hill
1 The chapels were listed in 1990

Manor Park
1 See *Pharos*, Vol. 22 No. 1 1956 pp.7–9

Mortlake Old

1 For a photo of the chapel see Brown, M. (Ed.) *Barnes and Old Mortlake Past with East Sheen,* (London, 1997) p.94

North Sheen

1 They were manufactured by Wainwright and Waring Ltd. See *Funeral Service Journal,* Vol. 68, No. 11, November, 1953, p.536

Nunhead

1 See Curl, J.S., 'Nunhead Cemetery, London: A History of the Planning, Architecture, Landscaping and Fortunes of a Great Nineteenth-Century Cemetery' *Ancient Monuments Society's Transactions, 1997,* ii pp.8–89. See also Curl, J.S. 'Saving a Victorian Burial Ground: Nunhead Cemetery, South London' *Country Life,* 17 July, 1975, pp. 146–8. The chapels, entrance gates and lodges were listed in 1972 along with many memorials.
2 Hone, William, in 1827, quoted by Woollacott, R. *Brief Guide to Nunhead Cemetery,* Newsletter 4, Peckham Society, Feb/March, 1976. See also *Nunhead Cemetery: An Illustrated Guide,* (London: 1998)
3 *The Times,* 19 July, 1969
4 See Batten, R. *The Leysdown Tragedy: An Account of the Deaths and Funeral of Eight Walworth Scouts in 1912,* (London, 1992)
5 See *The Times,* 11 May 1970 and 10 December 1970, 22 November 1974, 20 November 1975
6 See Brooks, C. *Mortal Remains: The History and Present State of the Victorian and Edwardian Cemetery* Ed. (Exeter,1989), pp.95–99

Paddington Willesden Lane

1 It is possible that the architect George Devey who worked in Little's office contributed to the plans.
2 The chapels were listed in 1982. Only one is still in use.
3 *The Builder,* Vol.13, 25 August 1855, p.402

Paines Lane

1 In the churchyard stands an obelisk erected by John Claudius Loudon in memory of his parents in 1843

Putney Vale

1 The brochure published by the Borough is undated
2 The entrance gates and lodge were listed in 1983

Queen's Road Croydon

1 *The Builder,* Vol. 20, 27 July 1861, p.511

Richmond
1. *The Richmond News*, undated (c.1879), in the local collection, Richmond Library

Rippleside
1. *The Builder*, Vol. 39, 6 August, 1881, p.192
2. See *The Times*, 13 January, 1899

St Marylebone
1. *The Builder*, Vol.12, 17 June, 1854, p.325
2. *The Illustrated London News* 17 March, 1855 p.245–6
3. See *The Builder*, Vol. 154, 14 January, 1938, pp.62–67

St Mary's R.C.
1. Eastlake, C. *A History of the Gothic Revival*, (London, 1872), p.348
2. See Nicholson, C. & Spooner, C. *Recent English Ecclesiastical Architecture* (London, 1911) p.138–39.

St Pancras and Islington
1. Brown, W. *A Series of Photographic Views of the St. Pancras and Islington Cemeteries*, n.d., p.6.
2. Brown, op.cit, p.8
3. *The Illustrated London News*, 29 July, 1854
4. See Puddlefoot, J.W. *The Finchley Cemeteries: A Series of Photographic Views of the St Pancras and Islington Cemeteries.*, n.d.
5. See *The Builder*, Vol. 153, 27 December 1937 p.1119–20. The executed design is very different from that proposed. See *The Undertakers' Journal*, May 1928 p.164 for an illustration. Freeman was cremated here in February 1938 and his ashes rest in the columbarium

Streatham
1. *The Architects' Journal*, Vol. 5, 23 April 1897, p.270

Streatham Park
1. *The Times*, 7 June 1890. *The Times* reprinted a news item from *The British Medical Journal* which noted, 'It appears to be a most undesirable proceeding to devote more land so near to our rapidly-increasing metropolis to burial purposes. The suburbs will soon be densely populated, and such a cemetery will soon become practically intramural and a source of danger.' See also *The Undertakers' and Funeral Directors' Journal* which commented, 'No doubt many undertakers have been struck with the value of the cemeteries which so often come under their notice, considered in the light of business investments. Cemeteries pay, there is no doubt about it; and an opportunity now offered for undertakers, if they please, to become part proprietors of a new fifty acre cemetery.' (22 May 1890, p.40)

St Thomas R.C.

1 *The Illustrated London News*, 14 February 1857, quoted by Evinson Denis in *St Thomas's, Fulham*, (London, 1976), p.11
2 Pevsner, Sir N. *The Buildings of England, London 3: North West*, (Harmondsworth, 1991), p.234

Teddington

1 *The Builder*, Vol 37, 2 May, 1879, p. 491. See also *The Building News*, Vol. 36, 2 May, 1879

Tottenham

1 Pevsner, Sir N. *The Buildings of England, Middlesex*, (Harmondsworth, 1951), p.155
2 *The Times*, 20 October 1855
3 The chapels and connecting tunnel were listed in 1995

Tottenham Park

1 See *The Undertakers' Journal*, September 1912, pp.255–56
2 See *The Undertakers' Journal*, May 1913, p.143, April 1915 and August 1915 p.xvi and p.214

Tower Hamlets

1 Holmes, Mrs B. op.cit,(ch.II,ref.4),p.303
2 Pevsner, Sir N. *The Buildings of England, London Vol.2*,(Harmondsworth, 1952), p.419
3 *The Illustrated London News*, 24 March 1849
4 Keeling, D. *The City of London and Tower Hamlets Cemetery*, East London Papers, (1969–70), p.124
5 For an account of this tragedy see Neal, W. *With Disastrous Consequences: London Disasters 1830–1917*, (London, 1992), pp.1–28. Others were buried at East London, West Ham and Woolwich
6 *The Illustrated London News*, 25 April, 1857
7 *The Times*, 19 December, 1887
8 Jones, B. *Design for Death*, (London, 1967), p.128.
9 Ibid

Twickenham

1 *The Builder*, Vol.25, 31 August, 1867, p.650

Walthamstow

1 Minutes of the Walthamstow Burial Board, 2 March 1871

West Ham

1 Minutes of the West Ham Vestry Burial Board, 14 November 1854
2 See Neal, W. *With Disastrous Consequences: London Disasters 1830–1917*, (London, 1992), pp.1–28. See also *The Illustrated London News* 14 September 1878. Most of

the victims were buried at Woolwich Cemetery, but others are at East London and Tower Hamlets
3   See Neal, W. op. cit, pp.183–210

Westminster Hanwell

1   Report of the Cemetery ground, in Westminster City Central Library, c.862/21
2   There are two 19th century architects named Robert Jerrard: father and son, and it is not clear which was involved here. In the 1830s they had built the Lansdowne estate in Cheltenham
3   The gate piers and railings were listed in 1981

West Norwood

1   Collison, G. *Cemetery Interment*, (ch.VI, ref.5), p.168
2   Jones. P.H. and Noble, G.E. (Eds.), *Cremation in Great Britain*, Second Edition (London, 1931), pp.56–58
3   See *Funeral Service Journal*, Vol. 71, No. 10, 1956, pp.158–9. The design won third prize at the International Arts Exhibition at Paris in 1956. See also *Pharos*, Vol.22 No. 4, 1956, p.8
4   A full history and description of the catacombs appears in the Friends of West Norwood Cemetery Newsletter No.14, April 1993. The Garden of Remembrance area is currently (May, 2006) covered temporarily prior to redevelopment that will incorporate protection and renovation of the catacombs
5   See F.O.W.N.C. newsletter article 'Maddick Edmund Distin' (May, 1999), pp. 6–10
6   An illustrated booklet on the Greek Cemetery by Don Bianco is obtainable from the Friends of West Norwood Cemetery.
7   Lambeth, London Borough of, *West Norwood Cemetery*, (London, 1971), p.4.
8   It is made of a fine grained, grey Rubislaw granite bed, pink Peterhead granite plinth, a body of dark carboniferous limestone probably from Wales, red marble column bases from Devon, yellow Siena marble column shafts, carved Portland stone capitals and statuary, all surmounted with a roof of Derbydene limestone
9   Over 60 monuments are listed in West Norwood including 7 that are grade II*
10 Lambeth, London Borough of, op.cit, p.1
11 Ashton, Algernon, *Truth, Wit and Wisdom*, (London, 1905), p.311
12 Lambeth, London Borough of, op.cit, p.4

Willesden

1   *The Builder*, Vol. 59, 10 October 1890, p. 294
2   From *The Willesden Chronicle* in a volume of 'cuttings' 1890–93 collected by F.A. Wood, in Brent Library, Grange Museum
3   See *The Times*, 28 December, 1928

WIMBLEDON
1   *The Builder,* Vol. 34, 18 March, 1876, p.276

WOODGRANGE PARK
1   See *The Architect,* Vol 41, 7 June 1889

WOOLWICH
1   Neal, W. *With Disastrous Consequences: London Disasters 1830–1917,* (London, 1992), pp.1–28. See also *The Illustrated London News* 14 September 1878. Two victims were also buried at West Ham Cemetery and others were buried at East London and Tower Hamlets.
2   Phipson-Wybrants' obituary appears in the Proceedings of The Royal Geographical Society, New Monthly, for Vol. 3 No. 4 (April 1881) pp.238–40

Bibliography

Abney Park Cemetery Company, *Hendon Park Cemetery* (London, 1903)
'An Act for establishing a Cemetery for the Interment of the Dead in the Neighbourhood of a Metropolis', 2 and 3 William IV *c*.110, local and personal. (This was the first of several similar Acts)
Andrews, W. *Curious Epitaphs Collected from the Graveyards of Great Britain and Ireland, with Biographical, Genealogical, and Historical Notes* (London, 1899)
The Architects' Journal, various dates
Ashton, A. *Truth, Wit and Wisdom* (London, 1905)
Ashton, A. *More Truth, Wit and Wisdom* (London, 1908)
The Architects' Journal, various dates
Arnold, C. *Necropolis: London and its Dead* (Simon & Schuster, 2006)
Austin, E. *Burial Grounds and Cemeteries: a practical guide to their Administration by Local Authorities* (London, 1907)
Bailey, C. *Harrap's Guide to Famous London Graves* (London, 1975)
Bakewell, J. and Drummond, J. *A Fine and Private Place* (London, 1977)
Barker, Rev. T. *Abney Park Cemetery: A complete Descriptive Guide to every part of this beautiful Depository of the Dead* (London, 1869)
Barker, F. *Highgate Cemetery: Victorian Valhalla* (London, 1984)
Beach, D. *London's Cemeteries* (London, 2006)
Bickley, F. *True Dialogues of the Dead* (London, 1925)
Blanch, W. *Ye Parish of Camberwell, A Brief Account of the Parish of Camberwell its History and Antiquities* (London, 1875)
Bond, P. 'The Celebration of Death, some thoughts on the design of crematoria', *Architectural Review* (April 1967)
British Institute of Industrial Art, *The Art of Graveyard Monuments* (London, 1925)
Brooks, C. *Mortal Remains: The History and Present State of the Victorian and Edwardian Cemetery* (Exeter, 1989)
Brown, M. (Ed) *Barnes and Old Mortlake Past with East Sheen* (London, 1997)
Brown, W. *A Series of Photographic Views of St. Pancras and Islington Cemeteries* (n.d.)

The Builder, various dates
Building News, various dates
Burial Law and Policy in the 21st Century: The Way Forward (London, 2007)
Cansick, F. *A Collection of Curious and Interesting Epitaphs, Copied from the Monuments of Distinguished and Noted Characters in the cemeteries and churches of St. Pancras, Middlesex* (London, 1872)
Chadwick, Sir E. *A Supplementary Report to Her Majesty's Secretary of State for the Home Department from the Poor Law Commissioners on the Results of a Special Inquiry into the Practice of Interment in Towns* (London, 1843)
Chapman, W. *Handbook of Kingston* (Kingston, 1877)
The City of London, *The City of London Cemetery and Crematorium* (London, n.d.)
Clark, B. *Handbook for Visitors to Kensal Green Cemetery* (London, 1843)
Clarke, B. *Parish Churches of London* (London, 1966)
Clarke, J.M. *London's Necropolis: A Guide to Bookwood Cemetery* (Stroud, 2005)
Clarke, J.M. *The Bookwood Necropolis Railway*, Fourth edition (Usk, 2006)
Cobb, G. *The Old Churches of London* (London, 1942)
Collison, G. *Cemetery Interment* (London, 1840)
Colloms, M. and Weindling, D. *The Good Grave Guide to Hampstead Cemetery,* (London, 2000)
Colvin, H. *A Biographical Dictionary of British Architects 1600–1840* (London, 1978)
Coones, P. 'Kensal Green Cemetery, London's first great Extramural Necropolis', *Transaction of the Ancient Monument Society* (1987)
Coussillan, A. *Les 200 Cimetières du vieux Paris par Jacques Hillairet,* (Paris, 1958)
Croft, H.J. *Guide to Kensal Green Cemetery,* Second edition (London, 1881)
Curl, J.S. *Death and Architecture (Stroud,* 2002)
Curl, J.S. *The Cemeteries and Burial Grounds of Glasgow* (Glasgow, 1974)
Curl, J.S. 'XIXth Century Funerary Architecture', *The Architect* (February, 1973)
Curl, J.S. 'Nunhead Cemetery', *Transaction of the Ancient Monument Society,* (1977)
Curl, J.S. *The Victorian Celebration of Death* (Newton Abbot, 1972)
Curl J.S. (Ed.) *Kensal Green Cemetery. The Origin and Development of the General Cemetery of All Souls, Kensal Green, London, 1824–2001* (Chichester, 2001)
Davey, R, *A History of Mourning,* Published by the House of Jay (London n.d.)
Davies, D & Shaw, A. *Reusing Old Graves* (Kent,1995)
Dawes, M. *The End of the Line: The Story of the Railway Service to the Great Northern London Cemetery* (Barnet, 2003)
Dean, C. *The Royal Hospital Chelsea* (London, 1950)
Delves, H.C. 'The Disposal of the Dead', *Journal of the Town Planning Institute (*September–October,1952)
Dickens, C. *Bleak House* (London, 1853)
Dickens, C. *The Uncommercial Traveller* (London, 1860)
Eastlake, C. *A History of the Gothic Revival* (London, 1872)
Elliot, B. 'The Landscape of the English Cemetery' *Landscape Design No.* 184 pp. 13–14 (October 1989)

English Heritage, *Paradise Preserved. An introduction to the assessment, evaluation, conservation and management of historic cemeteries* (London, 2007)

Francis, D. Kellaher, L. and Neophytou, G. *The Secret Cemetery* (Oxford, 2005)

The Fine Art Society, *Catalogue of British Sculpture, 1850–1914*, Exhibition Catalogue (London, September–October 1968)

Freeman, A. *Cremation, the Planning of Crematoria and Columbaria* (London, 1906)

French, Rev. J. *Walks in Abney Park* (London, 1883)

Friends of Highgate Cemetery, *Highgate Cemetery* (London, 1978)

Friends of Nunhead Cemetery, *Nunhead Cemetery, An Illustrated Guide* (London, 1988)

Funeral Service Journal, various dates

The Gentleman's Magazine, various dates

Gill, R.C. *A Dictionary of Local Celebrities*, Barnes and Mortlake History Society (London, 1980)

Gillon, E.V. Jr. *Victorian Cemetery Art* (New York, 1972)

Girouard, M. 'Highgate Cemetery', *Country Life* (5 August 1971)

Gomersall, Rev. W.J. *A Short History of Kensal Green and its Parish Church* (London, 1916)

Graham, H. *More Ruthless Rhymes for Heartless Homes*, (London, 1930)

Grainger, H.J. *Death Redesigned: British Crematoria: History, Architecture and Landscape* (Reading, 2005)

Gunnis, R. *Dictionary of British Sculptors 1660–1851*, Revised Edition (London, n.d.)

Hackman, H. *Wates's Book of London Churchyards. A Guide to the Old Churchyards and Burial–grounds of the City and Central London* (London, 1981)

Hakewill, A. *Modern Tombs, or gleanings from the Public Cemeteries of London* (London, 1851)

Hall, J. *Dictionary of Subjects and Symbols* (London, 1979)

Hare, A. *Walks in London*, 2 vols. Seventh edition (London, 1901)

Haywood, W. *Plans and Views of the City of London Cemetery at Little Ilford in the County of Essex* (London, 1856)

Hillman, E. (Ed.) *Attitudes to Life and Death*, Conference Report, the North East London Polytechnic (1978)

Holmes, Mrs B. *The London Burial Grounds. Notes on their History from the earliest times to the Present Day* (London, 1896)

Hyamson, A. *The Sephardim of England, A History of the Spanish and Portuguese Jewish Community 1492–1951* (London, 1951)

The Illustrated London News, various dates.

Joint Committee for the Memorial Industry, *Who wants Memorials* (Ealing, n.d)

Jones, B. *Design for Death* (London, 1967)

Jones, J. *How to Record Graveyards* (London, 1979)

Jones, P.H. and Noble, G. *Cremation in Great Britain* (London, 1931)

Joyce, P. *A Guide to Abney Park Cemetery*, Second edition (London, 1994) (Eds.)

Jupp, P.C. 'Enon Chapel: No Way for the Dead' in Jupp, P.C. and Howarth, G. (Eds) *The Changing Face of Death: Historical Accounts of Death and Disposal* (Basingstoke, 1997)

Jupp, P.C. and Grainger, H.J. (Eds.) *Golders Green Crematorium 1902–2002: A London Centenary in Context* (London, 2002)

Justyne, W. *Guide to Highgate Cemetery* (London, 1865)

Justyne, W. *Illustrated Guide to Kensal Green Cemetery* (London, 1858)

Kadish, S. *Jewish Heritage in England: An Architectural Guide* (London, 2006)

Keeling, D. 'The City of London and Tower Hamlets Cemetery', *East London Papers* (1969–70)

Kent, W. *Encyclopaedia of London* (London, 1937)

Knight, C. (Ed.) *London* (London, 1841–44)

Lambert, D. *The Cemetery in a Garden: 150 Years of the City of London Cemetery and Crematorium* (London, 2006)

Lambeth, London Borough of, *West Norwood Cemetery* (London, 1971)

Light, A. *Bunhill Fields*, 2 vols., (London, 1913–33)

Lindley, K. *Graves and Graveyards* (London, 1972)

Lloyd, J. *The History, Topography and Antiquities of Highgate, in the County of Middlesex* (Highgate, 1888)

Longworth, P. *The Unending Vigil, a History of the Commonwealth War Graves Commission 1917–67* (London, 1967)

Loudon, J. *On the laying out, planting and managing of Cemeteries and on the improvement of Churchyards* (London, 1843)

McDowell and Partners, *Victorian Catacombs, Nunhead Cemetery Southwark. Building Surveys and Structural Report* (Esher, 1976)

MacFarlane, W. *Illustrated Catalogue of MacFarlane's Castings*, Sixth edition (Glasgow, n.d.)

Manning, G. *The Listed Structures in West Norwood Cemetery* (London, 1989)

Marion, J. *Famous and Curious Cemeteries* (New York, 1977)

Morley, J. *Death, Heaven and the Victorians* (London, 1971)

Neal, W. *With Disastrous Consequences: London Disasters 1830–1917* (London, 1992)

Nierop–Reading, B. 'The Rosary Cemetery' *Landscape Design* No. 184 (October, 1989)

Ornstein, P. *Laws of the Burial Society of the United Synagogue . . . with an Historical preface of the Society and the United Synagogue Cemeteries* (London, 1902)

Parsons, B. *The London Way of Death* (Stroud, 2001)

Parsons, B. 'Mortlake and the Art Deco Influence' *Journal of the Institute of Burial and Cremation Administration* Vol. 71 No. 3 (2003) pp.20–23

Parsons, B. *Committed to the Cleansing Flame: The Development of Cremation in Nineteenth Century England* (Reading, 2005)

Pharos, various dates

Pickett, F. *History and Antiquities of Highgate, Middlesex* (London, 1842)

London Planning Advisory Committee *Planning for Burial Space in London* (London, 1997)

Pevsner, Sir N. *The Buildings of England: Essex*, 1954, *London Vol. 1*. 1973, *London Vol. 2, South*, 1983, *Middlesex*, 1951, *Surrey*, 1971. All Harmondsworth

Pugin, A.W.N. *An Apology for the Revival of Christian Architecture in England* (London, 1843)

Robinson, E. 'The Geology of Kensal Green Cemetery', Report on a Field Meeting in the *Proceedings of the Geology Association* (1979)
Robinson, E. 'Opening Unknown Doors', *Country Life,* (11 May 1989)
Robinson, W. *God's Acre Beautiful or the Cemeteries of the Future* (London, 1880)
Rugg J. 'The Origins and Progress of Cemetery Establishment in Britain' in the *Changing Face of Death: Historical Accounts of Death and Disposal* P.C. Jupp and G. Howarth (Eds.) (Basingstoke, 1997)
Rugg, J. 'Lawn Cemeteries: the emergence of a new landscape of death' *Urban History* vol.33, No.2 (2006) pp. 213–233
Samuel, L.J. *Samuel and Son, A Short History* (London, 1979)
Save Abney Park Cemetery Committee, 'Preliminary Proposals', typescript report (1978)
Sheppard, F.H.W. (ed.), *Survey of London, The Parish of St. Mary Lambeth,* 26, (London, 1956)
Sheppard, F.H.W. (ed.), *Survey of London, Northern Kensington,* Vol.37, (London, 1973)
Sims, G.R. (Ed.), *Living London* (London, 1906)
Simmonds, H. *All About Battersea* (London, 1882)
Smith, E. 'The South Metropolitan Cemetery, West Norwood and its Memorials', *London and Middlesex Archeological Society, Special Papers,* 2, pp. 436–52, (1978)
Southwark, London Borough of, 'Management Document N.C. (Nunhead Cemetery) J.S. 8/76–77', typescript report (1977)
Special Report: Memorial Safety in Local Authority Cemeteries Local Government Ombudsman (London, 2006)
Stone, Mrs, *God's Acre: or Historical Notes relating to Churchyards* (London, 1858)
Strang, J. *Necropolis Glasguensis with Osbervations (sic) on Ancient and Modern Tombs and Sepulture* (Glasgow, 1831)
Taylor, R. *Every Stone Tells a Story: A short History and History Trail of Tower Hamlets Cemetery Park* (London, 1996)
Tegg ,W. *The Last Act Being the Funeral Rites of Nations and Individuals* (London, 1876)
The Official Guide to Bunhill Fields (London, 1991)
Thorne, J. *Handbook to the Environs of London* (London, 1876)
Timbs, J. *Curiosities of London,* (London, 1885)
The Times, various dates
Trollope, Rev. E. *Manual of Sepulchral Monuments* (London, 1858)
The Undertakers' Journal, various dates
Vaes, G. *Les Cimetières de Londres,* (Brussels, 1978)
Victoria County History, various volumes on the Counties of Essex, Middlesex and Surrey.
Walford, E. *Old and New London* (London, 1887)
Walker, G. *Interment and Disinterment or a further exposition of the practices pursued in the metropolitan places of sepulture* (London, 1843)
Walker, G. *Gatherings from Graveyards, Particularly those of London, with a concise History of the Modes of Interment among different Nations, from the earliest Periods, and a Detail of dangerous and fatal Results produced by the Unwise and revolting custom of inhuming the Dead in the midst of the Living* (London, 1839)

Weller, S. *Landscape Design* No. 184, Cemetery Edition, (October 1989)
White, W. *History, Gazetteer and Directory of Essex,* Second edition (Essex, 1863)
Williamson, R. P. Ross, 'Victorian Necropolis – the cemeteries of London', *The Architectural Review,* (October 1942)
Willson, T. *The Pyramid, A General Metropolitan Cemetery to be erected in the Vicinity of Primrose Hill* (London, 1842)
Wilson, Sir A. and Levy, H. *Burial Reform and Funeral costs* (London, 1938)
Wilson, J. *The Story of Norwood* (London, 1973)
Wolfson, P. *Great London Cemeteries and Crematoria* (Sixth edition revised by Cliff Webb) (London, 1999)
Woollacott, R. *Nunhead Notables* (London, 1984)
Woollacott, R. *Camberwell Old Cemetery: London's Forgotten Valhalla* (London, 2000)
Wright, T. *History and Antiquities of London* (London, 1837)

BIOGRAPHICAL INFORMATION CAME FROM A WIDE RANGE OF SOURCES BUT THE BASIC REFERENCE WORKS USED WERE:

Boase, F. *Modern English Biography* Second impression, (London, 1965)
The Dictionary of National Biography
The Times obituaries.
Who Was Who 1897–1970 (six volumes).

Index of the Deceased

A

A'Beckett, Gilbert, 1811–56, Highgate
A'Beckett, Sir William, 1806–69, West Norwood
Abel, Sir Frederick, 1827–1902 Nunhead
Abel, Robert, 1857–1936, Nunhead
Ackland, William, 1820–95, Nunhead
Adams, Henry 1799–1887, Nunhead
Adler, Herman 1838–1911, Jewish, Willesden
Adler, Nathan, 1803–90, Jewish, Willesden
Aikman, Col. Frederick, 1828–88, Kensal Green
Ainsworth, Harrison, 1805–82, Kensal Green
Akerman, Sir John, 1825–1905, Westminster
Albery, James, 1838–89, Kensal Green
Alcock, Charles, 1842–1907, West Norwood
Alderson, Sir James, 1794–1882, West Norwood
Alexander, Maj.-Gen. Ernest, 1870–1934, Putney Vale
Alkins, Col.Sir John, 1875–1963, Putney Vale
Allder, Joshua, 1838–1904, Queen's Road Croydon
Allen, Sir Frederick, 1864–1934, Putney Vale
Allen, Thomas, 1861–98, Lambeth
Allen, William, 1888–1958, Golders Green
Allom, Thomas, 1804–77, Kensal Green
Anderson, Arthur, 1792–1868, West Norwood
Anderson, John, 1827–1907, Queen's Road, Croydon
Angelo, Henry, 1780–1852, Kensal Green
Anthony, Metropolitan of Sourozh, 1914–2003, Brompton
Apperley, Charles, 1778–1843, Kensal Green
Appold, John, 1800–65, West Norwood
Aracic, Milnoj, 1891–1951, Brompton
Archer, Fred, 1857–86, Hampstead
Armitage, Florence, –1915, West Norwood
Armstrong, Edward, 1878–1945, Golders Green
Armstrong, Robert, 1788–1867, Nunhead
Ashbee, Henry, 1834–1900, Kensal Green
Atherton, Sir William, 1806–64, Kensal Green
Augusta, Princess Edward de Ligne, –1872, St Mary's R.C. Kensal Green
Augustus, Duke of Sussex, 1773–1843, Kensal Green
Auldjo, John, 1805–86, Kensal Green
Ayrton, Acton, 1811–86, Brompton

B

Babbage, Charles, 1791–1871, Kensal Green
Babbage, Maj.Gen.Henry, 1825–1918, Beckenham
Bacon, John, 1740–99, Chingford Mount
Baggallay, Sir Richard, 1816–88, West Norwood
Bagration, Prince Alexandre, 1877–1955, Brompton
Baillie, Sir James, 1873–1951, Golders Green
Baily, Edward, 1788–1867, Highgate
Baird, Andrew, 1842–1908, Highgate
Baldwin, Albert, 1858–1936, Isleworth
Balfe, Michael, 1808–70, Kensal Green
Ball, John, 1818–89, St Thomas's R.C.
Bambrick, Pte. Valentine, 1837–64, St Pancras & Islington
Bancroft, Marie, 1840–1921, Brompton
Bancroft, Sir Squire, 1841–1926, Brompton
Banks, Charles, 1806–86, Nunhead
Banting, William, 1797–1878, Brompton
Banting, William, 1826–1901, Kensal Green
Barbirolli, Sir John, 1899–1970, St Mary's R.C., Kensal Green
Barclay, Sir George, 1862–1921, City of London
Barham, Sir George, 1836–1913, St. Marylebone
Barham, Rev. Richard, 1788–1845, Kensal Green
Baring–Gould, Baring, 1843–1917, Charlton
Barlow, Peter, 1776–1862, Charlton
Barlow, William, 1812–1902, Charlton
Barnard, Charles, 1935, Bandon Hill
Barnard, Frederick, 1846–96, Wimbledon
Barnato, Isaacs, 1852–97, Jewish, Willesden
Barnby, Sir Joseph, 1838–96, West Norwood
Barnes, Thomas, 1785–1841, Kensal Green
Barratt, Sir Albert, 1860–1941, Highgate
Barratt, Edward, 1844–91, West Norwood
Barraud, Francis, 1824–1900, Queen's Road, Croydon
Barrett, George & Catherine, –1878, West Ham
Barrow, Sir Reuben, 1838–1917, Queen's Road, Croydon
Barry, Edward, 1830–80, Paddington, Willesden Lane
Barry, Sir John, 1836–1918, Brookwood
Barry, 'James', 1795–1865, Kensal Green
Barth, Helmuth, 1906–46, Grove Park
Bartholomew, Anne, 1800–62, Highgate
Bartholomew, Valentine, 1799–1879, Highgate
Barthorpe, Sir Frederick, 1857–1942, West Norwood
Bartlett, Sir Herbert, 1842–1921, Highgate
Bartlett, Lavinia, 1806–75, Nunhead
Bartolozzi, Gaetano, 1757–1821, Kensal Green
Bassett, James (Charles Bertram), 1854–1907, West Norwood
Batchelor, Denzil, 1906–69, Gunnersbury
Bateman, Hezekiah, 1812–75, Kensal Green
Bates, Henry, 1825–92, St.Marylebone
Bates, Ralph, 1940–91, Chiswick New
Batten, Sir William, 1865–1938, Putney Vale
Bayes, Thomas, 1701–61, Bunhill Fields
Baylis, Lilian, 1874–1937, East London
Bayliss, Sir Wyke, 1835–1905, Streatham
Bayly, Mary, 1816–99, West Norwood
Baynes, Thomas, 1823–87, Hampstead
Bazoft, Farzad, 1958–90, Highgate
Beale, Thomas, 1828–94, West Norwood
Bearsted, Lord Marcus, 1853–1927, Jewish, Willesden
Beatty, Sir William, –1842, Kensal Green
Beaufoy, Henry, 1786–1851, West Norwood
Beck, Col.William, 1804–73, West Norwood

Beckett, Sir Albert, 1840–1904, Mortlake R.C.
Beckwith, Frederick, 1821–98, Nunhead
Beckwith, William, 1857–1892, Nunhead
Beech, Maj.Francis, 1885–1969, Eltham
Beer, Julius, 1836–80, Highgate
Beesley, Edward, 1831–1915, Paddington, Willesden Lane
Beeton, Isabella, 1836–65, West Norwood
Beeton, Samuel, 1831–77, West Norwood
Behnes, William, 1791–1806, Kensal Green
Belcher, Lady Diana, –1890, Highgate
Belcher, John, 1841–1913, West Norwood
Beldam, Asplan, 1841–1912, Ealing
Belilios, Emanuel, 1837–1905, Jewish, Golders Green
Bell, George, 1814–90, Highgate
Bellasis, Edward, 1800–73, Mortlake R.C.
Benedict, Sir Julius, 1804–85, Kensal Green
Benn, Sir Arthur, 1858–1937, Kensington Hanwell
Bennett, Sir William, 1852–1931, Putney Vale
Bennett William, 1820–95, Nunhead
Bennett, William, 1811–71, West Norwood
Bentley, Alfred, 1878–1923, St.Marylebone
Bentley, Derek, 1934–53, Croydon
Bentley, John, 1839–1902, Mortlake R.C.
Bentley, Sgt.Robert, –1910, City of London
Bentinck-Scott, William Cavendish, 5th Duke of Portland, 1800–79, Kensal Green
Berens, Alexander, –1858, West Norwood
Beresford, Adm.Lord Charles, 1846–1919, Putney Vale
Beresford Whyte, Rear Adm, William, 1863–1932, Gunnersbury
Berkley, James, 1819–62, Camberwell
Berliner, Isidore, 1869–1925, Jewish, East Ham

Berry, Lieut.James, 1843–1930, Royal Hospital, Greenwich
Bertolt, Ernestine, –1959, Gunnersbury
Bessemer, Sir Henry, 1813–98, West Norwood
Bethell, Richard, Lord Westbury, 1800–73, Great Northern
Betty, William, 1791–1874, Highgate
Bevin, Ernest, 1881–1951, Golders Green
Bicknell, Elhanen, 1788–1861, West Norwood
Biddulph, Gen.Sir Robert, 1835–1918, Charlton
Binney, Thomas, 1798–1874, Abney Park
Binks, George, 1793–1872, City of London
Birkbeck, George, 1776–1841, Kensal Green
Birkett, Lord William, of Ulverstone, 1883–1962, Golders Green
Bishop, Sir Henry, 1786–1855, St.Marylebone
Bishop, James, 1783–1854, Kensal Green
Bishop, William, 1903–61, Battersea St Mary's
Blackmore, Richard, 1825–1900, Teddington
Blackwood, Terence,Marquess of Dufferin and Ava. 1866–1918, Putney Vale
Bladen, Martin, Lord Hawke, 1860–1938, West Norwood
Blair, Sir Reginald, 1881–1962, Harrow
Blair, Sir Robert, 1859–1935, Hampstead
Blake, Rev. John, 1839–1906, Kensal Green
Blake, William, 1757–1827, Bunhill Fields
Blakeley, William, 1830–97, Fulham
Blakelock, Keith 1945–85, St Marylebone
Blanchard, Edward, 1820–89, Kensington Hanwell
Blanchard, Samuel, 1804–45, West Norwood
Blok, Arthur, 1882–1974, Jewish, Golders Green
Blondin, Emile, 1824–97, Kensal Green

Blore, Edward, 1787–1879, Highgate
Blount, Walter, 1807–94, Mortlake, R.C.
Blunt, Arthur Cecil, 1844–96, Old Mortlake
Bohn, Henry, 1796–1884, West Norwood
Boisragon, Brig.Gen.Guy, 1864–1931, Kensal Green
Bolton, Sir Frederick, 1851–1920, Hendon
Bonaparte, Prince Louis, 1813–91, St.Mary's R.C., Kensal Green
Bonham, Sir Samuel, 1803–63, Kensal Green
Bonington, Richard, 1802–28, Kensal Green
Bonomi, Joseph, 1796–1878, Brompton
Booth, Bramwell, 1856–1929, Abney Park
Booth, Catherine, 1829–90, Abney Park
Booth, Gen.William, 1829–1912, Abney Park
Booth–Clibborn, Catherine, 1858–1955, Highgate
Bòr–Komorowski, Gen.Tadeusz, 1895–1966, Gunnersbury
Borrow, George, 1803–81, Brompton
Borthwick, Algernon, Lord Glenesk, 1830–1908, St Marylebone
Bostock, Frank, 1866–1912, Abney Park
Boulter, Lieut.William, 1892–1955, Putney Vale
Bourne, Frank, –1945, Crystal Palace
Bovill, Sir William, 1814–73, Kingston
Bowater, Sir Thomas Vansittart, 1862–1938, Putney Vale
Bowden, Elizabeth, –1896, St Thomas's R.C.
Bowers, Robert, 1822–1908, Lambeth
Bowlby, Thomas, 1818–60, Paddington, Willesden Lane
Bowley, Al, 1890–1941, Westminster
Bowley, Robert, 1813–69, West Norwood
Boyd, Sir Harry, 1876–1940, Putney Vale
Boyd, Air Vice Marshal Owen, 1889–1944, Paddington, Mill Hill
Boyton, Sir James, 1855–1926, St Marylebone

Bradbury, Thomas, 1677–1759, Bunhill Fields
Bradlaugh, Charles, 1833–91, Brookwood
Bradley, Katherine, 1848–1914, Mortlake R.C.
Braham, John, 1774–1856, Kensal Green
Braidwood, James, 1800–61, Abney Park
Brain, Dennis, 1921–57, Hampstead
Braithwaite, Gen.Sir Walter, 1865–1945, Royal Hospital, Chelsea
Brake, Sir Francis, 1889–1960, Putney Vale
Bravo, Charles, 1846–76, Norwood
Brawne, Fanny, 1880–65, Brompton
Breese, John, 1817–89, Battersea St Mary's
Bridgeman, Henry, 1845–98, Highgate
Bright, Gerald, 1904–74, Jewish, Willesden
Brinsmead, John, 1836–1921, Highgate
Bristow, Francis, –1911, Nunhead
Bristowe, John, 1827–95, West Norwood
Bristowe, Thomas, 1833–92, West Norwood
Britton, John, 1771–1857, West Norwood
Broderip, William, 1789–1859, Kensal Green
Brodhurst, Bernard, 1822–90, Highgate
Brodie, Sir Harry, 1875–1956, Putney Vale
Brodie, Israel, 1895–1979, Jewish, Willesden
Bronowski, Jacob, 1908–74, Highgate
Brooks, Charles, 1816–74, Kensal Green
Broome, Sir Frederick, 1842–96, Highgate
Broome, Samuel, 1805–70, Nunhead
Brough, Lionel, 1836–1909, West Norwood
Broughshane, Lord William, of Kensington, 1872–1953, Gunnersbury
Brown, Charlie, –1932, Tower Hamlets
Brown, Horace, 1848–1925, Nunhead
Brown, John, 1830–1922, Hampstead
Brown, Robert, 1842–95, West Norwood

Brown, Samuel, 1810–75, West Norwood
Browning, William, 1797–1874, Nunhead
Bruce, Sir George, 1821–1908, Highgate
Bruce, Surg.Gen.Lewis Bruce, 1831–99, Ealing
Brunel, Isambard, 1806–59, Kensal Green
Brunel, Sir Marc, 1769–1849, Kensal Green
Brunton, Richard, 1841–1901, West Norwood
Brunton, Sir Thomas, 1844–1916, Highgate
Brydon, John, 1840–1901, Highgate
Buckland, Francis, 1826–80, Brompton
Buckley, Capt John, 1813–76, Tower Hamlets
Budge, Sir Ernest, 1857–1934, Nunhead
Bull, Sir William, 1863–1931, Hammersmith
Bumpus, Edward, 1832–96, West Norwood
Bunning, James, 1802–63, Highgate
Bunyan, John, 1628–88, Bunhill Fields
Burd, Constance, 1860–1939, Mortlake R.C.
Burden, Arthur, 1890–1915, Chiswick Old
Burden, Hugh, 1913–1985, Gunnersbury
Burder, George, 1752–1832, Bunhill Fields
Burge, Sir Charles, 1846–1921, Kingston
Burges, Elizabeth, –1855, West Norwood
Burges, William, 1827–81, West Norwood
Burke, Thomas, 1886–1943, Golders Green
Burne–Jones, Sir Philip 1861–1926, Golders Green
Burney, Charles, 1826–87, Royal Hospital, Greenwich
Burney, Charles, 1726–1814, Royal Hospital, Chelsea
Burnham, Robert, Lord Renwick, 1904–73, Putney Vale

Burns, Jabez, 1805–76, Paddington, Willesden Lane
Burns, Rt.Hon.John, 1858–1943, Battersea St Mary's
Burrowes, Peter, 1753–1841, Kensal Green
Burt, Sir Charles, 1832–1913, Richmond
Burton, Decimus, 1800–81, Kensal Green
Burton, Sir Richard, 1821–90, Mortlake R.C.
Busby, James, 1800–71, West Norwood
Butterfield, William, 1814–1900, Tottenham
Buzacott, Rev. Aaron, 1829–81, Abney Park
Byford, Roy, 1873–1939, Hammersmith
Byron, Anne, Lady, 1792–1860, Kensal Green
Byron, Henry, 1834–84, Brompton

C

Cafe, Gen.William 1826–1906, Brompton
Caffin, Adm.Sir Crawford, 1812–83, Charlton
Caird, Sir Andrew, 1870–1956, Putney Vale
Caird, Sir James, 1816–92, Highgate
Cairns, Sir William, 1828–88, Brompton
Calcott, Sir Augustus, 1779–1844, Kensal Green
Callcott, Maria, 1785–1842, Kensal Green
Callender, Sir Geoffrey, 1875–1945, Charlton
Callow, John, 1822–78, Nunhead
Calvert, Edward, 1799–1883, Abney Park
Campbell, Sir Edward, 1879–1945, Bromley Hill
Campbell, Gen. Sir Frederick, 1819–93, Charlton
Campbell–Johnson, Louis, 1862–1929, Brompton
Cansick, Frederick, 1928–18, Highgate
Capel, Henry, 1795–1887, Nunhead
Caradoc, John, Lord Howden, 1799–1873, Kensal Green

Carden, George, 1798–1874 Kensal Green
Cardwell, Viscount Edward, 1813–66, Highgate
Carmichael, Sir James, 1858–1934, Wandsworth
Carpenter, Charles, 1858–1938, Nunhead
Carpenter, Richard, 1812–55, Highgate
Carpenter, William, 1813–85, Highgate
Carter, Howard, 1874–1939, Putney Vale
Carter, Thomas, c.1818–67, Nunhead
Carroll, Brig.Gen.John, 1870–1927, Kensington Hanwell
Cartwright, Sir Henry, 1823–99, Kensington Hanwell
Carvajal, Antonio, –1659, Jewish, Old Sephardi, Mile End Road
Cary, Byron, Viscount Falkland, 1845–1922, Putney Vale
Casati, Marchesa Luisa, 1881–1957, Brompton
Cassavetti, Maria, 1843–1914, West Norwood
Casement, Gen.Sir William, 1780–1844, Kensal Green
Cassel, Sir Ernest, 1852–1921, Kensal Green
Cassell, John, 1817–65, Kensal Green
Castle, Rosanna, 1802–1906, Mortlake Old
Cattermole, George, 1800–68, West Norwood
Caulker, Thomas, 1846–59, Abney park
Causton, Sir Joseph, 1815–71, West Norwood
Chadwick, Sir Edwin, 1800–90, Mortlake Old
Chadwick, William, 1797–1852, Nunhead
Chalmers, Robert, Lord, 1858–1938, East Sheen
Chalon, Alfred, 1781–1860, Highgate
Chamberlain, Sir Austen, 1863–1937, St Marylebone
Chamberlain, Neville, 1869–1940, Golders Green

Chambers, Montagu, 1799–1886, Chiswick Old
Champness, Sir William, 1873–1956, Acton
Chaplin, Charles, –1901, Lambeth
Chapman, Edward, 1821–1904, Teddington
Charrington, Frederick, 1850–1936, Woodgrange Park
Chenery, Thomas, 1826–84, Brompton
Cherkassky, Shura, 1911–95, Highgate
Cheselden, William, 1688–1752, Royal Hospital, Chelsea
Chester Col Joseph, 1821–82, Nunhead
Cheyne, Charles, 1838–77, Nunhead
Cheyney, Peter, 1896–1951, Putney Vale
Chipp, Thomas, 1793–1890, Highgate
Chitty, Sir Joseph, 1828–99, Brookwood
Chorley, Henry, 1808–72, Brompton
Chubb, Charles, 1799–1845, Highgate
Chudleigh, Col. Thomas, 1664–1702, Royal Hospital, Chelsea
Church, Sir Arthur, 1834–1915, Richmond
Churchill, Marigold, 1918–21, Kensal Green
Cinquevalli, Paul, 1859–1918, West Norwood
Claflin, Austin, 1865–1928, St.Marylebone
Clarke, Sir Campbell, 1835–1902, Brompton
Clarke, Sir Casper, 1846–1911, Kensal Green
Clarke, Charles, 1849–1908, Nunhead
Clarke, William, 1798–1856, West Norwood
Clasper, Henry, 1858–1931, Putney Vale
Clery, Maj.Gen.Sir Francis, 1838–1926, Battersea New
Clifford, Sir Hugh, 1866–1941, Putney Vale
Clifford, John, 1836–1923, Kensal Green
Clipperton, Sir Charles, 1864–1927, Putney Vale
Clore, Sir Charles, 1904–79, Jewish, Willesden

INDEX OF THE DECEASED

Clowes, William, 1779–1847, West Norwood
Clutton, Henry, 1819–1891, Mortlake R.C.
Coates, Eric, 1886–1957, Golders Green
Cobb, Sir Cyril, 1861–1938, St.Marylebone
Cobbett, James, 1806–42, Kensal Green
Cock, James, 1737–1810, Royal Hospital, Chelsea
Cockburn, Adm.Sir George 1772–1853 Kensal Green
Cockle, Sir James 1809–95 Paddington, Willesden Lane
Coghlan, Sir Timothy, 1857–1926, St.Mary's R.C., Kensal Green
Cohen, Sir Bernard, 1886–1965 Jewish, Golders Green
Cohen, Sir John, 1898–1979 Jewish, Willesden
Cohen, Lord Lionel, of Walmer 1888–1973, Golders Green
Cole, George, Lord –1979 Gunnersbury
Cole, Sir Henry, 1808–82, Brompton
Coleridge–Taylor, Samuel 1875–1912 Bandon Hill
Coligny, Princess Diana 1922–73 Paddington, Mill Hill
Collard, William, 1776–1866, Highgate
Collins, Cecil, 1908–89 Highgate
Collingwood, Cuthbert, 1826–1908 Nunhead
Collins, Charles, 1828–73, Brompton
Collins, James, 1869–1934, Hammersmith New
Collins, Lizzie, 1870–1938, Streatham Park
Collins, Wilkie, 1824–89, Kensal Green
Collis, Gunner James, 1860–1918, Wandsworth
Colls, Benjamin, 1815–78, West Norwood
Colls, William, –1893, West Norwood
Collum, Robert, 1806–1900, Kensal Green
Collyer, William, 1782–1854, Nunhead
Colnaghi, Martin, 1821–1908, Highgate

Colvin Smith, Sir Colvin, 1829–1913, Kingston
Compton Burnett, Ivy 1892–1969 Putney Vale
Conder, John, 1714–81, Bunhill Fields
Conder, Josiah, 1789–1855, Abney Park
Cooch–Behar, H.H. The Majarajah of, 1862–1911 Golders Green
Cook, Sir Francis, 1817–1901, West Norwood
Cook, Sir Frederick, 1844–1920, Richmond
Cook, Thomas –1937 Bandon Hill
Cooke, Thomas, 1786–1864, Brompton
Coombes, Robert, 1808–60, Brompton
Cooper, Sir Edwin, 1873–1942, St. Marylebone
Cooper, Dame Gladys, 1888–1971, Hampstead
Cooper, Sir James, 1868–1936, Charlton
Cooper, Thompson, 1837–1904, West Norwood
Cooper–Key, Capt. Edmund, 1862–1933, Royal Hospital, Greenwich
Copley, John, Lord Lyndhurst, 1772–1863, Highgate
Corfield, Joseph, 1809–88 Abney Park
Cornell, George, c. 1928–1966 Camberwell New
Cornish, Walter, –1919, Woodgrange Park
Cornwell, James, 1812–1902 West Norwood
Cornwall, John, 1900–16, Manor Park
Costa, Ernestine, –1959, Gunnersbury
Costa, Sir Michael, 1808–84, Kensal Green
Costello, Tom, 1863–1943, Streatham Park
Cotton, Lieut. Gen. Sir Sydney, 1792–1874 Brompton
Coutts, Gen. Frederick, 1899–1986, Camberwell New
Cowen, Sir Frederick, 1852–1935, Jewish, Golders Green
Cowie, William, 1849–1910, Charlton
Cowper, Sir Charles, 1807–75, Highgate

Cox, David, 1809–85, West Norwood
Crace, Frederick, 1779–1859, West Norwood
Crace, John G., 1808–89 West Norwood
Crace, John D. 1838–1919 West Norwood
Crawford, Sir Thomas, 1824–95, Charlton
Crawley, George, 1833–79, Highgate West
Creagh, Gen.Sir O'Moore, 1848–1923, East Sheen
Crean, Maj.Thomas, 1875–1923, St.Mary's R.C. Kensal Green
Cremer, Sir William, 1838–1908, Hampstead
Cresswell, Sir Cresswell, 1793–1863 Kensal Green
Critchett, Sir Anderson, 1845–1925, Putney Vale
Crippen, Cora, 1875–1910, St Pancras & Islington
Critchett, George, 1817–82, Highgate
Crocker, Joseph, 1834–69, Brompton
Croft, Henry, 1862–1930, St.Pancras & Islington
Croft-Fraser, Thomas, –1956, Gunnersbury
Crompton, Richmal 1890–1969, Eltham
Cromwell, Hannah, 1653–1732, Bunhill Fields
Cromwell, Henry, 1658–1711, Bunhill Fields
Cromwell, William, Bunhill Fields
Crooks, Will 1852–1921 Tower Hamlets
Cross, Arthur –1965 Streatham Park
Crowe, Col. Joseph, 1826–76, West Norwood
Cruft, Charles, 1852–1938, Highgate
Crump, Sir William, 1851–1923, St.Pancras & Islington
Cubitt, Thomas, 1788–1855, West Norwood
Cubitt, Sir William, 1785–1861, West Norwood
Cunard, Sir Samuel, 1787–1865, Brompton
Cundy, Thomas   1820–95, Brompton

Cunningham, Allan, 1784–1842, Kensal Green
Cunningham, Marta, –1937, Kensington Hanwell
Cunningham, Peter 1789–1864 Nunhead
Cuppage, Lieut.Gen.Sir Burke, 1794–1877, Fulham
Cutbush, Herbert, –1918, Highgate
Cutbush, James, 1827–85, Highgate

D
Dadoo, Yusef, 1909–83 Highgate
Dalton, Lord Edward, of Forest & Frith, 1887–1962, Golders Green
Dalyell, Sir William, 1784–1865, Charlton
Dalzell, Robert, 15th Earl of Carnwath, 1847–1910, Fulham
Dalziel, Lord Davison, of Wooler, 1854–1928, Highgate
Dalziel, Edward, 1817–1905, Highgate
Dalziel, George, 1815–1902, Highgate
Dalziel, Thomas, 1823–1906, Highgate
Daniel, William, 1664–1739, Royal Hospital,Chelsea
Daniell, Thomas, 1749–1840, Kensal Green
Dark, James 1795–1871 Kensal Green
Darley, George, 1795–1846 Kensal Green
Davidge, George 1794–1842 West Norwood
Davies, Christiana, 1667–1739, Royal Hospital, Chelsea
Davies, 'Mutton', 1795–1867, Nunhead
Davis, Sir Charles, 1873–1938, Golders Green
Davison, James, 1813–85, Brompton
Dawber, Sir Guy, 1861–1938, Golders Green
Dawson, Charles 1850–1933 Rippleside
Dawson, Philip, 1825–90, Hampstead
Day, Sir John, 1826–1908 St.Mary's R.C. Kensal Green
Day, Lewis, 1845–1910, Highgate
Dear, Jeffrey, –1938, Kingston
de Blaquiere, Lord William 1778–1851 West Norwood

de Caceres, Simon, –1704 Jewish, Old Sephardi, Mile End Road
de Colyar, Henry, 1846–1925, Mortlake R.C.
de Courcy, John, Lord Kingsale, 1827–65 Kensal Green
de Ferranti, Sebastian, 1864–1930, Hampstead
Defoe, Daniel, 1661–1731, Bunhill Fields
de Keyser, Sir Polydor, 1832–98, Nunhead
Delargy, Hugh, 1908–76, St Mary's R.C. Kensal Green
de la Rue, Thomas 1793–1866 Kensal Green
de Montmorency, Sir Miles, 1893–1963, East Sheen
Denison, Lt.Gen.Sir William, 1804–71, Mortlake Old
d'Alcorn, Henry 1827–1905 St Pancras & Islington
d'Erlanger, Baron Frederic, 1868–1943, St. Mary's R.C., Kensal Green
de Morgan, William, 1839–1917 Brookwood
de Normandy, Alphonse, 1809–64, West Norwood
de Reuter, Baron Paul, 1816–99, West Norwood
de Rothschild, Sir Anthony, 1811–76, Jewish, Willesden
de Rothschild, Baroness Charlotte, 1819–84, Jewish, Willesden
de Rothschild, Evelina, 1839–66, Jewish, West Ham
de Rothschild, Ferdinand, 1839–98   Jewish, West Ham
de Rothschild, Meyer, 1818–74, Jewish, Willesden
de Sampayo, Baron, 1794–1860, Barnes Common
Devant, David, 1868–1941, Highgate
Devas, Anthony, 1911–58, Putney Vale
de Villiers, Sir Nicolas, 1902–58, St Marylebone
Dewar, Sir James, 1842–1943, Golders Green
Dickens, Catherine, 1815–70, Highgate

Dickens, Charles, 1837–96, Mortlake Old
Dickens, Sir Henry, 1849–1933, Putney Vale
Dickerson, I.P., –1900, Plumstead
Dickinson, Lowes 1819–1908 Kensal Green
Dickson, Gen.Sir Collingwood, 1817–1904, Kensal Green
Dilke, Charles 1789–1864 Kensal Green
Dimes, Albert, 1915–72, Bromley Hill
Disney, Gen.Sir Moore, 1766–1846, Kensal Green
Distant, William 1845–1922 Nunhead
Dixey, John –1953, Ealing
Dixon, Maj.Gen.Matthew, 1821–1905, Kensal Green
Dixon, Sir Pierson, 1904–65, Highgate
Dixon, William, 1821–79, Highgate
Dobbie, Gen.Sir William, 1879–1964, Charlton
Dobbs, Ernest, 1901–27, Chingford Mount
Dobson, Austin, 1840–1921, Kensington Hanwell
Dodd, George, –1854, West Norwood
Doherty, Laurie, 1876–1919, Putney Vale
Doherty, Reggie, 1874–1910, Putney Vale
Dolland, George 1774–1852 West Norwood
Don, Sir William, 1825–62, Kensal Green
Donaldson, Grp. Capt. Arthur 1915–1980 East Sheen
Donaldson, John, 1818–81 Royal Hospital, Greenwich
Donaldson, Thomas, 1795–1885, Brompton
Donkin, Bryan 1768–1855 Nunhead
Donkin, Sir Horatio 1845–1927 Nunhead
Doolittle, Thomas, 1632–1707, Bunhill Fields
Doughty, Charles, 1843–1926, Golders Green
Doulton, Sir Henry, 1820–97, West Norwood
Dove, Frederick, 1830–1923, Highgate
Downing, Henry, 1865–1947, Mitcham
Dowse, Rev. Charles, 1862–1934, Gunnersbury

Dowson, Ernest 1867–1900 Brockley
Dowton, William 1763–1851 West Norwood
Doyle, Richard, 1824–83, St.Mary's R.C. Kensal Green
Drew, Rev. George, 1818–80 Nunhead
Drewry, Lieut.George, 1894–1918, City of London
Druce, Thomas, 1793–1864, Highgate
Drughorn, Sir John, 1862–1943, Crystal Palace District
Dryden, Sir Alfred, 1821–1912, Putney Lower Common
Ducrow, Andrew, 1793–1842, Kensal Green
Duff, Edmund, 1869–1928, Queen's Road, Croydon
Dulcken, Maria, 1811–50, Highgate
Dundas, Gen.Sir David, 1735–1820, Royal Hospital, Chelsea
Dunn, Henry, 1801–78, West Norwood
Durandeau, Augustus 1848–93 Nunhead
Durham, Joseph, 1814–77, Kensal Green
Duveen, Sir Joseph, 1843–1908, Jewish, Willesden
Duveen, Lord Joseph, of Millbank, 1869–1939, Jewish Willesden
Dwyer, Sgt.Edward, –1916, St Thomas's R.C.
Dyer, George, 1755–1841, Kensal Green
Dyer, Major Gen. Godfrey, 1889–1977, Richmond

E

Eames, Sir William, 1821–1910, Brockley
Eassie, William, 1832–88, St Mary's R.C. Kensal Green
Eastlake, Sir Charles, 1793–1865, Kensal Green
Eaton, Henry, Lord Cheylesmore, 1816–91, Highgate
Ebbisham, Lord George, of Cobham, 1868–1953, Sutton
Edgar, William, 1791–1869, West Norwood
Edgington, Benjamin, 1794–1869 Nunhead
Elkington, George, –1897 Nunhead
Eddowes, Catherine, 1842–88 City of London
Edwards, Col. C.A., 1864–97, Mitcham
Edwards, Sgt. Frederick, 1894–1964 Richmond
Edwards, John, 1823–1911, Kensal Green
Edwards, Thomas 1879–1933 West Norwood
Effendi, Shogi, 1896–1957, Great Northern
Egan, Pierce, 1772–1849, Highgate
Elen, Gus, 1863–1940, Streatham Park
Elgar, Francis, 1845–1909, Highgate
Eliot, George, 1819–80, Highgate
Elkan, Benno, 1877–1960, Jewish, Pound Lane
Elkington, George 1824–97, Nunhead

Ellerman, Sir John, 1862–1933, Putney Vale
Ellis, Sir Arthur, 1883–1966, Chiswick Old
Ellis, Rev. William, 1795–1872, Abney Park
Ellis–Rees, Sir Hugh, 1900–74, Putney Vale
Ennis, Christopher, –1904, Mortlake R.C.
Ennis, Sir John, 1842–84, St.Thomas's R.C.
Enoch, Col. John, 1785–1855, West Norwood
Epps, James, –1907, West Norwood
Epstein, Sir Jacob, 1880–1959, Putney Vale
Eric, Douglas, 2nd Lord Hacking of Chorley, 1910–71, Putney Vale
Erichsen, Sir John, 1818–96, Hampstead
Esdaile, James, 1808–59, West Norwood
Espinosa, Edouard, 1871–1950, East Sheen
Espinosa, Louise, –1943, East Sheen
Eteson, Surg.Gen. Alfred, 1833–1910, Kensington Hanwell
Evans, Sir Edwin, 1855–1928, Wandsworth
Evans, George, 1876–1937 Ealing

INDEX OF THE DECEASED

Everest, Elizabeth, –1895, City of London
Eyre, Rev. John, 1754–1803, Chingford Mount

F

Fagge, Dr Charles 1838–83 West Norwood
Fairbrother, Sarah, 1816–90, Kensal Green
Fairlie, Robert, 1831–85, West Norwood
Falconer, Hugh, 1808–65, Kensal Green
Falk, Samuel 1708–82 Jewish, Alderney Road
Fanshawe, Henry, Lord Badeley, 1874–1951, Streatham Park
Faraday, Michael, 1791–1867, Highgate
Farey, Barnard, 1827–88, Nunhead
Farmer, L/Corp. Joseph, 1854–1930 Brompton
Farquhar, Horace, Earl, 1844–1923, Beckenham
Fauntleroy, Henry, 1785–1824, Bunhill Fields
Feller, Frank, 1848–1908, Kensington Hanwell
Fellowes, Sir Charles, 1799–1860, Highgate
Fellowes, Robert, 1770–1847, Kensal Green
Fenn, George 1831–1909 Isleworth
Fergusson, William, 1773–1846, Highgate
Ferrier, Kathleen, 1912–53, Golders Green
Field, Frederick, –1923, Streatham Park
Field, Henry, 1803–88, Nunhead
Field, James, 1845–1902, West Norwood
Field, Joshua, 1786–1863, West Norwood
Figgins, James, 1811–84, Nunhead
Figgins, Vincent, 1776–1844, Nunhead
Finberg, Alexander, 1866–1939, Barnes Common
Finney, Sir Stephen, 1852–1924, Putney Vale
Fischer, Harry, 1907–1977, Hampstead
Fisher, Andrew, 1862–1928, Hampstead

Fitch, Walter, 1817–92, Richmond
Fithian, Sir Edward, 1845–1936, Wandsworth
Fitzgerald, Richard, 1906–59, Streatham Park
Fitzgibbon, Edward, 1803–57, Highgate
Fitzherbert, Lord Alleyne of St. Helens, 1753–1839, Kensal Green
Fitzroy, Rt. Hon. Henry 1807–59 Westminster
Fleetwood, Charles, –1692, Bunhill Fields
Fleming, Sir Alexander, 1881–1955, Golders Green
Fletcher, Rev. Alexander, 1787–1860, Abney Park
Fletcher, Sir Banister, 1833–99, Hampstead
Flexmore, Richard, 1824–60, Kensal Green
Flynn, Sir Charles, 1884–1938, Croydon
Fogg, Eric, 1903–39, Golders Green
Foggo, George, 1793–1867, Highgate
Foggo, James, 1790–1860, Highgate
Foley, Patrick, 1836–1914, Hither Green
Foote, George, 1850–1915, City of London
Forrester, Alfred, 1804–72, West Norwood
Forster, John, 1812–76, Kensal Green
Forster, Sir Ralph, 1850–1930, Beckenham
Fortescue, George, 1847–1912, St. Pancras & Islington
Fortescue–Brickdale, Eleanor, 1872–1945, Brompton
Fowler, Sir John, 1817–98, Brompton
Fowler–Dixon, John, 1850–1943, Highgate
Fox, Sir Charles 1810–74 Nunhead
Fox, Sir John, 1874–1944, Golders Green
Fox, William, 1786–1864, Brompton
Foy, Tom, 1866–1917, Brompton
Foyle, William, 1885–1963, Highgate
Frampton, Sir George, 1860–1928, Golders Green
Francis, Francis, 1822–86, Twickenham
Frank, Sir Pierson, 1881–1951, Putney Vale

Frankau, Arthur, 1849–1904, Hampstead
Frankau, Pamela, 1908–67, Hampstead
Franks, Philas, 1722–65, Jewish, Alderney Road
Fraser, Reginald, –1966, Putney Vale
Fraser, William, 1st Lord Strathalmond, 1888–1970, Putney Vale
Fraser, William, 2nd Lord Strathalmond, 1916–76, Putney Vale
Freeling, Sir Francis, 1764–1836, Kensal Green
Fremantle, Sir Charles, 1800–69, Brompton
Freud, Sigmund, 1856–1939, Golders Green
Friese–Greene, William, 1855–1921, Highgate
Frinton, Freddie, 1916–68, Westminster
Fripp, George, 1813–96, Highgate
Fuller, Lt. Col. Francis, 1791–1853, Nunhead
Fulton, Sir Forrest, 1846–1925, Golders Green
Fury, Billy (Ronald Wycherley), 1941–1983, Paddington, Mill Hill
Fyfe, William, 1835–82, Paddington, Willesden Lane

G
Gabriel, Sir Thomas, 1811–73, West Norwood
Gaitskell, Hugh, 1906–63, Golders Green
Gale, Theophilus, 1628–78, Bunhill Fields
Gallup, Henry, –1885, West Norwood
Galsworthy, John, 1867–1933, Highgate
Galvin, George (Dan Leno), 1860–1904, Lambeth
Gandon, Charles, 1837–1902, Nunhead
Gardner, Benjamin, 1865–1948, City of London
Garrod Alfred, 1819–1907, Great Northern
Garnett, Richard, 1835–1906, Highgate
Garnier, Isaac, 1630–1711, Royal Hospital, Chelsea

Garstin, Sir William, 1849–1925, Golders Green
Garvice, Charles, 1851–1920, Richmond
Gassiot, John, 1797–1877, West Norwood
Gatti, Sir John, 1872–1929, St.Mary's R.C. Kensal Green
Gauntlett, Dr Henry, 1805–76, Kensal Green
Geary, Gen. Sir Henry, 1837–1918, Charlton
Geary, Stephen, 1797–1854, Highgate
Genée–Isitt, Adeline, 1878–1970, Golders Green
George, Duke of Cambridge, 1819–1904, Kensal Green
George, Ernest, 1839–1922, Golders Green
Gibbons, Caroll, 1903–54, Brookwood
Gibbons, Edward Stanley, 1840–1913, Twickenham
Gibson, John, 1817–92, Kensal Green
Gifford, Andrew, 1700–84, Bunhill Fields
Gilbart, James, 1794–1863, West Norwood
Gilbert, Alfred, 1828–1902, Paddington, Willesden Lane
Gilbert, Sir John, 1817–97, Brockley
Gilbert, Gen. Sir Walter, 1785–1853, Kensal Green
Glanville, Harold, 1854–1930, Nunhead
Glass, Joseph, 1791–1867 West Norwood
Glover, Brian, 1934–1997 Brompton
Glyn, Isabella, 1823–89 Kensal Green
Glyn, Elinor, 1864–1943, Golders Green
Godfrey, Francis, 1811–68, Mortlake Old
Godley, Pte. Sidney, 1889–1957, Manor Park
Godwin, George, 1815–88, Brompton
Goldie, Sir George, 1846–1925, Brompton
Golding, Benjamin, 1793–1863, Brompton
Goldsmid, Abraham,1756–1810, Jewish, Brady Street
Goldsmid, Benjamin,1753–1808, Jewish, Brady Street

Goldsmid, Sir Isaac, 1778–1858, Jewish, Kingsbury Road
Goldsmid, Sir Julian 1838–1934, Jewish, Kingsbury Road
Gollancz, Sir Israel, 1863–1930, Jewish, Willesden
Gomm. F.M. Sir Richard, 1784–1875 Nunhead
Goodman, Julia, 1812–1906, Jewish, Golders Green
Goodwin, Thomas, 1600–80, Bunhill Fields
Goossens, Sir Eugene, 1893–1962, St. Pancras & Islington
Gordon, Gen.Sir Thomas, 1832–1914, Brompton
Gorman, Albert, 1883–1959, Plumstead
Gorringe, Frederick, 1831–1909, Nunhead
Goss, Sir John, 1800–80, Kensal Green
Gosse, Sir Edmund, 1849–1928, St.Marylebone
Gough, Gen.Hugh, 1833–1909, Kensal Green
Gover, William, 1822–94, Nunhead
Govett, Samuel (Sam Polluski), 1866–1922, Lambeth
Grace, William, 1848–1915, Crystal Palace District
Gratten, Thomas, 1792–1864, Kensal Green
Granville, Christine, 1915–52, St.Mary's R.C. Kensal Green
Graves, Henry, 1808–92, Highgate
Greathead, James, 1844–96, West Norwood
Green, Charles, 1785–1870, Highgate
Green, Joseph, 1791–1863, Highgate
Greenaway, Kate, 1846–1901, Hampstead
Greenaway, Sir Percy, 1881–1956, Putney Vale
Greenough, George, 1778–1855, Kensal Green
Greenwood, Arthur, 1880–1954, Golders Green
Greenwood, Col.Harry, 1881–1948, Putney Vale

Gregory, Barnard, 1796–1852, Kensal Green
Gribble, Herbert, 1847–94, St.Thomas's R.C.
Grieve, Thomas, 1799–1882, West Norwood
Groom, John, 1845–1919, Highgate
Grossmith, George ,1847–1912, Kensal Green
Grove, Sir George, 1820–1900, Brockley
Grover, John, 1836–92, West Norwood
Guedalla, Philip, 1899–1944, Jewish, Golders Green
Gurney, Sir John, 1768–1845, Highgate
Gurney, William, 1777–1855, West Norwood
Gye, Sir Frederick, 1810–78, West Norwood

H
Habershon, Matthew, 1789–1852, Abney Park
Hackenschmidt, George, 1877–1968, West Norwood
Hafner, Frederick, –1907, Brompton
Haines, F.M. Sir Frederick, 1819–1909, Brompton
Haines, William, 1778–1848, West Norwood
Hall, Sir Douglas, 1866–1923, Putney Vale
Hall, John, 1774–1860, Abney Park
Hall, Radclyffe, 1880–1943, Highgate
Hall, Tommy, 1887–1949, Abney Park
Hamilton, Lord Claud, 1843–1925, Richmond
Hamilton, Adm.Sir Edward, 1772–1851, Kensal Green
Hampden, Rt Revd. Dickson 1793–1868 Kensal Green
Hampton, Sgt.Harry, 1870–1922, Richmond
Hancock, Thomas, 1786–1865, Kensal Green
Hann, Walter, 1838–1922, West Norwood
Hannen, Sir James, 1821–94, West Norwood

Hansard, Thomas, 1813–91, Kingston
Hansom, Joseph, 1803–82, St.Thomas's R.C.
Hansom, Joseph S., 1845–1931, St.Thomas's R.C.
Harben, Philip, 1906–70, Highgate
Harding, Gilbert, 1907–60, St.Mary's R.C. Kensal Green
Hardman, Sir William, 1828–90, Kingston
Hardwick, Arthur, –1922, Battersea St Mary's
Hardwick, Philip, 1822–92, Kensal Green
Hardy, Thomas, 1752–1832, Bunhill Fields
Hardy, Sir William, 1807–87, Brockley
Hargrave, John, 1894–1982, Hampstead
Harley, John, 1786–1858, Kensal Green
Harmsworth, Alfred, Lord Northcliffe 1865–1922 St Marylebone
Harmsworth, Cecil, 1st Lord Harmsworth, 1869–1948, St.Marylebone
Harmsworth, Sir Robert, 1870–1937, St.Marylebone
Harney, George, 1817–97, Richmond
Harris, Arthur, –1931, Charlton
Harris, Sir Augustus, 1852–96, Brompton
Harris, Rev. Dr. John 1802–56 Abney Park
Harris, Sir Percy, 1876–1952, Chiswick Old
Harrison, Reginald, 1837–1908, Highgate
Harrod, Henry, 1817–71, West Norwood
Harrold, Cdr. John, 1876–1948, Nunhead
Hart, Aaron, 1670–1756, Jewish, Alderney Road
Hart, Henry, 1818–91, Jewish, New Sephardi, Mile End Road
Hart, Joseph, 1712–68, Bunhill Fields
Hart, Moses, 1676–1757, Jewish, Alderney Road
Hart, Solomon, 1806–81, Jewish, Fulham Road
Hartley, Sir Charles, 1825–1915, Highgate

Harvey, William, 1796–1866, Richmond
Hastings, Sir George, 1853–1943, Teddington
Hawes, Sir Benjamin, 1797–1862, Highgate
Hawes, Sir Richard, 1893–1964, Kensington Hanwell
Hawke, Sir Edward, 1895–1964, Putney Vale
Hawke, Sir John, 1869–1941, Putney Vale
Hay, Sir James, 1839–1924, Brompton
Hay, Will, 1888–1949, Streatham Park
Hay–Drummond, Sir Robert, 1840–1926 Golders Green
Hayden, Joseph, 1786–1856, Highgate
Haynes, Arthur, 1914–66, Hammersmith New
Hayter, Sir George, 1792–1871, St.Marylebone
Hayward, Lt.Col.Reginald, 1881–1970, Putney Vale
Haywood, William, 1821–94, City of London
Hazell, Walter, 1843–1919, Beckenham
Head, Sir George, 1782–1855, Kensal Green
Hedgcock, Walter, 1864–1932, West Norwood
Hedmondt, Emanuel, 1857–1940, Golders Green
Henderson, Arthur, 1863–1935, Golders Green
Henderson, Dick, 1891–1958, St.Mary's R.C. Kensal Green
Henderson, Rev. Ebenezer, 1784–1858, Abney Park
Henderson, Sir Gerald, 1886–1963, Gunnersbury
Hendy, William, –1960, Battersea New
Hengler, Fredrick, 1820–87, Hampstead
Henriques, Sir Basil, 1890–1961, Jewish, Golders Green
Henry, William, –1928, Highgate
Henshaw, William, 1791–1877, Nunhead
Henry, William, –1928, Highgate

Henry, Sir Thomas, 1807–76, St.Thomas's R.C.
Henty, George, 1832–1902, Brompton
Herapath, John, 1790–1868, West Norwood
Herdman, Sir William, 1858–1924, Highgate
Herschell, Solomon, 1761–1842, Jewish, Brady Street
Hertslet, Lewis, 1787–1870, West Norwood
Hertz, Joseph –1946 Jewish, Willesden
Hewett, Samuel, –1904, Rippleside
Heywood, James, 1810–97, Barnes Common
Heywood, Peter, 1773–1831, Highgate
Hibberd, James, 1825–1890, Abney Park
Hickey, John, –1896, St. Pancras & Islington
Higgs, William, 1824–83, West Norwood
Hildyard, Thomas, 1821–88, Charlton
Hill, Francis, 1801–60, Nunhead
Hill, Sir George, 1855–1928, Royal Hospital, Greenwich
Hill, Jenny, 1850–96, Nunhead
Hill, Robert, 1811–78, Highgate
Hill, Sir Rowland, 1795–1879, Highgate
Hill, William, 1817–95, Westminster
Hillum, Mary, 1759–1864, Abney Park
Hilton, John, 1804–78, West Norwood
Hingston, Edward, c.1823–76, Kensal Green
Hiseland, William, 1620–1732, Royal Hospital, Chelsea
Hitch, Frederick, 1856–1913, Chiswick Old
Hobday, Sir Frederick, 1869–1939, Putney Vale
Hobhouse, Lord John, of Broughton de Gyfford, 1786–1869, Kensal Green
Hogarth, Georgina, 1827–1917, Mortlake Old
Hogarth, Mary, 1819–37, Kensal Green
Hogg, Quintin, 1845–1903, St.Marylebone
Hogg, Thomas, 1792–1862, Kensal Green

Holden, Gen.Sir Henry, 1856–1937, Highgate
Holl, Frank, 1845–88, Highgate
Holland, Gen.Sir Arthur, 1862–1927, Greenwich
Holland, Sir Edward, 1865–1939, Sutton
Holland, William, 1779–1856, Kensal Green
Hollingdale, Edward, –1956, St.Marylebone
Holloway, Sir Henry, 1857–1923, Wandsworth
Holman, James, 1786–1857, Highgate
Holman, John, 1824–83, Royal Hospital, Greenwich
Holmes, Maj.Thomas, 1808–93, Wandsworth
Holworthy, James, 1781–1841, Kensal Green
Holyoake, George, 1817–1906, Highgate
Hone, William, 1780–1842, Abney Park
Hood, Revd. Edwin, 1820–85, Abney Park
Hood, Tom, 1835–74, Nunhead
Hood, Thomas, 1799–1845, Kensal Green
Hooke, Robert, 1635–1703, City of London
Hore–Belisha, Lord Leslie, 1893–1957, Jewish, Golders Green
Horne, Rev Thomas, 1780–1862, Nunhead
Horniman, Rebekah, –1895, Camberwell
Horsley, William, 1774–1858, Kensal Green
Hose, Sir Charles, 1863–1929, Bandon Hill
Hosking, William, 1800–61, Highgate
Houston, Dame Fanny, 1857–1936, St.Marylebone
Hovenden, Robert, 1830–1908, Highgate
Howell, George, 1833–1910, Nunhead
Howell, James, 1787–1866, Nunhead
Hughes, Arthur, 1832–1915, Richmond
Hughes, David, 1830–1900, Highgate
Hughes, Col.Sir Edwin, 1832–1904, Plumstead

Hughes, Sir Thomas, 1856–1938, Streatham Park
Hullmandel, Charles, 1789–1850, Highgate
Hulton, Sir Edward, 1859–1925, Putney Vale
Hume, James, 1864–1932, Edmonton
Hume, Joseph, 1777–1855, Kensal Green
Humphreys, Sir George, 1863–1945, Gunnersbury
Hunt, James Leigh, 1784–1859, Kensal Green
Hunt, Sir John, 1859–1945, Westminster
Hunt, Walter, 1857–1946, Streatham Park
Hunter, Alfred, 1828–1911, West Norwood
Hunter, Robert, 1823–97, City of London
Hunter, Sir William, 1781–1856, West Norwood
Hurlstone, William, 1876–1906, Croydon
Hurwitz, Hyman, 1770–1844, Jewish, Brady Street
Hutchison, Leslie, 1900–69, Highgate
Huth, Frederick, 1777–1864, Kensal Green
Hutton, Sir John, 1841–1903, Highgate
Huxley, Thomas, 1825–95, St.Marylebone

I
Inglis, Sir James, 1851–1911, Kensington Hanwell
Ingram, Rev. Arthur, –1934, Gunnersbury
Innes, Charles, 1825–1907, Barnes Common
Irving, Henry, 1870–1919, Hampstead
Isaacs, Gerald, 2nd Marquess of Reading, 1889–1960, Jewish, Golders Green
Ismay, Bruce, 1862–1937, Putney Vale

J
Jack, George, 1855–1931, Golders Green
Jackson, Sir Charles, 1848–1923, Putney Vale
Jackson, Sir Henry, 1876–1937, Putney Vale
Jackson, John, 1769–1845, Brompton
Jackson, Rev. William, 1811–95, Ealing
Jacob, Jessie, 1890–1933, Golders Green
Jacob, Moses, –1781, Jewish, Brady Street
Jakobs, Josef 1898–1944 St Mary's R.C. Kensal Green
James, Sir William, 1807–81, Highgate
Jameson, Anna, 1794–1860, Kensal Green
Jameson, Sur.Gen.James, 1837–1904, Greenwich
Jeffrey, Julius, 1801–77, Richmond
Jenkins, William, –1778, Nunhead
Jenkyn, William, 1613–85, Bunhill Fields
Jerrold, Douglas, 1803–57, West Norwood
Jessel, Zadok, 1792–1864, Jewish, Fulham Road
Joel, Solomon, 1865–1931, Jewish, Willesden
John, Sir William, 1860–1952, Hampstead
Johns, Sir William, 1873–1937, Putney Vale
Johnson, Col.Sir Edwin, 1825–93, Kensington Hanwell
Johnson, John, 1661–1701, City of London
Johnson, Joseph, 1839–1906, Plaistow
Johnson, Ken, –1941, St Pancras & Islington
Johnson, Sir Walter, 1845–1910, Abney Park
Johnston, Sir Charles, 1848–1933, Putney Vale
Johnston, Lawson, 1839–1900, West Norwood
Jolowicz, Herbert, 1890–1954, Golders Green
Jones, George, 1786–1869, Highgate
Jones, Sir Horace, 1819–87, West Norwood
Jones, Capt.James, –1878, West Norwood
Jones, John, 1839–1929, Mortlake R.C.
Jones, John, 1800–82, Brompton
Jordan, Sir John, 1852–1925, Putney Vale
Joy, Henry, 1819–93, Chiswick Old

K

Kane, Adm.Sir Henry 1843–1917, St.Thomas's R.C.
Kanné, Joseph, –1888, Brompton
Kastrati, Quazim, 1908–74   East Sheen
Kay–Shuttleworth, Sir James, 1804–77, Brompton
Kearns, William 1794–1856 West Norwood
Keate, Thomas 1745–1821 Royal Hospital, Chelsea
Keeley, Robert, 1793–1869, Brompton
Keeling, Enoch Bassett, 1837–86, Abney Park
Kegan, Joseph 1862–1935 Bandon Hill
Kelly, Sir Fitzroy, 1796–1880, Highgate
Kelly, James, 1886–1920, Chiswick Old
Kelly, Mary, 1864–88, St.Patrick's R.C. Leystonstone
Kemble, Charles 1775–1854 Kensal Green
Kemp, Thomas, 1836–1905, Kensington Hanwell
Kendall, Henry 1776–1875 Kensal Green
Kendall, Surg.Gen.Henry, 1821–90, Bexley Heath
Kennedy, James, 1803–68, Highgate
Kennedy, William, 1839–85 Highgate
Kensit, John, 1853–1902, Hampstead
Kenyon, Harold, 1875–1959, St Marlebone
Kerensky, Alexander, 1881–1970, Putney Vale
Kershaw, Samuel, 1836–1914, West Norwood
Key, Sir John, 1794–1858, West Norwood
Kiffin, William, 1616–1701, Bunhill Fields
King, Thomas, 1835–88, West Norwood
King–Hall, Adm.Sir Herbert, 1862–1936, Putney Vale
Kingsley, George, 1827–92, Highgate
Kinloch–Cooke, Sir Clement, 1854–1944, Putney Vale
Kinnear, Roy, 1934–88, East Sheen
Kipling, Rudyard, 1865–1936, Golders Green
Kippis, Andrew, 1725–95, Bunhill Fields
Kitching, Theodore, 1866–1930, Abney Park
Kitching, Gen.Wilfred, 1893–1977, Camberwell New
Knight, Joseph, 1829–1907, Highgate
Knighton, Sir William, 1776–1836, Kensal Green
Knollys, Hanserd, 1599–1691, Bunhill Fields
Knollys, Gen.Sir William, 1797–1883, Highgate
Knowles, James, 1806–84, West Norwood
Knox, Dr Robert, 1791–1862, Brookwood
Kray, Charlie, 1927– 2000, Chingford Mount
Kray, Frances, 1944–67, Chingford Mount
Kray, Reggie, 1933–2000, Chingford Mount
Kray, Ronnie, 1933–1995, Chingford Mount
Kray, Violet, 1910–1982, Chingford Mount
Kunz, Charlie, 1896–1958, Streatham Park

L

Laidlaw, James, 1836–1921, Plaistow
Laing, Sir John, 1879–1978, Paddington, Mill Hill
Lambert, Constant, 1905–51, Brompton
Lambert, Percy, 1881–1913, Brompton
Landseer, John, 1769–1852, Highgate
Lane, Sarah, 1822–99, Kensal Green
Langham, Nat, 1820–71, Brompton
Lanner, Katherine, 1829–1908, West Norwood
Lardner, Nathaniel, 1684–1768, Bunhill Fields
Larpent, Sir George, 1786–1855, Kensal Green
Latey, John, 1808–91, Highgate
Laurie, Sir Peter, 1779–1861, Highgate
Lavery, Sir John, 1856–1941, Putney Vale
Lawson, Lionel, 1824–79, Jewish, Kingsbury Road

Leake, William, 1777–1860, Kensal Green
Learmore, Tom, 1866–1939, Streatham Park
Learmonth, Adm.Sir Frederick, 1866–1941, Gunnersbury
Lee, Alexander, 1802–51, West Norwood
Lee, Henry, 1817–98, Highgate
Lee, James, –1880, West Norwood
Lee, Sidney, 1866–1949, Gunnersbury
Leech, John, 1857–1942, Acton
Leech, John, 1817–64, Kensal Green
Leftley, Joseph, 1844–87, Rippleside
Leicester, Joseph 1825–1903 Nunhead
Lennox, Lord Alexander, 1825–92, St Thomas R.C.
Lepiankiewicz, Julius, 1910–73, Gunnersbury
Leslie, Charles, 1794–1859, Kensal Green
Letts, Thomas, 1803–72, West Norwood
Lettson, John, 1744–1815, Bunhill Fields
Levertoff, Rev. Paul, 1878–1954, Barkingside
Levey, Miriam, 1801–56, Jewish, Brady Street
Levi, Leone, 1821–88, Highgate
Levin, Bernard 1928–2004 Brompton
Levy, Sir Albert, 1864–1937, Jewish, Golders Green
Levy, Benjamin, –1705, Jewish, Alderney Road
Levy, David, 1740–99, Jewish, Alderney Road
Levy, Joseph, 1812–88, Jewish, Kingsbury Road
Lewis, Sir Charles, 1825–93, Putney Vale
Lewis, James, 1856–1924, Twickenham
Lewis, Sir Samuel, 1843–1903, Acton
Lewis, Ted 'Kid', 1896–1970, Jewish, East Ham
Lewis, Thomas, 1833–1915, Streatham
Lewis, Wyndham, 1779–1846, Kensal Green
Leybourne, George, 1842–84, Abney Park
Leyland, Frederick, 1831–92, Brompton
Liddell, Sir Adolphus, 1818–85, Mortlake Old
Liddell, Sir John, 1794–1868, Royal Hospital, Greenwich
Liebeschuetz, Hans, 1893–1978, Jewish, Golders Green
Lilly, Elizabeth, –1882, Highgate
Lillywhite, Frederick, 1792–1854, Highgate
Lima, Capt.Sir Bertram, 1886–1919, Hampstead
Limpus, Richard, 1824–75, West Norwood
Lindley, Robert, 1777–1855, Kensal Green
Lindo, Don Isaac, 1636–1712, Jewish, Old Sephardi, Mile End Road
Lindsay, Gen.Sir James, 1815–74, Mitcham
Lipton, Marcus, 1900–78, Jewish, East Ham
Lister, Joseph, Lord, 1827–1912, Hampstead
Liston, John, 1776–1864, Kensal Green
Liston, Robert, 1794–1847, Highgate
Livesey, Sir George, 1834–1908, Nunhead
Lloyd, Marie, 1870–1922, Hampstead
Lloyd, Maj.Gen.Sir Owen, 1854–1941, Kensal Green
Lobanov–Rostovsky, Princess Violette, 1893–1932, Brompton
Locke, Joseph 1805–60, Kensal Green
Lockhart, Charlotte, 1799–1837, Kensal Green
Lockwood, Sir Frank, 1847–97, Putney Vale
Loddiges, Conrad, 1821–65, Abney Park
Lodge, Gunner Isaac, 1866–1923 Hendon
Long, Edwin, 1829–91, Hampstead
Long, John St. John, 1798–1834, Kensal Green
Loraine, Robert, 1876–1935, Putney Vale
Losey, Joseph, 1909–84 Putney Vale
Loudon, John, 1783–1843, Kensal Green
Lover, Samuel, 1797–1868, Kensal Green
Low, Archibald, 1888–1956, Brompton
Lucas, Margaret, 1818–90, Highgate
Lucas, Samuel, 1811–65, Highgate

Lucey, William, –1893, Nunhead
Luckenbill, Daniel, 1881–1927, St.Marylebone
Lumley, Sir William, 1769–1850, Kensal Green
Lushington, Adm.Sir Stephen, 1803–77, Queen's Road, Croydon
Lusk, Sir Andrew, 1810–1909, Kensal Green
Lyle, Thomas, 1845–1931, Beckenham
Lyttleton, Gen.Sir Neville, 1845–1931, Royal Hospital, Greenwich

M
Maas, Joseph, 1847–86, Hampstead
McArthur, Hannibal, 1788–1861, West Norwood
McCall, Sir Robert, 1847–1934 Kensington Hanwell
McCallum, Capt.Kenneth, 1891–1963, Gunnersbury
McCarthy, Justin, 1830–1912, Hampstead
McCarthy, Rev.Wellbore, 1840–1925, Westminster
MacCartney, Sir Mervyn, 1853–1932, Golders Green
MacCaskie, Nicholas, 1881–1967, Gunnersbury
McCaul, Rev.Alexander, 1799–1863, City of London
Macchetta, Blanche, 1858–98, Brompton
McClintock, Adm.Sir Francis, 1819–1907 Kensington Hanwell
McCormack, Sir William, 1836–1901, Kensal Green
McCormick, William, 1801–78, Nunhead
McCulloch, John, 1789–1864, Brompton
MacDermott, G.H., 1845–1901, West Norwood
MacDonald, Col.Alexander, 1839–89, Teddington
MacDonald, Roderick, 1840–94, Charlton
MacDonnel, Lord Swinford, 1844–1925, Putney Vale
MacDougall, Sir John, 1844–1917, Charlton

MacDougall, Sir Patrick, 1819–94, Putney Vale
MacFadyean, Sir John, 1866–1929, Putney Vale
MacFarlene, Sir Donald 1830–1904, St.Thomas's R.C.
MacFarren, Sir George, 1813–87, Hampstead
MacGregor, Donald, 1839–1911, Mortlake R.C.
MacGregor, John, 1797–1856, West Norwood
McGrigor, Sir James, 1771–1858, Kensal Green
MacKay, Charles, 1814–89, Kensal Green
MacKay, Fulton, 1922–87, East Sheen
Mackenzie, A.B. Albert, 1898–1918, Camberwell
MacKenzie, Frederick, 1787–1854, Highgate
MacKenzie, Sir James, 1853–1925, Golders Green
MacLaine, Gen.Sir Archibald, 1773–1861, Highgate
MacLaren-Ross, Julian, 1912–64, Paddington Mill Hill
Maclauchlan, Hugh, 1852–99, Nunhead
Maclean, James, 1835–1906, Chiswick Old
MacLise, Daniel, 1806–70, Kensal Green
MacMillan, William, 1887–1977, Richmond
Macpherson, Maj.Gen.Sir William, 1858–1927, Brompton
McWhirter, Alan, 1925–75, Great Northern
Madden, Archibald, 1864–1928, Battersea St Mary's
Maddick, Edmund, –1939, West Norwood
Madge, Sir William, 1845–1927, Putney Vale
Madox–Brown, Ford, 1821–93, St.Pancras & Islington
Magnus, Sir Philip, 1842–1933, Jewish, Golders Green
Maher, Danny, 1881–1916, Paddington, Willesden Lane

Maitland, Sir Peregrine, 1777–1854, Kensal Green
Malcolmson, John, 1835–1902, Kensal Green
Mallett, Robert, 1810–81, West Norwood
Maltby, William, 1763–1854, West Norwood
Malynowski, Rt.Rev.Alexander, 1888–1957, Gunnersbury
Mancini, Al, 1903–68, St.Mary's R.C. Kensal Green
Mann, James, 1838–99, St.Mary's R.C. Kensal Green
Mann, Tom, 1856–1941, Golders Green
Manning, Cardinal Henry, 1808–92, St.Mary's R.C., Kensal Green
Manning, John, 1829–1908, Acton
Manns, Sir Augustus, 1823–1907, West Norwood
Mansell, George, 1805–70, Nunhead
Mantell, Gideon, 1790–1852, West Norwood
Manton, Joseph, 1766–1835, Kensal Green
Manzi, Frank, 1913–62, St. Pancras & Islington
Maple, John, 1815–1900, Highgate
Mappin, Edward, 1827–75, West Norwood
Marchand, P.O.Roy, 1918–40, Bromley Hill
Mare, Charles, 1814–98, Woodgrange Park
Marks, David, 1811–1909, Jewish, Kingsbury Road
Marks, Lord Simon, of Broughton 1888–1964, Golders Green
Marks, Henry, 1829–98, Hampstead
Marsden, William, 1796–1867, West Norwood
Marsh, Peter, 1828–1909, Nunhead
Marshall, Sir James, 1829–89, Mortlake R.C.
Marston, John, 1819–90, Highgate
Martin, Col. Albert, –1936, Manor Park
Martin, Sir Alec, 1884–1971, East Sheen
Martin, Air Marshal Sir Harold, 1918–88, Gunnersbury
Martin, Robert, 1821–1906, Twickenham
Martin, Sgt., –1981, Putney Vale
Martin, Adm.Sir Thomas, 1773–1854, Kensal Green
Martin–Harvey, Sir John, 1863–1944, East Sheen
Marx, Eleanor, 1855–98, Highgate
Marx, Karl, 1818–83, Highgate
Maryon–Wilson, Sir John, 1802–76, Charlton
Matcham, Frank, 1854–1920, Highgate
Mather, Rev.Robert, 1808–77, Abney Park
Matheson, Sir Alexander, 1861–1929, Putney Vale
Mathews, Sir Charles, 1850–1920, Putney Vale
Mattei, Titto, 1841–1914, St.Thomas's R.C.
Matz, Bertram, 1865–1925, Wandsworth
Maude, Gen.Frederick, 1821–87, Brompton
Maudslay, Joseph, 1801–67, West Norwood
Maule, Sir William, 1788–1858, Kensal Green
Maurice, Frederick, 1805–72, Highgate
Maxim, Sir Hiram, 1840–1916, West Norwood
Maxwell Brig. Gen. Sir Arthur, 1875–1935, St Marylebone
May, Adm.Henry, 1853–1904, Royal Hospital, Greenwich
May, Phil, 1864–1903, St. Mary's R.C. Kensal Green
Mayer, Carl, 1894–1944, Highgate
Mayhew, Augustus, 1826–75, Barnes Common
Mayhew, Henry, 1812–87, Kensal Green
Mayne, Sir Richard, 1796–1868, Kensal Green
Mays–Smith, Sir Alfred, 1861–1931, St.Marylebone
Meakin, James, 1866–1906, Highgate
Mears, Henry, –1912, Brompton
Medhurst, Rev.Walter, 1796–1857, Abney Park

Melia, Pius, 1800–83, St.Mary's R.C. Kensal Green
Mellish, William, –1834, Highgate
Mellon, Alfred, 1820–67, Brompton
Melville, Sir James, 1885–1931, St.Mary's R.C. Kensal Green
Mendes, Don Fernando, –1724, Jewish, Old Sephardi, Mile End Road
Mercury, Freddie, 1946–91, Kensal Green
Merewether, Sir Edward, 1858–1938, Brompton
Merivale, Herman, 1806–74, Brompton
Merryweather, Moses, 1791–1872, West Norwood
Messina, Alfredo, 1900–63, Gunnersbury
Messina, Guiseppe, 1879–1946, Gunnersbury
Meyer, Henry, 1797–1865, Battersea St Mary's
Meynell, Alice, 1847–1922, St.Mary's R.C. Kensal Green
Micklewright, George, 1817–76, City of London
Miers, Sir Henry, 1858–1942, Hampstead
Mikhailovich, Grand Duke Mikhail, 1861–1929, Hampstead
Miles, Frank, 1889–1912, Charlton
Millbourne, Sir Ralph, 1862–1942, Richmond
Miller, Sir Eric, 1927–77, Jewish, Willesden
Miller, Thomas, 1807–74, West Norwood
Miller, William, 1817–70, West Norwood
Mills, Sir Charles, 1825–95, Highgate
Mills, Freddie, 1919–65, Camberwell New
Mills, John, 1798–1879, Abney Park
Milman, Sir Francis, 1842–1922, Paines Lane
Milward, Thomas, 1826–74, Charlton
Mitchell, Air Chief Marshal Sir William, 1888–1944, Putney Vale
Mitra, Sid, 1856–1925, Golders Green
Mivart, St.George, 1827–1900, St. Mary's R.C. Kensal, Green
Mocatta, David, 1803–82, Jewish, Kingsbury Road

Moffat, Robert, 1795–1883, West Norwood
Moiseiwitch, Benno, 1890–1963, Golders Green
Mole, John, 1815–86, Brompton
Molesworth, Sir William, 1810–55, Kensal Green
Moloney, Joseph, –1896, Kingston
Molony, Sir Thomas, 1865–1949, Wimbledon
Monckton, Sir John, 1832–1902, Brompton
Monckton, Lionel, 1862–1924, Brompton
Mond, Alfred, Lord Melchett, 1868–1930, St. Pancras & Islington
Mond, Ludwig, 1839–1909, St.Pancras & Islington
Monk, William, 1823–89, Highgate
Montagu, Lord Robert, 1825–1902, Kensal Green
Montagu, Samuel,Lord Swaythling, 1832–1911, Jewish, Montagu Road
Montagu, Louis, 2nd Lord Swaythling, 1869–1927, Jewish, Willesden
Montefiore, Jacob, 1801–95, Jewish, New Sephardi, Mile End Road
Mooney, Sir John, 1874–1934, St. Mary's R.C. Kensal Green
Moor, Sir Ralph, 1860–1909, East Sheen
Moore, Bobby 1941–91 City of London
Moore, Edward, 6th Earl Mount Cashel, 1829–1915, Paddington, Willesden Lane
Morgan, Sir Benjamin, 1874–1937, East Sheen
Morgan, Charles, 1894–1958, Gunnersbury
Morgan, David, 1862–1937, Hampstead
Morgan, Lady Sydney, 1783–1859, Brompton
Mori, Nicholas, 1796–1839, Kensal Green
Morison, James, 1770–1840, Kensal Green
Morison, Rev. John, 1791–1859, Abney Park

Morley, Atkinson, 1781–1858, Highgate
Morley, Samuel, 1809–86, Abney Park
Morrell, Robert, 1823–1912, St. Pancras & Islington
Morris, John, 1812–80, Mortlake R.C.
Morris, John, 1810–86, Kensal Green
Morris, William 1808–74 Nunhead
Mortlock, William, 1832–81, West Norwood
Morton, Sir Desmond, 1891–1971, Gunnersbury
Morton, Fergus, Lord Henryton 1887–1973 Putney Vale
Moses, Nathan, 1692–1799, Jewish, Brady Street
Motley, John, 1814–77, Kensal Green
Mott, Thomas, 1841–1913, Royal Hospital, Greenwich
Mouat, Sur.Gen. Sir James, 1815–99, Kensal Green
Mountford, Edward, 1855–1908, Brookwood
Muir, Sir William, 1818–85, Charlton
Mullins, Edwin, 1848–1907, Hendon
Mullins, Thomas, 1839–99, Tower Hamlets
Mulready, William, 1786–1863, Kensal Grenn
Murchison, Dr Charles, 1830–75, West Norwood
Murchison, Sir Roderick, 1792–1871, Brompton
Murphy, Sir Dermod, 1914–75, Putney Vale
Murray, Alexander, –1888, West Norwood
Murray, Andrew 1845–1930 Bandon Hill
Murray, George, 1784–1843, Kensal Green
Murray, John, 1778–1843, Kensal Green
Musgrave, Thomas, 1788–60, Kensal Green
Myers, George, 1803–75, West Norwood
Mysore, Prince Hyder of, 1837–1923, Golders Green

N

Nabokoff, Constantine, 1871–1927, Golders Green
Nahum, Baron Sterling, 1906–56, Jewish, Golders Green
Nairne, Sir Charles, 1836–99, Charlton
Napier, Lt.Col.Sir William, 1785–1860, West Norwood
Nasmith, David, 1799–1839, Bunhill Fields
Navette, Nellie, 1865–1936, Streatham Park
Neal, Daniel, 1678–1743, Bunhill Fields
Neal, Edward, 1805–46, West Norwood
Neagle, Anna, 1904–86, City of London
Neilson, Lilian, 1848–80, Brompton
Nelson, Sir Thomas, 1826–85, Teddington
Nervo, Jimmy, 1897–1975, St.Marylebone
Neurath, Walter, 1903–67, Highgate
Newcomen, Thomas, 1663–1729, Bunhill Fields
Newman, Anthony, c.1774–1858, Nunhead
Newman, Edward, 1801–76, Nunhead
Newmann, Sir Sigismund, 1857–1916, Highgate
Newton, Sir Louis, 1867–1945, St.Marylebone
Newton, Richard, 1854–1926, Westminster
Nichols, John, 1779–1863, Kensal Green
Nichols, John, 1800–67, Battersea St Mary's
Nicholson, Francis, 1753–1844, Brompton
Nicholson, F.M.Lord William, 1845–1918, Brompton
Nicholson, Renton, 1809–61, Brompton
Nieto, David, 1654–1728, Jewish, Old Sephardi, Mile End Road
Nightingale, Joseph, 1827–82, Brompton
Nijinski, Vaslav, 1888–1950, St. Marylebone
Nisbet, Sir Alexander, 1812–92, Brockley
Noad, Henry, 1815–77, West Norwood
Noble, James, 1844–96, Wandsworth
Noble, Adm.James, 1774–1851, Kensal Green

Noble, Matthew, 1818–76, Brompton
Noble, Sir William, 1861–1943, Putney Vale
Nolan, Sir Sidney, 1917–92, Highgate
Nolloth, Adm. Matthew, 1810–82, Nunhead
Norman, F.M.Sir Henry, 1826–1904, Brompton
Northcott, Richard, 1871–1931, Golders Green
Nott, Cicely, 1832–1900, Nunhead
Novello, Ivor, 1893–1951, Golders Green
Nutter, William, 1759–1802, Chingford Mount

O
Oakley, Sir Henry, 1823–1915, Putney Vale
Oakley, John, 1813–87, West Norwood
O'Brien, James, 1797–1864, Abney Park
O'Brien, Sir Patrick, 1823–95, Kensal Green
O'Brien, Sir Tom, 1900–70, Hampstead
O'Connor, Fergus, 1794–1855, Kensal Green
O'Connor, Maj.Gen.Sir Luke, 1832–1915, St.Mary's, R.C., Kensal Green
O'Connor, Thomas, 1848–1929, St.Mary's R.C., Kensal Green
O'Connor, Dennis, 1840–83, St. Thomas's R.C.
Officer, Maj.Gen.William, –1988, East Sheen
Offor, George, 1787–1864, Abney Park
Ogle, Sir Thomas, 1618–1702, Royal Hospital, Chelsea
Ogdon, John, 1937–89, Gunnersbury
O'Gorman, Edith, 1842–1929, West Norwood
O'Gorman, Francis, –1923, St. Thomas's R.C.
O'Grady, Sir James, 1886–1934, Wandsworth
O'Leary, Maj. Michael, 1890–1961, Paddington, Mill Hill
Oke, George, 1821–74, Nunhead

Oliver, George, 1837–1901, West Norwood
Olpherts, Sir William, 1822–1902, Richmond
Ommaney, Adm.Sir Erasmus, 1814–1904, Mortlake Old
O'Neill, Norman, 1875–1934, Golders Green
Onoprienko, Gen.A.A., 1874–1922, Gunnersbury
Onslow, Sir Alexander, 1842–1908, Golders Green
Orchard, Mary, 1830–1906, Manor Park
Ordel, Harry, 1858–1914, Tower Hamlets
Ormsby, Gen.John, 1810–69, Charlton
Orton, Arthur, 1834–98, Paddington
Osbaldiston, David, 1794–1851 West Norwood
Osborn, George, 1808–91, Richmond
Osborn, Rear Adm.Sherard, 1822–75, Highgate
Osborne, William, 1814–91, Teddington
Ostafmedjy, Princess, –1934, Golders Green
Otway, Sir Loftus, 1774–1854, Highgate
Otway, Adm.Sir Robert, 1770–1846, Kensal Green
Overton, Robert, 1854–1924, Chingford Mount
Owen, Sir Hugh, 1804–81, Abney Park
Owen, John, 1616–83, Bunhill Fields
Owen, Thankful, 1620–81, Bunhill Fields
Owens, Sir Charles, 1845–1933, Putney Vale
Owen, Robert, 1771–1858, Kensal Green

P
Page, Vera, 1920–31, Gunnersbury
Paget, Gen.Sir Arthur, 1851–1928, Putney Vale
Paget, Gen.Sir Edward, 1775–1849, Royal Hospital, Chelsea
Paget, Sir James, 1814–99, St.Marylebone
Painter, Sir Frederick, 1844–1926, East Sheen
Palaeologu, Princess Eugenie, –1934, West Norwood

Palgrave, Francis, 1824–97, Barnes Common
Palgrave, William, 1826–88, St.Thomas's R.C.
Palliser, Sir William, 1830–82, Brompton
Palmer, Charles, 1819–1900, St.Mary's R.C. Kensal Green
Panizzi, Sir Anthony, 1797–1879, St.Mary's R.C. Kensal Green
Pankhurst, Emmeline, 1858–1928, Brompton
Panufnik, Sir Andrze, 1914–91, Richmond
Papworth, Wyatt, 1822–94, Highgate
Parker, Charles, 1799–1881, St.Thomas's R.C.
Parker, Sir Henry, 1825–94, St.Mary's R.C. Kensal Green
Parker, Capt.Henry, 1789–1873, Royal Hospital, Greenwich
Parker, John, 1792–1870, Highgate
Parker, Rev. Joseph, 1830–1902, Hampstead
Parker, William, 1823–90, Wandsworth
Parkes, Alexander, 1813–90, West Norwood
Parratt, James, –1878, Charlton
Parry, Joseph, 1841–1903, Hampstead
Paton, Sir George, 1859–1934, Putney Vale
Paton, Capt. George, 1895–1917, Putney Vale
Pavlova, Anna, 1881–1928, Golders Green
Pavy, Frederick, 1829–1911, Highgate
Payne, Joseph, 1808–78, Highgate
Payne, William, 1804–61, Highgate
Pearce, Matthew, –1775, Chingford Mount
Pearson, Sir Arthur, 1866–1921, Hampstead
Pearson, Charles, 1793–1862, West Norwood
Pearson, Frank, 1864–1947, Chiswick Old
Peart, Walter, –1898, Kensal Green
Peel, Rt.Hon.Jonathan, 1799–1879, Twickenham

Peile, James, 1833–96, Kensington Hanwell
Pelham, Rear Adm.Frederick, 1808–61, Highgate
Pelham–Clinton, Lord Edward 1836–1907 Brookwood
Pell, Adm.Sir Watkin, 1788–1869, Charlton
Pellegrini, Carlo, 1839–89, St.Mary's R.C., Kensal Green
Pennefather, Gen.Sir John, 1800–72, Brompton
Penton, Stephen, 1793–1873, Brompton
Pepper, John, 1821–99, West Norwood
Pepys, William, 1775–1856, Highgate
Perceval, Adm. George, 6th Earl of Egmont, 1794–1874, Charlton
Perceval, Sir Westby, 1854–1928, Wimbledon
Perry, Albert, –1915, Acton
Petersen, Sir William, 1856–1921, St Marylebone
Pettigrew, Thomas, 1791–1865, Brompton
Pettitt, Henry, 1848–93, Brompton
Phelps, Samuel, 1804–78, Highgate
Phelps, Rev. William, 1776–1856, West Norwood
Philip, John, 1817–67, Kensal Green
Philip, Dr Robert, 1791–1858, Abney Park
Phillips, Sir Benjamin, 1810–89, Jewish, West Ham
Phillips, Lawrence, 1842–1922, Jewish, Golders Green
Phillips, Morgan, 1902–63, North Sheen
Phillips, Philip, 1802–64, West Norwood
Philpot, Joseph, 1802–69, Queen's Road, Croydon
Pickering, William, 1796–1854, Kensal Green
Pickersgill, Henry, 1782–1875, Barnes Common
Pickersgill, Jeanette, –1885, Kensal Green
Pigott, John, –1923, Richmond
Pilsudska, Alexandra, 1867–1963, North Sheen

Pinwell, George, 1842–75, Highgate
Pirie, Sir John, 1781–1851, West Norwood
Pissarro, Felix, 1874–97, Richmond
Pitman, Sir Isaac, 1813–97, Golders Green
Platt, Sir Thomas, 1790–1862, Highgate
Plomley, Sir Roy, 1914–85, Putney Vale
Poland, Sir William, 1797–1884, Greenwich
Pollitt, Harry, 1890–1966, Golders Green
Pollock, Benjamin, 1856–1937, Chingford Mount
Pond, Christopher, 1826–81, West Norwood
Poole, Edward, 1830–67, West Norwood
Poole, Sophia, 1804–91, West Norwood
Poole, Paul, 1807–79, Highgate
Pope–Hennessy, James, 1916–74, Kensal Green
Porte, Col. John C., 1884–1919, West Norwood
Powell, Vavasour, 1617–70, Bunhill Fields
Powell, Revd. Baden, 1796–1860, Kensal Green
Power, Sir James, 1884–1914, St.Thomas's R.C.
Power, Sir Samuel, 1863–1932, Putney Vale
Powley, William, 1818–96, Chingford Mount
Praed, Winthrop, 1802–39, Kensal Green
Prain, Sir David, 1857–1944, Putney Vale
Prendergast, Gen.Sir Harry, 1834–1913, Richmond
Prendergast, Adm.Sir Robert, 1864–1946, Golders Green
Prevost, Louis, 1796–1858, Highgate
Price, Richard, 1723–91, Bunhill Fields
Prince, Arthur, 1881–1948, Hampstead
Prinsep, Valentine, 1838–1904, Brompton
Probyn, Mary, 1855–1909, Mortlake R.C.
Procter, Adelaide, 1825–64, Kensal Green
Prosser, Alfred, –1923, Highgate
Prout, Samuel, 1783–1852, West Norwood

Pudukota, H.H.the Rajah of, 1875–1928, Golders Green
Pugh, Hugh, 1812–40, Bunhill Fields
Pullum, William, 1887–1960, Camberwell New
Punshon, Rev. William, 1824–81, West Norwood
Purkiss, William, 1827–99, Paddington, Willesden Lane

Q

Quain, Sir John, 1816–76, St.Marylebone
Quain, Jones, 1796–1865, Highgate
Quain, Sir Richard, 1816–98, Hampstead
Quain, Richard, 1800–87, St. Marylebone
Quare, Daniel, 1648–1724, Bunhill Fields
Quaritch, Bernard, 1819–99, Highgate
Quinn, Sir Patrick, 1855–1936, Putney Vale

R

Raggi, Mario, 1821–1907, West Norwood
Raincock, Sophia, –1890, West Norwood
Ralli, Augustus, –1872, West Norwood
Ram, Rev.Stephen, –1746, Chingford Mount
Ramsbottom, James, 1891–1925, Richmond
Rank, Joseph, 1854–1943, Sutton
Rathbone, Eleanor, 1872–1946, West Norwood
Rattigan, Sir Terence, 1911–77, Kensal Green
Ranyard, Arthur, 1845–94, Kingston
Ravenscroft, Francis, 1828–1902, Nunhead
Ravenscroft, Humphrey, 1784–1851, Nunhead
Ravenshaw, Rev. Thomas, 1829–82, Nunhead
Rawlinson, Sir Robert, 1810–98, Brompton
Reach, Angus, 1821–56, West Norwood
Reed, Rev.Andrew, 1787–1862, Abney Park
Reed, Sir Carol, 1906–76, Gunnersbury
Reed, Sir Charles, 1819–81, Abney Park

Reed, Sir Edward, 1830–1906, Putney Vale
Reed, Talbot Baines, 1852–93, Abney Park
Reed, Thomas, 1817–88, Mortlake Old
Rees, Abraham, 1743–1825, Bunhill Fields
Regnart, Sir Horace, 1841–1912, St.Pancras & Islington
Reid, Sir George, 1845–1918, Putney Vale
Reid, Thomas Mayne, 1818–83, Kensal Green
Rendel, James, 1799–1856, Kensal Green
Rendle, William, 1820–81, Brompton
Rennie, John, 1794–1874, Kensal Green
Renton, Sir Thomas, 1665–1740, Royal Hospital, Chelsea
Renwick, Sir Harry, 1861–1932, Putney Vale
Repton, George, 1786–1858, Kensal Green
Reynolds–Stephens, Sir William, 1862–1943, Golders Green
Richard, Henry, 1812–88, Abney Park
Richards, Sgt.Alfred, 1879–1953, Putney Vale
Richards, Henry, 1819–85, Brompton
Richardson, Dorothy, 1873–1957, Streatham Park
Richardson, Joseph, 1790–1855, Kensal Green
Richardson, Sir Owen, 1879–1959, Brookwood
Richardson, Sir Ralph 1902–83 Highgate
Richardson, Thomas, 1870–1912, Richmond
Richmond, George, 1809–96, Highgate
Ricketts, Capt.Charles, 1788–1867, Kensal Green
Ridout, Maj.Gen.Sir Dudley, 1866–1941, Richmond
Rigby, Sir John, 1834–1903, St.Marylebone
Rippon, John, 1751–1836, Bunhill Fields
Ritson, Joseph, 1752–1803, Bunhill Fields
Roberts, David, 1796–1864, West Norwood

Roberts, Richard, 1789–1864, Kensal Green
Robertson, Thomas, 1858–95, Paddington, Willesden Lane
Robertson, Thomas, 1829–71, Abney Park
Robertson, Sir William, 1860–1933, Brookwood
Robins, Rev. Arthur 1834–89 Kensal Green
Robinson, Sir Bryan, 1808–87, Ealing
Robinson, Henry, 1775–1867, Highgate
Robinson, Peter, 1804–74, Highgate
Robinson, William, 1838–1935, Golders Green
Robinson, William, 1861–1918, East Sheen
Robson, Thomas, 1822–64, West Norwood
Rogers, Frederick, 1846–1915, Nunhead
Rogers, James, 1823–63, Brompton
Rogers, Nathaniel, 1808–84, Abney Park
Rolfe, Robert, 1855–1921, Richmond
Roll, Sir James, 1846–1927, City of London
Rolls, Charles, 1799–1885, Nunhead
Romilly, Lord John of Barry, 1802–74, Brompton
Rosa, Carl, 1843–89, Highgate
Rose, Sir William, 1820–81, Battersea St Mary's
Rosebery, Hannah, Countess of 1851–90, Jewish, Willesden
Rosen, Frederick, 1805–37, Kensal Green
Roseway, Sir David, 1890–1969, Pinner
Ross, Lt.Gen.Sir Alexander, 1840–1910, Ealing
Ross, Adm.Sir John, 1777–1856, Kensal Green
Ross, Sir Ronald, 1857–1932, Putney Vale
Ross, Sir William, 1794–1860, Highgate
Rossetti, Christina, 1830–94, Highgate
Rossetti, Gabriele, 1783–1854, Highgate
Rossetti, William, 1829–1919, Highgate
Roth, Camillo, –1888, Jewish, Kingsbury Road

Roth, Dr. Ernst, 1896–1971, Twickenham
Rothschild, Alfred, 1842–1918, Jewish, Willesden
Rothschild, Lord Lionel, 1868–1937, Jewish, Willesden
Rothschild, Lionel, 1808–79, Jewish, Willesden
Rothschild, Lord Nathan, 1840–1915, Jewish, Willesden
Rothschild, Nathan Meyer, 1777–1836, Jewish, Brady Street
Rothschild, The Hon. Nathanial, 1877–1927, Jewish, Willesden
Rothschild, Nathaniel, 3rd Lord, 1910–90 Jewish, Brady Street
Roupell, William, 1831–1909, West Norwood
Rous, Adm. Henry, 1795–1877, Kensal Green
Routledge, Edmund, 1843–99, Kensal Green
Routledge, William, 1859–1939, Putney Vale
Rowland, Christopher, 1929–67, Greenwich
Royds, Vice Adm.Sir Charles, 1876–1931, Golders Green
Russell, Adm.Lord Edward, 1805–87, Brompton
Russell, Henry, 1812–1900, Kensal Green
Russell, James, 1863–1939, Highgate
Russell, Rev. Joshua 1796–1870 Nunhead
Russell, Sir Peter, 1816–1905, St.Marylebone

S
Sabbat, Kazimierz, 1913–1989, Gunnersbury
Sabine, Joseph, 1770–1837, Kensal Green
Sadek, Napoleon, 1905–70, Jewish, Golders Green
St.Bobisch, Milosh, 1886–1951, Brompton
Saklatvala, Shapurji, 1874–1936, Brookwood
Salomons, David, 1797–1873, Jewish, West Ham
Salt, William, 1805–63, Highgate
Salviati, Giulio, c.1843–98, Brookwood
Sampayo, Anthony, 1818–62, Royal Hospital, Greenwich
Samuda, Joseph, 1813–85, Kensal Green
Samuel, Sir Harry, 1853–1934, Jewish, Golders Green
Samuel, Herbert, 1st Visct.Samuel, 1870–1963, Jewish, Willesden
Samuel, James, 1797–1866, Jewish, West Ham
Saponjic, Vladimir, 1896–1952, Brompton
Sargent, John Singer, 1856–1925, Brookwood
Sassoon, Sir Edward, 1853–1934, Jewish, Golders Green
Saunders, Albert, 1863–93, Crystal Palace District
Saunders, Sir Edwin, 1814–1901, Putney Vale
Saunders, John, 1867–1919, West Norwood
Saunders, William, 1825–1901, City of London
Sawa, Archbishop, 1898–1951, Brompton
Sayer, Frederic, –1868, Highgate
Sayers, Thomas, 1826–65, Highgate
Schiff, David, –1791, Jewish, Alderney Road
Schiller, Henry, 1807–71, Nunhead
Scoles, Joseph, 1798–1863, St.Thomas's R.C.
Scott, Sir Andrew, 1857–1939, Greenwich
Scott, Anne, 1803–33, Kensal Green
Scott, Maj.Gen. Douglas, 1848–1924, East Sheen
Scott, Sir Edward, 1842–83, Beckenham
Scott-Moncrieff, Sir Colin, 1836–1916, Wimbledon
Scratchley, Gen. Peter, 1835–85, Charlton
Scriven, Edward, 1775–1841, Kensal Green
Scriven, Mary, –1936, West Norwood
Seacole, Mary, 1805–81, St.Mary's R.C. Kensal Green

Seale, Edward, –1867, Camberwell
Seaman, Sir Owen, 1861–1938, Putney Vale
Searle, Edward, 1809–87, Hampstead
Seaton, Edward, 1815–80, Kensal Green
Selby, James, 1844–88, Highgate
Sell, Frederick, –1917, West Ham
Selwyn, Lord Justice Sir Charles, 1813–69, Nunhead
Semon, Sir Felix, 1849–1921, Golders Green
Semple, Col,.Sir David, 1856–1937, Westminster
Setty, Stanley, 1902–49, Jewish, Golders Green
Seymour, Dr Edward, 1796–1866, West Norwood
Sharpe, Sir Alfred, 1853–1935, Golders Green
Sharpe, Samuel, 1799–1881, Abney Park
Shaw, Sir Eyre, 1830–1908, Highgate
Shaw, John Byam, 1872–1919, Kensington Hanwell
Shaw, John, 1803–70, Kensal Green
Shaw–Lefevre, Charles, Viscount Eversley, 1794–1888, Kensal Green
Shenton, George, 1842–1908, West Norwood
Shepherd, Lord George of Spalding, 1881–1954, Golders Green
Shepherd, James,, 1835–1907 Royal Hospital, Greenwich
Shepherd, Mary, –1989, St Pancras & Islington
Sherry, Henry, 1850–1933, Kensal Green
Short, Albert, 1875–1932, Hampstead
Short, Horace, 1872–1917, Hampstead
Shute, Geoffrey, 1892–1951, Gunnersbury
Sibree, Deborah, –1920, Bromley Hill
Sibree, James, –1919, Bromley Hill
Sibree, Mary, –1926, Bromley Hill
Siddal, Elizabeth, 1829–62, Highgate
Sidney, Violet, –1929, Queen's Road, Croydon
Sieff, Lord Israel, 1890–1972, Golders Green
Siemens, Sir William, 1823–1883, Kensal Green
Sieveking, Sir Edward, 1816–1904, Abney Park
Sievier, Robert, 1794–1865, Kensal Green
Sim, John, 1810–75, Kingston
Sims, John, –1881, City of London
Simms, William, 1793–1860, West Norwood
Simon, Sir John, 1853–94, Jewish, Golders Green
Simpson, William, 1828–97, West Norwood
Singer, Simeon, 1846–1906, Jewish, Willesden
Sinnott, John, 1829–96, Battersea New
Skeffington, Sir Lumley, 1771–1850, West Norwood
Skerrett, Sir Charles, 1863–1929, St.Mary's R.C., Kensal Green
Slack, Wilf, 1953–89, Greenford Park
Smart, Dr. David, 1848–1913, Nunhead
Smart, Sir George, 1776–1867, Kensal Green
Smart, Henry, 1813–79, Hampstead
Smart, Adm.Sir Robert, 1796–1874, Chiswick Old
Smiles, Samuel, 1812–1904, Brompton
Smirke, Robert, 1753–1845, Kensal Green
Smirnove, Rev. James, 1756–1840, Kensal Green
Smith, Albert, 1816–60, Brompton
Smith, Alfred, 1828–91, Nunhead
Smith, Alfred, 1861–1932, Plumstead
Smith, Sir Allan, –1941, Hampstead
Smith, Donald, 1st Lord Strathcona & Mount Royal, 1820–1914, Highgate
Smith, Edgar, 1847–1916, Kensington Hanwell
Smith, Sir Francis, 1808–73, Brompton
Smith, George, –1784, Chingford Mount
Smith, John, 1774–1851, Abney Park
Smith, John, –1892, West Norwood
Smith, Sir John Mark, 1790–1874, Kensal Green

Smith, Sir Lumley, 1834–1918, West Norwood
Smith, Margaret, –1815, Chingford Mount
Smith, Martin, –1905, Golders Green
Smith, Sir Matthew, 1879–1959, Gunnersbury
Smith, Richard, 1786–1855, West Norwood
Smith, Richard, 1836–1900, Highgate
Smith, Robert, –1970, Sutton
Smith, Sydney, 1771–1845, Kensal Green
Smith, Sir Thomas, 1833–1909, St.Marylebone
Smith, William, 1792–1865, Kensal Green
Smith, Adm. William, 1799–1892, Brompton
Smith, Sir William, 1850–1932, Charlton
Smolenski, Gen. Jozef, 1894–1978, Gunnersbury
Smyly, Sir Philip, 1896–1953, Putney Vale
Smythe, George, Viscount Strangeford, 1818–57, Kensal Green
Snell, Hannah, 1723–92, Royal Hospital, Chelsea
Snell, Henry Saxon, 1830–1904, Putney Vale
Snell, Col. W.H., 1822–1910, Queen's Road, Croydon
Snow, John, 1813–58, Brompton
Sobolewski, Edmund, 1884–1974, Gunnersbury
Solander, Daniel, 1733–82, Brookwood
Solomon, Edward, 1855–90, Jewish, Willesden
Sophia, Princess, 1777–1848, Kensal Green
Sopwith, Thomas, 1803–79, West Norwood
Sotheby, Samuel, 1805–61, Brompton
Sowerby, George, 1788–1854, Highgate
Soyer, Elizabeth, 1813–42, Kensal Green
Spence, Rev. Dr. James, 1821–74, Abney Park
Spencer, Charles, 1837–90, Highgate

Spencer, Edward, 1833–78, Paddington, Willesden Lane
Spencer, George, –1916, St. Pancras & Islington
Spencer, Herbert, 1820–1903, Highgate
Spencer, Percival, 1864–1913, St.Pancras & Islington
Spencer Wells, Sir Thomas, 1818–97 Brompton
Spicer, James, 1807–88, Chingford Mount
Spielman, Sir Isidore, 1854–1925, Jewish, Willesden
Spielman, Sir Meyer, 1856–1936, Jewish, Willesden
Spreckley, Air Marshal Sir Herbert, 1904–63, Gunnersbury
Spring, Tom, 1795–1851, West Norwood
Spurgeon, Rev. Charles, 1834–92, West Norwood
Spurr, Alexander, –1873, Great Northern
Squires, Dorothy, 1915–98, Streatham Park
Stamp, Lord Josiah, of Shortlands, 1880–1941, Crystal Palace District
Stanfield, Clarkson, 1793–1867, St.Mary's R.C., Kensal Green
Steel, Alan, 1858–1914, Kensal Green
Stekel, William, 1868–1940, Golders Green
Stephens, Edward, –1861, West Norwood
Stephen, Sir Leslie, 1832–1904, Highgate
Stephens, William, 1817–71, Brockley
Stephenson, Rev. Bowman, 1839–1912, City of London
Stephenson, Mill, –1937, West Norwood
Stern, Aaron, 1820–85, City of London
Stern, Sir Frederick, 1884–1967, Jewish, Golders Green
Stevens, Alfred, 1818–75, Highgate
Stevens, Benjamin, 1833–1902, Kensal Green
Stevens, John, –1861, West Norwood
Stewart, Charles, 1840–1907, Highgate
Stewart, Charles, 1775–1837, Kensal Green
Stewart, F.M.Sir Donald, 1824–1900, Brompton

Stewart-Smith, Sir Dudley, 1857-1919, Putney Vale
Stiff, James, 1808-97, West Norwood
Stitch, Wilhelmina, 1888-1936, Golders Green
Stockley, Gen.Ernest, 1872-1946, Eltham
Stodare, Col., 1832-66, Highgate
Stoker, Bram, 1847-1912, Golders Green
Stokes, Leonard, 1858-1925, Mortlake R.C.
Stokowski, Leopold, 1882-1977, St.Marylebone
Stone, Capt.Walter, 1891-1917, Greenwich
Stopes, Marie, 1880-1958, Golders Green
Storey, Sir Thomas, 1851-1933, Putney Vale
Storks, Sir Henry, 1811-74, Highgate
Stothard, Thomas, 1755-1834, Bunhill Fields
Stoughton, Thomas, 1848-1917, West Norwood
Strang, William, 1859-1921, Kensal Green
Strange, Thomas, 1808-84, West Norwood
Stratton, Eugeen, 1861-1918, Bandon Hill
Stringer, Cecil, 1900-41, Mitcham
Stuart, John, 1815-66, Kensal Green
Stuart, Leslie, 1862-1928, Richmond
Summers, Rev. Montague, 1880-1948, Richmond
Sutcliffe, George, 1878-1943, East Sheen
Sutherland, Sir Iain, 1925-86, Highgate
Swan, Charles, -1923, Hendon
Swan, John, 1787-1869, Abney Park
Swanwick, Anna, 1813-99, Highgate
Sweny, Capt. Mark, 1783-1865, Royal Hospital, Greenwich
Swinburne-Hanham, John, 1860-1935, Golders Green
Swinfen, Lord of Chertsey, 1851-1919, Golders Green
Szlumper, Sir James, 1834-1914, Richmond

T

Tager, Marc, -1988, Jewish, Willesden
Talfourd, Sir Thomas, 1795-1854, West Norwood
Tasker, Helen Countess, -1888, St.Thomas's R.C.
Tasker, Joseph, -1848, St.Thomas's R.C.
Tate, Sir Henry, 1819-99, West Norwood
Tatham, Paton, Capt.G.H., 1895-1917, Putney Vale
Tao, Fau Kuang, -1976, Hendon
Tauber, Richard, 1891-1948, Brompton
Taylor, Sir Andrew, 1850-1937, Highgate
Taylor, Thomas, 1879-1932, Richmond
Taylor, Tom, 1817-80, Brompton
Taylor, Warrington, 1838-70, St. Thomas's R.C.
Tebbutt, Harriet, 1815-93 Nunhead
Temple, George, 1892-1914, Acton
Tenniel, Sir John, 1820-1914, Kensal Green
Terriss, William, 1847-97, Brompton
Terry, Fred, 1863-1933, Hampstead
Thackeray, William, 1811-63, Kensal Green
Thesiger, Alfred, 1838-80, Brompton
Thomas, Brandon, 1850-1914, Brompton
Thomas, David, 1813-94, West Norwood
Thomas, Edward, 1878-1917, Battersea New
Thomas, George, 1850-1923, Kensington Hanwell
Thompson, Edith, 1893-1923, Brookwood
Thompson, Francis, 1859-1907, St.Mary's R.C., Kensal Green
Thompson, Sir Henry, 1820-1904, Golders Green
Thompson, Percy, -1922, City of London
Thompson, Col. Robert, 1833-90, Twickenham
Thompson, Dr. Theophilus, 1807-60, West Norwood
Thoms, William, 1803-85, Brompton
Thomson, Alexander, -1905, Battersea New

Thomson, Charles, Lord Ritchie, 1838–1906, Kensal Green
Thomson, James, 1834–82, Highgate
Thornbury, George, 1828–76, Nunhead
Thornton, Harry, –1918, Highgate
Thornton, Henry, 1800–81, West Norwood
Thornton, Richard, 1776–1865, West Norwood
Thwaites, Sir John, 1815–70, Nunhead
Tietjens, Theresa, 1831–77, Kensal Green
Tighe, Lieut.Gen.Sir Michael, 1864–1925, East Sheen
Tilling, Robert, –1760, Bunhill Fields
Tilling, Thomas, 1825–93, Nunhead
Tilly, Vesta, 1864–1952, Putney Vale
Tindal, Sir Nicholas, 1776–1846, Kensal Green
Tinworth, George, 1843–1913, West Norwood
Tomlinson, Joseph, 1823–94, Nunhead
Topolski, Feliks, 1907–89, Highgate
Titcombe, Bishop Jonathan Holt, 1820–87, Brompton
Toumayan, Archbp. Bessak, 1912–81, Gunnersbury
Townsend, John, 1757–1826, Bunhill Fields
Towry–Law, William, 1809–86, Mortlake R.C.
Tracy, Adm.Sir Richard, 1837–1907, Kensal Green
Treloar, Sir William, 1843–1923, West Norwood
Trevor, Maj.Gen. William, 1831–1907, Kensal Green
Trollope, Anthony, 1815–82, Kensal Green
Troughton, Edward, 1753–1835, Kensal Green
Truelove, Edward, 1809–99, Highgate
Trunley, John, 1898–1944, Camberwell New
Truscott, Sir Francis, 1824–95, West Norwood
Tucker, Sgt. Charles, –1910, City of London
Turle, James, 1802–82, West Norwood
Turner, Charles, 1838–1913, Highgate
Turner, Sharon, 1768–1847, West Norwood
Turton, Thomas, 1780–1864, Kensal Green
Tussaud, Francis, 1829–58, St.Mary's R.C. Kensal Green
Tyler, Sir Alfred, 1870–1936, Bromley Hill
Tyrrell, William, Lord, 1866–1947, St.Thomas's R.C.
Tzokov, Dmitri, –1926, Golders Green

U

Unwins, David, 1780–1837, Kensal Green
Upton, Florence, 1873–1922, Hampstead
Ure, Andrew, 1778–1857, Highgate

V

Valentine, Isaac, 1822–98, Jewish, Lauriston Road
Valpy, Richard, 1754–1836, Kensal Green
Vance, Alfred, 1839–88, Nunhead
Vanne, Marda, 1896–1970, Gunnersbury
Van Praagh, Morris, 1809–71, Jewish, Lauriston Road
Van Zeller, Richard, 1844–92, Mortlake R.C.
Varley, Cromwell, 1828–83, Bexley Heath
Vaughan Williams, Ralph, 1872–1958, Golders Green
Veitch, James, 1815–69, Brompton
Verral, Charles, 1780–1843, Nunhead
Vernham, John, 1854–1921, Nunhead
Venn, Henry, 1796–1873, Mortlake Old
Verne, Matilde, 1865–1936, St.Marylebone
Vestris, Mme. Lucia, 1797–1836, Kensal Green
Vetch, James, 1815–69, Highgate
Vickers, Henry, –1917, West Ham
Vincent, Henry, 1813–78, Abney Park
Viscardini, Baldassare, 1830–96, Great Northern
Voysey, Charles, 1857–1941, Golders Green

Vsevolod, Prince, 1914–73, Gunnersbury
Vunivalu, Ravuama, 1921–64, Brookwood

W

Wadeson, Maj.Richard, 1826–85, Brompton
Wadsworth, Edward, 1889–1949, Brompton
Waechter, Sir Max, 1837–1924, Richmond
Wagland, John, –1892, Teddington
Wakley, Thomas, 1795–1862, Kensal Green
Walcott, Mackenzie, 1821–80, Brompton
Walcott, Sir Stephen, 1806–87, Ealing
Waldegrave, Adm.George, Lord Radstock, 1786–1857, Highgate
Waley, Arthur, 1889–1966, Highgate
Waley, Jacob, 1818–73, Jewish, Fulham Road
Waley, Simon, 1827–75, Jewish, Fulham Road
Walker, William, 1869–1918, Crystal Palace
Wall, Max, 1908–90, Highgate
Wallace Robert, 1831–99, Kensal Green
Wallace, William, 1814–70, Kensal Green
Waller, John, 1813–1905, Nunhead
Wallis, George, 1811–91, Highgate
Wallis, Joseph, 1825–83, Nunhead
Wallis, Richard, Camberwell
Walpole, Rt. Hon. Spencer, 1806–98, Ealing
Walter, Maj. Frederick, 1848–1931, Twickenham
Walter, Frederick, 1949–1931, Queen's Road, Croydon
Walter, Lionel, 29th Earl of Mar, 1891–1965, Ealing
Walters, Frederick, 1849–1931, Queen's Road, Croydon
Walters, Sir Tudor, 1868–1933, Putney Vale
Ward, Horatia Nelson, 1801–81, Paines Lane
Ward, James, 1800–84, Nunhead

Ward, James, 1769–1859, Kensal Green
Ward, Nathaniel, 1791–1868, West Norwood
Ward Ashton, Edward, –1880, Charlton
Warne, Frederick, 1825–1901, Highgate
Warneford, Lieut. Reginald, 1891–1915, Brompton
Warriner, John, 1860–1938, Nunhead
Waters, Charles, 1839–1910, Camberwell
Waters, Col.Marcus, 1794–1868, Kensal Green
Watkin, Maj.Gen.Sir Willoughby, 1859–1925, Twickenham
Watson, Sir Charles, 1844–1916, Putney Vale
Watson, Sir Frederick, 1773–1852, Kensal Green
Watson, Col. Thomas, 1867–1917, Golders Green
Watts, John, 1786–1858, West Norwood
Watts, Isaac, 1674–1748, Bunhill Fields
Watts–Dunton, Walter, 1832–1914, West Norwood
Waugh, Sir Andrew, 1810–78, Brompton
Waylett, Harriet, 1800–51, West Norwood
Waymouth, Adm. Arthur, 1864–1936, Gunnersbury
Weare, Lieut.Gen.Sir Henry, 1825–98, Kensington Hanwell
Weaver, Sir Lawrence, 1876–1930, Highgate
Webb, Sir Aston, 1849–1930, Gunnersbury
Webb, Stella, 1902–89, Highgate
Webb–Johnson, Alfred, Lord of Stoke on Trent, 1880–1958, Kingston
Webster, Benjamin, 1797–1882, Brompton
Webster, Richard, Lord Alverstone, 1842–1915, West Norwood
Webster, Thomas, 1773–1844, Highgate
Webster, Thomas, 1810–75, West Norwood
Weir, Rev. James, 1892–1971, St. Marylebone
Wells, James, 1803–72, Nunhead

Welman, Maj.Gen.William, 1827–1906, Beckenham
Welwitsch, Fredrich, 1806–72, Kensal Green
Wesley, Charles, 1793–1859, Highgate
Wesley, Susannah, 1670–1742, Bunhill Fields
West, Dame Rebecca, 1892–1983, Brookwood
Westhall, Charles, –1868, Brompton
Westmacott, James, 1823–1900, West Norwood
Weston, Edward, 1822–74, Nunhead
Westwood, Joseph, –1883, Tower Hamlets
Wheatley, John, 1892–1955, Putney Vale
Whistler, James, 1834–1903, Chiswick Old
Whitaker, Sir Cuthbert, 1873–1950, Golders Green
Whitaker, Joseph, 1820–95, West Norwood
White, Sir Arnold, 1830–93, West Norwood
White, Sir Edward, 1847–1914, St.Marylebone
White, Edward, c.1872–1952, Brookwood
White, Maj.Gen.Geoffrey, 1870–1959, Pinner
Whitefield, Elizabeth, 1704–68, Chingford Mount
Whitehead, George, 1636?–1723, Bunhill Fields
Whiteley, William, 1831–1907, Kensal Green
Wigan, Sir Frederick, 1827–1907, East Sheen
Wilcox, Sir Herbert, 1892–1977, City of London
Wilde, Lieut.Gen.Sir Alfred, 1819–78, Barnes Common
Wilkin, Sir Walter, 1842–1922, City of London
Williams, Daniel, 1643?–1716, Bunhill Fields
Williams, Edward, 1782–1855, Barnes Common
Williams, Fred, –1916, Twickenham
Williams, Sir George, 1821–1905, Highgate
Williams, Henry, 1811–65, Barnes Common
Williams, Sir Thomas, 1853–1941, Isleworth
Williams, Gen. Sir William, 1800–83, Brompton
Williams, William, 1820–92, West Norwood
Willis, Henry, 1810–84, Kensington Hanwell
Willock, Sir Henry, 1790–1858, Mortlake Old
Wilson, Charles –1990 Streatham
Wilson, Horace, 1786–1860, Kensal Green
Wilson, John, 1788–1870, Brompton
Wilson, Joseph, 1858–1929 Hendon
Wilson, Thomas, 1764–1843, Abney Park
Wimperis, John, 1829–1904, Wandsworth
Windsor, Frederick, 1763–1830, Kensal Green
Wing, Thomas, 1802–89, Nunhead
Wingate, Maj.Gen.Orde, 1903–44, Charlton
Wingfield, Maj.Walter, 1833–1912, Kensal Green
Wingham, Thomas, 1846–1903, St. Mary's R.C. Kensal Green
Winstedt, Sir Richard, 1878–1966, Putney Vale
Wisden, John, 1826–84, Brompton
Wiseman, Cardinal Nicholas, 1802–65, St.Mary's R.C., Kensal Green
Withers, John, 1823–1911, West Norwood
Wolseley, Frederick, 1837–99, Crystal Palace District
Wombwell, George, 1788–1850, Highgate
Wood, Sir Edward, 1854–1930, Hendon
Wood, Mrs Henry, 1814–87, Highgate
Wood, Capt.John, 1813–71, Highgate
Woodcroft, Bennet, 1803–79, Brompton

Woodgate, Sir Alfred, 1860–1943, Teddington
Woodriff, Capt John, 1791–1868, Nunhead
Woodington, William, 1806–93, West Norwood
Woods, Sir Albert, 1816–1904, West Norwood
Woodward, Joseph, 1872–1945, Golders Green
Woolley, Charles, 1846–1922, West Norwood
Worcell, Stanislaus, 1799–1857, Highgate
Worley, Sir Arthur, 1871–1937, St Marylebone
Wright, Sir George, 1848–1927, Acton
Wright, William, 1837–99, West Norwood
Wyatt, Matthew, 1777–1862, Highgate
Wyatt, Samuel, 1737–1807, Royal Hospital, Chelsea
Wyld, James, 1812–87, Kensal Green
Wylie, Alexander, 1815–87, Highgate
Wymark, Patrick, 1926–70, Highgate
Wyness, George, –1882, Brompton
Wynne, Greville, 1919–90, Gunnersbury
Wyon, Benjamin, 1802–58, Highgate
Wyon, William, 1795–1851, West Norwood

Y
Yanni, George, –1903, Camberwell
Yarrow, John, 1818–98, West Norwood
Yeates, John, 1814–1902, Nunhead
Yelverton, Roger, 1845–1912, Plaistow
Yorke, Albert, 6th Earl of Hardwicke, 1867–1904, St.Marylebone
Yorke, Charles, 5th Earl of Hardwicke, 1836–97, St.Marylebone
Young, Sir Allen, 1827–1915, Brookwood
Young, Col.Sir John, 1843–1932, Westminster
Young, Lady Ruth, 1930–93 Highgate
Young, William, –1901, Kingston

Index of architects, landscapers and sculptors whose work is represented in the cemeteries

Antoine Acket (1905–) 262
Aickin and Capes 251
Thomas Allom (1804–72) 341
H.H. Armstead (1828–1905) 37
John Ashdown (–1878), 253

Edward Baily (1788–1867) 385
John Bannen 317, 322, 325
Signor Bardi 245
Barnett and Birch 279
Edward Barry (1830–80) 341
F. Douglas Barton (1888–1966) viii, 42, 177
George Basevi (1794–1845) 228
Benjamin Baud (c. 1807–75) 248
William Behnes (1795–1900) 231
Charles Bell fl.(1875–1900) 178
William Bell 118
Sir Arthur Blomfield (1829–99) 290
Sir Reginald Blomfield (1836–1942) 27
Edward Blore (1787–1879) 228
C.E. Boast 141
Alfred A Bonella fl. (1859–1908) 185
Joseph Bonomi (1796–1878) 45, 61, 72
Darcy Braddell (1884–1970) 312
Lawrence Bradshaw (1917–91) 195
David Brandon (1813–96) 327
Josef Braunsteiner (1891–1963) 306
David Brown 281

Sir John Brown and A.E. Henson 331
James Bunning (1802–63) 263
William Burges (1827–81) 342
Timothy Butler (1806– c.1878) 99
William Butterfield (1814–1900) 325

Signor Cantagalli 317
Cecil R.W. Chapman 79
Robert M. Chart (1850–) 80
Chart & Sons 258
Church, Quick and Whinchop 279
Edward F.C. Clarke (1843–1904) 275
Robert Hampton Clucas fl. (1914–23) 177
C.R. Cockerell (1788–1863) 228
H.H. Collins (1933–05) 218
Sir Edwin Cooper (1873–1942) 300, 301
Edward Bainbridge Copnall (1903–73) 130
Frederick Cowell 185
R. Cox 155
E.W. Crickmay 322
John Cusworth fl.(1830–42) 235

Robert Davidson 132
E Guy Dawber (1861–38) 154
Charles J. Dawson (1850–1933) 39
Robert Donald (c.1826–66)
Sir Henry Doulton (1820–97) 33
Henry Downing (1865–1947) 257

INDEX OF ARCHITECTS

Daniel Ebbetts (–1921) 78
Joseph Edwards (1814–83) 190
Ernest J Elford (–1947) 281
Benno Elkan (1877–1960) 221
England and Brown viii, 44, 126

Aristide Fabbrucci (c.1859–1903) 34, 176
Farmer and Brindley 37
Benjamin Ferrey (1810–80) xi, 207
Isaac Finnemore 93
Banister Fletcher, snr. (1833–99) 180
Banister Fletcher, jnr. (1866–1953) 182
J.H. Foley (1818–74) 247
Thomas P. Francis 120
J. Dudley Forsyth (–1926) 178
Forsyth and Maule 88
H.H. Forward 209
Albert Freeman (1873–1938) 311

Stephen Geary (1797–1854) 92, 93, 187, 200
Sir Ernest George (1839–1922) 157
John Gibson (1817–92) 228, 236
Eric Gill (1882–1940) 228, 234, 254
George Godwin (1815–88) 241
T. Goodchild (–1885) 323
Richard Goulden 251
J.W. Griffiths (1796–1888) 228
W.P. Griffith (1815–84) 269
Prof. Ludwig Grüner (1801–82) 229

John Hall 156
William Haywood (1821 94) 132, 133
Evelyn Hellicar (1862–1929) 91
Alexander G. Hennell (1838–1915) 144
S. Hewitt 121
Thomas J. Hill 256
E. Hodgkinson 88
Arthur Holden 263
William Hosking (1800–61) 72

Robert Jerrard jnr.(–1861) 339
F. Lynn Jenkins (1870–1927) 301
Ernest Joseph (1876–1960) 221
W. Goscombe John (1860–1952) 179
Charles Jones 145, 333

Owen Jones (1809–74) 145, 333
Nathan Joseph (1834–1909) 224

A.E. Kates 263
Arthur Knapp-Fisher (1888–1965) 173
T.E. Knightley (1823–1905) 338

F.M. Lander fl. (1840–55) 234
T. Lavender 278
Charles Lee 85
Thomas Little (1802–59) 264, 275
George Loddiges 1786–1846, 71
Eric E. Lofting 274
J.C. Loudon (1873–43) 93
Sir Edwin Lutyens (1869–1944) 106, 158

Sir Edgar MacKennal (1863–1931) 300
W.R. Mallet fl. (1884–96) 279
Sydney March (1876–1967) 150
Edward Maufe 106, 158
Arthur Messer (1863–1934) 105
William Milligan (1812–78) 241
Edward Milner (1819–94) 208
Thomas Milnes (1813–88) 245
Mitchell and Bridgewater 158
H. Morley Lawson 171
Morphew and Green 89
Joseph R. Musto (1880–1941) 129

Francesco Nagni (1897–1977) 36
William Newton–Dunn (1859–1934) 315
Samuel Nicholl (1827–1905) 305, 314
Matthew Noble (1817–76) 101

O'Shea brothers, James and John 77

Thomas H.Nowell Parr (1864–1933) 262
G.L. Paling 251
J.B. Papworth (1775–1847) 228
J.L. Pearson (1817–97) 143, 343
Henry Pegram (1862–1937) 158, 160
William Poole 83
George Pritchett (1824–1912) 325, 326
A.W.N. Pugin (1796–1832) 22, 23, 72, 202
E.W. Pugin (1834–75) 310

C.H.B. Quennell (1872–1935) 306, 307

Sir William Reid-Dick (1879–61) 299, 302
S.W. Richardson 54
C.E. Robins 288
William Robinson (1838–1935) 164, 157
Augustus Rovendino fl. (1852–1900) 210
D.J. Ross 135
Douglas W Rowntree 148
Reginald Rowell (1875–1966) 149

George Saunders 176
Sir G.G. Scott (1811–78) 116
W Gilbee Scott (1857–1930) 361
J.O. Scott (1842–1913) 26, 37
Seagrave, Bravett and Taylor 311
Charles J. Shoppe (1823–97) 207
Robert Sievier (1794–1865) 224, 227, 228
Sydney Smirke (1798–1877) 245
C.H. Smith (1792–1864) 244
Raymond Smith fl. (1842–76) 242
Alexander Spurr (–1873) 166, 168
Leonard Stokes (1858–1925) 260, 261
G.E. Street (1824–81) 342
R.C. Sutton (1833–1915) 110
Egerton Swartwout 106
Godfrey Sykes (1824–66) 241

H.W. Tee (1899–1948) 153
Albert Thomas (1875–1964) 256
Cecil Thomas 291
William B Thomas (1811–98) 105
Francis Thorne (–1885) 208, 209

Sir William Tite (1798–1873) xxiv, 339, 340
C.S. Trapp 79
C.A. Trim (–1972) 251
George Truefitt (1824–1902) 87
Cyril Tubbs (1858–1927) 105

Alwyn Underdown 340

R. Vanlinden 306
Francis Verheyden 106

Lilian Wade 106
Alfred Waterhouse (1830–1905) 72
Sir Aston Webb (1849–1930) 39, 118, 175
Maurice Webb (1880–1939) 118
Philip Webb (1831–1915) 319, 321
William Webster 208
Frederick Wehnert (1801–71) 253
Richard Westmacott (1799–1872) 358, 100
Edward White (1873–1952) 106, 108
Major L Milner White (–1977) 318
A.H. Wilds fl. (1822–48) 342
G Berkeley Willis (1882–1979) 229
J. Winter 255
Paul Woodroffe 306
Charles H. Worley (–1906) 359
Matthew D. Wyatt (1820–77) 223
Thomas Wyatt (1807–80) xii, 327

Alfred Yeates (1867–1944) 157
H.W. Young 334

Sutton: *Sans Peur*

Printed in Great Britain
by Amazon